Program Development in Java

Program Development in Java

Abstraction, Specification, and Object-Oriented Design

Barbara Liskov

with John Guttag

⋀⋁ Addison-Wesley

Boston • San Francisco • New York • Toronto • Montreal
London • Munich • Paris • Madrid
Capetown • Sydney • Tokyo • Singapore • Mexico City

The publisher offers discounts on this book when ordered in quantity for special sales. For more information, please contact:

Pearson Education Corporate Sales Division
201 W. 103rd Street
Indianapolis, IN 46290
(800) 428-5331
corpsales@pearsoned.com

Visit us on the Web at *www.awl.com/cseng/*

Library of Congress Cataloging-in-Publication Data

Liskov, B.
 Program development in Java : abstraction, specification, and object-oriented design / Barbara Liskov and John Guttag.
  p. cm.
 ISBN 0-201-65768-6 (alk. paper)
 1. Java (Computer program language) 2. Object-oriented programming (Computer science) I. Guttag, John. II. Title.
 QA76.73.J38 L58 2000
 005.13'3—dc21   00-036277

Text printed on recycled and acid-free paper.

ISBN 0201657686

3 4 5 6 7 8 CRW 05 04 03 02

3rd Printing May 2002

To Nate and Moses

Contents

7 — Type Hierarchy   147

8 — Polymorphic Abstractions   189

Contents

9 — Specifications   207

10 — Testing and Debugging   221

Contents

Preface

Constructing production-quality programs—programs that are used over an extended period of time—is well known to be extremely difficult. The goal of this book is to improve the effectiveness of programmers in carrying out this task. I hope the reader will become a better programmer as a result of reading the book. I believe the book succeeds at improving programming skills because my students tell me that it happens for them.

What makes a good programmer? It is a matter of efficiency over the entire production of a program. The key is to reduce wasted effort at each stage. Things that can help include thinking through your implementation before you start coding, coding in a way that eliminates errors before you test, doing rigorous testing so that errors are found early, and paying careful attention to modularity so that when errors are discovered, they can be corrected with minimal impact on the program as a whole. This book covers techniques in all these areas.

Modularity is the key to writing good programs. It is essential to break up a program into small modules, each of which interacts with the others through a narrow, well-defined interface. With modularity, an error in one part of a program can be corrected without having to consider all the rest of the code, and a part of the program can be understood without having to understand the entire thing. Without modularity, a program is a large collection of intricately interrelated parts. It is difficult to comprehend and to modify such a program, and also difficult to get it to work correctly.

The focus of this book therefore is on modular program construction: how to organize a program as a collection of well-chosen modules. The book relates modularity to abstraction. Each module corresponds to an abstraction, such as an index that keeps track of interesting words in a large collection of documents or a procedure that uses the index to find documents that match a particular query. Particular emphasis is placed on object-oriented programming—the use of data abstraction and objects in developing programs.

The book uses Java for its programming examples. Familiarity with Java is not assumed. It is worth noting, however, that the concepts in this book are language independent and can be used to write programs in any programming language.

How Can the Book Be Used?

Program Development in Java can be used in two ways. The first is as the text for a course that focuses on an object-oriented methodology for the design and implementation of complex systems. The second is use by computing professionals who want to improve their programming skills and their knowledge of modular, object-oriented design.

When used as a text, the book is intended for a second or third programming course; we have used the book for many years in the second programming course at MIT, which is taken by sophomores and juniors. At this stage, students already know how to write small programs. The course builds on this material in two ways: by getting them to think more carefully about small programs, and by teaching them how to construct large programs using smaller ones as components. This book could also be used later in the curriculum, for example, in a software engineering course.

A course based on the book is suitable for all computer science majors. Even though many students will never be designers of truly large programs, they may work at development organizations where they will be responsible for the design and implementation of subsystems that must fit into the overall structure. The material on modular design is central to this kind of a task. It is equally important for those who take on larger design tasks.

What Is This Book About?

Roughly two-thirds of the book is devoted to the issues that arise in building individual program modules. The remainder of the book is concerned with how to use these modules to construct large programs.

Program Modules

This part of the book focuses on abstraction mechanisms. It discusses procedures and exceptions, data abstraction, iteration abstraction, families of data abstractions, and polymorphic abstractions.

Three activities are emphasized in the discussion of abstractions. The first is deciding on exactly what the abstraction is: what behavior it is providing to its users. Inventing abstractions is a key part of design, and the book discusses how to choose among possible alternatives and what goes into inventing good abstractions.

The second activity is capturing the meaning of an abstraction by giving a specification for it. Without some description, an abstraction is too vague to be useful. The specification provides the needed description. This book defines a format for specifications, discusses the properties of a good specification, and provides many examples.

The third activity is implementing abstractions. The book discusses how to design an implementation and the trade-off between simplicity and performance. It emphasizes encapsulation and the need for an implementation to provide the behavior defined by the specification. It also presents techniques—in particular, the use of representation invariants and abstraction functions—that help readers of code to understand and reason about it. Both rep invariants and abstraction functions are implemented to the extent possible, which is useful for debugging and testing.

The material on type hierarchy focuses on its use as an abstraction technique—a way of grouping related data abstractions into families. An important issue here is whether it is appropriate to define one type to be a subtype of another. The book defines the substitution principle—a methodical way for deciding whether the subtype relation holds by examining the specifications of the subtype and the supertype.

This book also covers debugging and testing. It discusses how to come up with a sufficient number of test cases for thorough black box and glass box tests, and it emphasizes the importance of regression testing.

Programming in the Large

The latter part of *Program Development in Java* is concerned with how to design and implement large programs in a modular way. It builds on the material about abstractions and specifications covered in the earlier part of the book.

The material on programming in the large covers four main topics. The first concerns requirements analysis—how to develop an understanding of what is wanted of the program. The book discusses how to carry out requirements analysis and also describes a way of writing the resulting requirements specification, by making use of a data model that describes the abstract state of the program. Using the model leads to a more precise specification, and it also makes the requirements analysis more rigorous, resulting in a better understanding of the requirements.

The second programming in the large topic is program design, which is treated as an iterative process. The design process is organized around discovering useful abstractions, ones that can serve as desirable building blocks within the program as a whole. These abstractions are carefully specified during design so that when the program is implemented, the modules that implement the abstractions can be developed independently. The design is documented by a design notebook, which includes a module dependency diagram that describes the program structure.

The third topic is implementation and testing. The book discusses the need for design analysis prior to implementation and how design reviews can be carried out. It also discusses implementation and testing order. This section compares top-down and bottom-up organizations, discusses the use of drivers and stubs, and emphasizes the need to develop an ordering strategy prior to implementation that meets the needs of the development organization and its clients.

This book concludes with a chapter on design patterns. Some patterns are introduced in earlier chapters; for example, iteration abstraction is a major component of the methodology. The final chapter discusses patterns not covered earlier. It is intended as an introduction to this material. The interested reader can then go on to read more complete discussions contained in other books.

Barbara Liskov

Acknowledgments

John Guttag was a coauthor of an earlier version of this book. Many chapters still bear his stamp. In addition, he has made numerous helpful suggestions about the current material.

Thousands of students have used various drafts of the book, and many of them have contributed useful comments. Scores of graduate students have been teaching assistants in courses based on the material in this book. Many students have contributed to examples and exercises that have found their way into this text. I sincerely thank all of them for their contributions.

My colleagues both at MIT and elsewhere have also contributed in important ways. Special thanks are due to Jeannette Wing and Daniel Jackson. Jeannette Wing (CMU) helped to develop the material on the substitution principle. Daniel Jackson (MIT) collaborated on teaching recent versions of the course and contributed to the material in many ways; the most important of these is the data model used to write requirements specifications, which is based on his research.

In addition, the publisher obtained a number of helpful reviews, and I want to acknowledge the efforts of James M. Coggins (University of North Carolina), David H. Hutchens (Millersville University), Gail Kaiser (Columbia University), Gail Murphy (University of British Columbia), James Purtilo (University of Maryland), and David Riley (University of Wisconsin at LaCrosse). I found their comments very useful, and I tried to work their suggestions into the final manuscript.

Finally, MIT's Department of Electrical Engineering and Computer Science and its Laboratory for Computer Science have supported this project in important ways. By reducing my teaching load, the department has given me time to write. The laboratory has provided an environment that enabled research leading to many of the ideas presented in this book.

Introduction

This book will develop a methodology for constructing software systems. Our goal is to help programmers construct programs of high quality—programs that are reliable, efficient, and reasonably easy to understand, modify, and maintain.

A very small program, consisting of no more than a few hundred lines, can be implemented as a single monolithic unit. As the size of the program increases, however, such a monolithic structure is no longer reasonable because the code becomes difficult to understand. Instead, the program must be decomposed into a number of small independent programs, called *modules*, that together provide the desired function. We shall focus on this decomposition process: how to decompose large programming problems into small ones, what kinds of modules are most useful in this process, and what techniques increase the likelihood that modules can be combined to solve the original problem.

Doing decomposition properly becomes more and more important as the size of the program increases for a number of reasons. First, many people must be involved in the construction of a large program. If just a few people are working on a program, they naturally interact regularly. Such contact reduces the possibility of misunderstandings about who is doing what and lessens the seriousness of the consequences should misunderstandings occur. If many people work on a project, regular communication becomes impossible because it consumes too much time. Instead, the program must be decomposed into pieces that the individuals can work on independently with a minimum of contact.

The useful life of a program (its *production* phase) begins when it is delivered to the customer. Work on the program is not over at this point, however. The code will probably contain residual errors that will need attention, and program modifications will often be required to upgrade the program's serviceability or to provide services better matched to the user's needs. This activity of program *modification* and *maintenance* is likely to consume more than half of the total effort put into the project.

For modification and maintenance, it is rarely practical to start from scratch and reimplement the entire program. Instead, one must retrofit modifications within the existing structure, and it is therefore important that the structure accommodate change. In particular, the pieces of the program must be independent, so that a change to one piece can be made without requiring changes to all pieces.

Finally, most programs have a long lifetime. Programmers often have to deal with programs long after they have first worked on them. Moreover, there is likely to be substantial turnover of personnel over the life of any project, and program modification and maintenance are typically done by people other than the original implementors. All of these factors require that programs be structured in such a way that they can be understood easily.

In the methodology we shall describe in this book, programs will be developed by means of problem decomposition based on a recognition of useful abstractions. *Decomposition* and *abstraction*, the two key concepts in this book, form our next subject.

1.1   Decomposition and Abstraction

The basic paradigm for tackling any large problem is clear—we must "divide and rule." Unfortunately, merely deciding to follow Machiavelli's dictum still leaves us a long way from solving the problem at hand. Exactly how we choose to divide the problem is of overriding importance.

Our goal in decomposing a program is to create modules that are themselves small programs that interact with one another in simple, well-defined ways. If we achieve this goal, different people will be able to work on different modules independently, without needing much communication among themselves, and yet the modules will work together. In addition, during program modification and maintenance, it will be possible to modify some of the modules without affecting all of the others.

When we decompose a problem, we factor it into separable subproblems in such a way that

- Each subproblem is at the same level of detail.

- Each subproblem can be solved independently.

- The solutions to the subproblems can be combined to solve the original problem.

Sorting using merge sort is an elegant example of problem solving by decomposition. It breaks the problem of sorting a list of arbitrary size into the two simpler problems of sorting a list of size two and merging two sorted lists of arbitrary size.

Decomposition is a time-honored and useful technique in many disciplines. From Babbage's day onward, people have recognized the utility of such things as macros and subroutines as decomposition devices for programmers. It is important to recognize, however, that decomposition is not a panacea and when used improperly, it can have a harmful effect. Furthermore, large or poorly understood problems are difficult to decompose properly. The most common problem is creating individual components that solve the stated subproblems but do not combine to solve the original problem. This is one of the reasons why system integration is often difficult.

For example, imagine creating a play by assembling a group of writers, giving each a list of characters and a general plot outline, and asking each of them to write a single character's lines. The authors might accomplish their individual tasks admirably, but it is highly unlikely that their combined efforts will be an admirable play. It would probably lack any sort of coherence or sense. Individually acceptable solutions simply cannot be expected to combine properly if the original task has been divided in a counterproductive way.

Abstraction is a way to do decomposition productively by changing the level of detail to be considered. When we abstract from a problem, we agree to ignore certain details in an effort to convert the original problem to a simpler one. We might, for example, abstract from the problem of writing a play to the problem of deciding how many acts it should have, or what its plot will be, or even the sense (but not the wording) of individual pieces of dialog. After this has been done, the original problem (of writing all of the dialog) remains, but it has been considerably simplified—perhaps even to the point where it could be turned over to another or even several others. (Alexandre Dumas *père* churned out novels in this way.)

The paradigm of abstracting and then decomposing is typical of the program design process: decomposition is used to break software into components that can be combined to solve the original problem; abstractions assist in making a good choice of components. We alternate between the two processes until we have reduced the original problem to a set of problems we already know how to solve.

1.2   Abstraction

The process of abstraction can be seen as an application of a many-to-one mapping. It allows us to forget information and consequently to treat things that are different as if they were the same. We do this in the hope of simplifying our analysis by separating attributes that are relevant from those that are not. It is crucial to remember, however, that relevance often depends upon context. In the context of an elementary school classroom we learn to abstract both $(\frac{8}{3}) \times 3$ and $5 + 3$ to the concept we represent by the numeral 8. Much later we learn, often under unpleasant circumstances, that on many computing machines this abstraction can get us into a world of trouble.

For example, consider the structure shown in Figure 1.1, in which the concept is "mammal." All mammals share certain characteristics, such as the fact that females produce milk. At this level of abstraction, we focus on these common characteristics and ignore the differences between the various types of mammals.

At a lower level of abstraction, we might be interested in particular instances of mammals. However, even here we can abstract by considering not individuals, or even species, but groups of related species. At this level, we would have groupings such as primates or rodents. Here again, we are interested in common characteristics rather than the differences between, say, humans and chimpanzees. Such differences are relevant at a still lower level of abstraction.

Figure 1.1   An abstraction hierarchy

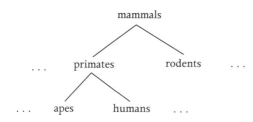

The abstraction hierarchy of Figure 1.1 comes from the field of zoology, but it might well appear in a program that implemented some zoological application. A more specifically computer-oriented example that is useful in many programs is the concept of a "file." Files abstract from raw storage and provide long-term, online storage of named entities. Operating systems differ in their realizations of files; for example, the structure of the filenames differs from system to system, as does the way in which the files are stored on secondary storage devices.

In this book, we are interested in abstraction as it is used in programs in general. The most significant development to date in this area is high-level languages. By dealing directly with the constructs of a high-level language, rather than with the many possible sequences of machine instructions into which they can be translated, the programmer achieves a significant simplification.

In recent years, however, programmers have become dissatisfied with the level of abstraction generally achieved even in high-level language programs. Consider, for example, the program fragments in Figure 1.2. At the level of abstraction defined by the programming language, these fragments are clearly different: if there is an occurrence of e in a, one fragment finds the index of the first occurrence and the other, the index of the last. If e does not occur in a, one sets i to a.length and the other to -1. It is not improbable, however, that both were written to accomplish the same goal: to set found to false if there is no occurrence of e in a and, otherwise, to set found to true and z to the index of some occurrence of e in a. If this is what we want, it is not evident from the program fragments by themselves.

One approach to dealing with this problem lies in the invention of "very-high-level languages" built around some fixed set of relatively general data structures and a powerful set of primitives that can be used to manipulate

Figure 1.2   Two program fragments

```
// search upwards
found = false;
for (int i = 0; i < a.length; i++)
   if (a[i] == e) {
      z = i;
      found = true;
   }

// search downwards
found = false;
for (int i = a.length-1; i >= 0; i--)
   if (a[i] == e) {
      z = i;
      found = true;
   }
```

them. For example, suppose a language provided isIn and indexOf as primitive operations on arrays. Then we could accomplish the task outlined in Figure 1.2 simply by writing

```
found = a.isIn(e);
if (found)
    z = a.indexOf(e);
```

The flaw in this approach is that it presumes that the designer of the programming language will build into the language most of the abstractions that users of the language will want. Such foresight is not given to many; and even if it were, a language containing so many built-in abstractions might well be so unwieldy as to be unusable.

A preferable alternative is to design into the language mechanisms that allow programmers to construct their own abstractions as they need them. One common mechanism is the use of *procedures*. By separating procedure definition and invocation, a programming language makes two important methods of abstraction possible: *abstraction by parameterization* and *abstraction by specification*. These abstraction mechanisms are summarized in Sidebar 1.1.

Sidebar 1.1 Abstraction Mechanisms

- *Abstraction by parameterization* abstracts from the identity of the data by replacing them with parameters. It generalizes modules so that they can be used in more situations.

- *Abstraction by specification* abstracts from the implementation details (how the module is implemented) to the behavior users can depend on (what the module does). It isolates modules from one another's implementations; we require only that a module's implementation supports the behavior being relied on.

1.2.1 Abstraction by Parameterization

Abstraction by parameterization, through the introduction of parameters, allows us to represent a potentially infinite set of different computations with a single program text that is an abstraction of all of them. For example,

$$x * x + y * y$$

describes a computation that adds the square of the value stored in the variable x to the square of the value stored in the variable y.

On the other hand, the *lambda expression*

$$\lambda\, x, y\colon \mathrm{int}.(x * x + y * y)$$

describes the set of computations that square the value stored in some integer variable, which we shall temporarily refer to as x, and add to it the square of the value stored in another integer variable, which we shall temporarily call y. In such a lambda expression, we refer to x and y as the *formal parameters* and $x * x + y * y$ as the *body* of the expression. We invoke a computation by binding the formal parameters to arguments and then evaluating the body. For example,

$$\lambda\, x, y\colon \mathrm{int}.(x * x + y * y)(w, z)$$

is identical in meaning to

$$w * w + z * z$$

In more familiar notation, we might denote the previous lambda expression by

```
int squares (int x, y)
{
    return x * x + y * y;
}
```

and the binding of actual to formal parameters and evaluation of the body by the procedure call

```
u = squares(w, z);
```

Programmers often use abstraction by parameterization without even noticing that they are doing so. For example, suppose we need a procedure that sorts an array of integers a. At some time in the future, we shall probably have to sort some other array, perhaps even somewhere else in this same program. It is highly unlikely, however, that every array we need to sort will be named a; we therefore invoke abstraction by parameterization to generalize the procedure and thus make it more useful.

Abstraction by parameterization is an important means of achieving generality in programs. A sort routine that works on any array of integers is much more generally useful than one that works only on a particular array of integers. By further abstraction, we can achieve even more generality. For example, we might define a sort abstraction that works on arrays of reals as well as arrays of integers, or even one that works on arraylike structures in general.

Abstraction by parameterization is an extremely powerful mechanism. Not only does it allow us to describe a large (even infinite) number of computations relatively simply, but it is easily and efficiently realizable in programming languages. Nonetheless, it is not a sufficiently powerful mechanism to describe conveniently and fully the abstraction that the careful use of procedures can provide.

1.2.2   Abstraction by Specification

Abstraction by specification allows us to abstract from the computation (or computations) described by the body of a procedure to the end that procedure was designed to accomplish. We do this by associating with each procedure a *specification* of its intended effect and then considering the meaning of a

Figure 1.3   The sqrt procedure

```
float sqrt (float coef) {
    // REQUIRES: coef > 0
    // EFFECTS: Returns an approximation to the square root of coef
    float ans = coef/2.0;
    int i = 1;
    while (i < 7) {
        ans = ans - ((ans * ans - coef)/(2.0*ans));
        i = i + 1;
    }
    return ans;
}
```

procedure call to be based on this specification rather than on the procedure's body.

We are making use of abstraction by specification whenever we associate with a procedure a comment that is sufficiently informative to allow others to use that procedure without looking at its body. A good way to write such comments is to use pairs of *assertions*. The *requires assertion* (or *precondition*) of a procedure specifies something that is assumed to be true on entry to the procedure. In practice, what is most often asserted is a set of conditions sufficient to ensure the proper operation of the procedure. (This is often simply the vacuous assertion "true.") The *effects assertion* (or *postcondition*) specifies something that is supposed to be true at the completion of any invocation of the procedure for which the precondition was satisfied.

Consider, for example, the sqrt procedure in Figure 1.3. Because a specification is provided, we can ignore the body of the procedure and take the meaning of the procedure call y = sqrt(x) to be "If x is greater than zero when the procedure is invoked, then after the execution of the procedure, y is an approximation to the square root of x." Notice that the requires and effects assertions permit us to say nothing about the value of y if x is not greater than zero. This is important, since a user might otherwise quite reasonably assume that sqrt(0) returned a meaningful answer.

In using a specification to reason about the meaning of a procedure call, we follow two distinct rules:

1. After the execution of the procedure, we can assume that the postcondition holds provided the precondition held when the call was made.

2. We can assume *only* those properties that can be inferred from the post-condition.

The two rules mirror the two benefits of abstraction by specification. The first asserts that users of the procedure need not bother looking at the body of the procedure in order to use it. They are thus spared the effort of first understanding the details of the computations described by the body and then abstracting from these details to discover that the procedure really does compute an approximation to the square root of its argument. For complicated procedures, or even simple ones using unfamiliar algorithms, this is a nontrivial benefit.

The second rule makes it clear that we are indeed abstracting from the procedure body, that is, omitting some supposedly irrelevant information. This insistence on forgetting information is what distinguishes abstraction from decomposition. By examining the body of sqrt, users of the procedure could gain a considerable amount of information that cannot be gleaned from the postcondition and therefore should not be relied on—for example, that sqrt(4) will return +2. In the specification, however, we are saying that this information about the returned result is to be ignored. We are thus saying that the procedure sqrt is an abstraction representing the set of all computations that return "an approximation to the square root of x."

In this book, abstraction by specification will be the major method used in program construction. Abstraction by parameterization will be taken almost for granted; abstractions will have parameters as a matter of course.

1.2.3   Kinds of Abstractions

Abstraction by parameterization and by specification are powerful methods for program construction. They enable us to define three different kinds of abstractions: procedural abstraction, data abstraction, and iteration abstraction. In general, each procedural, data, and iteration abstraction will incorporate both methods within it.

For example, sqrt is like an operation: it abstracts a single action or task. We shall refer to abstractions that are operationlike as *procedural abstractions*. Note that sqrt incorporates both abstraction by parameterization and abstraction by specification.

Procedural abstraction is a powerful tool. It allows us to extend the virtual machine defined by a programming language by adding a new operation. This kind of extension is most useful when we are dealing with problems that are conveniently decomposable into independent functional units. However, it is often more fruitful to think of adding new kinds of data objects to the virtual machine.

The behavior of the data objects is expressed most naturally in terms of a set of operations that are meaningful for those objects. This set includes operations to create objects, to obtain information from them, and possibly to modify them. For example, push and pop are among the meaningful operations for stacks, integers need the usual arithmetic operations, and a bank account object in a banking system would have operations to deposit and withdraw money. Thus a *data abstraction* (or *data type*) consists of a set of objects and a set of operations characterizing the behavior of the objects.

As an example, consider MultiSets. MultiSets are like ordinary sets except that elements can occur more than once in a MultiSet. MultiSet operations might include empty, insert, delete, numberOf, and size. These operations create an empty MultiSet, add and delete elements from a MultiSet, tell how many times a particular element occurs in a MultiSet, and tell how many elements are in a MultiSet, respectively. The operations might be implemented within the runtime environment of the programming language by calls to various procedures. Programmers using MultiSets, however, need not worry about how these procedures are implemented. To them empty, insert, delete, numberOf, and size are abstractions defined by such statements as

- The size of the MultiSet insert(s, e) is equal to size(s) + 1.

- For all e, the numberOf times e occurs in the MultiSet empty( ) is 0.

The key thing to notice is that each of these statements deals with more than one operation. We do not present independent definitions of each operation, but rather define them by showing how they relate to one another. The emphasis on the relationships among operations is what makes a data abstraction something more than just a set of procedures. The importance of this distinction is discussed throughout this book.

In addition to procedural and data abstraction, we shall also deal with *iteration* abstraction. Iteration abstraction is used to avoid having to say more than is relevant about the flow of control in a loop. A typical iteration abstraction might allow us to iterate over all the elements of a MultiSet without constraining the order in which the elements are to be processed.

Sidebar 1.2   Kinds of Abstractions

- *Procedural abstraction* allows us to introduce new operations.

- *Data abstraction* allows us to introduce new types of data objects.

- *Iteration abstraction* allows us to iterate over items in a collection without revealing details of how the items are obtained.

- *Type hierarchy* allows us to abstract from individual data types to families of related types.

Finally, we shall sometimes abstract groups of data abstractions into *type families*. All members of the family have operations in common; these common operations are defined in the *supertype*, the type that is the ancestor of all the others, which are its *subtypes*. For example, there might be a family of types that provide the ability to read from input streams. The supertype would provide basic operations to open a stream, to read a character or a string, and to close a stream. The subtypes will then provide additional operations, for example, allowing data to be streamed from a file. Type families abstract from the details that distinguish members of a family from one another, to their commonalities. They allow programmers to ignore the differences most of the time.

Sidebar 1.2 summarizes the kinds of abstractions.

1.3   The Remainder of the Book

This book is concerned with how to do program decomposition based on abstraction. Our emphasis will be on data abstraction. We believe that while procedural and iteration abstraction have valuable roles to play, it is data abstraction that most often provides the primary organizational tool in the programming process. Data abstraction is the basis of object-oriented programming and design.

However, before we can decompose intelligently, we need a thorough understanding of the kinds of abstractions we are aiming for. The next several chapters are concerned with this topic. Since we will be using Java as our implementation mechanism, we begin by providing a brief introduction to Java and the way it supports object-oriented programming. Then we discuss the various kinds of abstractions—what they are, how to specify their behavior, and how to implement them in Java.

Our discussion shall emphasize how to get things right: how to develop a good abstraction, how to specify it clearly, and how to implement it correctly. Our programs ultimately will consist of many modules, each corresponding to the implementation of an abstraction. Unless each of these modules works individually as required, the program as a whole will not function properly. Therefore, understanding how to program at the module level—called *programming in the small*—is essential to achieving our ultimate goal of developing complete programs—called *programming in the large*.

The latter portion of the book focuses on programming in the large and in particular on the use of abstractions in program construction. We discuss the phases of program construction, how to do program design, and how to carry on into implementation. The book concludes with a discussion of a number of techniques, called *design patterns*, for organizing the structure of a program to improve its flexibility or performance.

Exercises

1.1 Describe an abstraction hierarchy with which you are familiar.

1.2 Select a procedure that you have written or used and discuss how it supports abstraction by specification and by parameterization.

Understanding Objects in Java

2

Java is an object-oriented language. This means that most of the data manipulated by programs are contained in *objects*. Objects contain both state and operations; the operations are called *methods*. Programs interact with objects by invoking their methods. The methods provide access to the state, allowing using code to observe the current state of an object or to modify it. Sidebar 2.1 provides information about the origins of Java.

This chapter provides some basic information about Java and its support for object-oriented programming and design. We shall concentrate primarily on the language *semantics*, that is, on the meaning of constructs in the language. For a complete, detailed description of the language, you should consult a Java text or reference manual. A Java reference manual is available online.

2.1   Program Structure

Java programs are made up of classes and interfaces. *Classes* are used in two different ways: to define collections of procedures (this use is discussed in Chapter 3) and to define new data types, such as MultiSet (this use is discussed in Chapter 5). *Interfaces* are also used to define new data types.

The majority of the content of both classes and interfaces consists of definitions of *methods*. A class that defines a group of procedures provides a method for each procedure; for example, a class providing procedures that manipulate integer arrays might contain a method to sort an array and another method to search an array for a match with a particular integer. A class or interface that defines a data type provides methods for the operations associated with the objects of that type. For example, in the case of a MultiSet, there might be an insert method to add an integer in the MultiSet and a numberOf method to determine how many times a given integer appears in the MultiSet.

An example of a class that defines a group of procedures is given in Figure 2.1. (Comments begin with the // symbol and continue to the end of the line.) Such methods are named by indicating their class and then their method name. Here are examples of calls of the methods in class Num:

```
int x = Num.gcd(15, 6);
if (Num.isPrime(y)) ...
```

A method takes zero or more arguments and returns a single result. Its *header* indicates this information. The arguments are often referred to as the *formal parameters* or *formals* of the call. For example, gcd has two formals, x and y, both of which are integers; it returns an integer result. A method may also terminate by throwing an exception. Exceptions will be discussed in detail in Chapter 4.

Because Java requires that every method have a result, a special form is used when there is no result. Such a method indicates that its return type is void. For example, suppose the Arrays class provides routines that are useful in manipulating arrays, among them a way of sorting arrays:

Figure 2.1   The Num class

```
public class Num {
   // class providing useful numeric routines

   public static int gcd (int n, int d) {
      // REQUIRES: n and d to be greater than zero
      // the gcd is computed by repeated subtraction
      while (n != d)
         if (n > d) n = n - d; else d = d - n;
      return n;
   }

   public static boolean isPrime(int p) {
      // implementation goes here
   }
}
```

```
public static void sort (int[ ] a)
```

(The form int [ ] indicates that the argument is an array of integers of unspec-ified length.) This method doesn't return a result; instead, it sorts its argument array in place. It can be called as follows:

```
Arrays.sort(a); // a call; assume a is an array of ints
```

2.2   Packages

Classes and interfaces are grouped into *packages*. Packages serve two purposes. First, they are an *encapsulation* mechanism; they provide a way to share information within the package while preventing its use on the outside.

Each class and interface has a declared *visibility*. Only classes and interfaces declared to be *public* can be used by code in other packages—for example, the Num class in Figure 2.1 can be used outside its package. The remaining definitions can be used only within the package.

In addition, the declarations within a class have a declared visibility. Only entities declared to be public, such as the gcd and isPrime methods in the Num class, are accessible to code in other packages. Other kinds of declared

17

visibility limit the code that can access the entity—for example, to just its class or just its package; the details will be discussed in later chapters.

The other use of packages is for *naming*. Each package has a hierarchical name that distinguishes it from all other packages. Classes and interfaces within the package have names that are relative to the package name. This means that there are no name conflicts between classes and interfaces defined in different packages.

Code in a package can refer to other classes and interfaces of its own package by using their class or interface name. For example, if the `mathRoutines` package contains the class `Num`, code within that package can refer to that class by using the name `Num`. Definitions in other packages can be referred to using their *fully qualified names*—that is, their name appended to their package's hierarchical name. For example, the fully qualified name for the `Num` class might be `mathRoutines.Num`. It is also possible to use short names to refer to definitions in other packages by using the *import* statement, to either import all public definitions from a package, or to import specific public definitions from a package. In either case, the imported definition can be referred to using its class or interface name.

One problem with short names is the possibility of name conflicts. For example, suppose two packages both define classes, named `Num`. In this case, if code uses both classes, it cannot use a short name for each. Either it could use a fully qualified name for each or it could import one of the classes and use a long name for the other.

Sometimes there is a conflict between encapsulation and naming. It is convenient to group many definitions in the same package because then code outside the package has access to all of them by importing the whole package. But this kind of grouping may be wrong from the point of encapsulation because code within a package can sometimes access internal information of other definitions within that package. In general, such a conflict should be resolved in favor of encapsulation.

2.3   Objects and Variables

All data are accessed by means of *variables*. *Local variables*, such as those declared within methods, reside on the runtime *stack*; space is allocated for them when the method is called and deallocated when the method returns.

Figure 2.2   Objects and variables

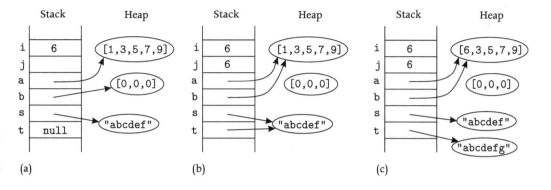

Every variable has a declaration that indicates its *type*. *Primitive types*, such as int (integers), boolean, and char (characters), define sets of values, such as 3, false, or c. All other types define sets of objects. Some object types will be provided for you, in packages defined by others. One such package is java.lang, which provides a number of useful types such as String; the types defined by this package can be used without importing the package. Others you will define yourselves. Chapter 5 describes how to define new types.

Variables of primitive types contain *values*. For example, the following:

```
int i = 6;
```

stores the value 6 in variable i. Variables of all other types, including strings and arrays, contain *references* to *objects* that reside on the *heap*. Objects are created on the heap by use of the new operator. Thus,

```
int [ ] a = new int[3];
```

causes space for a new array of integers object, with room for three integers, to be allocated on the heap and a reference to the new object to be stored in a.

Local variables can be initialized when they are declared. They *must* be initialized before their first use. Furthermore, if the compiler cannot prove that a variable is initialized before first use, it will cause compilation to fail.

Objects and variables are illustrated in Figure 2.2a, which shows the stack and heap after processing the following declarations:

```
int i = 6;
int j; // uninitialized
int [ ] a = {1,3,5,7,9}; // creates a 5-element array
int [ ] b = new int[3];
String s = "abcdef"; // creates a new string
String t = null;
```

Here all variables except j have been given an initial value. Variable t has been initialized to null; this special value provides a way of initializing a variable that will eventually refer to an object.

This example shows a number of object creations. Strings are created by indicating their content; thus, s refers to a string object containing "abcdef". Arrays can be created similarly, by indicating their elements; thus, a refers to a five-element array. The assignment to b shows the usual way of creating a new object, by calling the built-in new operator. This operator creates an object of the indicated class on the heap and then initializes it by running a special kind of method, called a *constructor*, for that class. For example, the array constructor initializes each element of a new array of integers to 0. Thus, b refers to a three-element array of integers, where each element of the array is 0.

Every object has an identity that is distinct from that of every other object. That is, when an object is created by a call to new, or through use of the special forms such as "abcdef" for strings and {1,3,5,7,9} for arrays, what is obtained is an object that is distinct from any other object in existence.

An assignment

```
v = e;
```

copies the value obtained by evaluating the expression e into the variable v. If the expression evaluates to a reference to an object, the reference is copied. This situation is illustrated in Figure 2.2b, which shows the results of the following assignments:

```
j = i;
b = a;
t = s;
```

Note that in the case of the string and array variables, we now have two variables pointing to the same object. Thus, assignment involving references causes variables to *share* objects.

The == operator can be used to determine whether two variables contain the same value. This operator is used primarily for primitive types—for example, to compare two ints, as in j == i, or to determine whether a variable that might refer to an object instead contains null, such as t == null. It can also be used to determine whether two variables refer to the same object; in the situation in Figure 2.2a, for example, a == b will not be true, whereas in the situation in Figure 2.2b, a == b is true.

Objects in the heap continue to exist as long as they are reachable from some variable on the stack, either directly or via a path through other objects. When an object is no longer reachable, its storage becomes available for reclamation by the garbage collector. For example, in the state shown in Figure 2.2b, the array formerly referred to by b is no longer reachable and is therefore available for reclamation by the garbage collector.

2.3.1   Mutability

All objects are either *immutable* or *mutable*. The state of an immutable object never changes, while the state of a mutable object can change.

Strings are immutable: there are no String methods that cause the state of a String object to change. For example, strings have a concatenation operator +, but it does not modify either of its arguments; instead, it returns a new string whose state is the concatenation of the states of its arguments. If we did the following assignment to t with the state shown in Figure 2.2b:

```
t = t + "g";
```

the result as shown in Figure 2.2c is that t now refers to a new String object whose state is "abcdefg" and the object referred to by s is unaffected.

On the other hand, arrays are mutable. The assignment

```
a[i] = e;
```

causes the state of array a to change by replacing its ith element with the value obtained by evaluating expression e. (The modification occurs only if i is in bounds for a; otherwise, an exception is thrown.)

If a mutable object is shared by two or more variables, modifications made through one of the variables will be visible when the object is used through the other variable. For example, suppose the shared array in Figure 2.2b is modified by

---

Sidebar 2.2 Mutability and Sharing

- An object is *mutable* if its state can change. For example, arrays are mutable.
- An object is *immutable* if its state never changes. For example, strings are immutable.
- An object is *shared* by two variables if it can be accessed through either of them.
- If a mutable object is shared by two variables, modifications made through one of the variables will be visible when the object is used through the other.

```
b[0] = i;
```

This causes the zeroth element of the array to contain 6 (instead of the 1 it used to contain), as shown in Figure 2.2c. Furthermore, the change is visible when the array is used later, via either variable b or variable a; for example, in

```
if (a[0] == i) ...
```

the expression will evaluate to true, and therefore, the then branch will be executed.

Sidebar 2.2 summarizes mutability and sharing.

2.3.2 Method Call Semantics

An attempt to call a method, e.m(...), first evaluates e to obtain the class or object whose method is being called. Then the expressions for the arguments are evaluated to obtain *actual parameter* values; this evaluation happens left to right. Next an *activation record* is created for the call and pushed onto the stack; the activation record contains room for the formal parameters of the method (as discussed earlier, the formals are the variables declared in the method header) and any other local storage the method requires. Then the actual parameters are assigned to the formals; this kind of parameter passing is called *call by value*. Finally, control is *dispatched* to the called method e.m; Section 2.5 discusses how this works.

Just as was the case for assignment to variables, if an actual parameter value is a reference to an object, that reference is assigned to the formal. This means that the called procedure shares objects with its caller. Furthermore, if

Figure 2.3   Method call

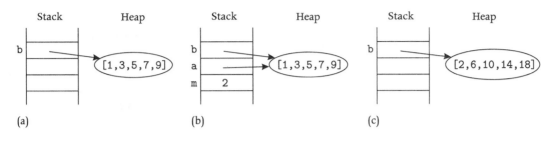

(a)   (b)   (c)

these objects are mutable, and the called procedure changes their state, these changes are visible to the caller when it returns.

For example, suppose the Arrays class mentioned earlier contained a method, multiples, that multiplies each element of its array argument a by its multiplier argument m:

```
public static void multiples (int [ ] a, int m) {
    if (a == null) return;
    for (int i = 0; i < a.length; i++) a[i] = a[i]*m;
}
```

This method works on any size array; it uses a.length to determine the length of the array. Figure 2.3 shows what happens when the method is called by the following code:

```
int [ ] b = {1,3,5,7,9};
Arrays.multiples(b, 2);
```

Figure 2.3a shows the situation just before the call. Figure 2.3b shows the situation just after the call has occurred; the stack now contains the activation record for the call, and the formals have been initialized to contain the actuals. Thus, the formal a of Arrays.multiples refers to the same array as b does. Finally, Figure 2.3c shows the situation just after Arrays.multiples returns. At this point, the activation record created for the call has been discarded. However, the argument array has been modified, and this modification is visible to the caller through variable b.

In a call e.m in which e is supposed to evaluate to an object, it is possible that e might instead evaluate to null and thus not refer to any object. If this happens, the call is not made, but instead the NullPointerException is raised (exceptions are discussed in Chapter 4).

2.4   Type Checking

Java is a *strongly typed* language, which means that the Java compiler checks the code to ensure that every assignment and every call is type correct. If a type error is discovered, compilation fails with an error message.

Type checking depends on the fact that every variable declaration gives the type of the variable, and the header of every method and constructor defines its *signature*: the types of its arguments and results (and also the types of any exceptions it throws). This information allows the compiler to deduce an *apparent type* for any expression. And this deduction then allows it to determine the legality of an assignment.

For example, consider

```
int y = 7;
int z = 3;
int x = Num.gcd (z, y);
```

When the compiler processes the call to Num.gcd, it knows that Num.gcd requires two integer arguments, and it also knows that expressions z and y are both of type int. Therefore, it knows the call of gcd is legal. Furthermore, it knows that gcd returns an int, and therefore it knows that the assignment to x is legal.

Java has an important property: legal Java programs (that is, those accepted by the compiler) are guaranteed to be *type safe*. This means that there cannot be any type errors when the program runs: it is not possible for the program to manipulate data belonging to one type as if it belonged to a different type. Type safety is achieved by three mechanisms: compile-time type checking, automatic storage management, and array bounds checking. Type safety is summarized in Sidebar 2.3.

2.4.1   Type Hierarchy

Java types are organized into a *hierarchy* in which a type can have a number of *supertypes*; we say the type is a *subtype* of each of its *supertypes*. (Other texts may use the term *superclass* [*subclass*] to mean supertype [subtype]; in addition, some texts say a type *extends* another type to mean it is a subtype of the other type.) Type hierarchy provides a way of abstracting from the

Sidebar 2.3 Type Safety

- One important difference between Java and C and C++ is that Java provides type safety. This is accomplished by three mechanisms:

  - Java is a strongly typed language. This means that type errors such as using a pointer as an integer are detected by the compiler.
  - Java provides automatic storage management for all objects. In C and C++, programs manage storage for objects in the heap explicitly. Explicit management is a major source of errors such as *dangling references*, in which storage is deallocated while a program still refers to it.
  - Java checks all array accesses to ensure they are within bounds.

- These techniques ensure that type mismatches cannot occur at runtime. In this way an important source of errors is eliminated from your code.

differences among subtypes to their common behavior, which is captured by their supertype.

The subtype relation is transitive: if R is a subtype of S, and S is a subtype of T, then R is a subtype of T. The relation is also reflexive: type S is a subtype of itself.

If S is a subtype of T, its objects are intended to be usable in any context that expects to use objects belonging to T. For S objects to be usable, they must have all the methods that T objects have; this requirement is enforced by the Java compiler. In addition, all the method calls must behave the same way on S and T objects; this requirement is *not* enforced by Java, nor could it be, since it requires processing beyond the abilities of a compiler (it requires proving that the two programs behave in the same way). We will discuss this requirement in greater detail in Chapter 7 when we discuss how to define sub- and supertypes. For now, you will only make use of predefined type hierarchies, and you can assume that subtypes are defined properly.

The special type Object is at the top of the type hierarchy in Java; all object types, including String and array types, are subtypes of this type. This means all objects have certain methods—namely, the ones specified for Object. For example, Object methods include equals and toString, with the following headers:

```
boolean equals (Object o)
String toString ( )
```

Object and its methods will be discussed further in Chapter 5.

Since objects of a subtype behave like those of a supertype, it makes sense to allow them to be referred to by a variable whose declared type is a supertype. This usage is permitted by Java: an assignment v = e is legal if the type of e is a subtype of the type of v. For example, the following is legal:

```
Object o1 = a;
Object o2 = s;
```

Here a is an array, and s is a string, as shown in Figure 2.2.

An implication of the assignment rule is that the *actual type* of an object obtained by evaluating an expression is a subtype of the apparent type of the expression deduced by the compiler using declarations. For example, the apparent type of o2 is Object, but its actual type is String.

Type checking is always done using the apparent type. This means, for example, that any method calls made using the object will be determined to be legal based on the apparent type. Therefore only Object methods like equals can be called on o2; string methods like length (which returns a count of the number of characters in the string) cannot be called:

```
if (o2.equals("abc")) // legal
if (o2.length( )) // illegal
```

Furthermore, the following is illegal:

```
s = o2; // illegal
```

because the apparent type of o2 is not a subtype of String. Compilation will fail when the program contains illegal code as in these examples.

Sometimes a program needs to determine the actual type of an object at runtime, for example, so that a method not provided by the apparent type can be called. This can be done by *casting*. For example,

```
if (((String)o2.length()) == 0)
s = (String) o2; // legal
```

The use of a cast causes a check to occur at runtime; if the check succeeds, the indicated computation is allowed, and otherwise, the ClassCastException will be raised. In the example, the casts check whether o2's actual type is the

---

Sidebar 2.4 Type Hierarchy

- Java supports *type hierarchy*, in which one type can be the *supertype* of other types, which are its *subtypes*. A subtype's objects have all the methods defined by the supertype.

- All object types are subtypes of Object, which is the top of the type hierarchy. Object defines a number of methods, including equals and toString. Every object is guaranteed to have these methods.

- The *apparent type* of a variable is the type understood by the compiler from information available in declarations. The *actual type* of an object is its real type—the type it receives when it is created.

- Java guarantees that the apparent type of any expression is a supertype of its actual type.

---

same as the indicated type String; these checks succeed, and therefore, the assignment in the first statement or the method call in the second statement is allowed.

Sidebar 2.4 summarizes this discussion.

2.4.2 Conversions and Overloading

The determination of type correctness is actually not as simple as described previously, for two reasons. First, Java allows certain implicit *conversions* of a value of one type to a value of another type. Implicit conversions involve only the primitive types. For example, Java allows chars to be *widened* to numeric types. Thus, the assignment to n in the following is legal:

```
char c = 'a';
int n = c;
```

In general, conversions involve computation—that is, they cause the production of a new value (of the variable's type) that is then assigned to the variable. After the compiler determines the conversion needed to make the assignment legal, it generates the code needed to produce the new value. You can learn what conversions are legal, and what computations they involve, by consulting a Java text.

In addition, Java allows *overloading*. This means that there can be several method definitions with the same name. Most languages allow overloaded definitions of operators; for example, + is defined for both integers and floats. Java allows overloading of operators, but in addition, it allows programmers to overload method names as well.

For example, consider a class C with the following methods:

```
static int comp(int, long)   // defn. 1
static float comp(long, int) // defn. 2
static int comp(long, long)  // defn. 3
```

This class provides three overloaded definitions of comp.

When there are overloaded definitions, several of them might work for a particular call. For example, suppose you have the declarations

```
int x;
long y;
float z;
```

In Java, an int can be widened to a long, and also a float can be widened to a long. Therefore a call C.comp(x, y) could go to either the first definition of comp (since here the types match exactly) or the third definition of comp (by widening x to a long). The second definition is not possible since it isn't possible to widen a long to an int.

The rule used to determine which method to call when there are several choices, as in this example, is "most specific." A method m1 is more specific than another method m2 if any legal call of m1 would also be a legal call of m2 if more conversions were done. For example, the first definition of comp would be selected for the call C.comp(x, y) since it is more specific than the third definition.

If there is no most specific method, a compile time error occurs. For example, all three definitions are possible matches for the call C.comp(x, x). However, none of these is most specific, and therefore, the call is illegal. The programmer can resolve the ambiguity in a case like this by making the conversion explicit; for example, C.comp((long) x, x) selects the second definition.

Overloading decisions also take into account assignments from sub- to supertypes. For example, consider

```
void foo (T a, int x)   // defn. 1
void foo (S b, long y)  // defn. 2
```

Then C.foo(e, 3), where S is a subtype of T and e is a variable of type S, is not legal since neither definition is most specific.

2.5   Dispatching

When a method is called on some object, it is essential that the call go to the code provided by that object for that method, because only that code can do the right thing. For example, consider

```
String t = "ab";
Object o = t + "c";  // concatenation
String r = "abc";
boolean b = o.equals(r);
```

Here the intention is to find out whether o's value is the string "abc". This desire will be satisfied if the call goes to the string's code for equals, since this will compare the values of the two strings. If instead the call goes to Object's code for equals, we will only learn whether o and r are the very same object.

The problem is that the compiler doesn't necessarily know what code to call at compile time because it only knows the apparent type of the object and not its actual type. This is illustrated in the example: the compiler only knows that o is an Object. If the apparent type were used to determine the code to call, the wrong result would happen; for example, b would contain false because o and r are distinct objects.

Therefore, we need a way to *dispatch* a method call to the code of the actual object. This requires a runtime mechanism since the compiler cannot figure out what to do at compile time.

Figure 2.4 illustrates one way that dispatching works. Each object contains a reference to a *dispatch vector*. The dispatch vector contains an entry for each of the object's methods. The compiler generates code to access the location in the vector that points to the code of the method being called and branch to that code. The figure shows the situation for object o; a call to the equals method would branch to the code referred to by the first location in the table, and thus the call will go to the implementation provided by String.

Figure 2.4   Dispatching.

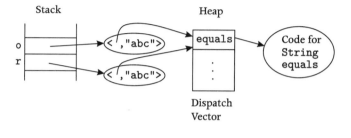

2.6   Types

This section describes a few object types that are nonstandard (i.e., they don't appear in other languages) and that we will use throughout the book.

2.6.1   Primitive Object Types

Primitive types like int and char are not subtypes of Object, and their values, such as 3 and c, cannot be used in contexts where objects are required. For example, such values cannot be stored in Vectors; Vectors are discussed in Section 2.6.2.

Primitive values can be used in contexts requiring objects by *wrapping* them in objects. Each primitive type has an associated object type (e.g., Integer for int, Character for char). Such a type provides a constructor for producing one of its objects by wrapping a value of the associated primitive type, and a method to do the reverse transformation. For example, for Integer we have

```
public Integer(int x) // the constructor
public int intValue( ) // the method
```

These types also provide methods to produce objects of their associated types from strings. Thus,

```
int n = Integer.parseInt(s);
```

will return the int described by string s. For example, if s is the string "1024", n will contain the integer 1024. If s cannot be interpreted as an integer, the method will throw NumberFormatException.

The primitive object types have a number of other useful methods; consult a Java text to learn about them. They are defined in the package java.lang. This package defines a number of types that are so central to Java that the package can be used without needing to import it. For example, the types String and Object are defined in java.lang.

2.6.2   Vectors

Vectors are extensible arrays; they are empty when first created and can grow and shrink on the high end. Vectors are defined in the java.util package. Here we discuss some of their methods; for more information, consult a Java text.

Like an array, a vector contains elements numbered from zero up to one less than its current length. The length of a vector can be determined by calling its size method.

Each element in the vector has the apparent type Object. This means that vectors can be heterogeneous: different elements of a vector can be objects of different types. However, vectors typically are used in a more limited ways, so that all elements of a vector are of the same type or of a few closely related types.

When a vector is created, it is empty, and its length is zero; for example,

```
Vector v = new Vector( );   // creates a new, empty Vector
if (v.size( )== 0) // true
```

A vector can be made to grow by using the add method to add an element to its high end; for example,

```
v.add("abc");
```

This method increases the size of the vector by 1 and stores its argument in the new location.

Vector elements can be accessed for legal indices. The get method fetches the indexed element; for example,

```
String s = (String) v.get(0);
```

Note that get returns an `Object`, and the using code must then cast the result to the appropriate type. If the given index is not within bounds, get throws the `IndexOutOfBoundsException`.

```
String t = (String) v.get(1); // throws IndexOutOfBoundsException
```

The set method is used to change a particular element; for example,

```
v.set(0, "def"); // now v contains the single element "def"
```

Finally, the vector can be caused to shrink by using the `remove` method; for example,

```
v.remove(0);
```

Because all elements of a vector must belong to types that are subtypes of `Object`, vectors cannot contain elements of primitive types such as int and char. Such values can be stored in a vector by using the associated object types. For example,

```
v.add(3); // a compile time error
v.add(new Integer(3)); // legal
```

To use such an element later it must be both cast and converted to a value; for example,

```
int x = ((Integer) v.get(2)).intValue( );
```

2.7 Stream Input/Output

The package java.io provides a number of types of input and output streams. These facilities are briefly described here; more detail can be found in a Java text.

Input/output (I/O) is done using character streams. Input is done using objects that belong to type Reader or one of its subtypes. For example, BufferedReader objects can be used to read characters from a stream. (The term *buffered* indicates that input is done in larger chunks than individual characters, and the data are then kept in a buffer until they are used.) The content of a file can be read by using subtype FileReader; for example,

```
FileReader in = new FileReader(filename);
```

where the string, `filename`, is the pathname of the file.

Output occurs on objects of type `Writer` or a subtype of this type. Subtype `PrintWriter` can be used to print values and objects to an output device, while subtype `FileWriter` can be used to send output to a file.

Java also provides some predefined objects for doing standard I/O; these objects are defined in class `System` of package `java.lang`:

`System.in`	*// Standard input to the program.*
`System.out`	*// Standard output from the program.*
`System.err`	*// Error output from the program.*

These objects are *not* character stream objects (since they were defined in Java 1.0, before character streams, which were introduced in Java 1.1, had been invented). In particular, `System.in` is an `InputStream`, while `System.out` and `System.err` are `PrintStream`s. However, this difference need not concern you very much because `InputStream`s behave like `Reader`s (i.e., have the same methods), and `OutputStream`s are similar to `Writer`s. Furthermore, you can use them as character streams by wrapping them; for example,

```
PrintWriter myOut = new PrintWriter(System.out);
BufferedReader myIn = new BufferedReader(System.in);
```

Most methods on streams do error checking (e.g., to check for end of file when data is being input from a file) and throw `IOException` if an error is detected.

2.8   Java Applications

There are two kinds of Java applications: those run from the command line on a terminal, and those run by interacting with a user interface. We will discuss the latter kind of application in Chapters 11 through 14.

Applications that run from the command line provide a `main` method. This method takes an array of strings as an argument:

```
public static void main(String[ ])
```

where the argument array contains the command-line arguments.

The following example is a trivial complete program that prints the string `"Hello world"` followed by a newline to standard output:

```
public class HelloWorld {

   public static void main(String[ ] args) {
      System.out.println("Hello world");
   }
}
```

Since the name of the method is `main`, the program can be run from the command line.

The next example reads an integer from an input stream and prints its factorial to an output stream. It shows how to read and write integers from streams; other built-in types can be read/written similarly.

```
public class computeFactorial {

   public static void main (String[ ] args) {
      PrintWriter out = new PrintWriter(System.out);
      BufferedReader in =
            new BufferedReader(new InputStreamReader(System.in));
      PrintWriter err = new PrintWriter(System.err);
      out.println("Enter an integer: ");
      String s = null;
      try {
         s = in.readLine( );
         int n = Integer.parseInt(s);
         if (n > 0) {
            out.print(n);
            out.print(" != ");
            out.println(Num.fact(n));
         } else err.println("input not positive");
      } catch (Exception e) { err.println("bad input"); }
   }
}
```

Note that the code does not check directly for badly formatted input. Instead, it relies on the checking done within the call to the `Integer.parseInt` method; recall that this method will throw the `NumberFormatException` if there is a formatting problem. If this exception, or `IOException`, occurs, it is handled by the `try-catch` construct (as discussed further in Chapter 4), and the code produces an appropriate error message.

Although these examples perform a single computation that transforms an input into an output and then terminates, more generally applications run for a long time and interact with a user or other programs to determine what to do. We will discuss long-lived applications in Chapters 11 through 14.

Exercises

2.1 Consider the following code:

```
String s1 = "ace";
String s2 = "f";
String s3 = s1;
String s4 = s3 + s2; // concatenation
```

Illustrate the effect of the code on the heap and stack by drawing a diagram similar to that in Figure 2.2.

2.2 Consider the code:

```
int[ ] a = {1,2,3};
int[ ] b = new int[2];
int[ ] c = a;
int x = c[0];
```

Illustrate the effect of this code on the heap and stack by drawing a diagram similar to that in Figure 2.2.

2.3 Extend the diagram you produced in question 2.2 to show the effect of the following code:

```
b[0] = x;
a[1] = 6;
x = b[1];
y = a[1];
```

2.4 Consider the routine:

```
void sums (int[ ] z) {
    if (z == null || z.length == 0) return;
        for (int i = 1; i < z.length; i++)
            z[i] = z[i-1] + z[i];
    }
```

This routine modifies its argument z so that when the routine returns, each element z[i] contains the sum of the values z[0],...,z[i] as of the time of the call. Show the effect of the following code:

```
int[ ] d = {2, 4, 6, 8};
Arrays.sums(d);
```

by providing diagrams similar to those in Figure 2.3. Show the state of the program right before the call of sums, right after the call of sums starts running, and right after sums returns.

2.5 Consider the following code:

```
Object o = "abc";
```

For each of the following statements, indicate whether or not a compile-time error will occur, and for those statements that are legal at compile time, indicate whether they will return normally or by throwing an exception; if the return is normal, also indicate the result.

```
boolean b = o.equals("a, b, c");
char c = o.charAt(1);
Object o2 = b;
String s = o;
String t = (String) o;
c = t.charAt(1);
c = t.charAt(3);
```

2.6 Consider the following code:

```
int[ ] a = [1,2,3];
Object o = "123";
String t = "12";
String w = t + "3";
boolean b = o.equals(a);
boolean b2 = o.equals(t);
boolean b3 = o.equals(w);
boolean b4 = (o == w);
```

Show the effect of executing this code by means of a diagram similar to that in Figure 2.2. Also explain how the the code arrived at the results in b, b1, b2, and b3.

2.7 Consider the following definitions:

```
void m (Object o, long x, long y)  // defn 1
void m (String s, int x, long y)   // defn 2
void m (Object o, int x, long y)   // defn 3
void m (String s, long x, int y)   // defn 4
```

and suppose you have the following variable declarations:

```
Object u;
String v;
int a;
long b;
```

For each of the following calls, determine which definitions would match a particular call; also decide whether the call is legal, and if so, which of the preceding definitions is selected:

```
m(v, a, b);
m(v, a, a);
m(v, b, a);
m(v, b, b);
m(o, b, b);
m(o, a, a);
```

Procedural Abstraction

In this chapter, we discuss the most familiar kind of abstraction used in programming, the *procedural abstraction*, or *procedure* for short. Anyone who has introduced a subroutine to provide a function that can be used in other programs has used procedural abstraction. Procedures combine the methods of abstraction by parameterization and specification in a way that allows us to abstract a single action or task, such as computing the greatest common demoninator (gcd) of two integers or sorting an array.

A procedure provides a transformation from input arguments to output arguments. More precisely, it is a mapping from a set of input arguments to a set of output results, with possible modifications of the inputs. The set of inputs or outputs, or both, might be empty. For example, gcd has two inputs and one output, but it does not modify its inputs. By contrast, a sort procedure might have one input (the array to be sorted) and no output, and it does modify its input (by sorting it).

We begin with the benefits of abstraction and, in particular, of abstraction by specification. Next we discuss specifications and why they are needed. Then we discuss how to specify and implement *standalone procedures*; these are procedures that are independent of particular objects. We conclude with some general remarks about their design.

3.1   The Benefits of Abstraction

An abstraction is a many-to-one map. It "abstracts" from "irrelevant" details, describing only those details that are relevant to the problem at hand. Its *realizations* must all agree in the relevant details but can differ in the irrelevant ones. Of course, distinguishing what is relevant from what is irrelevant is not always easy. A major portion of this book will be concerned with how this is done.

In abstraction by parameterization, we abstract from the identity of the data being used. The abstraction is defined in terms of formal parameters; the actual data are bound to these formals when the abstraction is used. Thus, the identity of the actual data is irrelevant, but the presence, number, and types of the actuals are relevant. Parameterization generalizes abstractions, making them useful in more situations. A virtue of such generalizations is that they decrease the amount of code that needs to be written and, thus, modified and maintained.

In abstraction by specification, we focus on the behavior that the user can depend on and abstract from the details of implementing that behavior. Therefore, the behavior—"what" is done—is relevant, while the method of realizing that behavior—"how" it is done—is irrelevant. For example, for an isPrime procedure, the fact that the procedure determines whether or not its argument is a prime is relevant, but the details of how this is determined are irrelevant.

A key advantage of abstraction by specification is that it allows us to change to another implementation without affecting the meaning of any program that uses the abstraction (Figure 3.1). For example, we could change the algorithm used to implement the isPrime procedure, and programs us-

Figure 3.1   The general structure of abstraction by specification

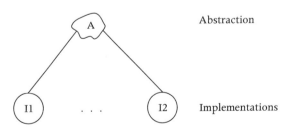

Sidebar 3.1   Benefits of Abstraction by Specification

- *Locality*—The implementation of an abstraction can be read or written without needing to examine the implementations of any other abstractions.

- *Modifiability*—An abstraction can be reimplemented without requiring changes to any abstractions that use it.

ing isPrime would continue to run correctly with this new implementation (although some change in performance might be noticed). The implementations could even be written in different programming languages, provided that the data types of the arguments are treated the same in these languages. For example, in many systems implemented in higher-level languages, it is common to implement some abstractions in machine language to improve performance.

Abstraction by specification provides a method for achieving a program structure with two advantageous properties. These benefits are summarized in Sidebar 3.1. The first property is *locality*, which means that the implementation of one abstraction can be read or written without needing to examine the implementation of any other abstraction. To write a program that uses an abstraction, a programmer need understand only its behavior, not the details of its implementation.

Locality is beneficial both when a program is being written and later when someone wants to understand it or reason about its behavior. Because of locality, different abstractions that make up a program can be implemented by people working independently. One person can implement an abstraction that uses another abstraction being implemented by someone else. As long as both people agree on what the used abstraction is, they can work independently and still produce programs that work together properly. Also, understanding a program can be accomplished one abstraction at a time. To understand the code that implements one abstraction, it is necessary to understand what the used abstractions are, but not the code that implements them. In a large program, the amount of information that is not needed can be enormous; we can ignore not only the code of the used abstractions but also the code of any abstractions they use, and so on.

The second property is *modifiability*. Abstraction by specification helps to bound the effects of program modification and maintenance. If the implementation of an abstraction changes but its specification does not, the rest of the program will not be affected by the change. Of course, if the number of abstractions that must be reimplemented is large, making a modification will still be a lot of work. As will be discussed later, the workload can be reduced by identifying potential modifications while designing the program and then trying to limit their effects to a small number of abstractions. For example, if the effects of machine dependencies can be limited to just a few abstractions, the result will be software that can be transported readily to another machine.

Modifiability leads to a sensible method of tuning performance. Programmers are notoriously bad at predicting where time will actually be spent in a complex system, probably because it is difficult to anticipate where bottlenecks will arise. Since it is unwise to invest effort in inventing techniques that avoid nonexistent bottlenecks, a better method is to start with a simple set of abstractions, run the system to discover where the bottlenecks are, and then reimplement the abstractions that are bottlenecks.

3.2   Specifications

It is essential that abstractions be given precise definitions; otherwise, the advantages discussed in Section 3.1 cannot be achieved. For example, we can replace one implementation of an abstraction by another only if everything that was depended on by users of the old implementation is supported by the new one. The entity depended on and supported is the abstraction. Therefore, we must know what the abstraction is.

We shall define abstractions by means of *specifications*, which are written in a *specification language* that can be either formal or informal. The advantage of formal specifications is that they have a precise meaning. However, we shall use informal specifications in this book, in which the behavior of the abstraction is given in English. Informal specifications are easier to read and write than formal ones, but giving them a precise meaning is difficult because the informal specification language is not precise. Despite this, informal specifications can be very informative and can be written in such a way that readers will have little trouble understanding their intended meaning.

A specification is distinct from any implementation of the abstraction it defines. The implementations are all similar because they implement the same abstraction; they differ because they implement it in different ways. The specification defines their commonality.

A specification language is *not* a programming language. Thus, our specifications will not be written in Java. Furthermore, specifications are usually quite different from programs because they focus on describing what the abstraction is rather than how it is implemented. This allows them to be much shorter and easier to read than the corresponding implementation.

3.3   Specifications of Procedural Abstractions

The specification of a procedure consists of a header and a description of effects. The *header* gives the name of the procedure, the number, order, and types of its parameters, and the type of its result; it also lists any exceptions thrown by the procedure, but we defer discussion of exceptions to Chapter 4. In addition, names must be given for the parameters. For example, the header for removeDupls is

```
void removeDupls (Vector v);
```

while the header of sqrt is

```
float sqrt (float x);
```

The information in the header is syntactic; it describes the "form" of the procedure. It is similar to a description of the "form" of a mathematical function, as in

$$f : integer \rightarrow integer;$$

In neither case is the meaning—what the procedure or the function does—described. The meaning is captured in the semantic part of the specification, in which the behavior of the procedure is described in English, possibly extended with convenient mathematical notation. This description makes use of the names of the inputs.

Figure 3.2 shows a template of a procedure specification. The semantic part of a specification consists of three parts: the requires, modifies, and effects clauses. These clauses should appear in the order shown, although the requires

Figure 3.2   Specification template for procedural abstractions

```
return_type pname (...)
    // REQUIRES: This clause states any constraints on use
    // MODIFIES: This clause identifies all modified inputs
    // EFFECTS: This clause defines the behavior
```

and modifies clauses are optional. The clauses are shown as comments because they should always appear in your code.

The clauses describe a relation between the procedure's inputs and results. For most procedures, the inputs are exactly the parameters that are listed in the procedure header. However, some procedures have additional *implicit* inputs. For example, a procedure might read a file and write some information on System.out; the file and System.out are also inputs of the procedure.

The *requires clause* states the constraints under which the abstraction is defined. The requires clause is needed if the procedure is *partial*—that is, if its behavior is not defined for some inputs. If the procedure is *total*—that is, if its behavior is defined for all type-correct inputs—the requires clause can be omitted. In this case, the only restrictions on a legal call are those implied by the header—that is, the number and types of the arguments.

The *modifies clause* lists the names of any inputs (including implicit inputs) that are modified by the procedure. If some inputs are modified, we say the procedure has a *side effect*. The modifies clause can be omitted when no inputs are modified. The absence of the modifies clause means that none of the inputs is modified.

Finally, the *effects clause* describes the behavior of the procedure for all inputs not ruled out by the requires clause. It must define what outputs are produced and also what modifications are made to the inputs listed in the modifies clause. The effects clause is written under the assumption that the requires clause is satisfied, and it says nothing about the procedure's behavior when the requires clause is not satisfied.

In Java, standalone procedures are defined as *static methods* of classes. To use such a method, it is necessary to know its class. Therefore, we need to include this information with the specification, giving us the expanded template shown in Figure 3.3. We have simply added a little information about the class: its name and a brief description of its purpose. Additionally, the specification indicates the visibility of the class and each standalone

Figure 3.3   Specification template for class providing standalone procedures

```
visibility cname {
    // OVERVIEW: This clause defines the purpose of the class as a whole.

    visibility static p1 ...
    visibility static p2 ...
}
```

Figure 3.4   Standalone procedure specifications

```
public class Arrays {
    // OVERVIEW: This class provides a number of standalone procedures that
    //     are useful for manipulating arrays of ints.

    public static int search (int[ ] a, int x)
        // EFFECTS: If x is in a, returns an index where x is stored;
        //     otherwise, returns -1.

    public static int searchSorted (int[ ] a, int x)
        // REQUIRES: a is sorted in ascending order
        // EFFECTS: If x is in a, returns an index where x is stored;
        //     otherwise, returns -1.

    public static void sort (int[ ] a)
        // MODIFIES: a
        // EFFECTS: Rearranges the elements of a into ascending order
        //     e.g., if a = [3, 1, 6, 1] before the call, on return a = [1, 1, 3, 6].
}
```

procedure; the visibility of the class and the procedures usually will be public, so that the standalone procedures can be used in other packages.

A partial specification of a class, Arrays, which provides a number of standalone procedures that are useful for manipulating arrays of integers, is given in Figure 3.4. Since the class and the methods are public, the methods can be used by code outside the package containing the class definition.

In the specification, we can see that search and searchSorted do not modify their inputs, but sort modifies its input, as indicated in the modifies clause. Note the use of an example in the sort specification. Examples can clarify a specification and should be used whenever convenient.

Note also that sort and search are *total*, since their specifications do not contain a requires clause. searchSorted, however, is *partial*; it only does its job if its argument array is sorted. Note that the effects clause does not state what searchSorted does if the argument does not meet this constraint. In this case, the implementor can do whatever is convenient; for example, the implementation could even run forever. Obviously, this is not a very desirable situation, and therefore you should avoid the use of the requires clause as much as possible. This issue is discussed further in Section 3.5.

When a procedure modifies the state of some input, the specification needs to relate the state of the object at return with its state at the time of call. This is what happens in the specification of sort. Writing such specifications can be simplified by having notation to identify these different states explicitly. We will make use of the following notation: the name of a formal argument— for example, x denotes its state at the time of call and x_post denotes its state at return. Thus, an alternative way of writing the specification for sort is

```
public static void sort (int[ ] a)
    // MODIFIES: a
    // EFFECTS: Rearranges the elements of a into ascending order.
    //    For example, if a = [3, 1, 6, 1], a_post = [1, 1, 3, 6].
```

Sometimes a procedure must produce a new object. For example, consider

```
public static int[ ] boundArray (int[ ], int n)
    // EFFECTS: Returns a new array containing the elements of a in the
    //    order they appear in a except that any elements of a that are
    //    greater than n are replaced by n.
```

You might wonder whether boundArray could return its argument array if none of its elements exceed n. However, this possibility is ruled out by the specification, which indicates that boundArray must return a *new* object. And obviously this requirement is important, since arrays are mutable: if boundArray returned its argument, the using code is likely to notice the sharing.

In Figure 3.4, all procedures use only formal parameters as inputs. Here is an example of a specification of a procedure that has implicit inputs, namely System.in and System.out:

```
public static void copyLine( )
    // REQUIRES: System.in contains a line of text
    // MODIFIES: System.in and System.out
    // EFFECTS: Reads a line of text from System.in, advances the cursor in
    //     System.in to the end of the line, and writes the line on System.out.
```

Note that the specification describes what the procedure does to the implicit inputs.

Typically, specifications are written first, in advance of writing the code that implements them. At that point, the class should be given a skeleton implementation, consisting of just the method headers and specifications. The bodies of the routines will be missing; code will be provided for these bodies at a later time.

3.4   Implementing Procedures

The implementation of a procedure should produce the behavior defined by its specification. In particular, it should modify only those inputs that appear in the modifies clause; and if all inputs satisfy the requires clause, it should produce the result in accordance with the effects clause.

Figure 3.5 shows a Java method that implements searchSorted (specified in Figure 3.4) using linear search. Note that the implementation of search-Sorted returns −1 when passed null in place of the argument array. This behavior is consistent with what is described in its specification. However, a better specification might have treated this case specially, by indicating that an exception should be thrown. Exceptions will be discussed in Chapter 4. Note also that we have included a comment in the code explaining the algorithm in use; such a comment is not needed if the algorithm is straightforward but should be included if it is not.

As a second example, consider the sort procedure specified in Figure 3.4. One possible method is quick sort, which partitions the elements of the array into two contiguous groups such that all the elements in the first group are no larger than those in the second group; it continues to partition recursively until the entire array is sorted. To carry out these steps, we use two subsidiary procedures: quickSort, which causes the partitioning of smaller and smaller subparts of the array, and partition, which performs the partitioning of a designated subpart of the array.

Figure 3.5   An implementation of searchSorted

```
public class Arrays {
    // OVERVIEW: This class provides a number of standalone procedures that
    //    are useful for manipulating arrays of ints.

    public static int searchSorted (int[ ] a, int x) {
        // REQUIRES: a is sorted in ascending order.
        // EFFECTS: If x is in a, returns an index where x is stored;
        //    otherwise, returns -1.
        // uses linear search
        if (a == null) return -1;
        for (int i = 0; i < a.length; i++)
            if (a[i] == x) return i; else if (a[i] > x) return -1;
        return -1;
    }

    // other static methods go here
}
```

Figure 3.6 shows the sort implementation. Note that the quickSort and partition routines are *not* declared to be public; instead, their use is limited to the Arrays class. This is appropriate because they are just helper routines and have little utility in their own right. Nevertheless, we have provided specifications for them; these specifications are of interest to someone interested in understanding how quickSort is implemented but not to a user of quickSort.

As another example, consider a class Vectors that is similar to Arrays but instead provides useful routines for vectors (recall that vectors are extensible arrays of objects). One routine provided by this class removes duplicates from a vector. Figure 3.7 on page 50 contains the specification and implementation of this routine. Note that the specification explains what "duplicate" means: it is determined by using the equals method to compare elements of the vector.

Figure 3.6   Quick sort implementation

```
public class Arrays {
   // OVERVIEW: ...

   public static void sort (int[ ] a) {
      // MODIFIES: a
      // EFFECTS: Sorts a[0], ..., a[a.length - 1] into ascending order.
      if (a == null) return;
      quickSort(a, 0, a.length-1); }

   private static void quickSort(int[ ] a, int low, int high) {
      // REQUIRES: a is not null and 0 <= low & high < a.length
      // MODIFIES: a
      // EFFECTS: Sorts a[low], a[low+1], ..., a[high] into ascending order.
      if (low >= high) return;
      int mid = partition(a, low, high);
      quickSort(a, low, mid);
      quickSort(a, mid + 1, high); }

   private static int partition(int[ ] a, int i, int j) {
      // REQUIRES: a is not null and 0 <= i < j < a.length
      // MODIFIES: a
      // EFFECTS: Reorders the elements in a into two contiguous groups,
      //    a[i],...,a[res] and a[res+1],...,a[j], such that each
      //    element in the second group is at least as large as each
      //    element of the first group. Returns res.
      int x = a[i];
      while (true) {
         while (a[j] > x) j--;
         while (a[i] < x) i++;
         if (i < j) { // need to swap
            int temp = a[i]; a[i] = a[j]; a[j] = temp;
            j--; i++; }
         else return j; }
   }
}
```

Figure 3.7   Removing duplicates from a vector

```
public class Vectors {
   // OVERVIEW: Provides useful standalone procedures for manipulating vectors.

   public static void removeDupls (Vector v) {
      // REQUIRES: All elements of v are not null.
      // MODIFIES: v
      // EFFECTS: Removes all duplicate elements from v; uses equals to
      //    determine duplicates. The order of remaining elements may change.
      if (v == null) return;
      for (int i = 0; i < v.size( ); i++) {
         Object x = v.get(i);
         int j = i + 1;
         // remove all dupls of x from the rest of v
         while (j < v.size( ))
            if (!x.equals(v.get(j))) j++;
            else { v.set(j, v.lastElement( ));
               v.remove(v.size( )-1); }
      }
   }
}
```

3.5   Designing Procedural Abstractions

In this section, we discuss a number of issues that arise in designing procedural abstractions.

Procedures are introduced during program design to shorten the calling code and clarify its structure. In this way, the calling code becomes easier to understand and to reason about. However, it is possible to introduce too many procedures. For example, the partition procedure in Figure 3.6 is worth introducing because it has a well-defined purpose and because it allows us to separate the details of partitioning the array from controlling the partitioning, thus making quickSort easier to understand. Further decomposition is probably counterproductive, however. For example, the loop body in partition could be made into a procedure, but its purpose would be difficult to state, and neither partition itself nor the new procedure would do much.

Procedures, as well as the other kinds of abstractions that we shall discuss later, should be designed to be *minimally constraining*; care should be taken to constrain details of the procedure's behavior only to the extent necessary. In this way, we leave more freedom to the implementor, who may be able to provide a more efficient implementation as a result. However, details that matter to users must be constrained or the procedure will not be what is needed.

One kind of detail that is almost certainly left undefined is the algorithm to be used in the implementation. Generally, users do not depend on such details. (There are exceptions, however; for example, a numerical procedure may be constrained to use a well-known numerical method so that its behavior with respect to rounding errors will be well defined.) Some details of what the procedure does may also be left undefined, leading to a procedure that is *underdetermined*. This means that for certain inputs, instead of a single correct output, there is a set of acceptable outputs. An implementation is constrained to produce some member of that set, but any member will do.

The search and searchSorted procedures are underdetermined because we did not state exactly what index should be returned if x occurs in the array more than once. This means that implementations can differ in this regard. For example, Figure 3.8 shows another implementation of search-Sorted using binary search. This implementation differs from the one using linear search (see Figure 3.5) in many details. For example, for all but very small arrays, binary search is faster than linear search. Moreover, if x appears in a more than once, the two procedures may return different indices. Finally, if x is contained in a but a is not sorted, the implementation using binary search may return -1 when the other implementation finds the index of x or vice versa (as an example, consider a = [1, 7, 6, 4, 9] and x = 7). Nevertheless, both implementations are correct realizations of the search-Sorted abstraction since both provide behavior that is consistent with the specification.

removeDupls (see Figure 3.7) is also underdetermined, since it does not necessarily preserve the order of elements in its input vector. This lack of constraint may be a mistake, because users may care about the order; if the input vector is sorted, for example, it might be desirable to preserve the order. The important point is that what matters depends on what users need. Details that matter to users should be specified; the others can be left undefined.

An underdetermined abstraction usually has a *deterministic* implementation; that is, one that, if called twice with identical inputs, behaves identically

Figure 3.8   Implementing searchSorted using binary search

```
public class Arrays {
   // OVERVIEW: ...

   public static int searchSorted (int[ ] a, int x) {
      // uses binary search
      if (a == null) return -1;
      int low = 0;
      int high = a.length - 1;
      while (low <= high) {
         int mid = (low + high) / 2;  // computes the floor
         if (x == a[mid]) return mid;
         if (x < a[mid]) high = mid - 1; else low = mid + 1;
      }
   return -1;
   }
}
```

on the two calls. Both implementations of searchSorted are deterministic. (Nondeterministic implementations require the use of nondeterministic primitives, global data, or static variables; for example, the implementation might read the system clock each time it is called and use that value as a way of producing a different result from any previous call.)

In addition to minimality, another important property of procedures is *generality*, which is often achieved by using parameters instead of specific variables or assumptions. For example, a procedure that searches for an arbitrary integer in an array, where the integer is an argument of the procedure, is more general than one that works only for a specific integer. Similarly, a procedure that works on any size array is more general than one that works only on arrays of some fixed size. Generalizing a procedure is only worthwhile, however, if doing so increases its usefulness. This is almost always true when size assumptions are eliminated, since by doing so we ensure that a minor change in the context of use (for example, doubling the size of an array) requires little, if any, program modification. See Sidebar 3.2 for a summary of the properties of procedural abstractions. Generalization is discussed further in Chapter 8.

Sidebar 3.2 Properties of Procedures and Their Implementations

- *Minimality*—One specification is more minimal than another if it contains fewer constraints on allowable behavior.

- *Underdetermined behavior*—A procedure is underdetermined if for certain inputs its specification allows more than one possible result.

- *Deterministic implementation*—An implementation of a procedure is deterministic if, for the same inputs, it always produces the same result. Implementations of underdetermined procedures are almost always deterministic.

- *Generality*—One specification is more general than another if it can handle a larger class of inputs.

Another important property of procedures is simplicity. A procedure should have a well-defined and easily explained purpose that is independent of its context of use. A good check for simplicity is to give the procedure a name that describes its purpose. If it is difficult to think of a name, there may be a problem with the procedure.

Some of the procedures discussed earlier are partial, while others are total. This dichotomy leads to the question of when it is appropriate to define a partial abstraction. Partial procedures are not as safe as total ones, since they leave it to the user to satisfy the constraints in the requires clause. When the requires clause is not satisfied, the behavior of a partial procedure is completely unconstrained; and this can cause the using program to fail in mysterious ways. For example, searchSorted might not return or it might return the wrong index when its input array is not sorted. In the latter case, the error may not be noticed until long after searchSorted returns. By then, the reason for the error may be obscure, and important objects may have been damaged.

On the other hand, partial procedures can be more efficient to implement than total ones. For example, if searchSorted had to work even when the input array was not sorted, then neither implementation (in Figure 3.5 or Figure 3.8) would be correct; only a less-efficient implementation that examined all elements of the array could be used.

Sidebar 3.3   Total versus Partial Procedures

- A procedure is *total* if its behavior is specified for all legal inputs; otherwise, it is *partial*. The specification of a partial procedure always contains a requires clause.

- Partial procedures are less safe than total ones. Therefore, they should be used only when the context of use is limited or when they enable a substantial benefit, such as better performance.

- When possible, the implementation should check the constraints in the requires clause and throw an exception if they are not satisfied.

In choosing between a partial and a total procedure, we have to make a trade-off. On the one hand is efficiency; on the other is safe behavior, with fewer potential surprises at runtime. How is such a choice to be made? An important consideration is the expected context of use. If the procedure is intended for general use (for example, if it is to be made available as part of a program library), safety considerations should be given great weight. In such a situation, it is impossible to examine all code that calls the procedure to ensure that the calls satisfy the constraints. Therefore, it is wise to avoid the constraints if possible.

Alternatively, some procedures are intended to be used only in a limited context. This was the situation with `partition` and `quickSort`, which can be used only within the `Arrays` class. In a limited context, it is easy to establish that constraints are satisfied. For example, `partition` assumes that i is less than j, but this condition is established by `quickSort`, which is its only caller. Therefore, we might choose a partial procedure in such a case if this can improve performance or lead to a simpler implementation.

Another point is that the implementation of an abstraction is not forbidden to check the constraint given in a requires clause. If the check indicates that the requires clause is not satisfied, the procedure could produce an error message, but a better approach is usually to throw an exception; exceptions are discussed in the next chapter. Sidebar 3.3 summarizes our discussion of total versus partial procedures.

Of course, it doesn't make sense to check a constraint when the checking is very expensive, for example, as it would be in the `searchSorted` routine.

But sometimes a constraint is not expensive to check; this is the case for removeDupls, which requires all elements of the vector to be non-null. In such a case it is a good idea to do the check and throw an expection if it fails. Since such checks aren't required by the specification, they can be disabled later, when the program is in production use, if this becomes necessary to achieve good performance.

Finally, it is worth noting that a specification is the only record of its abstraction. Therefore, it is crucial that the specification be clear and precise. How to write good specifications is the subject of Chapter 9.

3.6   Summary

This chapter has been concerned primarily with procedures: what they are, how to describe their behavior, and how to implement them. We also discussed two important benefits of abstraction and the need for specifications.

A procedure is a mapping from inputs to outputs, with possible modifications of some of the inputs. Its behavior, like that of any other kind of abstraction, is described by a specification, and we presented a form for informal specifications of procedures. A procedure is implemented in Java by a static method; in other languages, it would be implemented by a function or subroutine.

Abstraction provides the two key benefits of locality and modifiability. Both are based on the distinction between an abstraction and its implementations. Locality means that each implementation can be understood in isolation. An abstraction can be used without having to understand how it is implemented, and it can be implemented without having to understand how it is used. Modifiability means that one implementation can be substituted for another without disturbing the using programs.

To obtain these benefits, we must have a description of the abstraction that is distinct from any implementation. To this end, we introduced the specification, which describes the behavior of an abstraction using a special specification language. This language can be formal or informal; we used an informal language but with a fixed structure consisting of the requires, modifies, and effects clauses. Users can assume the behavior described by the specification, and implementors must provide this behavior. Thus, the specification serves as a contract between users and implementors.

Since we are interested in design and how to invent good abstractions, we concluded the chapter with a discussion of what procedures should be like. Desirable properties include minimality, simplicity, and generality. Minimality often gives rise to underdetermined abstractions. We also discussed the pros and cons of partial and total procedures. We shall continue to discuss desirable properties in the following chapters as we introduce additional kinds of abstractions.

Exercises

3.1 Computing the greatest common divisor by repeated subtraction (see Figure 2.1 in Chapter 2) is not very efficient. Reimplement gcd to use division instead.

3.2 Specify and implement a method with the header

```
public static int sum (int[ ] a)
```

that returns the sum of the elements of a.

3.3 Specify and implement a procedure isPrime that determines whether an integer is prime.

3.4 Specify and implement a procedure that determines whether or not a string is a palindrome. (A *palindrome* reads the same backward and forward; an example is "deed.")

3.5 You are to choose between two procedures, both of which compute the minimum value in an array of integers. One procedure returns the smallest integer if its array argument is empty. The other requires a nonempty array. Which procedure should you choose and why?

3.6 Suppose that the implementation of sorting by quick sort shown in Figure 3.6 were changed as follows: Procedure partition is retained, but quickSort is eliminated, so that its work is done directly in sort. Is this change a good idea? What purpose does quickSort have? Discuss.

3.7 Suppose the implementation of partition in Figure 3.6 were changed to return i instead of returning j. Would this work? Explain your reasoning.

Exceptions

4

A procedural abstraction is a mapping from arguments to results, with possible modification of some of the arguments. The arguments are members of the *domain* of the procedure, and the results are members of its *range*.

A procedure often makes sense only for arguments in a subset of its domain. For example, a procedure that computes the factorial makes sense only if its argument is positive. As another example, the search procedure can return the index of the element only if the element appears in the array.

One way of coping with such a situation is to use partial procedures, as discussed in Chapter 3. For example, we might define gcd only when its arguments are positive:

```
public static int gcd (int n, int d)
    // REQUIRES: n, d > 0
    // EFFECTS: Returns the greatest common divisor of n and d.
```

The caller of a partial procedure must ensure that the arguments are in the permitted subset of the domain, and the implementor can ignore arguments outside this subset. Thus, in implementing gcd, we could ignore the case of nonpositive arguments.

Partial procedures are generally a bad idea, however, since there is no guarantee that their arguments are in the permitted subset and the procedure may therefore be called with arguments outside the subset. When this happens, the procedure is allowed to do anything: it might loop forever or return an erroneous result. The latter case is especially bad since it can lead to an obscure error that is difficult to track down. For example, the calling code might continue to run, using the erroneous result, and possibly damage important databases.

Partial procedures lead to programs that are not robust. A *robust* program is one that continues to behave reasonably even in the presence of errors. If an error occurs, the program may not be able to provide exactly the same behavior as if there were no error, but it should behave in a well-defined way. Ideally, it should continue after the error by providing some approximation of its behavior in the absence of an error; a program like this is said to provide *graceful degradation*. At worst, it should halt with a meaningful error message and without causing damage to permanent data.

A method that enhances robustness is to use *total* procedures: procedures whose behavior is defined for all inputs in the domain. If the procedure is unable to perform its "intended" function for some of these inputs, at least it can inform its caller of the problem. In this way, the situation is brought to the attention of the caller, which may be able to do something about it, or at least avoid harmful consequences of the error.

How should the caller be notified if a problem arises? One possibility is to use a particular result to convey the information. For example, a factorial procedure might return zero if its argument is not positive:

```
public static int fact (int n)
    // EFFECTS: If n > 0 returns n! else returns 0.
```

This solution is not very satisfactory. Since the call with illegal arguments is probably an error, it is more constructive to treat this case in a special way, so that a programmer who uses the procedure is less likely to ignore the error by mistake. Also, returning a special result may be inconvenient for the calling code, which then must check for it. For example, rather than writing:

```
z = x + Num.fact(y);
```

the calling code instead must do the check:

```
int r = Num.fact(y);
if (r > 0) z = x + r; else ...
```

Furthermore, if every value of the return type is a possible result of the procedure, the solution of returning a special result is impossible, since there is no leftover value to use. For example, the get method of Vector returns the value of the vector's i^{th} element, and that value can be any object or null. Therefore, we can't convey information about the index being out of bounds by returning a particular object or by returning null.

What is needed is an approach that conveys information about unusual situations in all cases, even when every value of the return type is a legitimate result. In addition, it is desirable for the approach to distinguish these situations in some way, so that users can't ignore them by mistake. It would also be nice if the approach allowed the handling of these situations to be separated from the normal program control flow.

An exception mechanism provides what we want. It allows a procedure to terminate either *normally*, by returning a result, or *exceptionally*. There can be several different exceptional terminations. In Java, each exceptional termination corresponds to a different *exception type*. The names of the exception types are selected by the definer of the procedure to convey some information about what the problem is. For example, the get method of Vector has IndexOutOfBoundsException.

In this chapter, we discuss how to specify, implement, and use procedures with exceptions. We also discuss a number of related design issues.

4.1   Specifications

A procedure that can terminate exceptionally is indicated by having a *throws clause* in its header:

```
throws < list_of_types >
```

For example,

```
public static int fact (int n) throws NonPositiveException
```

states that fact can terminate by throwing an exception; and in this case, it throws an object of type NonPositiveException.

A procedure can throw more than one type of exception; for example,

```
public static int search (int[ ] a, int x)
      throws NullPointerException, NotFoundException
// EFFECTS: If a is null throws NullPointerException; else if x is not
//    in a throws NotFoundException; else returns i such that x = a[i].
```

Figure 4.1   Some specifications with exceptions

```
public static int fact (int n) throws NonPositiveException
    // EFFECTS: If n is non-positive, throws NonPositiveException, else
    //    returns the factorial of n.

public static int search (int[ ] a, int x)
        throws NullPointerException, NotFoundException
    // REQUIRES: a is sorted
    // EFFECTS: If a is null throws NullPointerException; else if x is not
    //    in a, throws NotFoundException; else returns i such that a[i] = x.
```

states that search can throw two exceptions: NullPointerException (if a is null) and NotFoundException (if a is not null and x is not in a).

The specification of a procedure that throws exceptions must make it clear to users exactly what is going on. First, we require that its header list *all* exceptions that it can throw as part of its "ordinary" behavior, for example, for all inputs that meet its requires clause.

Second, the effects clause must explain what causes each exception to be thrown. As before, the effects clause should define the behavior of the procedure for all inputs not ruled out by the requires clause. Since this behavior includes exceptions, the effects section must define what causes the procedure to terminate with each exception, and what its behavior is in each case. Furthermore, if a procedure signals an exception for a certain subset of arguments, that subset should *not* be excluded in the requires clause. Termination by throwing an exception is part of the ordinary behavior of the procedure.

Figure 4.1 shows specifications of fact and search. Note that the specification of search contains a requires clause and that, as usual, its effects section assumes that the requires clause is satisfied.

When a procedure has side effects, its specification must make clear how these interact with exceptions. The modifies section of a specification indicates that an argument may be modified but does not say when this will happen. If there are exceptions, it is likely that the modification will happen only for some of them. Exactly what happens must be described in the effects section. Modifications must be described explicitly in each case where they occur; if no modifications are described, this means none happens. For example, the following specification indicates that v is modified only when addMax returns normally:

```
public static void addMax (Vector v, Integer x)
        throws NullPointerException, NotSmallException
// REQUIRES: All elements of v are Integers.
// MODIFIES: v
// EFFECTS: If v is null throws NullPointerException; if v contains an
//    element larger than x throws NotSmallException; else adds x to v.
```

4.2 The Java Exception Mechanism

This section provides a brief discussion of how exceptions are supported in Java.

4.2.1 Exception Types

Exception types are subtypes of either Exception or RuntimeException, both of which are subtypes of type Throwable. Figure 4.2 shows the hierarchy of exception types. The main point to note is that there are two kinds of exceptions: *checked* exceptions and *unchecked* exceptions. Unchecked exceptions are subtypes of RuntimeException; checked exceptions are subtypes of Exception but not of RuntimeException.

Figure 4.2   The exception type hierarchy

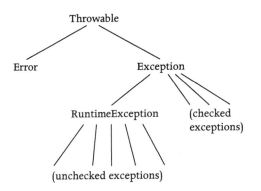

Most exceptions that are defined by Java are unchecked (e.g., Null-PointerException, IndexOutOfBoundsException) but others are checked (e.g., IOException). User-defined exceptions can similarly be either checked or unchecked.

There are two differences in how checked and unchecked exceptions can be used in Java:

1. If a procedure might throw a checked exception, Java requires that the exception be listed in the procedure's header; otherwise, there will be a compile-time error. Unchecked exceptions need not be listed in the header.

2. If code calls a procedure that might throw a checked exception, Java requires that it handle the exception as explained in Section 4.2.4; otherwise, there will be a compile-time error. Unchecked exceptions need not be handled in the calling code.

These differences between checked and unchecked exceptions make it necessary to think carefully when defining a new exception type about whether or not it should be checked. We will discuss this design issue in Section 4.4.2.

We will deviate from the Java rules in one important way: we require that the header of a procedure list *all* exceptions it throws, whether checked or unchecked. For example, the header of search in Figure 4.1 lists NullPointerException even though this is an unchecked exception. The reason for listing unchecked exceptions is that from the point of view of someone using the procedure, any exception that can occur is of interest; you can't understand how to use a procedure without this information. Of course, you could obtain the information from the effects clause of the specification, but including the information in the header brings it to the attention of the user in a very direct way. It also provides a good approach for the specifier: list all exceptions in the header, and then make sure the effects clause explains each of them.

4.2.2   Defining Exception Types

When a new exception type is defined, its declaration indicates whether it is checked or unchecked by indicating its supertype: if the supertype is Exception, it is checked; while if the supertype is RuntimeException, it is unchecked. For example, Figure 4.3 gives a definition of a new exception

Figure 4.3   Defining a new exception type

```
public class NewKindOfException extends Exception {

    public NewKindOfException( ) { super( ); }
    public NewKindOfException(String s) { super(s); }
}
```

type. The header of the class states that the new type, NewKindOfException, is a subtype of type Exception; this is the meaning of

```
extends Exception
```

Therefore, the exception being defined in the figure is a checked exception. The definition of an unchecked exception differs only in that its header contains

```
extends RuntimeException
```

As illustrated in Figure 4.3, a class defining a new exception type need only define constructors; recall that constructors are special methods that are used to initialize newly created objects of the class. Defining a new exception type requires very little work because most of the code for the new type is inherited from the class that implements its supertype. We will discuss inheritance, and also provide more detail about the special forms used in this definition, in Chapter 7.

The exception type provides two constructors; in other words, the constructor name is overloaded as discussed in Section 2.4.2. The second constructor initializes the exception object to contain the string provided as its argument; as we shall see in Section 4.2.3, this string will explain why the exception was thrown. For example,

```
Exception e1 = new NewKindOfException("this is the reason");
```

causes exception object e1 to contain the string "this is the reason". The first constructor initializes the object to contain the empty string, for example,

```
Exception e2 = new NewKindOfException( );
```

The string, together with the type of exception, can be obtained by calling the toString method on the exception object. For example,

```
String s = e1.toString( );
```

causes s to contain the string

```
"NewKindOfException: this is the reason"
```

Exception types must be defined in some package. One possibility is to define them in the same package that contains the class of the methods that throw them. However, in this case, we would need a longer name, for example, `NotFoundFromSearchException`, to avoid name conflicts with exception types defined for other procedures. A better alternative, therefore, is to have a package that defines exception types. This allows the same exception type to be used in many routines.

Java does not require that exception types have the form `EnameException`. However, it is good programming style to follow this convention since it makes it easy to distinguish exception types, which should be used only for throwing and handling exceptions, from ordinary types.

4.2.3   Throwing Exceptions

A Java procedure can terminate by *throwing* an exception. It does this by using the **throw** statement. For example, in `fact` we might have

```
if (n <= 0) throw new NonPositiveException("Num.fact");
```

Here we are throwing an object of type `NonPositiveException`; we actually construct this object as part of the throw, by calling `new`.

The main issue when throwing exceptions is what to use for the string argument. To answer this question, we need to understand the purpose of the string. The string is used primarily to convey information to a person when the program isn't able to handle the exception and therefore stops with an error message, or writes an error message to a log.

Therefore, the string must enable the user to find out what went wrong. A good way to accomplish this is to have the string identify the procedure that threw the exception, since in general many procedures will throw the same exception type. The information should allow a person to find the specification of that procedure. Giving the class and method name is usually sufficient; however, if the method is overloaded, the types of its arguments must also be given.

4.2.4   Handling Exceptions

When a procedure terminates with an exception, execution does *not* continue right after the call. Instead, control is transferred to some code that handles the exception.

Code deals with an exception in two ways. The first is to handle it explicitly by using the try statement. For example, the following code uses a try statement to handle NonPositiveException should it be thrown by the call of fact.

```
try { x = Num.fact(y); }
catch (NonPositiveException e) {
    // in here can use e
}
```

If the call of fact throws NonPositiveException, the catch clause is executed: the exception object is assigned to variable e so that this object can be used while handling the exception.

This example has one catch clause; however, several catch clauses can be attached to the try statement so that several different exceptions can be handled. Also, try statements can be nested. If an exception thrown by the body of the inner try statement is not caught by one of its catch clauses, it can be caught by one of the catch clauses of the outer try statement. For example, in

```
try { ...;
    try { x = Arrays.search(v, 7); }
    catch (NullPointerException e) {
        throw new NotFoundException( ); }
} catch (NotFoundException b) { ... }
```

the catch clause in the outer try statement will handle NotFound Exception if it is thrown by the call of Arrays.search or by the catch clause for NullPointerException.

The catch clauses do not have to identify the actual type of an exception object. Instead, the clause can list a supertype of the type. For example, in

```
try { x = Arrays.search(v, y); }
catch (Exception e) { s.println(e); return; }
```

the catch clause will handle both `NullPointerException` and `NotFound-Exception`. (Here s is a `PrintWriter`, and `println` uses e's `toString` method to obtain the information to print.)

The second way to deal with an exception is to propagate it. This occurs when a call within some procedure P signals an exception that is not handled by a catch clause of any containing `try` statement in P. In this case, Java automatically propagates the exception to P's caller provided one of the following is true:

- that exception type or one of its supertypes is listed in P's header,
- the exception type is unchecked.

Otherwise, there is a compile-time error.

A procedure should only raise exceptions that are listed in its specification since this is what a person writing code that uses the procedure relies on. Unfortunately, Java does not enforce this requirement for unchecked exceptions. Therefore, you must enforce it yourself: make sure that any exception your code raises, either by automatic propagation or by an explicit throw, is listed in the header of the procedure you are implementing (even if the exception is unchecked) and described in that procedure's specification.

4.2.5   Coping with Unchecked Exceptions

Any call can potentially throw any unchecked exception. This means we have a problem in catching unchecked exceptions because it's hard to know where they come from. For example, in

```
try { x = y[n]; i = Arrays.search(z, x); }
catch (IndexOutOfBoundsException e) {
    // handle IndexOutOfBoundsException from the array access y[n]
}
// code here continues assuming problem has been fixed
```

`IndexOutOfBoundsException`, which is an unchecked exception, might have occurred because of an error in the implementation of `search`.

The only way to be certain about the origin of an unchecked exception is to narrow the scope of the `try` statement. For example, it is certain the exception comes from the array access in the following code:

```
try { x = y[n]; }
catch (IndexOutOfBoundsException e) {
   // handle IndexOutOfBoundsException from the array access y[n]
}
i = Arrays.search(z, x);
```

We will discuss these issues further in Section 4.4.2.

4.3   Programming with Exceptions

When implementing a procedure with exceptions, the programmer's job, as always, is to provide the behavior defined by the specification. If this behavior includes exceptions, the program must throw the proper exceptions at the proper times with the meaning described in the specification. To accomplish this task, the program may need to handle exceptions that are thrown by procedures it calls.

Some exceptions are handled *specifically*: the catch clause attempts to respond to the specific situation that gave rise to the exception. Other exceptions are handled *generically*. In this case, the catch clause does not attempt to deal with the exception in any specific way. Instead, it takes a generic action. It might stop the program after reporting the problem to a user, or it might "restart" the program by reverting to an earlier state, without an attempt to fix the exact problem. For example, such a program might carry out some kind of shutdown, followed by a clean restart. (The shutdown should also be logged, so that if it was due to a program error, the error can be fixed.)

4.3.1   Reflecting and Masking

There are two ways to deal with an exception. Sometimes an exception is *reflected* up another level; that is, the caller also terminates by throwing an exception. Reflecting an exception can be accomplished by automatic propagation, as discussed in Section 4.2.4, or by explicitly catching an exception and then throwing an exception. The former is more limited because the same exception object is thrown. More commonly, we want to throw a different object, of a different exception type, because the meaning of the information has changed. Another point is that before reflecting an exception, the caller may need to do some local processing in order to satisfy its specification.

For example, many programs that iterate through arrays need to "prime" the iteration by obtaining an initial value from the array. This is the case in the min procedure shown in Figure 4.4. min simply fetches the zeroth element of the array. If the array argument is null, the call will raise NullPointerException, and this is reflected to the caller of min by being propagated automatically. If the array is empty, the call will raise IndexOutOfBoundsException. It would not make sense to reflect this exception to min's caller, since we want exceptions that are related to the min abstraction rather than exceptions having to do with how min is implemented. Instead, min throws EmptyException, which is an exception that is meaningful for it. Note that the string in the exception object identifies Arrays.min as the thrower.

A second possibility is that the caller *masks* the exception—that is, handles the exception itself and then continues with the normal flow. This situation is illustrated in the sorted procedure in Figure 4.4. Again, the code is priming the loop; but in this case, if the array is empty, it simply means it is sorted.

One point to note about both examples is how we used exceptions to control program flow. This is perfectly acceptable programming practice: exceptions can be used to avoid other work. For example, in both min and sorted, the code does not need to check the length of the array explicitly. (However, depending on how the exception mechanism is implemented, it may be expensive to handle exceptions, and you should weigh this cost against the benefit of using exceptions to avoid the extra work.)

4.4   Design Issues

Now we consider how to decide about the use of exceptions when designing abstractions. There are two main issues: when to use an exception, and whether to use a checked or unchecked exception.

An important point is that exceptions are not synonymous with errors. Exceptions are a mechanism that allows a method to bring some information to the attention of its caller. That information might not concern an error. For example, there isn't anything erroneous about search being called on an element that isn't in the array; instead, this is just an interesting situation

Figure 4.4   Reflecting and masking exceptions

```
public class Arrays {

    public static int min (int[ ] a) throws NullPointerException, EmptyException {
        // EFFECTS: If a is null throws NullPointerException else if a is empty
        //     throws EmptyException else returns the minimum value of a
        int m;
        try { m = a[0]; }
        catch (IndexOutOfBoundsException e) {
            throw new EmptyException("Arrays.min"); }
        for (int i = 1; i < a.length; i++)
            if (a[i] < m) m = a[i];
        return m; }

    public static boolean sorted (int[ ] a) throws NullPointerException {
        // EFFECTS: If a is null throws NullPointerException else if a is
        //     sorted in ascending order returns true else returns false.
        int prev;
        try { prev = a[0]; }
        catch (IndexOutOfBoundsException e) { return true; }
        for (int i = 1; i < a.length; i++)
            if (prev <= a[i]) prev = a[i]; else return false;
        return true; }
}
```

that the caller should be informed about. We convey this information through an exception because we want to distinguish it from the other possibility. The classification of one possibility as normal and the others as exceptional is somewhat arbitrary.

Also, even when an exception is associated with what appears to be an error at a lower level of abstraction, the situation is not necessarily an error at a higher one. For example, within the get method of Vector, it appears to be erroneous if the given index isn't within bounds. However, from the perspective of the caller of get, this situation may simply indicate that a loop should terminate. Thus, it can be just as "correct" for a call to terminate with an exception as to terminate normally. Exceptions are simply a means for allowing several kinds of behavior and informing the caller about the different cases.

Furthermore, not every error leads to an exception. Consider an erroneous record in a large input file, where it is possible to continue processing the file by skipping that record. In such a case, it may be appropriate to inform a person (not a program) about the error by writing an error message on some output device. Note, by the way, that what is done when an error occurs must be defined in the abstraction's specification, even when no exception is thrown.

4.4.1 When to Use Exceptions

Exceptions should be used to eliminate most constraints listed in requires clauses. The requires clause should remain only for efficiency reasons or if the context of use is so limited that we can be sure the constraint is satisfied. For example, search might still require that the array be sorted, since it can then be implemented much more efficiently. Also, the partition procedure used in quick sort (Figure 3.6) should require its argument i to be less than its argument j, since the context of use is so limited.

Exceptions should also be used to avoid encoding information in ordinary results. For example, instead of returning -1 if the element is not in the array, search signals an exception. It is better to convey this information with an exception, since the result returned in this case cannot be used like a regular result. By using an exception, we make it easy to distinguish this result from a regular one, thus avoiding a potential error. Using exceptions instead of encoding information in results is particularly important for procedures intended for general use. For procedures that will be used in a limited context (e.g., that aren't public), encoding information in ordinary results may be acceptable.

The rules for using exceptions are summarized in Sidebar 4.1.

4.4.2 Checked versus Unchecked Exceptions

Suppose you have decided that you need to define a new exception type. How do you choose between a checked or an unchecked exception?

Checked exceptions either must be handled in calling code or must be listed in the throws clause of the procedure header; otherwise, there will be a compile-time error. This provides a certain amount of protection. If you forget

Sidebar 4.1   Rules for Using Exceptions

- When the context of use is local, you need not use exceptions because you can easily verify that requires clauses are satisfied by calls and that special results are used properly.

- However, when the context of use is nonlocal, you should use exceptions instead of special results. And you should use exceptions instead of requires clauses unless a requirement cannot be checked or is very expensive to check.

to handle a checked exception that is thrown by some call in your code, the compiler will warn you so that you can get rid of the error.

However, unchecked exceptions will be implicitly propagated to the caller even if they aren't listed in the header. This means that procedures can raise unchecked exceptions even when this isn't mentioned in their header and specification. For example, if search is implemented incorrectly so that it accesses its argument array, a, out of bounds and doesn't handle the resulting IndexOutOfBoundsException, it will throw that exception to its caller, even though that possibility is not mentioned in its specification.

It may seem that this really isn't a problem, since using code can handle the exception, for example, at the top level. But code isn't very good at coping with programmer errors, which are usually the reason unchecked exceptions propagate. (Exceptions also propagate because of resource problems—for example, the heap ran out of room; programs aren't good at coping with those errors either.)

Furthermore, there is a danger that the exception will be *captured*. For example, in:

```
try { x = y[n]; i = Arrays.search(z, x); }
catch (IndexOutOfBoundsException e) {
    // handle IndexOutOfBoundsException from use of array y
}
// code here continues assuming problem has been fixed
```

the catch clause might handle IndexOutOfBoundsException from search by mistake. Whatever corrective action is taken by the catch clause will fix only the problem with y and n, but not the problem with search. It is unlikely that the code after the catch clause will work in this case, and when the error is finally discovered, it may be very difficult to track down.

Why does Java have unchecked exceptions when they are a problem? The reason is that checked exceptions are also a problem: if your code is certain not to cause one to be raised, you still must handle it! This is why many exceptions defined by Java are in fact unchecked.

So there are good reasons on both sides here. This means that there is a design issue: when you define a new exception type, you must think carefully about whether it should be checked or unchecked.

Choosing between checked and unchecked exceptions should be based on expectations about how the exception will be used. If you expect using code to avoid calls that raise the exception, the exception should be unchecked. This is the rationale behind `IndexOutOfBoundsException`: arrays are supposed to be used primarily in `for` loops that control the indices and thus ensure that all calls on array methods have indices within bounds.

Otherwise, exceptions should be checked. For example, it is likely that many calls of `search` will be made without knowledge of whether the searched-for integer is in the array. In such a case, it would be an error for the calling code not to handle the exception. Therefore, the exception type should be checked so that such errors can be detected by the compiler.

The question of whether the exception is "usually" avoided often has to do with the cost and convenience of avoiding it. For example, it is convenient and inexpensive to determine the size of a vector (by calling the `size` method, which returns in constant time); therefore, using code is likely to use this method to avoid `IndexOutOfBoundsException`. But sometimes there is no convenient way to avoid the exception, or avoiding the exception is costly. Both situations arise for `search`. There may be no other procedure to determine whether the element is in the array, since this is (partly) the purpose of `search`. Furthermore, if such a procedure existed, its call would be costly.

The rules for choosing between checked and unchecked exceptions are summarized in Sidebar 4.2.

4.5   Defensive Programming

Exceptions can be used to support the practice of *defensive programming*— that is, writing each procedure to defend itself against errors. Errors can be

---

Sidebar 4.2 Checked versus Unchecked Exceptions

- You should use an unchecked exception only if you expect that users will usually write code that ensures the exception will not happen, because
  - There is a convenient and inexpensive way to avoid the exception.
  - The context of use is local.
- Otherwise, you should use a checked exception.

---

introduced by other procedures, by the hardware, or by the user entering data; these latter errors will continue to exist even if the software is error free. An exception mechanism provides a means for conveying information about errors and a way to handle errors without cluttering the main flow of a routine. Therefore, it encourages a methodology of writing code that checks for problems and reports them in an orderly way.

For example, the implementation of a procedure with a requires clause should check, if possible, whether the requires clause is satisfied. This raises the question of what to do if the requires clause is not satisfied. One possibility is to halt the program with an error message if the check fails. However, this is not a very robust approach. It's better to use the exception mechanism because then, if the call occurs in a context in which a higher level can recover from problems in a generic way (e.g., by doing a restart), it will be able to do this for the failed check as well.

It's a good idea to have a particular exception type devoted to situations such as the requires clause not being satisfied. A good name for this type is `FailureException`; it is an unchecked exception.

Headers of procedures should *not* list `FailureException`, and their specifications should not mention throwing it. The reason is that this exception is used for situations that do not correspond to what is described in a procedure's specification. Instead, the exception indicates that something is broken so that the procedure is unable to satisfy its specification.

There are many other situations in which `FailureException` should be thrown. For example, suppose you are using search in a context in which you know x is in the array, yet your call of search throws `NotFoundException`. Since this is a checked exception, you must catch it; your code can then throw `FailureException`. The string within the `FailureException`, as usual, should indicate what the problem is. One easy way to do this is to concatenate information about your class and method with the string obtained from `NotFoundException`, for example,

```
catch (NotFoundException e) {
    throw new FailureException("C.p" + e.toString( )); }
```

More generally, `FailureException` should be raised whenever your code checks an assumption that should hold and discovers it doesn't. We will see examples of this in later chapters.

Of course, checking for problems takes time, and it is tempting not to bother with the checks, or to use them only while debugging and disable them during production. This is generally an unwise practice. Defensive programming is particularly valuable during production because it can prevent a small error from causing a large problem, such as a damaged database. Disabling checks during production is analogous to disconnecting warning lights in an airplane; a pilot would never do this because the results could be catastrophic. Checks should be disabled only if we have proved that the errors can never occur or if the checks are costly.

4.6   Summary

In this chapter, we have extended procedures to include exceptions. Exceptions are needed in robust programs because they provide a way to respond to errors and unusual situations. If an argument is not what is expected, a procedure can notify the caller of this fact rather than simply failing or encoding the information in a special result. Since this notification is distinct from the normal case, the caller cannot confuse the two.

Exceptions are introduced when procedures are designed. Most procedures should be defined over the entire input domain; exceptions are used to take care of situations in which the "usual" behavior cannot happen. Partial procedures are suitable only when it is either too expensive or not possible to check the condition, or when the procedure is used in a limited context in which it can be proved that all calls have proper arguments.

In implementing a procedure, the programmer must ensure that it terminates as specified in all situations. Only exceptions permitted by the specification should be signaled, and each should be signaled only in the situation indicated in the specification. In addition, it is a good idea to practice defensive programming by checking for errors in as many cases as possible; Failure-Exception can be used to report such errors. An example is checking in a partial procedure for inputs that do not satisfy the requires clause.

Exercises

4.1 Implement a standalone procedure to read in a file containing words and white space and produce a compressed version of the file in an output file. The compressed version should contain all of the words in the input file and none of the white space, except that it should preserve lines.

4.2 Implement search as specified in Figure 4.1 in two ways: using for loops, and using while (true) loops that are terminated when accessing the array raises IndexOutOfBoundsException. Which implementation is better? Discuss.

4.3 A specification for a procedure that computes the sum of the elements in an array of integers might require a nonempty array, return 0 if the array is empty, or throw an exception if the array is empty. Discuss which alternative is best and provide the specification for the procedure.

4.4 Consider a procedure

```
static void combine (int[ ] a, int[ ] b)
```

that multiplies each element of a by the sum of the elements of b; for example, if a = [1, 2, 3] and b = [4, 5], then on return a = [9, 18, 27]. What should this procedure do if a or b is null or empty? Give a specification for combine that answers these questions and explain why your specification is a good one.

Data Abstraction

5

This chapter discusses the most important abstraction mechanism, data abstraction. Data abstraction allows us to abstract from the details of how data objects are implemented to how the objects behave. This focus on the behavior of objects forms the basis of object-oriented programming.

Data abstraction allows us to extend the programming language in use (e.g., Java), with new data types. What new types are needed depends on the application domain of the program. For example, in implementing a compiler or interpreter, stacks and symbol tables are useful, while accounts are a natural abstraction in a banking system. Polynomials arise in a symbolic manipulation system, and matrices are useful in defining a package of numeric functions. In each case, the data abstraction consists of a set of objects—for example, stacks or polynomials—plus a set of operations. For example, matrix operations include addition, multiplication, and so on, and deposit and withdraw are operations on accounts.

The new data types should incorporate abstraction both by parameterization and by specification. Abstraction by parameterization can be achieved in the same way as for procedures—by using parameters wherever it is sensible to do so. We achieve abstraction by specification by making the operations part of the type. To understand why the operations are needed, consider what happens if we view a type as just a set of objects. Then all that is needed to implement the type is to select a storage representation for the objects; all the using programs can be implemented in terms of this representation. However, if the representation changes, or even if its interpretation changes, all programs that use the type must be changed: there is no way to limit the impact of the change.

On the other hand, suppose we include operations in the type, obtaining

$$\text{data abstraction} = \langle \text{objects, operations} \rangle$$

and we require users to call the operations instead of accessing the representation directly. Then to implement the type, we implement the operations in terms of the chosen representation, and we must reimplement the operations if we change the representation. However, we need not reimplement any using programs because they did not use the representation. Now we have abstracted from the representation details; using code depends only on the specified behavior of the type with its operations. Therefore, we have achieved abstraction by specification.

If enough operations are provided, lack of access to the representation will not cause users any difficulty—anything they need to do to the objects can be done, and done efficiently, by calls on the operations. In general, there will be operations to create and modify objects and to obtain information about their values. Of course, users can augment the set of operations by defining standalone procedures, but such procedures would not have access to the representation.

Data abstraction allows us to defer decisions about data structures until the uses of the data are fully understood. Choosing the right data structures is crucial to achieving an efficient program. In the absence of data abstraction, data structures must be defined too early; they must be specified before the implementations of using modules can be designed. At this point, however, the uses of the data are typically not well understood. Therefore the chosen structure may lack needed information or be organized in an inefficient way.

We use data abstraction to avoid defining the structure immediately: we introduce the abstract type with its objects and operations. Implementations of using modules can then be designed in terms of the abstract type. Decisions about how to implement the type are made later, when all its uses are understood.

Data abstraction is also valuable during program modification and maintenance. In this phase, data structures are particularly likely to change, either to improve performance or to accommodate changing requirements. Data abstraction limits the changes to just the implementation of the type; none of the using modules need be changed.

In this chapter, we describe how to specify and implement data abstractions in Java. We also discuss ways to reason about the correctness of programs that use and implement types, and we describe some issues that arise in designing new types.

5.1   Specifications for Data Abstractions

Just as was the case for procedures, the meaning of a type should not be given by any of its implementations. Instead, a specification should define its behavior. Since objects of the type are used only by calling the operations, most of the specification consists of explaining what the operations do.

In Java, new types are defined by classes or interfaces. For now, we will consider only classes; interfaces will be discussed in Chapter 7.

Each class defines a type by defining a name for the type, a set of *constructors*, and a set of *instance methods* or *methods*. Constructors are used to initialize new objects of the type; these are the *instances*. Once an object has been created (and initialized by a constructor), users can access it by calling its methods.

The form of a data abstraction specification is shown in Figure 5.1. The header class dname indicates that a new data type called dname is being defined. The header contains a declaration of the visibility of the class; almost

Figure 5.1   The form of a data abstraction specification

```
visibility class dname {
    // OVERVIEW: A brief description of the behavior of the type's objects goes here.

    // constructors
    // specs for constructors go here

    // methods
    // specs for methods go here
}
```

all classes have public visibility so that they can be used by code outside of their containing package.

The specification has three parts. The *overview* gives a brief description of the data abstraction, including a way of viewing the abstract objects in terms of "well-understood" concepts. It usually presents a model for the objects; that is, it describes the objects in terms of other objects that the reader of the specification can be expected to understand. For example, stacks might be defined in terms of mathematical sequences. The overview section also states whether objects of the type are mutable, so that their state can change over time, or immutable.

The *constructors* part of the specification defines the constructors that initialize new objects, while the *methods* part defines the methods that allow access to the objects once they have been created. All the constructors and methods that appear in the specification will be public.

Constructors and methods are procedures, and they are specified using the specification notation presented in Chapters 3 and 4, with the following differences:

- Methods and constructors both belong to objects, rather than to classes. Therefore, the keyword `static` will not appear in the methods' headers (since this keyword means that the method belongs to the class rather than to an object of the class).

- The object a method or constructor belongs to is available to it as an implicit argument, and this object can be referred to in the method or constructor specification as `this`.

As was the case for specifications of procedures, specifications for data abstractions take the form of comments in the code. When a data abstraction is first invented, all that exists is the specification; almost all code in the class, such as the bodies of the methods, is missing. Later, when the data abstraction is implemented, this code is added.

5.1.1   Specification of IntSet

Figure 5.2 gives a specification for the `IntSet` data abstraction. `IntSet`s are unbounded sets of integers with operations to create a new, empty `IntSet`, test whether a given integer is an element of an `IntSet`, and add or remove elements. The overview indicates that `IntSet`s are mutable. It also indicates

Figure 5.2   Specification of the IntSet data abstraction

```
public class IntSet {
    // OVERVIEW: IntSets are mutable, unbounded sets of integers.
    //    A typical IntSet is {x₁, . . . , xₙ}.

    // constructors
    public IntSet ( )
        // EFFECTS: Initializes this to be empty.

    // methods
    public void insert (int x)
        // MODIFIES: this
        // EFFECTS: Adds x to the elements of this, i.e., this_post = this + { x }.

    public void remove (int x)
        // MODIFIES: this
        // EFFECTS: Removes x from this, i.e., this_post = this – { x }

    public boolean isIn (int x)
        // EFFECTS: If x is in this returns true else returns false.

    public int size ( )
        // EFFECTS: Returns the cardinality of this.

    public int choose ( ) throws EmptyException
        // EFFECTS: If this is empty, throws EmptyException else
        //    returns an arbitrary element of this.
}
```

that we will model IntSets in terms of mathematical sets. In the rest of the specification, we specify each operation using this model.

Figure 5.2 uses set notation in the specifications of the methods. In particular, it uses + for set union, and – for set difference. Figure 5.3 summarizes the set notation used in this book.

The IntSet type has a single constructor that initializes the new set to be empty; note that the specification refers to the new set object as this. Since a constructor always modifies this (to initialize it), we do not bother to indicate the modification in the modifies clause. In fact, this modification is invisible

Figure 5.3   Set notation

> A set is denoted as $\{x1, \ldots, xn\}$. The xi's are the elements of the set. There are no duplicates in a set.
>
> set union: $t = s1 + s2$ is the set containing all the elements of set $s1$ and all the elements of set $s2$. If $s1$ and $s2$ contain an element in common, there will be only one occurrence of that element in t.
>
> set difference: $t = s1 - s2$ is the set containing all the elements of $s1$ that are not also elements of $s2$.
>
> set intersection: $t = s1 \& s2$ is the set containing all elements that are members of both $s1$ and $s2$.
>
> cardinality: $|s|$ stands for the size of set s.
>
> set membership: x in s is true if x is an element of s.
>
> set former: $t = \{x \mid p(x)\}$ is the set of all elements x such that $p(x)$ is true.

to users: they do not have access to the constructor's object until after the constructor runs, and therefore, they cannot observe the state change.

Once an `IntSet` object exists, elements can be added to it by calling its `insert` method, and elements can be removed by calling `remove`; again, the specifications refer to the object as `this`. These two methods are *mutators* since they modify the state of their object; their specifications make it clear that they are mutators because they contain a modifies clause stating that `this` is modified. Note that the specifications of `insert` and `remove` use the notation `this_post` to indicate the value of `this` when the operation returns. An input argument name without the *post* qualifier always means the value when the operation is called.

The remaining methods are *observers*: they return information about the state of their object but do not change the state. Observers do not have a modifies clause. (More accurately, an observer does not have a modifies clause stating that `this`, or some argument object of its type, is modified; however, observers typically don't modify anything.)

The `choose` method returns an arbitrary element of the `IntSet`; thus, it is underdetermined. It throws an exception if the set is empty. This exception can be unchecked since users can call the `size` method before calling `choose` to cheaply and conveniently ensure that the set is nonempty.

Note that `insert` does not throw an exception if the integer is already in the set, and similarly, `remove` does not throw an exception if the integer is not in the set. These decisions are based on assumptions about how sets will be used. We expect that users will add and remove set elements without concern for whether they are already there. Therefore, the methods do not throw exceptions. If we expected a different pattern of usage, we might change the specifications and headers of these methods (to throw an exception), or we might provide additional methods that throw an exception (e.g., `insertNonDup` and `removeIfIn`), so that users can choose the method that best fits their needs.

In the `IntSet` specification, we are relying on the reader knowing what mathematical sets are; otherwise, the specification would not be understandable. In general, this reliance on informal description is a weakness of informal specifications. It is probably reasonable to expect the reader to understand a number of mathematical concepts, such as sets, sequences, and integers. However, not all types can be described nicely in terms of such concepts. If the concepts are inadequate, we must describe the type as best we can, even by using pictures; but of course, there is always the danger that the reader will not understand the description or will interpret it differently than we intended. Techniques for writing understandable specifications will be discussed in Chapter 9.

Note that the specification takes the form of a preliminary version of the class. This code could be compiled if the methods and constructors were given empty bodies (except that methods that return results will need a type-correct return statement). This will allow you to compile code that uses the abstraction, so that you'll be able to get rid of errors that the compiler catches, such as type errors. You probably won't be able to run the using code, however, until after the new type is implemented.

5.1.2   The Poly Abstraction

A second example of a data abstraction specification is given in Figure 5.4. `Poly`s are polynomials with integer coefficients. Unlike `IntSet`s, `Poly`s are immutable: once a `Poly` has been created (and initialized by a constructor), it cannot be modified. Operations are provided to create a one-term `Poly` and to add, subtract, and multiply `Poly`s.

Figure 5.4   Specification of the Poly data abstraction

```
public class Poly {
    // OVERVIEW: Polys are immutable polynomials with integer coefficients.
    //    A typical Poly is c_0 + c_1 x + ...

    // constructors
    public Poly ( )
        // EFFECTS: Initializes this to be the zero polynomial.

    public Poly (int c, int n) throws NegativeExponentException
        // EFFECTS: If n < 0 throws NegativeExponentException else
        //    initializes this to be the Poly cx^n.

    // methods
    public int degree ( )
        // EFFECTS: Returns the degree of this, i.e., the largest exponent
        //    with a non-zero coefficient. Returns 0 if this is the zero Poly.

    public int coeff (int d)
        // EFFECTS: Returns the coefficient of the term of this whose exponent is d.

    public Poly add (Poly q) throws NullPointerException
        // EFFECTS: If q is null throws NullPointerException else
        //    returns the Poly this + q.

    public Poly mul (Poly q) throws NullPointerException
        // EFFECTS: If q is null throws NullPointerException else
        //    returns the Poly this * q.

    public Poly sub (Poly q) throws NullPointerException
        // EFFECTS: If q is null throws NullPointerException else
        //    returns the Poly this − q.

    public Poly minus ( )
        // EFFECTS: Returns the Poly − this.
}
```

The `Poly` type has two constructors, one to create the zero polynomial, and one to create an arbitrary monomial. In general, a type can have a number of constructors. All constructors have the same name, the type name, and therefore, if there is more than one constructor, this name is *overloaded*.

Java allows method names to be overloaded as well. Java requires that overloaded definitions differ from one another in the number of arguments and/or their types; otherwise, a compile-time error occurs. The two definitions for the `Poly` constructor are legal since one has no arguments and the other has two arguments.

`Poly` has no mutator methods: no method has a `modifies` clause. This is what we expect to see for an immutable data abstraction. Furthermore, the method specifications do not use the *post* notation that was used in the `IntSet` specification. This notation is not needed for immutable abstractions: since object state doesn't change, the pre and post states of objects are identical.

As part of defining `Poly`, we need to decide whether `NegativeExponent-Exception` is checked or unchecked. Since it seems likely that users will avoid calls with a negative exponent, it is appropriate to make the exception unchecked.

5.2   Using Data Abstractions

Figure 5.5 gives examples of procedures that use data abstractions. (The classes of the procedures aren't shown in the figure.) The `diff` method returns a new `Poly` that is the result of differentiating its argument `Poly`. The `getElements` routine returns an `IntSet` containing the integers in its array argument `a`; there are no duplicates in the returned set (since sets do not contain duplicates) even if there are duplicates among the elements of `a`.

These routines are written based on the specifications of the used abstractions and can use only what is described in the specifications. They are not able to access the implementation details of the abstract objects since, as we shall see, this access is limited to implementations of the objects' constructors and methods. They can use methods to access object state and to modify that state if the object is mutable, and they can use constructors to initialize new objects.

Figure 5.5   Using abstract data types

```
public static Poly diff (Poly p) throws NullPointerException {
    // EFFECTS: If p is null throws NullPointerException
    //     else returns the Poly obtained by differentiating p.
    Poly q = new Poly ( );
    for (int i = 1; i <= p.degree( ); i++)
        q = q.add(new Poly(p.coeff(i)*i, i - 1));
    return q;
}

public static IntSet getElements (int[ ] a)
        throws NullPointerException {
    // EFFECTS: If a is null throws NullPointerException else returns a set
    //     containing an entry for each distinct element of a.
    IntSet s = new IntSet( );
    for (int i = 0; i < a.length; i++) s.insert(a[i]);
    return s;
}
```

5.3   Implementing Data Abstractions

A class both defines a new type and provides an implementation for it. The specification constitutes the definition of the type. The remainder of the class provides the implementation.

To implement a data abstraction, we select a *representation*, or *rep*, for its objects and then implement the constructors to initialize the representation properly and the methods to use/modify the representation properly. The chosen representation must permit all operations to be implemented in a reasonably simple and efficient manner. In addition, if some of the operations must run quickly, the representation must make this possible. A representation that is fast for some operations often will be slower for others. We might, therefore, require multiple implementations of the same type; we will discuss how to achieve this in Chapter 7.

For example, a plausible representation for an IntSet object is a vector, where each integer in the IntSet occurs as an element of the vector. We could choose to have each element of the set occur exactly once in the vector or allow it to occur many times. The latter choice makes the implementation of insert run faster but slows down remove and isIn. Since isIn is likely to be called frequently, we will make the former choice, and therefore, there will be no duplicate elements in the vector.

5.3.1 Implementing Data Abstractions in Java

A representation typically has a number of components; in Java, each of these is an *instance variable* of the class implementing the data abstraction. The implementations of the constructors and methods access and manipulate the instance variables.

Thus, when considered from an implementation point of view, objects have both methods and instance variables. To support abstraction, however, it is important to restrict access to the instance variables to the implementation of the methods and constructors; this allows you, for example, to reimplement an abstract type without affecting any code that uses the type. Therefore, the instance variables should not be visible to users; code that uses the objects can refer only to their methods.

The instance variables are prevented from being visible to users by declaring them to be private. Java allows instance variables to have other than private visibility. It is generally not a good idea to have public instance variables; this point will be discussed in more detail in Sections 5.6.2 and 5.9. The one exception to this rule occurs when defining record types; record types are discussed in Section 5.3.4.

Declarations of instance variables do not have the static qualifier. These variables belong to objects; there is a separate set of them for each object. It is also possible to declare static variables within a class. Such variables belong to the class itself, rather than to specific objects, just as static methods belong to the class. Static variables are not used very often in implementing data abstractions; some examples of their use will be given in Chapter 15.

5.3.2 Implementation of IntSet

This section gives a first example of an implementation—for the IntSet data abstraction. The implementation is given in Figure 5.6.

The first point to note here is the definition of the IntSet rep, preceding the implementations of the constructors and methods. In this case, the rep

Figure 5.6   Implementation of `IntSet`

```
public class IntSet {
    // OVERVIEW: IntSets are unbounded, mutable sets of integers.
    private Vector els; // the rep

    // constructors
    public IntSet ( ) {
        // EFFECTS: Initializes this to be empty.
        els = new Vector( ); }

    // methods
    public void insert (int x) {
        // MODIFIES: this
        // EFFECTS: Adds x to the elements of this.
        Integer y = new Integer(x);
        if (getIndex(y) < 0) els.add(y); }

    public void remove (int x) {
        // MODIFIES: this
        // EFFECTS: Removes x from this.
        int i = getIndex(new Integer(x));
        if (i < 0) return;
        els.set(i, els.lastElement( ));
        els.remove(els.size( ) - 1); }

    public boolean isIn (int x) {
        // EFFECTS: Returns true if x is in this else returns false.
        return getIndex(new Integer(x)) >= 0; }

    private int getIndex (Integer x) {
        // EFFECTS: If x is in this returns index where x appears else returns - 1.
        for (int i = 0; i < els.size( ); i++)
            if (x.equals(els.get(i))) return i;
        return -1; }

    public int size ( ) {
        // EFFECTS: Returns the cardinality of this.
        return els.size( ); }

    public int choose ( ) throws EmptyException {
        // EFFECTS: If this is empty throws EmptyException else
        // returns an arbitrary element of this.
            if (els.size( ) == 0) throw new EmptyException("IntSet.choose");
            return els.lastElement( ); }
}
```

consists of a single instance variable. Since this variable has private visibility, it can be accessed only by code inside its class.

The constructors and methods belong to a particular object of their type. The object is passed as an additional, implicit argument to the constructors and methods, and they can refer to it using the keyword this. For example, the instance variable els can be accessed using the form this.els. (The code cannot assign to this.) However, the prefix is not needed: the code can refer to methods and instance variables of its own object by just using their names. Thus, in the methods and constructors in the figure, els refers to the els instance variable of this.

The implementation of IntSet is straightforward. The constructor initializes its object by creating the vector that will hold the elements and assigning it to els; since the vector is empty, no more work need be done. The insert, remove, and isIn methods all make use of the private method, getIndex, to determine whether the element of interest is already in the set. Doing this check allows insert to preserve the no-duplicates condition. This condition is relied on in size (since otherwise the size of the vector would not be the same as the size of the set) and in remove (since otherwise there might be other occurrences of the element that would need to be removed).

Note that getIndex has private visibility; therefore, it cannot be called outside the class. The design takes advantage of this fact by having getIndex return −1 when the element is not in the vector rather that using an exception. As discussed in Chapter 4, this is a satisfactory approach here, since getIndex is used only within this class.

Since vectors cannot store ints, the methods use Integer objects instead to contain the set elements. This approach is somewhat awkward. An alternative is to use arrays of ints; but this has its own difficulties, since then the implementation of IntSet would need to switch to bigger arrays as the set grows. The implementation of Vector takes care of this problem in an efficient manner.

getIndex uses the equals method to check for membership. This check is correct because equals for Integer objects returns true only if the two objects being compared are both Integers and both contain the same integer value.

5.3.3   Implementation of Poly

Now we consider the implementation of the Poly data abstraction. Unlike IntSets, Polys are immutable, and therefore, their size does not change over time. Therefore, we can represent a Poly as an array rather than a vector. The ith element of the array will contain the coefficient of the ith exponent; this representation makes sense only if the Poly is dense. The zero Poly can be represented either as an empty array or as a one-element array containing zero; we will use the latter approach. In addition, we will have an instance variable that keeps track of the degree of the Poly since this is convenient.

Figures 5.7 and 5.8 show the implementation of Poly. The main point to note here is that several of the methods (e.g., add and mul) make use of instance variables of other Poly objects in addition to their own object. Code in a method is allowed to access private information in other objects of its class as well as private information in its own object.

Note how sub and mul are implemented in terms of other Poly methods. Another point is the use of the Poly constructor in the implementations of add, mul, and minus. All of these methods actually initialize the new Poly themselves; this is allowed since the new Poly is just another object of the class, which can be accessed in the method. These methods create the new Poly using the private constructor (which cannot be called by users) to get an array of the right size. In the case of mul, we rely on the fact that the array constructor initializes all elements of an array of ints to zero. Also, note the care taken to ensure that the new Poly object is the right size. This requires a precomputation in the add method to handle the case of trailing zeros.

5.3.4   Records

Suppose polynomials are going to be sparse rather than dense. In this case, the previous implementation would not be a good one, since the array is likely to be large and full of zeros. Instead, we would like to store information only for the coefficients that are nonzero.

This could be accomplished by using two vectors:

```
private Vector coeffs; // the non-zero coefficients
private Vector exps; // the associated exponents
```

However, the implementation in this case must ensure that the two arrays are lined up, so that the ith element of coeffs contains the coefficient that goes with the exponent stored in the ith element of exps. It would be more convenient if instead we could use just one vector, each of whose elements contained both the coefficient and the associated exponent.

Figure 5.7   First part of Poly implementation

```
public class Poly {
    // OVERVIEW: ...
    private int[ ] trms;
    private int deg;

    // constructors
    public Poly ( ) {
        // EFFECTS: Initializes this to be the zero polynomial.
        trms = new int[1]; deg = 0; }

    public Poly (int c, int n) throws NegativeExponentException {
        // EFFECTS: If n < 0 throws NegativeExponentException else
        //    initializes this to be the Poly cxⁿ.
        if (n < 0)
            throw new NegativeExponentException("Poly(int,int) constructor");
        if (c == 0) { trms = new int[1]; deg = 0; return; }
        trms = new int[n+1];
        for (int i = 0; i < n; i++) trms[i] = 0;
        trms[n] = c;
        deg = n; }

    private Poly (int n) { trms = new int[n+1]; deg = n; }

    // methods
    public int degree ( ) {
        // EFFECTS: Returns the degree of this, i.e., the largest exponent
        //    with a non-zero coefficient. Returns 0 if this is the zero Poly.
        return deg; }

    public int coeff (int d) {
        // EFFECTS: Returns the coefficient of the term of this whose exponent is d.
        if (d < 0 || d > deg) return 0; else return trms[d]; }

    public Poly sub (Poly q) throws NullPointerException {
        // EFFECTS: If q is null throws NullPointerException else
        //    returns the Poly this − q.
        return add (q.minus( )); }

    public Poly minus ( ) {
        // EFFECTS: Returns the Poly −this.
        Poly r = new Poly(deg);
        for (int i = 0; i < deg; i++) r.trms[i] = − trms[i];
        return r; }
```

Figure 5.8   Rest of the implementation of the Poly data abstraction

```
public Poly add (Poly q) throws NullPointerException {
    // EFFECTS: If q is null throws NullPointerException else
    //    returns the Poly this + q.
    Poly la, sm;
    if (deg > q.deg) {la = this; sm = q;} else {la = q; sm = this;}
    int newdeg = la.deg;  // new degree is the larger degree
    if (deg == q.deg)  // unless there are trailing zeros
        for (int k = deg; k > 0; k--)
            if (trms[k] + q.trms[k] != 0) break; else newdeg--;
    Poly r = new Poly(newdeg);  // get a new Poly
    int i;
    for (i = 0; i <= sm.deg && i <= newdeg; i++)
        r.trms[i] = sm.trms[i] + la.trms[i];
    for (int j = i; j <= newdeg; j++) r.trms[j] = la.trms[j];
    return r; }

public Poly mul (Poly  q) throws NullPointerException {
    // EFFECTS: If q is null throws NullPointerException else
    //    returns the Poly this * q.
    if ((q.deg == 0 && q.trms[0] == 0) ||
        (deg == 0 && trms[0] == 0)) return new Poly( );
    Poly r = new Poly(deg+q.deg);
    r.trms[deg+q.deg] = 0;  // prepare to compute coeffs
    for (int i = 0; i <= deg; i++)
        for (int j = 0; j <= q.deg; j++)
            r.trms[i+j] = r.trms[i+j] + trms[i]*q.trms[j];
    return r; }
}
```

This can be accomplished by using a *record*. Most languages provide records as a built-in feature. For example, in C and C++, you can define a struct with named fields of various types. Java, however, does not provide this ability. Instead, record types must be defined using classes.

A record is simply a collection of fields, each with a name and type. The class implementing such a type has a public or *package-visible* instance variable for each field; package visibility means the fields can be accessed by other code in the same package but nowhere else. The class provides

Figure 5.9   A record type

```
class Pair {
    // OVERVIEW: A record type
    int coeff;
    int exp;
    Pair(int c, int n) { coeff = c; exp = n; }
}
```

a constructor for creating a new object of the type; the constructor takes arguments to define the initial values of the fields. An example is given in Figure 5.9. Since no visibility is explicitly indicated for the class and its instance variables, they are package visible.

Note that no specification is given for this class, other than to indicate that it is a record type. Such a minimal specification is sufficient: knowing that the class defines a record type indicates that the type simply provides the fields defined by the instance variables.

We can use Pair in an implementation of sparse polynomials:

```
private Vector trms; // the terms with non-zero coefficients
```

Here each element of trms is a Pair. This representation is simpler than the one using two vectors. An additional benefit is that it allows us to avoid the use of the intValue method. For example, consider the implementation of the coeff method. If we are using two vectors, we have:

```
public int coeff (int x) {
    for (int i = 0; i < exps.size( ); i++)
        if (((Integer) exps.get(i)).intValue( ) == x)
            return ((Integer) coeffs.get(i)).intValue( );
    return 0; }
```

If we use the vector of pairs, however, we have

```
public int coeff (int x) {
    for (int i = 0; i < trms.size( ); i++) {
        Pair p = (Pair) trms.get(i);
        if (p.exp == x) return p.coeff; }
    return 0; }
```

5.4   Additional Methods

So far, we have ignored some additional methods that all objects have. These are methods defined by Object. All classes define subtypes of Object, and therefore, they must provide all the Object methods. Furthermore, classes will inherit the implementations of these methods unless they implement the methods explicitly (inheritance will be discussed in detail in Chapter 7). Inheriting the Object methods is fine if the inherited implementation is correct for the new type; otherwise, the class must provide its own implementation. This section discusses some of these methods and how they ought behave. Of particular interest are the methods equals, clone, and toString. (See Sidebar 5.1.)

Two objects should be equals if they are *behaviorally equivalent*. This means that it is not possible to distinguish between them *using any sequence of calls to the objects' methods*. In the case of mutable objects, all distinct objects are distinguishable (i.e., equals has the same meaning as ==). For example, consider the following code:

```
IntSet s = new IntSet( );
IntSet t = new IntSet( );
if (s.equals(t)) ...; else ...
```

Sidebar 5.1 equals, clone, **and** toString

- Two objects are equals if they are behaviorally equivalent. Mutable objects are equals only if they are the same object; such types can inherit equals from Object. Immutable objects are equals if they have the same state; immutable types must implement equals themselves.

- clone should return an object that has the same state as its object. Immutable types can inherit clone from Object, but mutable types must implement it themselves.

- toString should return a string showing the type and current state of its object. All types must implement toString themselves.

At the time the if is executed, both s and t have the same state (the empty set). However, s and t are nevertheless distinguishable, because of mutations; for example, if the code now does s.insert(3), s and t will have different states. Therefore, the call to equals in the if statement must return false. In other words, for mutable objects s and t, s.equals(t) (or t.equals(s)) should return false if s and t are different objects even when they have the same state.

On the other hand, if two immutable objects have the same state, they should be considered equal because there will not be any way to distinguish among them by calling their methods. For example, consider

```
Poly p = new Poly(3, 4);
Poly q = new Poly(3, 4);
if (p.equals(q)) ...; else ...
```

When the if statement is executed, p and q have the same state (the polynomial $3x^4$). Furthermore, because Polys are immutable, p and q will always have the same state. Therefore, the call p.equals(q) in the if statement should return true.

The default implementation of equals provided by Object tests whether the two objects have the same identity. This is the right test for IntSet: s and t are not equivalent even though they have the same state. However, it is the wrong test for Poly, and it will be the wrong test for any immutable type.

Therefore, when you define an immutable type, you need to provide your own implementation of equals. However, you need not worry about equals for mutable types; objects of these types will have an equals method—namely, the one they inherit from Object—that does the right thing.

Object also provides a hashCode method. The specification of hashCode indicates that if two objects are equivalent according to the equals method, hashCode should produce the same value for them. Yet the default implementation for hashCode will not do this for immutable types. hashCode is needed only for types that are intended to be keys in hash tables. If your immutable type is one of these, you must implement hashCode in a way that observes this constraint on its behavior.

There is a weaker equality notion that we will call *similarity*. Two objects are similar if it is not possible to distinguish between them using any observers of their type. Just as it is useful to have a standard name equals for the method that does equivalence testing, it is also useful to have a standard name for the method that provides similarity testing. We will call this method similar.

There is no requirement to provide this method in a new type, but you can do so if you wish.

For immutable types, similar and equals are the same. However, for mutable types, similarity is weaker than equivalence. For example, in

```
IntSet s = new IntSet( );
IntSet t = new IntSet( );
if (s.similar(t)) ...; else ...
```

the call to similar should return true.

The clone method makes a copy of its object. The copy it produces should have the same state as its object; that is, it should be similar to the object being cloned. The default implementation provided by Object simply assigns from the instance variables of the old object to those of the new one. This is often not a correct implementation. For example, in the case of IntSet, it would cause the els components of the two objects to share the same vector. Then, when a modification is done to one of them (e.g., an insert), the state of the other will also change, which is incorrect. On the other hand, the default implementation is correct for Poly; again there is sharing (of the array that is the trms component), but the sharing doesn't matter because that array is never modified.

If you want a type to provide a clone method, you must provide your own implementation if the default implementation is not correct. In general, the default implementation will be correct for immutable types and incorrect for mutable ones. If the default implementation is correct, you can inherit it by putting implements Cloneable in the class header. If a class neither includes this clause in its header nor provides an implementation of clone, then if the clone method is called on one of its objects, the code will throw CloneNotSupportedException.

For example, the implementations of IntSet and Poly shown earlier do not support clone and, therefore, should the clone method be called on an Int-Set or Poly object, it will raise CloneNotSupportedException. If we wanted these types to provide clone, we would need to reimplement it for IntSet, but we could inherit it for Poly. The situation is illustrated in Figure 5.10, which shows how to provide clone and equals for Poly and IntSet. Note that no specification is given for these methods since they have standard meanings.

Poly implements equals but inherits clone from Object because of the implements Cloneable in its header. Note that Poly provides two (over-

Figure 5.10   The clone and equals methods

```
public class Poly implements Cloneable {
   // as given before, plus

   public boolean equals (Poly q) {
      if (q == null || deg != q.deg) return false;
      for (int i = 0; i <= deg; i++)
         if (trms[i] != q.trms[i]) return false;
      return true; }

   public boolean equals (Object z) {
      if (!(z instanceof Poly)) return false;
      return equals((Poly) z); }
}

public class IntSet {
   // as given before, plus

   private IntSet (Vector v) { els = v; }

   public Object clone ( ) {
      return new IntSet((Vector) els.clone( )); }
}
```

loaded) definitions for equals, one overriding the Object method and an extra one:

```
boolean equals (Object) // header of Object method
boolean equals (Poly)   // header of Poly method
```

The second one is an optimization; it avoids the cast and the call on instanceof, which are expensive, in contexts in which both the object and the argument are known by the compiler to be Polys. For example, consider

```
Poly x = new Poly(3, 7);
Object y = new Poly(3, 7);
   .
   .
   .
if (x.equals(new Poly(3,7))) ...
if (x.equals(y)) ...
```

In the first if statement, the call will go to the optimized implementation of equals because the compiler knows both x and the argument are Polys, but the second call will go to the unoptimized implementation because the compiler doesn't know that y is a Poly.

IntSet implements clone but inherits equals from Object. Note that the implementation uses an additional constructor so that it can initialize the newly created object with the right vector; since this constructor is private, it can be called only inside the class.

The signature of the clone method in a subtype must be identical to the signature of clone for Object:

```
Object clone ( );
```

Unfortunately, this means that calls to the method aren't very convenient or efficient. For example, most likely the caller of s.clone( ), where s is an IntSet, wants to get an IntSet object as a result. And, in fact, IntSet's clone method produces an IntSet object. However, clone's return type indicates that an Object is being returned. Since Object is not a subtype of IntSet (in fact the opposite is true), the object returned by clone cannot be assigned to an IntSet variable; instead the caller must cast the result, for example,

```
IntSet t = (IntSet) s.clone( );
```

The toString method produces a string that represents the current state of its object, together with an indication of its type. For example, for an IntSet, we might want to see a representation like

```
IntSet: {1, 7, 3}
```

while for a Poly we might want

```
Poly: 2 + 3x + 5x**2
```

The implementation of toString provided by Object is not very informative; it provides the type name of the object and its hash code. Therefore, almost every type should provide its own implementation of toString.

Figure 5.11 shows the toString method for IntSet. Again no specification is given, since the meaning is standard. The implementation identifies the type of object being produced; all toString implementations should follow this convention.

Figure 5.11   toString method for IntSet

```
public String toString ( ) {
    if (els.size( ) == 0) return "IntSet:{ }";
    String s = "IntSet: {" + els.elementAt(0).toString( );
    for (int i = 1; i < els.size( ); i++)
        s = s + " , " + els.elementAt(i).toString( );
    return s + "}"; }
```

5.5   Aids to Understanding Implementations

In this section, we discuss two pieces of information, the abstraction function and the representation invariant, that are particularly useful in understanding an implementation of a data abstraction.

The *abstraction function* captures the designer's intent in choosing a particular representation. It is the first thing you decide on when inventing the rep: what instance variables to use and how they relate to the abstract object they are intended to represent. The abstraction function simply describes this decision.

The *rep invariant* is invented as you investigate how to implement the constructors and methods. It captures the common assumptions on which these implementations are based; in doing so, it allows you to consider the implementation of each operation in isolation of the others.

The abstraction function and rep invariant together provide valuable documentation, both to the original implementor and to others who read the code. They capture the reason why the code is the way it is: for example, why the implementation of choose can return the $zero^{th}$ element of els (since the elements of els represent the elements of the set), or why size can simply return the size of els (because there are no duplicates in els).

Because they are so useful, both the abstraction function and rep invariant should be included as comments in the code. This section describes how to define them and also how to provide them as methods.

5.5.1   The Abstraction Function

Any implementation of a data abstraction must define how objects belonging to the type are represented. In choosing the representation, the implementor

Figure 5.12   An example of an abstraction function

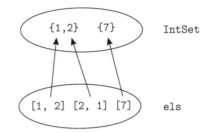

has in mind a relationship between the rep and the abstract objects. For example, in the implementation in Figure 5.6, IntSets are represented by vectors, where the elements of the vector are the elements of the set.

This relationship can be defined by a function called the *abstraction function* that maps from the instance variables that make up the rep of an object to the abstract object being represented:

$$AF: \mathcal{C} \to \mathcal{A}$$

Specifically, the abstraction function *AF* maps from a *concrete state* (i.e., the state of an object of the class $\mathcal{C}$) to an *abstract state* (i.e., the state of an abstract object). For each object *c* belonging to $\mathcal{C}$, *AF(c)* is the state of the abstract object $a \in \mathcal{A}$ that *c* represents.

For example, the abstraction function for the IntSet implementation maps the instance variables of objects of the IntSet class to abstract IntSet states. Figure 5.12 illustrates this function at some points; it shows how objects with various els components map to IntSet states. This abstraction function is *many-to-one*: many els components map to the same abstract element. For example, the IntSet {1, 2} is represented by an object whose els vector contains the Integer with value 1 followed by the Integer with value 2, and also by an object whose els vector contains the two integers in the opposite order. Since the process of abstraction involves forgetting irrelevant information, it is not surprising that abstraction functions are often many-to-one. In this example, the order in which the elements appear in the els component is irrelevant.

The abstraction function is a crucial piece of information about an implementation. It defines the meaning of the representation, the way in which the objects of the class are supposed to implement the abstract objects. It should always be described in a comment in the implementation.

In writing such a description, however, we are hampered by the fact that if the specification of the type is informal, the range of the abstraction function (the set $\mathcal{A}$) is not really defined. We shall overcome this problem by giving a description of a "typical" abstract object. This allows us to define the abstraction function in terms of this typical object. The description of the typical abstract object state is part of the specification; it is provided in the overview section. For example, the overview for IntSet stated:

// A typical IntSet is $\{x1, \ldots, xn\}$

(Recall that we are using mathematical sets to denote IntSet states.) Then we can say

// The abstraction function is
//   AF(c) = { c.els[i].intValue | 0 <= i < c.els.size }

The notation $\{x \mid p(x)\}$ describes the set of all x such that the predicate $p(x)$ is true; this notation was defined in Figure 5.3. For example, here it says that the elements of the set are exactly the integer values contained in the els vector.

Note that in defining the abstraction function, we use some convenient abbreviations: we use the notation c.els[i] to stand for use of the get method of Vector, and we omit the ( ) when we use methods with no arguments (like intValue and size). We also omit casting and simply assume the elements of the els vector are Integers.

As a second example, consider the Poly implementation. We chose to represent a Poly as an array in which the ith element held the ith coefficient up to the degree. We can describe this representation as follows:

// A typical Poly is $c_0 + c_1x + c_2x^2 + \cdots$
// The abstraction function is
//   AF(c) $= c_0 + c_1x + c_2x^2 + \cdots$
//   where
// c_i = c.trms[i] if $0 <= i < $ c.trms.size
// $= 0$ otherwise

Abstraction functions need not be provided for record types. A record type provides no abstraction over its rep; its rep is a collection of fields and so are its abstract objects. Therefore, its abstraction function is always the identity map.

5.5.2   The Representation Invariant

In Java, type checking guarantees that whenever a method or constructor is called, its object this belongs to its class. Frequently, however, not all objects of the class are legitimate representations of abstract objects. For example, the representation of IntSet given in Figure 5.6 could potentially include objects whose els vector contained more than one entry with the same integer value. However, we decided that each element of the set would be entered in the vector exactly once. Therefore, legitimate representations of IntSets do not contain duplicate entries.

A statement of a property that all legitimate objects satisfy is called a *representation invariant*, or *rep invariant*. A rep invariant $\mathbb{I}$ is a predicate

$$\mathbb{I}: \mathcal{C} \rightarrow \text{boolean}$$

that is true of legitimate objects. For example, for IntSet, we might state the following rep invariant:

```
// The rep invariant is:
//    c.els ≠ null &&
//    for all integers i . c.els[i] is an Integer &&
//    for all integers i , j . (0 <= i < j < c.els.size ⇒
//        c.els[i].intValue ≠ c.els[j].intValue )
```

Thus, $\mathbb{I}$ is false if els contains duplicates; additionally, it rules out a rep in which els does not refer to a vector, as well as a rep in which the els vector contains something other than an Integer. This rep invariant is written using predicate calculus notation. Figure 5.13 summarizes the notation we will use in this book.

The rep invariant can also be given more informally:

```
// The rep invariant is:
//    c.els ≠ null &&
//    all elements of c.els are Integers &&
//    there are no duplicates in c.els
```

As a second example, consider an alternative representation of IntSets that consists of an array of 100 booleans plus a vector:

Figure 5.13   Predicate calculus notation

&& will be used for conjunction: p && q is true if p is true and q is true

|| will be used for disjunction: p || q is true if either p is true or q is true

$\Rightarrow$ will be used for implication: $p \Rightarrow q$ means that if p is true, then q is also true. Note that false $\Rightarrow$ anything, i.e., if p is false, then we can deduce whatever we like.

iff (if and only if) will be used for double implication: p iff q means that $p \Rightarrow q$ and $q \Rightarrow p$

for all x in s . $p(x)$ means that predicate $p(x)$ is true for all x in set s.

there exists x in s . $p(x)$ means that there is at least one x in set s for which the predicate $p(x)$ is true

---

```
private boolean[100] els;
private Vector otherEls;
private int sz;
```

The idea here is that for an integer i in the range 0...99, we record membership in the set by storing true in els[i]. Integers outside this range will be stored in otherEls in the same manner as in our previous implementation of IntSet. Since it would be expensive to compute the size of the IntSet if we had to examine every part of the els array, we also store the size explicitly in the rep. This representation is a good one if almost all members of the set are in the range 0 . . . 99 and if we expect the set to have quite a few members in this range. Otherwise, the space required for the els array will be wasted.

For this representation we have

```
// The abstraction function is
//    AF(c) = { c.otherEls[i].intValue | 0 <= i < c.otherEls.size }
//        +
//        { j | 0 <= j < 100 && c.els[j] }
```

In other words, the set is the union of the elements of otherEls and the indexes of the true elements of els. Also, we have

```
// The rep invariant is
// c.els ≠ null && c.otherEls ≠ null && c.els.size = 100 &&
//    all elements in c.otherEls are Integers &&
//    all elements in c.otherEls are not in the range 0 to 99 &&
```

```
//   there are no duplicates in c.otherEls &&
//   c.sz = c.otherEls.size + ( count of true entries in c.els )
```

Note that the `sz` instance variable of this rep is redundant: It holds information that can be computed directly from the other instance variables. Whenever there is redundant information in the rep, the relationship of this information to the rest of the rep should be explained in the rep invariant (for example, in the last line of this rep invariant).

It is sometimes convenient to use a helping function in the rep invariant or abstraction function. For example, the last line of the preceding rep invariant could be rewritten

```
// c.sz = c.otherEls.size + cnt(c.els, 0)
//   where cnt(a, i) = if i >= a.size then 0
//     else if a[i] then 1 + cnt(a, i+1)
//     else cnt(a, i+1)
```

The helping function `cnt` is defined by a recurrence relation.

The implementation of `Poly` in Figure 5.7 has an interesting rep invariant. Recall that we chose to store coefficients only up to the degree, without any trailing zeros except in the case of the zero polynomial. Therefore, we do not expect to find a zero in the high element of the `trms` component unless the component has just one element. In addition, these arrays always have at least one element. Furthermore, `deg` must be one less than the size of `trms`. Thus we have

```
// The rep invariant is
//   c.trms ≠ null && c.trms.length >= 1 && c.deg = c.trms.length-1
//   && c.deg > 0 ⇒ c.trms[deg] ≠ 0
```

Recall that the implementation of the `coeff` operation depended on the length of the array being one greater than the degree of the `Poly`; now we see this requirement spelled out in the rep invariant.

Sometimes all concrete objects are legal representations. Then we have simply

```
// The rep invariant is
//   true
```

This is what happens for record types: record objects are used by accessing their fields directly. This means that using code will be able to modify the fields, which in turn means that the class implementing the record cannot constrain the rep in any way. Of course, there might be some constraints on how the record objects are used that define a stronger relationship between the fields, but these constraints would be ensured by the code that uses the record objects and would show up in the rep invariant for that code. For example, the rep invariant for the sparse polynomial implementation discussed in Section 5.3.4 would include

```
// for all elements e of c.trms
//    e is a Pair and e.exp >= 0 and e.coeff ≠ 0
```

Rep invariants need not be given for record types because all these classes have exactly the same rep invariant. They must be given for all other types, even those for which the invariant is simply true. Giving the invariant may prevent the implementor from depending on a stronger, unsatisfied invariant.

5.5.3   Implementing the Abstraction Function and Rep Invariant

In addition to providing the abstraction function and rep invariant as comments in your code, you should also provide methods to implement them. (The only exception to this rule is record types, which do not need these methods.) These methods are useful for finding errors in your code; in addition, the implementation of the abstraction function can be used to do output. Sidebar 5.2 summarizes the abstraction function and rep invariant.

The `toString` method is used to implement the abstraction function. The method that checks the rep invariant is called `repOk`. It has the following specification:

```
public boolean repOk( )
    // EFFECTS: Returns true if the rep invariant holds for this;
    //    otherwise returns false.
```

The method is public because we want it to be callable by code outside of its class. Every type should provide this method, but a specification need not be given for it, since the specification is identical for every type.

Figure 5.14 gives implementations of the `repOk` methods for the classes we have seen so far. Note the use of the `instanceof` operator in `repOk` for `IntSet` to check that the element is an `Integer`.

The `repOk` method is used in two ways. Test programs can call it to check whether an implementation is preserving the rep invariant. Or you can use

- The abstraction function explains the interpretation of the rep. It maps the state of each legal representation object to the abstract object it is intended to represent. It is implemented by the toString method.

- The representation invariant defines all the common assumptions that underlie the implementations of a type's operations. It defines which representations are legal by mapping each representation object to either true (if its rep is legal) or false (if its rep is not legal). It is implemented by the repOk method.

Figure 5.14   Implementations of repOk methods

```
// for Poly:
public boolean repOk( ) {
    if (trms == null || deg != trms.length - 1 ||
        trms.length == 0) return false;
    if (deg == 0) return true;
    return trms[deg] != 0; }

// for IntSet:
public boolean repOk( ) {
    if (els == null) return false;
    for (int i = 0; i < els.size( ); i++) {
        Object x = els.get(i);
        if (!(x instanceof Integer)) return false;
        for (int j = i + 1; j < els.size( ); j++)
            if (x.equals(els.get(j))) return false;
    }
    return true; }
```

it inside method and constructor implementations. In this case, if the rep invariant does not hold, you can throw FailureException. Constructors would call it before they return to ensure the rep invariant holds on the newly initialized object. Also any methods that modify the rep of either old or newly created objects would call it on these objects before they return. For example, in `Poly`, the `add`, `mul`, and `minus` routines would call it, but `sub` need not since it doesn't access the reps of objects directly, and `coeff` need not since it doesn't modify the rep. In `IntSet`, the mutators `insert` and `remove` would call it. If the calls on `repOk` are costly, they can be disabled when the program is in production.

5.5.4   Discussion

A rep invariant is "invariant" because it always holds for the reps of abstract objects; that is, it holds whenever an object is used outside its implementation. The rep invariant need not hold all the time, since it can be violated while executing one of the type's operations. For example, the `Poly mul` method produces a `trms` component with zero in the high element, but the element is overwritten with a nonzero value before `mul` returns. The rep invariant must hold whenever operations return to their callers.

There is a relationship between the abstraction function and the rep invariant. The abstraction function is of interest only for legal representations, since only these represent the abstract objects. Therefore, it need not be defined for illegal representations. For example, both `IntSet` and `Poly` have abstraction functions that are defined only if the `els` and `trms` components, respectively, are non-null, and furthermore, the abstraction function for `IntSet` makes sense only if all elements of the `Vector` are `Integers`.

There is an issue concerning how much to say in a rep invariant. A rep invariant should express all constraints on which the operations depend. A good way to think of this is to imagine that the operations are to be implemented by different people who cannot talk to one another; the rep invariant must contain all the constraints that these various implementors depend on. However, it need not state additional constraints. We will see an example of unstated constraints in Section 6.6.

When a data abstraction is implemented, the rep invariant is one of the first things the programmer thinks about. It must be chosen before any operations are implemented, or the implementations will not work together harmoniously. To ensure that it is understood, the rep invariant should be written down and included as a comment in the code (in addition to the abstraction function). Writing the rep invariant forces the implementor to articulate what is known and increases the chances that the operations will be implemented correctly.

All operations must be implemented in a way that *preserves* the rep invariant. For example, suppose we implemented `insert` by

```
public void insert (int x) {
    els.addElement(new Integer(x));
}
```

This implementation can produce an object with duplicate elements. If we know that the rep invariant prohibits such objects, then this implementation is clearly incorrect.

The rep invariant is also useful for the reader of an implementation. For example, in an alternative implementation of `IntSet`, we might have decided to keep the rep array sorted. In this case, we would have

```
// The rep invariant is
//    c.els ≠ null && all elements of c.els are Integers
//    && for all i, j such that 0 <= i < j < c.els.size
//        c.els[i].intValue < c.els[j].intValue
```

and the operations would be implemented differently than in Figure 5.6. The rep invariant tells the reader why the operations are implemented as they are.

5.6 Properties of Data Abstraction Implementations

This section discusses some properties of implementations of data abstractions: benevolent side effects and exposing the rep. These properties are summarized in Sidebar 5.3.

5.6.1 Benevolent Side Effects

A mutable abstraction must have a mutable rep or it will not be possible to provide the required mutability. However, an immutable abstraction need not have an immutable rep. (It is possible to have an immutable rep in Java by declaring all the instance variables to be `final`.)

For example, `Poly`s are immutable, but they have a mutable rep. A mutable rep is not a problem so long as modifications made to the rep cannot be

---

Sidebar 5.3 Properties of Data Abstraction Implementations

- An implementation performs a *benevolent side effect* if it modifies the rep without affecting the abstract state of its object. Benevolent side effects are possible only when the abstraction function is many-to-one.

- An implementation *exposes the rep* if it provides users of its objects with a way of accessing some mutable component of the rep.

---

observed by the abstraction's users. For example, sometimes it is useful to initialize an object by incrementally mutating its rep, though once the object is fully initialized, its rep is never modified again. This is the way `Poly`s are created in some of the `Poly` methods.

Mutability is also useful for *benevolent side effects*, which are modifications that are not visible outside the implementation. For example, suppose rational numbers are represented as a pair of integers:

```
int num, denom;
```

The abstraction function is

```
// A typical rational is n/d
// The abstraction function is
//    AF(c) = c.num/c.denom
```

Given this rep, several choices must be made: what to do with a zero denominator, how to store negative rationals, and whether or not to keep the rational in reduced form (that is, with the numerator and denominator reduced so that there are no common terms). Suppose we choose to rule out zero denominators, to represent negative rationals by means of negative numerators, and *not* to keep the rep in reduced form (to speed up operations like multiplication). Thus we have

```
// The rep invariant is
//    c.denom > 0
```

However, to test whether two rationals are equal, it is useful to compute reduced forms; they can be computed using the following gcd procedure:

Figure 5.15   A benevolent side effect

```
public class rat {
    private int num;
    private int denom;

    public boolean equals(rat r) {
        if (r == null) return false;
        if (num == 0) return r.num == 0;
        if (r.num == 0) return false;
        reduce( );
        r.reduce( );
        return (num == r.num && denom == r.denom); }

    private void reduce ( ) {
        // REQUIRES: This.num != 0
        // MODIFIES: This
        // EFFECTS: Changes this to its reduced form.
        int temp = num;
        if (num < 0) temp = -num;
        int g = Num.gcd(temp, denom);
        num = num/g;
        denom = denom/g; }
}
```

```
static public int gcd (int n, int d) throws NonPositiveException
    // EFFECTS: If n or d is not positive throws NonPositiveException
    //     else returns the greatest common divisor of n and d.
```

The implementation of the equals method is shown in Figure 5.15. Once computed, the reduced forms are stored in the rep because this will speed up the next equality test.

The modification of the rep performed by the equals method is a benevolent side effect. Such side effects are often performed for reasons of efficiency. They are possible whenever the abstraction function is many-to-one, since then many rep objects represent a particular abstract object. It is sometimes useful within an implementation to switch from one of these rep objects to another. Such a switch is safe since the rep still maps to the same abstract object.

5.6.2 Exposing the Rep

A key issue in implementing data abstractions is to obtain the ability to do local reasoning: we want to be able to ensure that a class is correct just by examining the code of that class. Local reasoning is valid only if the representations of abstract objects cannot be modified outside their implementation. If local reasoning is not supported, we say the implementation *exposes the rep*. Exposing the rep means that the implementation makes mutable components of the rep (e.g., instance variables) accessible to code outside of the class.

One way to expose the rep is to have instance variable declarations that are not declared to be private. However, even if all instance variables are private, it is still possible to expose the rep!

For example, suppose IntSet had an allEls method with the following specification:

```
public Vector allEls ( )
    // EFFECTS: Returns a vector containing the elements of this, each
    //    exactly once, in arbitrary order.
```

and suppose this method were implemented (as part of the implementation given in Figure 5.6) as follows:

```
public Vector allEls ( ) {
    return els; }
```

This implementation would allow users of IntSet to access the els component directly; since this component is mutable, users can modify it. To avoid this problem, the allEls implementation must return a copy of the els component.

Exposing the rep is an implementation error. It can happen either because a method returns a mutable object in the rep, as discussed previously, or because a constructor or method makes a mutable argument object part of the rep. For example, suppose IntSet had the following constructor:

```
public IntSet(Vector elms) throws NullPointerException
    // EFFECTS: If elms is null throws NullPointerException else
    //    initializes this to contain as elements all the ints in elms.
```

and suppose the implementation were

```
public IntSet (Vector elms) throws NullPointerException {
    if (elms == null)
        throw new NullPointerException
            ("IntSet 1 argument constructor");
    els = elms;
}
```

Again, we have an implementation error that results in the rep being exposed.

5.7   Reasoning about Data Abstractions

Whenever you write a program, you think in an informal way about whether it is correct. This reasoning is so basic that you may not be aware that you are doing it! In addition, you often want to convince others of the correctness of your code—for example, as part of a code inspection. This process of "convincing" also involves an informal correctness argument. Finally, when you read someone else's code to determine if it is correct, you also go through an informal correctness argument.

Reasoning about the correctness of standalone procedures is relatively straightforward: you assume the precondition holds and examine the code to convince yourself that the procedure does what its effects clause requires. Reasoning about data abstraction implementations is a little trickier because you have to consider the entire class. Furthermore, you have to reason about code written at the concrete level (i.e., it manipulates the rep), yet convince yourself that it satisfies the specification, which is written in terms of abstract objects.

This section discusses how to carry out this reasoning. First we discuss how to show that an implementation *preserves the rep invariant*, that is, ensures the invariant is true for an object whenever it is being used outside of its class. Then we discuss how to reason that operations do the right thing. We also discuss how to reason about properties of a data abstraction by showing that certain abstract invariants hold. Sidebar 5.4 summarizes the reasoning process.

Sidebar 5.4 Reasoning about Data Abstractions

- Data type induction is used to reason about whether an implementation preserves the rep invariant. For each operation, we assume the rep invariant holds for any inputs of the type, and show it holds at return for any inputs of the type and any new objects of the type.

- To prove the correctness of an operation, we make use of the abstraction function to relate the abstract objects mentioned in its specification to the concrete objects that represent them.

- Data type induction is also used to reason about abstract invariants. However, in this case, the reasoning is based on the specification, and observers can be ignored.

5.7.1   Preserving the Rep Invariant

As part of showing that a type is implemented correctly, we must show that the rep invariant holds for all objects of the class. We do this as follows. First, we show that the invariant holds for objects returned by constructors. For methods, we can assume when they are called that the invariant holds for this and also for all argument objects of the type; we must show that it holds when the method returns for this and any arguments of the type and also for returned objects of the type.

For example, the `IntSet` implementation of Figure 5.6 has invariant

```
// c.els ≠ null &&
// for all integers i . c.els[i] is an Integer &&
// for all integers i, j . ( 0 <= i < j < c.els.size =>
//   c.els[i].intValue ≠ c.els[j].intValue )
```

The `IntSet` constructor establishes this invariant because the newly created vector is empty. The `isIn` method preserves it because we can assume that the invariant holds for this when `isIn` is called and `isIn` does not modify this; the same is true for `size` and `choose` and private method `getIndex`. Method `insert` preserves the invariant because the following conditions are met:

- The invariant holds for this at the time of the call.

- The call to `getIndex` by `insert` preserves the invariant.

- insert adds x to this only if x is not already in this (i.e., getIndex(x) returns −1); therefore, since this satisfies the invariant at the time of the call, it still satisfies the invariant after the call.

As a second example, consider the Poly implementation in Figure 5.7 and recall that the invariant is

```
//   c.trms ≠ null && c.trms.length >= 1 && c.deg = c.trms.length - 1
//   && c.deg > 0 ⟹ c.trms[deg] ≠ 0
```

The Poly constructor that produces the zero polynomial preserves the invariant because it creates a one-element array; the other Poly constructor preserves the invariant because it explicitly tests for the zero polynomial. The mul operation preserves the invariant because the following conditions are met:

- The invariant holds for this at the time of the call; it also holds for q if q is not null.

- If either this or q is the zero Poly, this is recognized and the proper rep constructed.

- Otherwise, neither this nor q contains a zero in its high term—therefore, the high term of the trms array in the returned Poly, which contains the product of the high terms of trms and q.trms, cannot be zero.

This kind of reasoning is called *data type induction*. The induction is on the number of procedure invocations used to produce the current value of the object. The first step of the induction is to establish the property for the constructor(s); the induction step establishes the property for the methods.

5.7.2　Reasoning about Operations

Proving that the operations preserve the rep invariant is only part of what is needed to convince yourself that your implementation is correct. In addition, you need to show that each operation does what it is supposed to do.

The difficulty is that the specifications are written in terms of abstract objects, but the implementation manipulates concrete representations. Therefore, we need a way to relate the two. This is done by using the abstraction function.

For example, suppose we wanted to argue that the implementation of IntSet is correct. This would consist of arguing that each operation is implemented correctly:

- *The constructor*. The `IntSet` constructor returns an object whose `els` component is an empty vector. This is correct because the abstraction function maps the empty vector to the empty set.

- *The* `size` *method*. When this method is called, we know that the size of the `els` vector is the cardinality of the set because the abstraction function maps the elements of the vector to the elements of the set *and* because the rep invariant, which can be assumed to hold when `size` is called, ensures that there are no duplicates in `els`. Therefore, returning this size is correct.

- *The* `remove` *method*. This method first checks whether the element to be removed is in the vector and simply returns if it is not. This is correct because if the element isn't in the vector, it isn't in the set (because of the way the abstraction function maps the vector to the set), and therefore, when `remove` returns, `this_post` maps to `this` − { x }. Otherwise, the method removes the element from the vector, and again we get the right result because the rep invariant guarantees that there are no duplicates in `els`.

This process would continue until every operation had been considered. Note that we make use of the rep invariant in these proofs; that is, we are able to assume it holds on entry.

An important point about these proofs is that we are able to reason about each operation independently, which is possible because of the rep invariant. It captures the common assumptions between the operations and, in this way, stands in place of all the other operations when we consider the proof of any particular operation. Of course, this reasoning is valid only if all operations preserve the rep invariant, since that is what allows it to take the place of the other operations in the reasoning process.

5.7.3   Reasoning at the Abstract Level

The preceding sections have discussed how we reason about the correctness of an implementation of a data abstraction. It is also useful to reason about a data abstraction at an abstract level. In this case, the reasoning is based only on the type's specification; we can ignore its implementation.

One kind of property that it is useful to show is an *abstract invariant*, which is the abstract analog of the rep invariant. For example, we relied on abstract invariants for vectors and arrays in our reasoning about the correctness of the `IntSet` and `Poly` implementations. For both vectors and arrays, we assumed that their size was greater than or equal to zero and, furthermore, that all indexes that were greater than or equal to zero, and less than the size, were in bounds.

There are similar abstract invariants for sets and polynomials. For example, the size of an `IntSet` is always greater than or equal to zero. This property can be established as follows:

- It clearly holds for the constructor since it returns a new, empty `IntSet`.
- It holds for `insert` since this only increases the size of the `IntSet`.
- It holds for `remove` since this removes an element from the set only if the element was in the set at the time of the call.

Note that we completely ignore the observers in this proof. Since they do not modify their objects (in a way that users can notice), they cannot affect the property.

Note that we are reasoning at an abstract level, not at an implementation level. We are not concerned with how `IntSets` are implemented. Instead, we work directly with the `IntSet` specification. Working at the abstract level greatly simplifies the reasoning.

5.8 Design Issues

In this section, we discuss some issues that arise when defining a data abstraction: mutability, kinds of operations, and adequacy. Sidebar 5.5 summarizes the properties of data abstractions.

5.8.1 Mutability

Data abstractions are either mutable, with objects whose values can change, or immutable. Care should be taken in deciding on this aspect of a type. In general, a type should be immutable if its objects would naturally have unchanging values. This might be the case, for example, for such mathematical objects as integers, `Polys`, and complex numbers. A type should usually be mutable if it is modeling something from the real world, where it is natural for the values of objects to change over time. For example, an automobile in

---

Sidebar 5.5 Properties of Data Abstractions

- A data abstraction is mutable if it has any mutator methods; otherwise, the data abstraction is immutable.

- There are four kinds of operations provided by data abstractions: *creators* produce new objects "from scratch"; *producers* produces new objects given existing objects as arguments, *mutators* modify the state of their object; and *observers* provide information about the state of their object.

- A data type is *adequate* if it provides enough operations so that whatever users need to do with its objects can be done conveniently and with reasonable efficiency.

---

a simulation system might be running or stopped, and contain passengers or not. Similarly, a type modeling storage, such as an array or a set, is likely to be mutable. However, we might still prefer to use an immutable type in such a case because of the greater safety immutability provides, or because immutability can allow sharing of subparts. We will see an example of such an immutable type (lists) in Chapter 7.

In deciding about mutability, it is sometimes necessary to make a trade-off between efficiency and safety. Immutable abstractions are safer than mutable ones because no problems arise if their objects are shared. However, new objects may be created and discarded frequently for immutable abstractions, which means that storage management work (e.g., garbage collection) is done more frequently. For example, representing a set as a list is probably not a good choice if insert and remove are used frequently.

In any case, note that mutability or immutability is a property of the type and not of its implementation. An implementation must simply support this aspect of its abstraction's behavior.

5.8.2   Operation Categories

The operations of a data abstraction fall into four categories:

1. *Creators*. These operations create objects of their type "from scratch" without taking any objects of their type as inputs. All creators are constructors. Most constructors are creators—for example, all the ones in the

examples in this chapter. But sometimes constructors take arguments of their type, and these are *not* creators.

2. *Producers*. These operations take objects of their type as inputs and create other objects of their type. They may be either constructors or methods. For example, add and mul are producers for Poly.

3. *Mutators*. These are methods that modify objects of their type. For example, insert and remove are mutators for IntSets. Clearly, only mutable types can have mutators.

4. *Observers*. These are methods that take objects of their type as inputs and return results of other types. They are used to obtain information about objects. Examples are size, isIn, and choose for IntSets, and coeff and degree for Polys.

The creators usually produce some but not all objects; for example, the Poly creators (the two constructors) produce only single-term polynomials, while the IntSet constructor produces only the empty set. The other objects are produced by producers or mutators. Thus, the producer add can be used to obtain Polys with more than one term, while the mutator insert can be used to obtain sets containing many elements.

Mutators play the same role in mutable types that producers play in immutable ones. A mutable type can have producers as well as mutators; for example, if IntSet had a clone method, this method would be a producer. Sometimes observers are combined with producers or mutators; for example, IntSet might have a chooseAndRemove method that returns the chosen element and also removes it from the set.

5.8.3   Adequacy

A data type is *adequate* if it provides enough operations so that everything users need to do with its objects can be done both conveniently and with reasonable efficiency. It is not possible to give a precise definition of adequacy, although there are limits on how few operations a type can have and still be useful. For example, if we provide only the IntSet constructor and the insert and remove methods, programs cannot find out anything about the elements in the set (because there are no observers). On the other hand, if we add just the size method to these three operations, we can learn about elements in the set (for example, we could test for membership by deleting the integer and seeing if the size changed), but the type would be costly and inconvenient to use.

A very rudimentary notion of adequacy can be obtained by considering the operation categories. In general, a data abstraction should have operations from at least three of the four categories discussed in the preceding section. It must have creators, observers, and producers (if it is immutable) or mutators (if it is mutable). In addition, the type must be *fully populated*. This means that between its creators, mutators, and producers, it must be possible to obtain every possible abstract object state.

However, the notion of adequacy additionally must take context of use into account: a type must have a rich enough set of operations for its intended uses. If the type is to be used in a limited context, such as a single package, then just enough operations for that context need be provided. If the type is intended for general use, a rich set of operations is desirable.

To decide whether a data abstraction has enough operations, identify everything users might reasonably expect to do. Next, think about how these things can be done with the given set of operations. If something seems too expensive or too cumbersome (or both), investigate whether the addition of an operation would help. Sometimes a substantial improvement in performance can be obtained simply by having access to the representation. For example, we could eliminate the isIn operation for IntSets because this operation can be implemented outside the type by using the other operations. However, testing for membership in a set is a common use and will be faster if done inside the implementation. Therefore, IntSet should provide this operation.

There can also be too many operations in a type. When considering the addition of operations, you need to consider how they fit in with the purpose of the data abstraction. For example, a storage abstraction like Vector or IntSet should include operations to access and modify the storage, but not operations unrelated to this purpose, such as a sort method or a method to compute the sum of the elements of the vector or set.

Having too many operations makes an abstraction harder to understand. Also, implementation is more difficult, and so is maintenance, because if the implementation changes, more code is affected. The desirability of extra operations must be balanced against these factors. If the type is adequate, its operations can be augmented by standalone procedures that are outside the type's implementation (i.e., static methods of some other class).

5.9   Locality and Modifiability

The benefits of locality and modifiability apply to data abstractions as well as to procedures. However, these benefits can be achieved only if we have abstraction by specification.

Locality (the ability to reason about a module by just looking at its code and not any other code) requires that a representation be *modifiable* only within its type's implementation. If modifications can occur elsewhere, then we cannot establish the correctness of the implementation just by examining its code; for example, we cannot guarantee locally that the rep invariant holds, and we cannot use data type induction with any confidence.

Modifiability (the ability to reimplement an abstraction without having to reimplement any other code) requires even more than locality—all access to a representation, even to immutable components, must occur within its type's implementation. If access occurs in some other module, we cannot replace the implementation without affecting that other module. This is why all the instance variables must be declared `private`.

Thus, it is crucial that access to the representation be restricted to the type's implementation. It is desirable to have the programming language help here so that restricted access is guaranteed provided the implementor does not expose the rep. Otherwise, restricted access is another property that must be proved about programs. Java provides support for restricted access via its encapsulation mechanisms.

Sidebar 5.6 summarizes the discussion about locality and modifiability.

Sidebar 5.6   Locality and Modifiability for Data Abstraction

- A data abstraction implementation provides locality if using code cannot modify components of the rep; that is, it must not expose the rep.

- A data abstraction implementation provides modifiability if, in addition, there is no way for using code to access any part of the rep.

5.10   **Summary**

This chapter has discussed data abstractions: what they are, how to specify their behavior, and how to implement them, both in general and in Java. We discussed both mutable abstractions, such as IntSet, and immutable ones, such as Poly.

We also discussed some important aspects of data type implementations. In general, we want all objects of the class to be legal representations of the abstract objects; the rep invariant defines the legal representations. The abstraction function defines the meaning of the rep by stating the way in which the legal class objects represent the abstract objects. Both the rep invariant and the abstraction function should be included as comments in the implementation (in the private section of the class declaration). They are helpful in developing the implementation since they force the implementor to be explicit about assumptions. They are also helpful to anyone who examines the implementation later since they explain what must be understood about the rep. Furthermore, the rep invariant and abstraction function should be implemented (as repOk and toString, respectively) since this makes debugging and testing easier.

In addition, we explored some issues that must be considered in designing and implementing data types. Care must be taken in deciding whether or not a type is mutable; an immutable abstraction can have a mutable rep, however, and observers can even modify the rep, provided these modifications are "benevolent" (i.e., not visible to users). Also, care is needed in choosing a type's operations so that it serves the needs of its users adequately. We also discussed data type induction and how it is used to prove properties of objects. Furthermore, we discussed how having an encapsulated rep is crucial for obtaining the benefits of locality and modifiability.

Exercises

5.1 Implement a toString method for Polys (as part of the implementation in Figure 5.7).

5.2 Suppose IntSets were implemented using a Vector as in Figure 5.6, but the els component was kept sorted in increasing size. Give the rep invariant and abstraction function for this implementation. Also implement repOk and toString.

5.3 Suppose Polys (Figure 5.4) were implemented with the zero Poly represented by the empty array. Give the rep invariant and abstraction function for this implementation, and implement repOk and toString.

5.4 Suppose we wanted a way to create a Poly (Figure 5.4) by reading a string from a BufferedReader. Specify and implement such an operation. Does the operation need to be implemented inside the Poly class (e.g., the one in Figure 5.7), or can it be in a separate class?

5.5 Bounded queues have an upper bound, established when a queue is created, on the number of integers that can be stored in the queue. Queues are mutable and provide access to their elements in first-in/first-out order. Queue operations include

```
IntQueue(int n);
void enq(int x);
int deq ( );
```

The constructor creates a new queue with maximum size n, enq adds an element to the front of the queue, and deq removes the element from the end of the queue. Provide a specification of IntQueue, including extra operations as needed for adequacy. Implement your specification. Give the rep invariant and abstraction function and implement repOk and toString.

5.6 Implement sparse polynomials. Be sure to include the rep invariant and abstraction function and to implement repOk and toString.

5.7 Specify and implement a rational number type. Give the rep invariant and abstraction function and implement repOk and toString.

5.8 Consider a map data abstraction that maps Strings to ints. Maps allow an existing mapping to be looked up. Maps are also mutable: new pairs can be added to a map, and an existing mapping can be removed. Give a specification for maps. Be sure your data type is adequate, and if any operations throw exceptions, explain whether they are checked or unchecked. Also implement your specification. Give the rep invariant and abstraction function and implement repOk and toString.

5.9 Discuss whether the implementations of bounded queues and maps should provide their own implementations of equals and clone and implement these operations if they are needed.

5.10 Give an informal argument that the implementation of Poly in Figure 5.7 preserves the rep invariant.

5.11 Give an informal argument that the implementation of Poly in Figure 5.7 is correct.

5.12 Give an informal argument that the following abstract invariant holds for Polys:

$$p.degree > 0 \Rightarrow p.coeff(p.degree) \neq 0$$

5.13 Provide correctness arguments for your implementations of the types mentioned previously (rational numbers, sparse polynomials, bounded queues, and maps).

5.14 Suppose we wanted to evaluate a Poly (Figure 5.4) at a given point:

```
int eval(Poly p, int x) throws NullPointerException
    // EFFECTS: If p is null throws NullPointerException else
    //    returns the value of p at x, e.g., eval(x² + 3x, 2) = 10.
```

Should eval be an operation of Poly? Discuss.

5.15 A student proposes a type matrix with operations to add and multiply matrices and to invert a matrix. These matrices are mutable; for example, the invert operation modifies its argument to contain the inverse of the original matrix. A second student claims that a matrix abstraction ought not to be mutable. Discuss.

5.16 A student says that as long as programs outside a type's implementation cannot modify the rep, we have achieved as much as is possible from data abstraction. Discuss.

Iteration Abstraction

6

This chapter discusses our final abstraction mechanism, the *iteration abstraction*, or *iterator* for short. Iterators are a generalization of the iteration mechanisms available in most programming languages. They permit users to iterate over arbitrary types of data in a convenient and efficient way.

For example, an obvious use of a set is to perform some action for each of its elements:

```
for all elements of the set
    do action
```

Such a loop might go through the set completely—for example, to sum all elements of a set. Or it might search for an element that satisfies some criterion, in which case the loop can stop as soon as the desired element has been found.

IntSets as we have defined them so far provide no convenient way to perform such loops. For example, suppose we want to compute the sum of the elements in an IntSet:

```
public static int setSum (IntSet s) throws NullPointerException
    // EFFECTS: If s is null throws NullPointerException else
    //     returns the sum of the elements of s.
```

The implementation of setSum shown in Figure 6.1 illustrates the two main defects of our IntSet abstraction. First, to loop through all elements, we delete each element returned by choose so that it will not be chosen

Figure 6.1   An implementation of setSum

```
public static int setSum (IntSet s) throws NullPointerException {
   int[ ] a = new int[s.size( )];
   int sum = 0;
   for (int i = 0; i < a.length; i++) {
      a[i] = s.choose( );
      sum = sum + a[i];
      s.remove(a[i]); }
   // restore elements of s
   for (int i = 0; i < a.length; i++) s.insert(a[i]);
   return sum;
}
```

again. Thus, two operations, choose and remove, must be called on each iteration. This inefficiency could be avoided by having choose remove the chosen element, but we still have the second problem, which is that iterating over an IntSet destroys it by removing all its elements. Such destruction may be acceptable at times but cannot be satisfactory in general. Although we can collect the removed elements and reinsert them later, as is done in Figure 6.1, the approach is clumsy and inefficient.

If setSum were an IntSet operation, we could implement it efficiently by manipulating the rep of IntSet. However, setSum does not make sense as an IntSet operation; it seems peripheral to the concept of a set. Furthermore, even if we could justify making it an operation, what about other similar procedures we might want? There must be a way to implement such procedures efficiently outside the type.

To support iteration adequately, we need to access all elements in a collection efficiently and without destroying the collection. How might we do this for IntSets? One possibility is to provide a members method:

```
public int[ ] members ( )
   // EFFECTS: Returns an array containing the elements of this,
   //    each exactly once, in some arbitrary order.
```

Given this operation, we can implement setSum as shown in Figure 6.2. Since members does not modify its argument, we no longer need to rebuild the IntSet after iterating.

Figure 6.2   Implementation of setSum using the members method

```
public static int setSum (IntSet s) {
    int[ ] a = s.members( );
    int sum = 0;
    for (int i = 0; i < a.length; i++) sum = sum + a[i];
    return sum;
}
```

Although members makes it easier to use IntSets, it is inefficient, especially if the IntSet is large. First, we have two data structures—the IntSet itself and the array—and, if the set is large, so is the array. Second, in the case of a search loop, we have probably done too much work since the loop need not examine all elements of the collection being searched. For example, if we were searching an IntSet for a negative element, we could stop as soon as we encountered the first negative element. However, we must process the entire collection to build the array.

An alternative to members is an operation that simply returns the representing vector. However, this solution is very bad since it destroys abstraction by exposing the rep.

Yet another possibility is to change the IntSet abstraction to encompass the notion of indexing. However, such an IndexedSet is a more complicated abstraction than IntSet, and the added complexity does not seem intrinsic to the notion of a set.

What is needed is a general mechanism of iteration that is convenient and efficient and that preserves abstraction. Iterators provide the needed support. An iterator is a special kind of procedure that causes the items we want to iterate over to be produced incrementally. The produced items can be used in other modules that specify actions to be performed for each item. The using code will contain some sort of looping structure,

> for each *result item* i *produced by iterator* A
>   do *perform some action on* i

Each iteration of the loop produces a new item, which is then acted on by the body of the loop.

Note the separation of concerns in such a form. The iterator is responsible for producing the items, while the code containing the loop defines the action to be performed on them. The iterator can be used in different modules that perform different actions on the items, and it can be implemented in different ways without affecting these modules.

Since the iterator causes items to be produced one at a time, it avoids the space and time problems discussed earlier. We need not construct a potentially large data structure to contain the items. Moreover, if the using code is performing a search loop, the iterator can be stopped as soon as the item of interest is found.

As mentioned earlier, iterators are a generalization of the iteration mechanisms available in most programming languages. In addition to some form of while loop, programming languages typically provide a for loop for iterating over integers. Such iteration is useful in conjunction with arrays, which are indexed, but does not mesh well with nonindexed collections like IntSet. Iterators provide convenient iteration even over nonindexed collections.

6.1   Iteration in Java

Java does not provide direct support for iteration abstraction. Instead, we will provide iteration by a special kind of procedure, which we will refer to as an *iterator*. Some iterators are methods of data abstractions, and a data abstraction can provide several iterator methods. In addition, there can be standalone iterators.

An iterator returns a special kind of data object called a *generator*. A generator keeps track of the state of an iteration in its rep. It has a hasNext method that can be used to determine whether more elements remain to be produced, and a next method to get the next element and advance the state of the generator object to record the returning of that element.

All generators belong to types that are subtypes of the Iterator interface (interfaces will be discussed in detail in Chapter 7). This interface is described in Figure 6.3; it is defined by the java.util package. (The Iterator interface provides some additional methods to what are shown in the figure, but we will not use them in this book.) The specification provides a generic description of all generator types; all such types have objects with the two methods and the indicated behavior. NoSuchElementException is an unchecked exception because of the expectation that most uses of a generator will avoid causing the exception to be raised.

Figure 6.3   Specification of Iterator interface

```
public interface Iterator {

    public boolean hasNext ( );
        // EFFECTS: Returns true if there are more elements to yield
        //    else returns false

    public Object next ( ) throws NoSuchElementException;
        // MODIFIES: this
        // EFFECTS: If there are more results to yield, returns the next result
        //    and modifies the state of this to record the yield.
        //    Otherwise, throws NoSuchElementException
}
```

Figure 6.4   Using generators

```
// loop controlled by hasNext
Iterator g = primesLT100( );
while (g.hasNext( )) {
    int x = ((Integer) g.next( )).intValue( );
    // use x
    }

// loop controlled by exception
Iterator g = primesLT100( );
try {
    while (true) {
        int x = ((Integer) g.next( )).intValue( );
        // use x
        }
catch (NoSuchElementException e) { }
```

Figure 6.4 shows how to use generators to do iteration. First, a generator is created by calling an iterator; in this example, the iterator primesLT100 returns a generator that will produce all prime numbers less than 100. The generator is typically used in a while loop. The loop body uses the next method to get the next value produced by the iteration. Either the loop is controlled by the hasNext method or the loop can be terminated when next throws an exception.

6.2   Specifying Iterators

The specification of an iterator explains the whole iteration: how the iterator uses its arguments to produce a generator, *and* the behavior of the generator. (See Sidebar 6.1.) The specification given in Figure 6.3 explains what the generator methods do but is otherwise generic: it doesn't explain exactly what any particular generator does. We capture the missing information in the specification of the iterator.

Figure 6.5 gives the specifications of two iterators, both of which are methods of data abstractions. The terms iterator is a method of Poly that provides the ability to iterate through the terms of the Poly. The specification explains that the returned generator allows iteration over this, producing all the exponents of its Poly for nonzero terms up to the degree. Note that the specification indicates the type of object (Integer) that will actually be produced by the generator.

The figure also specifies an elements iterator for sets; this method would replace the choose method described earlier. Two points are of interest here. First, note that the specification of elements includes a requirement on the code using the generator. It is not clear what the generator would do if the set

Sidebar 6.1   Iterators and Generators

- An *iterator* is a procedure that returns a *generator*. A data abstraction can have one or more iterator methods, and there can also be standalone iterators.

- A generator is an object that produces the elements used in the iteration. It has methods to get the next element and to determine whether there are any more elements. The generator's type is a subtype of Iterator.

- The specification of an iterator defines the behavior of the generator; a generator has no specification of its own. The iterator specification often includes a requires clause at the end constraining the code that uses the generator.

Figure 6.5   Two iterator methods

```
public class Poly {
    // as before plus:

    public Iterator terms ( )
        // EFFECTS: Returns a generator that will produce exponents
        //    of nonzero terms of this (as Integers) up to the degree,
        //    in order of increasing exponent.
}

public class IntSet {
    // as before plus:

    public Iterator elements ( )
        // EFFECTS: Returns a generator that will produce all the elements of
        //    this (as Integers), each exactly once, in arbitrary order.
        // REQUIRES: this must not be modified while the generator is in use.
}
```

were modified while the generator is being used. Therefore, we rule out such modifications in the specification of `elements`. Almost always a generator over a mutable object will have such a requirement. We state the requirement in a requires clause as usual, but since this is a requirement on the *use* of the generator, rather than on the call to the iterator, we place the requires clause at the end of the specification. Normally, a requires clause is the very first part of a specification. In fact, an iterator might have two requires clauses: one ruling out certain arguments and the other stating constraints on using the returned generator.

The second point is that, unlike the `choose` method, the `elements` iterator does not throw any exceptions. It is typical that the use of iterators eliminates problems associated with certain arguments (like the empty set) that would arise for related procedures such as `choose`.

Although both of these data abstractions provide only one iterator, a data abstraction can have many iterators. Also, neither `terms` nor `elements` modifies anything: the iterator doesn't modify `this`, and neither does the generator it returns. Iterators are usually like this, but modifications are occasionally useful. If there is a modification, the iterator specification must explain what it is, and whether the iterator or the generator does the modification.

Figure 6.6   Specification of `allPrimes` iterator

```
public class Num {

    public static Iterator allPrimes ( )
        // EFFECTS: Returns a generator that will produce all primes
        //     (as Integers), each exactly once, in increasing order.
}
```

In addition to iterator methods, it is also possible to have standalone iterators; they will be static methods. Figure 6.6 gives a specification of such an iterator, the `allPrimes` iterator. The generator returned by `allPrimes` will keep producing results without any bound, and therefore it will need to be used in a loop that bounds the iteration.

6.3   Using Iterators

Figure 6.7 gives some examples of using iterators and the generators they return. The `diff` routine differentiates a `Poly`. Note that the code does not catch the `NegativeExponentException` of the `Poly` constructor because it never calls the constructor with a negative exponent (and the exception is unchecked). The `printPrimes` routine uses the `allPrimes` iterator. This routine uses a searching loop: the iteration stops as soon as enough primes have been printed. The `max` routine returns the largest element provided by its generator. This implementation illustrates additional ways to use generators. Generators can be passed as arguments to routines. In such a case, the routine has abstracted away where the elements are coming from: they might be coming from a collection like `IntSet` or from a standalone iterator like `all-Primes`. Also, the code in `max` *primes* the generator: it uses it before the loop to initialize the iteration.

Note that all using code is written in terms of the generic `Iterator` type described in Figure 6.3. As we shall see in Section 6.4, iterators actually return objects belonging to classes that implement this type, but these classes are never visible to using code.

Sidebar 6.2 on page 134 summarizes the use of generators.

Figure 6.7   Using iterators and generators

```
public class Comp {
    public static Poly diff (Poly p) throws NullPointerException {
        // EFFECTS: If p is null throws NullPointerException else
        //    returns the poly obtained by differentiating p.
        Poly q = new Poly( );
        Iterator g = p.terms( );
        while (g.hasNext( )) {
            int exp = ((Integer) g.next( )).intValue( );
            if (exp == 0) continue; // ignore the zero term
            q = q.add(new Poly(exp*p.coeff(exp), exp-1)); }
        return q;
    }

    public static void printPrimes (int m) {
        // MODIFIES: System.out
        // EFFECTS: Prints all the primes less than or equal to m on System.out
        Iterator g = Num.allPrimes( );
        while (true) {
            Object p = g.next( );
            if (p > m) return;
            System.out.println("The next prime is: " + p.toString( )); }
    }

    public static int max (Iterator g) throws EmptyException,
        NullPointerException {
        // REQUIRES: g contains only Integers
        // MODIFIES: g
        // EFFECTS: If g is null throws NullPointerException; if g is empty,
        //    throws EmptyException; else consumes all elements of g
        //    and returns the largest int in g.
        try {
            int m = ((Integer) g.next( )).intValue( );
            while (g.hasNext( )) {
                int x = g.next( );
                if (m < x) m = x; }
            return m; }
        catch (NoSuchElementException e)
            { throw new EmptyException("Comp.max"); }
    }
}
```

Sidebar 6.2   Using Generators

- Using code interacts with a generator via the `Iterator` interface.

- Using code must obey the constraint imposed on it by the iterator's requires clause.

- Generators can be passed as arguments and returned as results.

- It is sometimes useful to *prime* the generator: to consume some of the produced items before looping over the rest of them.

6.4   Implementing Iterators

To implement an iterator, one needs to write its code *and* define and implement a class for its generator. There will be a separate generator class for each iterator. These classes aren't visible to users: users don't see their class declarations. Instead, user code is written in terms of the generic `Iterator` type, as was illustrated in Figure 6.7.

Each new class implements the `Iterator` interface. Such classes define subtypes of types defined by the `Iterator` interface. Therefore, code written in terms of `Iterator` types will be able to use objects of the class. This is why users don't need to know about the new class; knowing about the `Iterator` interface is sufficient, together with the specification of the iterator.

Figure 6.8 gives the implementation of the `terms` iterator of Poly, using the rep described in Figure 5.7. The generator object it returns is an object of type `PolyGen`; the return is legal because `PolyGen` is a subtype of `Iterator`.

The `PolyGen` class is also shown in the figure. It is implemented as an *static inner class*—that is, as a class that is nested inside another class. Because `PolyGen` is private, no code outside the `Poly` class will be able to name it; therefore, using code will be unable to declare variables of type `PolyGen` or construct `PolyGen` objects. Instead, using code will obtain `PolyGen` objects only by calling the `terms` iterator and will use them via the `Iterator` interface.

Because `PolyGen` is an inner class, its constructor can be called by code within the `Poly` class, and its code can access private instance variables and methods of `Poly` objects. This is appropriate since `PolyGen` is really part of the

Figure 6.8   Implementation of the terms iterator

```
public class Poly  {
   private int[ ] trms;
   private int deg;

   public Iterator terms ( ) { return new PolyGen(this); }

   // inner class
   private static class PolyGen implements Iterator {
      private Poly p;   // the Poly being iterated
      private int n;   // the next term to consider

      PolyGen (Poly it) {
         // REQUIRES: it != null
         p = it;
         if (p.trms[0] == 0) n = 1; else n = 0; }

      public boolean hasNext ( ) { return n <= p.deg; }

      public Object next ( ) throws NoSuchElementException {
         for (int e = n; e <= p.deg; e++)
            if (p.trms[e] != 0) { n = e + 1; return new Integer(e); }
         throw new NoSuchElementException("Poly.terms"); }
   } // end PolyGen
}
```

Poly implementation—the part that provides the terms iterator. Furthermore, the inner class must preserve the representation invariant of Poly just like other Poly code.

Note that no specification is given for PolyGen. This is because it is fully specified already: its objects must be generators, and they must obey the specification of the terms iterator.

Note also that the exception thrown in the next method identifies the terms iterator as the source of the problem. This is appropriate because users are aware of the iterator but not the inner class that implements the associated generator; therefore, the information is being conveyed at a level that makes sense to users.

Figure 6.9   Implementation of allPrimes iterator

```
public class Num {

    public static Iterator allPrimes( ) { return new PrimesGen( ); }

    // inner class
    private static class PrimesGen implements Iterator {
        private Vector ps;   // primes yielded
        private int p;  // next candidate to try

        PrimesGen ( ) { p = 2; ps = new Vector( ); }

        public boolean hasNext ( ) { return true; }

        public Object next ( ) {
            if (p == 2) { p = 3; return 2; }
            for (int n = p; true; n = n + 2)
                for (int i = 0; i < ps.size( ); i++) {
                    int el = ((Integer) ps.get(i)).intValue( );
                    if (n%el == 0) break; // not a prime
                    if (el*el > n) { // have a prime
                        ps.add(new Integer(n)); p = n + 2; return n; }
                }
        }
    }
} // end PrimesGen
}
```

Figure 6.9 contains an implementation of the allPrimes iterator that was specified in Figure 6.6. Since all primes are odd except for 2, the loop only considers odd numbers as potential primes, and 2 is handled specially. The implementation keeps all the odd primes generated so far in the ps array and uses them to determine whether the next candidate is a prime.

Note that the header of the PrimesGen next method does not list No-SuchElementException since it does not throw this exception. However, the specification of Iterator indicates that this exception can be raised by next. It is acceptable for the subtype method to have fewer exceptions than the corresponding supertype method. From the point of view of the user, this rule makes sense: when the call happens, the user is prepared to handle the ex-

---

Sidebar 6.3 Implementing Iterators

- An iterator's implementation requires the implementation of a class for the associated generator.

- The generator class is a *static inner class*: it is nested inside the class containing the iterator and can access the private information of its containing class.

- The generator class defines a subtype of Iterator.

- The implementation of the generator assumes using code obeys constraints imposed on it by the requires clause of the iterator.

---

ceptions listed in the header of the method he or she knows about. If some of those exceptions do not happen, it is not a problem. We will discuss this issue further in Chapter 7.

Sidebar 6.3 summarizes the implementation of iterators.

6.5 Rep Invariants and Abstraction Functions for Generators

We need to define rep invariants and abstractions functions for generators, just as we do for ordinary abstract types. This section explains how to do this.

Rep invariants for generators are similar to those for ordinary abstract types; the only difference is that we will not provide a method to check them. The rep invariant for PolyGen is

$$// \ c.p \neq null \ \&\& \ (0 <= c.n <= c.p.deg)$$

Note how this rep invariant is expressed using instance variables of Poly. Note also how the requirement that c.p not be null is satisfied because of the requires clause of the constructor of PolyGen.

The rep invariant for `PrimesGen` is

// `c.ps` *is not* `null` *and*
//   *all elements of* `c.ps` *are primes, and they are sorted in ascending order,*
//   *and they include all primes* < `c.p` *and* > 2.

Note that this invariant would be quite expensive to check!

To define the abstraction function for a generator, we need to understand what the abstract state of a generator is. All generators have the same abstract state: a sequence of the items that remain to be generated. The abstraction function thus needs to map the rep to this sequence.

Here are the abstraction functions for `PrimesGen` and `PolyGen`:

// *abstraction function for* `PrimesGen`
//   `AF(c) = [ p1, p2, ... ]` *such that*
//   *each* `pi` *is an* `Integer` *and* `pi` *is a prime and* `pi >= c.p` *and*
//   *every prime* >= `c.p` *is in the sequence and*
//   `pi > pj` *for all* `i > j >= 1`.

// *abstraction function for* `PolyGen`
//   `AF(c) = [ x1, ..., xn ]` *such that*
//   *each* `xi` *is an* `Integer` *and*
//   *every index* `i >= n` *of a nonzero element of* `c.p.trms` *is in*
//   *the sequence and no other elements are in the sequence*
//   *and* `xi > xj` *for all* `i > j >= 1`.

6.6 Ordered Lists

This section provides another example of an iterator. This iterator is part of `OrderedIntList`—a mutable abstraction that keeps its elements in sorted order. The `smallToBig` iterator will produce the elements of the list in this order. Note that `OrderedIntList` would not be adequate without the iterator because there would be no convenient way to find out what is in the list without removing elements from the list.

The specification of `OrderedIntList` is given in Figure 6.10. The `addEl` and `remEl` methods throw an exception when the element is already in the ordered list. This choice reflects a belief that users will want to know about the situation, without having to check for it explicitly (by calling `isIn`).

Figure 6.10   Specification of ordered lists

```
public class OrderedIntList {
    // OVERVIEW: An ordered list is a mutable ordered list of integers.
    //     A typical list is a sequence [x1, ..., xn] where xi < xj if i < j.

    // constructors
    public OrderedIntList ( )
    // EFFECTS: Initializes this to be an empty ordered list.

    // methods
    public void addEl (int el) throws DuplicateException
        // MODIFIES: this
        // EFFECTS: If el is in this, throws DuplicateException;
        //     otherwise, adds el to this.

    public void remEl (int el) throws NotFoundException
        // MODIFIES: this
        // EFFECTS: If el is not in this, throws NotFoundException;
        //     otherwise, removes el from this.

    public boolean isIn (int el)
        // EFFECTS: If el is in this returns true else returns false.

    public boolean isEmpty ( )
        // EFFECTS: Returns true if this is empty else returns false.

    public int least ( ) throws EmptyException
        // EFFECTS: If this is empty, throws EmptyException;
        //     otherwise, returns the smallest element of this.

    public Iterator smallToBig ( )
        // EFFECTS: Returns a generator that will produce the elements of this
        //     (as Integers), each exactly once, in order from smallest to largest.
        // REQUIRES: this must not be modified while the generator is in use.

    public boolean repOk ( )
    public String toString ( )
    public Object clone ( )
}
```

139

Furthermore, since users are likely to make calls that throw the exceptions, the exceptions should be checked.

The implementation of OrderedIntList uses a sorted tree. The idea is that each node of the tree contains a value and two subnodes, one on the left and one on the right. The two subnodes are themselves ordered lists, and therefore the rep is recursive. The tree is sorted so that all the values in the left subnode are less than the value in the parent node, and all values in the right subnode are greater than the value in the parent node.

Figure 6.11 gives part of the implementation of ordered lists. Note that the implementation of addEl implicitly propagates the DuplicateException raised by its recursive calls; the implementation of remEl is similar.

The smallToBig iterator is implemented in Figure 6.12. The generator starts by producing the elements of the left subtree. When all these elements have been produced, it returns the value of the top node of the tree and then produces the elements of the right subtree. Because it is important for both generator methods, and especially the hasNext method, to execute efficiently, the implementation keeps track of how many elements are left to be produced. It does this by computing how many elements are in the list at the time the iteration begins.

The abstraction function and rep invariant for OrderedIntList are

```
// the abstraction function is:
//    AF(c) = if c.empty then [ ] else AF(c.left) + [ c.val ] + AF(c.right)
// the rep invariant is:
//    I(c) = c.empty || ( c.left ≠ null && c.right ≠ null &&
//       I(c.left) && I(c.right) &&
//       (!c.left.isEmpty => c.left.greatest < c.val) &&
//       (!c.right.isEmpty => c.val < c.right.least) )
```

Here [ ] is the empty sequence, + concatenates sequences, and c.left. greatest is the largest element of c.left. Note that both the abstraction function and the rep invariant are defined recursively. This is what you would expect for a recursive implementation!

The abstraction function and rep invariant for the generator are

```
// the abstraction function is:
//    AF(c) = if c.cnt = 0 then [ ]
//       else if |AF(c.child)| = c.cnt then AF(c.child)
//       else AF(c.child) + [Integer(c.me.val)] + AF(OLGen(c.right))
```

Figure 6.11 Part of the implementation of ordered list

```
public class OrderedIntList {
   private boolean empty;
   private OrderedIntList left, right;
   private int val;

   public OrderedIntList ( ) { empty = true; }

   public void addEl (int el) throws DuplicateException {
      if (empty) {
         left = new OrderedIntList( ); right = new OrderedIntList( );
         val = el; empty = false; return; }
      if (el ==val)
         throw new DuplicateException("OrderedIntList.addEl");
      if (el < val) left.addEl(el); else right.addEl(el); }

   public void remEl (int el) throws NotFoundException {
      if (empty) throw new NotFoundException("OrderedIntList.remEl");
      if (el == val)
         try { val = right.least( ); right.remEl(val); }
         catch (EmptyException e) { empty = left.empty; val = left.val;
            right = left.right; left = left.left; return; }
      else if (el < val) left.remEl(el); else right.remEl(el); }

   public boolean isIn (int el) {
      if (empty) return false;
      if (el == val) return true;
      if (el < val) return left.isIn(el); else return right.isIn(el);
   }

   public boolean isEmpty ( ) { return empty; }

   public int least ( ) throws EmptyException {
      if (empty) throw new EmptyException("OrderedIntList.least");
      try { return left.least( ); }
      catch (EmptyException e) { return val; }
}
```

Figure 6.12   Implementation of ordered list iterator

```
public Iterator smallToBig ( ) { return new OLGen(this, count( )); }

private int count ( ) {
   if (empty) return 0;
   return 1 + left.count( ) + right.count( );   }

// inner class
private static class OLGen implements Iterator {
   private int cnt; // count of number of elements left to generate
   private OLGen child; // the current sub-generator
   private OrderedIntList me; // my node

   OLGen (OrderedIntList o, int n) {
   // REQUIRES: o != null
      cnt = n;
      if (cnt > 0) { me = o;
         child = new OLGen(o.left, o.left.count( )); }
   }

   public boolean hasNext ( ) { return cnt > 0; }

   public Object next ( ) throws NoSuchElementException {
      if (cnt == 0)
         throw new NoSuchElementException("OrderedIntList.smallToBig");
      cnt--;
      try { return new Integer(child.next( )); }
      catch (NoSuchElementException e) { }
      // if get here, must have just finished on the left;
      child = new OLGen(me.right, cnt);
      return new Integer(me.val);   }
} // end of OLGen
```

```
// the rep invariant is:
//   I(c) = c.cnt = 0 || (c.cnt > 0 &&
//      c.me ≠ null && c.child ≠ null &&
//      (c.cnt = c.child.cnt + 1 ||
//         c.cnt = c.child.cnt + c.me.right.count + 1))
```

Note how the rep invariant depends on the requires clause of the `smallToBig` iterator that the ordered list not be modified while the generator is in use.

6.7   Design Issues

Most data types will include iterators among their operations, especially types like IntSet and OrderedIntList whose objects are collections of other objects. Iterators are frequently needed for adequacy; they make elements of a collection accessible in a way that is both efficient and convenient.

A type might have several iterators. For example, OrderedIntList might have the method,

```
public Iterator bigToSmall ( )
    // EFFECTS: Returns a generator that will produce the elements of this
    //    (as Integers), each exactly once, in order from largest to smallest.
    // REQUIRES: this must not be modified while the generator is in use.
```

in addition to the smallToBig method discussed earlier.

For mutable collections, we have consistently required that the loop body not modify the collection being iterated over. If we omit this requirement, the generator returned by the iterator must behave in a well-defined way even when modifications occur. For example, suppose integer n is deleted from an IntSet while the generator returned by elements is in use; should n be produced by the generator or not?

One approach is to require that a generator produce the elements contained in its collection argument at the time it is created by the iterator, even if modifications occur later. The behavior of a generator specified in this way is well defined, but the implementation is likely to be inefficient. For example, if the elements iterator had to return this sort of generator, its implementation would have to provide the generator with a copy of the els array—just what we objected to in the members method. Because the approach of constraining the loop body avoids such inefficiencies, it will be preferred most of the time. A related issue is whether the iterator or the generator it returns can modify the collection. As a general convention, such modifications should be avoided.

Modifications by the loop body or the iterator or generator can sometimes be useful. For example, consider a program that performs tasks waiting on a task queue:

```
Iterator g = q.allTasks( );
while (g.hasNext( )) {
   Task t = (Task) g.next( );
```

```
        // perform t
        // if t generates a new task nt, enqueue it by performing q.enq(nt)
    }
```

When the task being performed generates another task, we simply enqueue it to be performed later; the generator returned by iterator allTasks will present it for execution at the appropriate time. However, examples like this are rare; usually neither the generator nor the loop body will modify the collection.

6.8   Summary

This chapter identified a problem in the adequacy of data types that are collections of objects. Since a common use of a collection is to perform some action for its elements, we need a way to access all elements. This method should be efficient in space and time, convenient to use, and not destructive of the collection. In addition, it should support abstraction by specification.

Iterators solve this problem. They return a special kind of object, called a generator, that produces the items in the collection one at a time. Producing items incrementally means that extra space to store the items is not needed, and production can be stopped as soon as the desired object has been found. Iterators support abstraction by specification for the containing type by encapsulating the way the items are produced; the approach depends on knowledge of the rep, but using programs are shielded from this knowledge.

Generators are objects of Iterator types. Such types are subtypes of the type defined by the Iterator interface. Users of the generator are not aware of the class that implements the interface; using code is written entirely in terms of the Iterator interface.

Iterators are useful in their own right, as was illustrated by the allPrimes example. However, their main use is as operations of data types. We shall see other examples of such use in the rest of the book.

Exercises

6.1 Specify a procedure, isPrimes, that determines whether an integer is prime, and then implement it using allPrimes (Figure 6.6).

6.2 Implement the elements iterator for IntSet (see Figure 6.5). Be sure to give the rep invariant and abstraction function.

6.3 Complete the implementation of OrderedIntList provided in Figures 6.11 and 6.12 by providing implementations for clone, toString, repOk, and equals (if necessary).

6.4 Implement the bigToSmall iterator for OrderedIntLists as an extra method in the implementation provided in Figures 6.11 and 6.12. bigToSmall was specified in Section 6.6. Also discuss whether this iterator is needed in order for OrderedIntLists to be adequate.

6.5 Specify and implement an iterator that provides all the nonzero unit polynomials of a Poly in order of increasing degree. For example, for the Poly $x + 7x^3$, it would produce the Polys x and $7x^3$. You can define this either as a Poly operation or not as you prefer, but you should justify your choice.

6.6 Implement the following iterator:

```
static Iterator filter (Iterator g, Check x)
    throws NullPointerException
        // REQUIRES: g contains only Integers
        // MODIFIES: g
        // EFFECTS: If g is null throws NullPointerException else
        //    returns a generator that produces in order, each exactly once,
        //    all elements e produced by g for which x.checker(e) is true.
```

Here Check is a type whose objects have a method:

```
public boolean checker(Integer)
```

that determines whether its argument satisfies some predicate.

6.7 Implement the following iterator and associated generator:

```
static Iterator perms (int[ ] a) throws NullPointerException
    // EFFECTS: If a is null throws NullPointerException, else
    //    returns a generator that will produce the permutations of a,
    //    each exactly once, in arbitrary order.
    //    All objects in the generator will be int arrays.
    // REQUIRES: a not be modified while generator is in use.
```

Be sure to give the rep invariant and abstraction function for the generator.

6.8 Discuss the adequacy of Poly without the terms iterator. How would the adequacy be affected by providing an iterator allCoeffs that produced all nonzero coefficients up to the degree? How about adding an iterator allTerms that provided all the exponents up to the degree?

6.9 Consider a Table type that maps Strings to ints; this type was discussed in the exercises in Chapter 5. Is this type adequate without iterators? Define any iterators that are needed and implement them as an extension to your implementation of Table.

6.10 Consider the bounded queue type that was discussed in the exercises in Chapter 5. Is this type adequate without iterators? Define any iterators that are needed and implement them as an extension to your implementation of bounded queues.

6.11 Consider an IntBag type. Bags are like sets except that they can contain the same integer multiple times. Define an IntBag type by giving a specification for it and justify the adequacy of your definition. Then provide an implementation for the type including the rep invariant and abstraction functions for the type and for any generator types. Also discuss the performance of your implementation.

Type Hierarchy

This chapter discusses a way to enhance the utility of data abstraction by defining families of related types. All members of a family have similar behavior: they all have certain methods, and calls on those methods behave in similar ways. Family members may differ by extending the behavior of the common methods or by providing additional methods.

A type family might correspond to the kind of hierarchy found in the real world; for example, Busses and Cars are both specialized kinds of Vehicles, or Dogs and Cats are special kinds of Mammals. Or it might correspond to concepts that only exist within programs; for example, a BufferedReader is a specialized kind of Reader.

A type family is defined by a *type hierarchy* (see Sidebar 7.1). At the top of the hierarchy is a type whose specification defines the behavior common to all family members, including the signatures and behavior of all the common methods. Other family members are defined to be *subtypes* of this type, which is referred to as their *supertype*. The hierarchy can be more than two levels: subtypes can themselves have subtypes, and so on.

Type families are used in two different ways. They can be used to define *multiple implementations* of a type. In this case, the subtypes do not add any new behavior, except that each of them has its own constructors. Rather, the class implementing the subtype implements exactly the behavior defined by

Sidebar 7.1 Type Hierarchy

- Type hierarchy is used to define type families consisting of a supertype and its subtypes. The hierarchy can extend through many levels.

- Some type families are used to provide multiple implementations of a type: the subtypes provide different implementations of their supertype.

- More generally, though, subtypes extend the behavior of their supertype, for example, by providing extra methods.

- The substitution principle provides abstraction by specification for type families by requiring that subtypes behave in accordance with the specification of their supertype.

the supertype. For example, we could use a type family to provide both sparse and dense polynomials, so that the most efficient representation could be used for each polynomial object.

More generally, though, the subtypes in a type family extend the behavior of their supertypes, for example, by providing additional methods. The hierarchy defining such a type family can be multilevel. Furthermore, at the bottom of the hierarchy there might be multiple implementations of some subtype.

Type hierarchy requires the members of the type family to have related behavior. In particular, the supertype's behavior must be supported by the subtypes: subtype objects can be substituted for supertype objects without affecting the behavior of the using code. This property is referred to as the *substitution principle*. It allows using code to be written in terms of the supertype specification, yet work correctly when using objects of the subtype. For example, code can be written in terms of the `Reader` type, yet work correctly when using a `BufferedReader`.

The substitution principle provides abstraction by specification for a type family. It allows us to abstract from the differences among the subtypes to the commonalities, which are captured in the supertype specification. The substitution principle is discussed in Section 7.9.

7.1   Assignment and Dispatching

The utility of type hierarchy rests on a loosening of the rules governing assignment and argument passing and on the way calls are dispatched to code. Both of these issues were discussed in Chapter 2, but we discuss them again here since they are central to understanding how hierarchy works.

7.1.1   Assignment

A variable declared to belong to one type can actually refer to an object belonging to some subtype of that type. In particular, if S is a subtype of T, S objects can be assigned to variables of type T, and they can be passed as arguments or results where a T is expected.

For example, suppose that DensePoly and SparsePoly are subtypes of Poly. (The idea is that DensePoly provides a good implementation of Polys that have relatively few zero coefficients below the degree term, and Sparse-Poly is good for the Polys that don't match this criterion.) Then the following code is permitted:

```
Poly p1 = new DensePoly( ); // the zero Poly
Poly p2 = new SparsePoly(3, 20); // the Poly 3x^20.
```

Thus, variables of type Poly can refer to DensePoly and SparsePoly objects.

Having assignments like these means that the type of object referred to by a variable is not necessarily the same as what is declared for the variable. For example, p1 is declared to have type Poly but in fact refers to a DensePoly object. To distinguish these two types, we refer to an object's *apparent* type and its *actual* type. The apparent type is what the compiler can deduce given the information available to it (from declarations); the actual type is the type the object really has. For example, the object referred to by p1 has apparent type Poly but actual type DensePoly. The actual type of an object will always be a subtype of its apparent type. (As discussed in Chapter 2, recall that we consider that a type is a subtype of itself.)

The compiler does type checking based on the information available to it: it uses the apparent types, not the actual types, to do the checking. In particular, it determines what method calls are legal based on the apparent type. For example,

```
int d = p1.degree( );
```

is considered to be legal since `Poly`, the apparent type of p1, has a method named degree that takes no arguments and returns an `int`.

The goal of the checking is to ensure that when a method call is executed, the object actually has a method with the appropriate signature. For this to make sense, it is essential that the object p1 refers to has all the methods indicated by the supertype with the expected signatures. Thus, `DensePoly` and `SparsePoly` must have all the methods declared for `Poly` with the expected signatures. Java ensures that this condition is satisfied.

In the preceding example, suppose that `Poly` did not have a degree method. In this case, the call will be rejected by the compiler even if the object referred to by p1 actually has such a method. An object belonging to a subtype is created in code that knows it is dealing with the subtype. That code can use the extra subtype methods. But code written in terms of the supertype can only use the supertype methods.

7.1.2   Dispatching

The compiler may not be able to determine what code to run when a method is called. The code to run depends on the actual type of the object, while the compiler knows only the apparent type. For example, consider the compilation of

```
static Poly diff(Poly  p) {
    // differentiates p
    Iterator g = p.terms( );
    ...
}
```

When this routine is compiled, the compiler does not know whether the actual type of the object p refers to is a `DensePoly` or a `SparsePoly`, yet it must call the implementation of `terms` for `DensePoly` if p is a `DensePoly`, and the implementation of `terms` for `SparsePoly` if p is a `SparsePoly`. (It must call the code determined by the actual type since the representations are different and the code works differently in the two cases.)

As discussed in Chapter 2, calling the right method is achieved by a runtime mechanism called *dispatching*. The compiler does not generate code to call the method directly. Instead, it generates code to find the method's code and then branch to it.

There are several ways to implement dispatching. One approach is to have objects contain, in addition to their instance variables, a pointer to a *dispatch vector*, which contains pointers to the implementations of the object's methods. This structure is illustrated in Figure 7.1. Code to call a method retrieves the dispatch vector from the object, retrieves the address of the method's code from the appropriate slot of the dispatch vector, and then branches to that address. For example, to call the `terms` method of `Poly p`, the calling code would call the code pointed at by the fourth slot of p's dispatch vector.

Sidebar 7.2 summarizes assignment and dispatching.

Figure 7.1   A Poly object with a dispatch vector

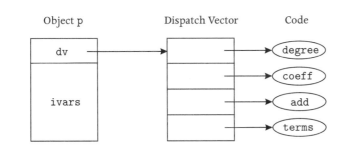

Sidebar 7.2   Assignment and Dispatching

- The compiler deduces an *apparent* type for each object by using the information in variable and method declarations.

- Each object has an *actual* type that it receives when it is created: this is the type defined by the class that constructs it.

- The compiler ensures the apparent type it deduces for an object is always a supertype of the actual type of the object.

- The compiler determines what calls are legal based on the object's apparent type.

- Dispatching causes method calls to go to the object's actual code—that is, the code provided by its class.

7.2   Defining a Type Hierarchy

The first step in defining a type hierarchy is to define the type at the top of the hierarchy. This type has a specification like those we are familiar with, except that it may be incomplete—for example, lacking constructors.

Specifications of subtypes are given relative to those of their supertypes. Rather than restate the parts of the supertype specification that don't change, subtype specifications focus on what is new. Therefore, the subtype specification must define the subtype constructors, plus any extra methods provided by the subtype. In addition, if the subtype changes the behavior of some supertype methods, specifications must be provided for those methods. Only limited changes to the behavior of supertype methods are allowed; this point is discussed in Section 7.9.

Implementations of supertypes are usually somewhat different from what we have seen so far. Some supertypes aren't implemented at all; others may have only partial implementations, in which some methods are implemented but others are not. Furthermore, a supertype implementation may provide extra information to potential subtypes, giving them access to instance variables or to methods that users can't call.

When supertypes are implemented, even only partially, subtypes are then implemented as extensions of the supertype implementation. Reps of subtype objects contain within them the instance variables defined in the implementation of the supertype. Some subtype methods are inherited from the supertype's implementation and need not be implemented by the subtype's implementation. However, the subtype implementation can also reimplement these methods.

7.3   Defining Hierarchies in Java

Type hierarchies are defined in Java using the *inheritance* mechanism. This mechanism allows a class to be a *subclass* of one other class (its *superclass*) and to implement zero or more interfaces.

Supertypes in Java are defined by both classes and interfaces. In either case, the class or interface provides a specification for the type. An interface only defines a specification; it does not contain any code implementing the supertype. Interfaces are discussed in Section 7.7. When a supertype is defined by a class, then in addition to the specification, the class may provide a full or partial implementation.

There are two kinds of classes in Java: *concrete classes* and *abstract classes*. Concrete classes provide a full implementation of the type. Abstract classes provide at most a partial implementation of the type. They have *no* objects (since some of their methods are not yet implemented), and using code cannot call their constructors.

Both kinds of classes can contain normal methods (like we have seen so far) and *final methods*. Final methods cannot be reimplemented by subclasses; we will not use them in this book, but they are occasionally useful to ensure that the behavior of a method is fixed by the supertype and cannot be changed in any subtype. Abstract classes may in addition have *abstract methods*; these are methods that are not implemented by the superclass and, therefore, must be implemented by some subclass. However, the distinction between these categories of methods is of interest *only* to implementors of subclasses; it is *not* of interest to users.

A subclass declares its superclass by stating in its header that it extends that class. This will automatically cause it to have all the methods of its superclass with the same names and signatures as defined in the superclass. In addition, it may provide some *extra methods*.

A concrete subclass must contain implementations of the subclass constructors and the extra methods. In addition, it must implement the abstract methods of its superclass and may reimplement, or *override*, the normal methods. It *inherits* from its superclass the implementations of the final methods and any normal methods that it does not override. Any methods it overrides must have signatures identical to what the superclass defines, except that the subclass method can throw fewer exception types.

The representation of a subclass object consists of the instance variables declared for the superclass *and* those declared for the subclass. When implementing the subclass, it may be necessary to have access to the representation details of the superclass implementation. This will be possible only if the superclass made parts of its implementation accessible to the subclass. An important issue in designing a superclass is to determine the interface it provides to its subclasses. It's best if subclasses can interact with superclasses entirely via the public interface since this preserves full abstraction and allows the superclass to be reimplemented without affecting the implementations of its subclasses. But that interface may be inadequate to permit efficient subclasses. In that case, the superclass can declare *protected* methods, constructors, and

---

Sidebar 7.3 Defining a Hierarchy

- A supertype is defined by either a class or an interface, which provides its specification and, in the case of the class, provides a partial or complete implementation.

- An abstract class provides only a partial implementation; it has no objects and no constructors that users can call.

- A subclass can *inherit* the implementations of its superclass's methods, but it can also *override* those implementations (for nonfinal methods).

- The rep of a subclass consists of its own instance variables and those of its superclass, but it can access the superclass instance variables only if they are declared to be *protected*.

---

instance variables that are visible to subclasses. However, protected members are also package visible: they are accessible to other parts of the superclass's package. Therefore, their visibility is not as limited as one might want: the rep is exposed to other code in the package.

Sidebar 7.3 summarizes this discussion.

Every class that does not explicitly extend some other class implicitly extends Object. Thus, every class is a subclass of Object and must provide correct implementations for the Object methods, as discussed in Chapter 5.

7.4   A Simple Example

The first example concerns a family of integer set types. In this case, the class at the top of the hierarchy is not abstract: IntSet provides a minimal (adequate) set of methods; subtypes will provide additional methods. IntSet has only normal methods that it implements and that its subclasses can override. A specification for IntSet is given in Figure 7.2; it is similar to ones we have seen for IntSet in earlier chapters, except that it defines a subset method.

A portion of the implementation of IntSet is given in Figure 7.3 (a more complete implementation for IntSet can be found in Figure 5.6). The elements of the IntSet are stored in the els vector. The main point to note is that

Figure 7.2   Specification for IntSet

```
public class IntSet {
    // OVERVIEW: IntSets are mutable, unbounded sets of integers.
    //    A typical IntSet is {x₁, . . . , xₙ}.

    // constructors
    public IntSet ( )
        // EFFECTS: Initializes this to be empty.

    // methods
    public void insert (int x)
        // MODIFIES: this
        // EFFECTS: Adds x to the elements of this.

    public void remove (int x)
        // MODIFIES: this
        // EFFECTS: Removes x from this.

    public boolean isIn (int x)
        // EFFECTS: If x is in this returns true else returns false.

    public int size ( )
        // EFFECTS: Returns the cardinality of this.

    public Iterator elements ( )
        // EFFECTS: Returns a generator that produces all elements of this
        //    (as Integers), each exactly once, in arbitrary order.
        // REQUIRES: this not be modified while the generator is in use.

    public boolean subset (IntSet s)
        // EFFECTS: Returns true if this is a subset of s else returns false.

    public boolean repOk ( )
}
```

there are no protected members. This means that subclasses of IntSet have no special access to the components of the superclass part of their rep. This lack of access is acceptable here because the elements iterator provides adequate power.

Figure 7.3   Partial Implementation of `IntSet`

```
public class IntSet {
   private Vector els;  // the elements

   public IntSet ( ) { els = new Vector ( ); }

   private int getIndex (Integer x) { ... }

   public boolean isIn (int x) {
      return getIndex(new Integer(x)) >= 0; }

   public boolean subset (IntSet s) {
      if (s == null) return false;
      for (int i = 0; i < els.size( ); i++)
         if (!s.isIn(((Integer) els.get(i)).intValue( )))
         return false;
         return true; }

   // implementations of other methods go here
}
```

Now consider a type `MaxIntSet`, which is a subtype of `IntSet`. An `MaxIntSet` object behaves just like an `IntSet` object except that it has an extra method that returns the largest element of the set. The specification for `MaxIntSet` is given in Figure 7.4. Note that the specification relies on the `IntSet` specification and only defines what is new, both in the overview clause and in the specifications of operations. In the case of `MaxIntSet`, no specifications of the supertype methods have changed, and therefore only the new operations, the `max` method and the `MaxIntSet` constructor, have been specified. All other methods have the specifications provided for them in the specification of `IntSet`.

An easy way to implement `MaxIntSet` is to allow `IntSet` to keep track of the elements of the set. However, to make it easy to find the maximum element, it is desirable for the subclass to have an instance variable:

`private int biggest;` // the maximum element (if set is not empty)

Thus, `MaxIntSet` objects have two instance variables: `els` (from the superclass) and `biggest` (from the subclass). When a new element is inserted, if it is

Figure 7.4   Specification for MaxIntSet

```
public class MaxIntSet extends IntSet {
    // OVERVIEW: MaxIntSet is a subtype of IntSet with an additional
    //     method, max, to determine the maximum element of the set.

    // constructors
    public MaxIntSet ( )
        // EFFECTS: Makes this be the empty MaxIntSet.

    // methods
    public int max ( ) throws EmptyException
        // EFFECTS: If this is empty throws EmptyException else returns the
        //     largest element of this.
}
```

bigger than the current biggest, the value of biggest is changed. When an element is removed, if it is the biggest, we need to reset biggest to hold the new maximum. Computing the new maximum can be accomplished using the elements iterator.

Figure 7.5 shows the implementation of MaxIntSet. The class implements the constructor and the max method. In addition, it overrides the implementations of insert, remove, and repOk. However, the implementations of size, isIn, elements, subset, and toString are inherited from IntSet.

First, note the implementation of the constructor. The very first thing a subclass constructor must do is to call a superclass constructor to initialize the superclass instance variables; here we make the call explicitly (using the syntax super( )). If the subclass constructor does not contain this call, Java will automatically insert a call to the superclass constructor with no arguments. Thus, in this case, the call could have been omitted, for example,

```
    public MaxIntSet ( ) { }
```

is also a correct implementation of the constructor. However, if a call to a superclass constructor that has arguments is needed, the call must be made explicitly. In either case, by the time the rest of the MaxIntSet constructor starts to run, the els array has already been initialized. There is no work for the MaxIntSet constructor to do at this point, since biggest has no value when the set is empty.

Figure 7.5   Implementation of MaxIntSet

```
public class MaxIntSet extends IntSet {
   private int biggest; // the biggest element if set is not empty

   public MaxIntSet ( ) { super( ); }

   public void insert (int x) {
      if (size ( ) == 0 || x  > biggest) biggest = x;
      super.insert(x); }

   public void remove (int x) {
      super.remove(x);
      if (size( ) == 0 || x < biggest) return;
      Iterator g = elements( );
      biggest = ((Integer) g.next( )).intValue( );
      while (g.hasNext( ) {
         int z = ((Integer) g.next( )).intValue( );
         if (z > biggest) biggest = z; }
   }

   public int max ( ) throws EmptyException {
      if (size( ) == 0) throw new EmptyException ("MaxIntSet.max");
      return biggest; }

   public boolean repOk ( ) {
      if (!super.repOk( )) return false;
      if (size( ) == 0) return true;
      boolean found = false;
      Iterator g = elements ( );
      while (g.hasNext( )) {
         int z = ((Integer) g.next( )).intValue( );
         if (z > biggest) return false;
         if (z == biggest) found = true; }
      return found;
   }
}
```

To implement the methods of MaxIntSet, we need to make use of the overridden methods of IntSet. For example, for insert, we want IntSet's insert method to do the actual work. Within a subclass, all the overridden methods of the superclass are available. However, there is a naming issue: how do we distinguish the overriding method (the one being implemented for MaxIntSet) from the overridden method? Java resolves this issue by using a compound form: for example, super.insert, to name the overridden method. A name without the prefix—for example, insert—means the overriding one, and so does the form this.insert. Examples of uses of overridden methods occur in the implementations of insert and remove.

Although the overridden methods are visible to the subclasses, they are *not* accessible to users of subclass objects. For example, if x is a MaxIntSet object, x.insert names the implementation of insert provided by MaxIntSet, and there is no way for using code to name the insert method provided by IntSet.

The rep invariant and abstraction function for a subclass are typically defined in terms of those for the superclass. Thus, we have

```
// The abstraction function is:
//    AF_MaxIntSet(c) = AF_IntSet(c)
```

Here we have introduced notation to distinguish the two abstraction functions; the one for IntSet is AF_IntSet, and the one for MaxIntSet is AF_MaxIntSet. In this example, the biggest field does not affect what set a MaxIntSet object represents; therefore, AF_MaxIntSet simply produces the same set as AF_IntSet. (Note that it is reasonable to apply AF_IntSet to an MaxIntSet object since such an object has all the IntSet instance variables.) The fact that the two abstraction functions are the same reflects the fact that MaxIntSet relies on IntSet to store the set elements.

The rep invariant for MaxIntSet is

```
// the rep invariant is:
//    I_MaxIntSet(c) = c.size > 0 =>
//       (c.biggest in AF_IntSet(c) &&
//          for all x in AF_IntSet(c) (x <= c.biggest))
```

Thus, the rep invariant is defined in terms of the abstraction function for IntSet. Note that it does not include the rep invariant of IntSet for the simple reason that preserving that rep invariant is the job of IntSet's implementation, and there is no way that the implementation of MaxIntSet can interfere since it has only public access to the IntSet part of its rep. On the other hand, the implementation of repOk for a subclass should always check the invariant for the superclass since the subclass rep cannot be correct if the superclass part of the rep is not correct. This point is illustrated by the implementation of repOk shown in Figure 7.5.

We might not be happy with the implementation of remove since it sometimes has to go through the els array twice—once to remove x and again to recompute biggest. To do better, however, MaxIntSet would require access to the IntSet rep, which could be accomplished by having IntSet declare els to be protected. In this case, the rep invariant of MaxIntSet must include the rep invariant of IntSet (since the implementation of MaxIntSet could cause the rep invariant to be violated), giving:

```
// the rep invariant is:
// I_MaxIntSet(c) = I_IntSet(c) && c.size > 0 =>
//    (c.biggest in AF_IntSet(c) &&
//      for all x in AF_IntSet(c) (x <= c.biggest) )
```

Sidebar 7.4 summarizes the definitions of the abstraction function and rep invariant for subclasses of concrete classes.

Sidebar 7.4   Rep Invariant and Abstraction Function for Subclasses of Concrete Superclasses

- The abstraction function for a subclass, AF_sub, is typically defined using AF_super, the abstraction function of the superclass.

- The subclass rep invariant, I_sub, needs to include a check on the superclass rep invariant, I_super, only if the superclass has some protected members. However, repOk for the subclass should always check repOk for the superclass.

Figure 7.6   An exception type with more information

```
public MyException extends Exception {
    // OVERVIEW: MyException objects contain an int as well as a string.
    private int val;

    public MyException (String s, int v) { super(s); val = v; }
    public MyException (int v) { super( ); val = v; }
    public int valueOf ( ) { return val; }
}
```

7.5   Exception Types

Now we have introduced enough material to explain exception types. Exception types are subtypes of Throwable, and the implementation of Throwable provides methods that access the string within the exception object. New exception types can therefore be implemented just by defining their constructors. It is also possible to define an exception type that has additional methods and that has more information in its objects. Figure 7.6 shows such a type. Its constructors require an int argument, and its method, valueOf, allows programs to access the int.

7.6   Abstract Classes

An *abstract class* provides only a partial implementation of a type. It may have some instance variables, and if it does, it will also have one or more constructors. These constructors cannot be called by its users, since an abstract class has no objects, but the constructors can be used by subclasses to initialize the superclass's part of the rep.

Typically, an abstract class contains both abstract methods and regular (nonabstract) methods. It provides implementations of the nonabstract methods. These implementations often make use of the abstract methods, which allows the superclass to define the generic part of the implementation, with the subclasses filling in the details. (This is referred to as the *template pattern* as discussed further in Chapter 15.) Implementing methods in the superclass is desirable: we implement them just once, even though there may be many subclasses. Not only will subclasses have less code, but they will be easier to get correct.

For example, suppose we wanted to define a type `SortedIntSet`, which is like an `IntSet` except that the `elements` iterator provides access to the elements in sorted order. A specification is given in Figure 7.7. Note that a specification is given for `elements` since its specification has changed: it produces the elements in sorted order. Note also that `SortedIntSet` provides an additional subset method, and therefore its subset method is overloaded. It has two subset methods:

```
public boolean subset (IntSet s) // inherited
public boolean subset (SortedIntSet s) // extra
```

Since no specification is given for the extra subset method, it must have the same specification as the inherited subset method. The reason a second subset method is provided is to obtain better performance in the case where the argument is known to be a `SortedIntSet`.

To implement `SortedIntSet`, we might like to use an ordered list. However, if `SortedIntSet` is implemented by a subclass of `IntSet` as defined in Figure 7.3, we have a problem: every `SortedIntSet` object will contain within it instance variables inherited from `IntSet`. These instance variables are no longer interesting, since we do not want to keep elements of a `SortedIntSet` in the `els` vector.

We can obtain efficient subtypes whose objects do not contain unused instance variables by not having these variables in the superclass. However, if the `IntSet` class does not have a way to store the set elements, it can't actually have any objects. Therefore, it must be abstract.

Figure 7.8 shows part of the implementation of an abstract class for `IntSet`. Here `insert`, `remove`, `elements`, and `repOk` are abstract. `isIn`, `subset`, and `toString` are implemented by using one of the abstract methods (`elements`). Although `size` could be implemented using `elements`, this would be inefficient. Furthermore, all subclasses will need a way to implement `size` efficiently. Therefore, `IntSet` has an instance variable, `sz`, to track the size. This means the definer of `IntSet` must decide whether to make it accessible to

Figure 7.7   Specification of SortedIntSet

```
public class SortedIntSet extends IntSet {
    // OVERVIEW: A sorted int set is an int set whose elements are
    // accessible in sorted order.

    // constructors:
    public SortedIntSet( )
        // EFFECTS: Makes this be the empty sorted set.

    // methods:
    public Iterator elements ( )
        // EFFECTS: Returns a generator that will produce all elements of this,
        //    each exactly once, in ascending order.
        // REQUIRES: this not be modified while the generator is in use.

    public int max ( ) throws EmptyException
        // EFFECTS: If this is empty throws EmptyException else returns
        //    the largest element of this.

    public boolean subset (SortedIntSet s)
}
```

subclasses, or to hide it, providing access through protected methods. If we hide it, IntSet can maintain the invariant

```
sz >= 0
```

However, this is quite uninteresting: what matters is that sz is the size of the set and this can only be maintained by the subclasses. Therefore, we will allow subclasses direct access to sz; this is why it is declared to be protected. Since no rep invariant is guaranteed by IntSet, its repOk method is abstract. Note that the class has no abstraction function; this is typical for an abstract class since the real implementations are provided by the subclasses.

Figure 7.9 shows a partial implementation of SortedIntSet as a subclass of IntSet as defined in Figure 7.8. This subclass must implement all the abstract methods but can inherit the nonabstract methods such as size. The subclass uses the OrderedIntList type defined in Figure 6.10. Note that the

Figure 7.8   Implementation of abstract `IntSet`

```
public abstract class IntSet {
    protected int sz; // the size

    // constructors
    public IntSet ( ) { sz = 0; }

    // abstract methods
    public abstract void insert (int x);
    public abstract void remove (int x);
    public abstract Iterator elements ( );
    public abstract boolean repOk ( );

    // methods
    public boolean isIn (int x) {
        Iterator g = elements ( );
        Integer z = new Integer(x);
        while (g.hasNext( ))
            if (g.next( ).equals(z)) return true;
        return false; }

    public int size ( ) { return sz; }

    // implementations of subset and toString go here
}
```

implementation for the extra subset method can be more efficient than that of the inherited subset method; the extra method will be called when the object and the argument both have the apparent type `SortedIntSet`. Note also that the inherited method is overridden so that the more efficient implementation can be provided when the argument is a `SortedIntSet`.

The rep invariant and abstraction function for `SortedIntSet` are given in Figure 7.9. The abstraction function maps the `els` ordered list to a set; it treats the ordered list as a sequence, as described in the specification of `Ordered-IntList`, and uses the `[ ]` notation to access the elements of the sequence. The rep invariant constrains both the `SortedIntSet` instance variable, `els`,

Figure 7.9   Partial implementation of SortedIntSet

```
public class SortedIntSet extends IntSet {
    private OrderedIntList els;
    // the abstraction function is:
    //    AF(c) = c.els[1],...,c.els[c.sz]
    // the rep invariant is: c.els != null && c.sz = c.els.size

    public SortedIntSet ( ) { els = new OrderedIntList( ); }

    public int max ( ) throws EmptyException {
        if (sz == 0) throw new EmptyException("SortedIntSet.max");
        return els.greatest( );
    }

    public Iterator elements ( ) { return els.elements( ); }

    public boolean subset (IntSet s) {
        try { return subset((SortedIntSet) s); }
            catch (ClassCastException e) { return super.subset(s); }
    }

    public boolean subset (SortedIntSet s) {
        // implementation in here takes advantage of fact that
        // smallToBig of OrderedIntList returns els in ascending order.
        ...
    }

    // implementations of insert, remove, and repOk go here
}
```

and the IntSet instance variable, sz. Note that it assumes els is sorted since
this is true of all OrderedIntList objects.

Subclasses can also be abstract. They might continue to list some of the
abstract superclass methods as abstract, or they might introduce new ones of
their own.

Sidebar 7.5 summarizes the use of protected members.

Sidebar 7.5   Use of Protected Members

- It is desirable to avoid the use of protected members for two reasons: without them, the superclass can be reimplemented without affecting the implementation of any subclasses; and protected members are package visible, which means that other code in the package can interfere with the superclass implementation.

- Protected members are introduced to enable efficient implementations of subclasses. There can be protected instance variables, or the instance variables might be private, with access given via protected methods. The latter approach is worthwhile if it allows the superclass to maintain a meaningful invariant.

7.7   Interfaces

A class is used to define a type and also to provide a complete or partial implementation. By contrast, an interface defines only a type. It contains only nonstatic, public methods, and all of its methods are abstract. It does not provide any implementation. Instead, it is implemented by a class that has an `implements` clause in its header.

For example, the interface defining the `Iterator` type is given in Figure 7.10. Since this is an interface, we do not need to declare that its methods are public; however, we will continue to declare the methods to be public as a convention.

In addition to being more convenient when all the methods are abstract, interfaces also provide a way of defining types that have multiple supertypes. A class can extend only one class, but it can, in addition, implement one or more interfaces. For example, a `SortedIntSet` might implement a `Sorted-Collection` interface. This can be expressed by

```
public class SortedIntSet extends IntSet
    implements SortedCollection { ... }
```

`SortedIntSet` is a subtype of both `IntSet` and `SortedCollection`.

Figure 7.10   Iterator interface

```
public interface Iterator {

    public boolean hasNext ( );
        // EFFECTS: Returns true if there are more items to produce
        //    else returns false.

    public Object next ( ) throws NoSuchElementException;
        // MODIFIES: this
        // EFFECTS: If there are no more items to produce, throw
        //    NoSuchElementException. Otherwise returns the next item
        //    and changes the state of this to reflect the return.
}
```

7.8   Multiple Implementations

Hierarchy can be used to provide multiple implementations of a type. This use can be thought of as defining a very constrained type family, in which all members have exactly the same methods and behavior.

For example, there might be both sparse and dense implementations of polynomials. Furthermore, in a program that uses polynomials, it might be desirable to use both implementations. This allows each Poly to be represented in the way that is best for it. Yet one wants to consider objects from different implementations as belonging to the same type.

When inheritance is used to provide multiple implementations, the type being implemented will be defined either by an interface or by an abstract class: the whole point is to defer implementation details to subclasses. Furthermore, the subclasses will provide exactly the behavior defined by the specification of the interface or abstract class, except that they must provide constructors.

The implementation subclasses are largely invisible to users. The only place where users need to be aware of them is when they create new objects. At that point, the code must call the constructor of the appropriate subclass. For example, the programmer of code that uses Poly must decide whether to create a sparse or dense Poly whenever a new Poly object is created.

7.8.1   Lists

As a first example, consider the IntList abstraction specified in Figure 7.11. Here we will use one subclass to implement the empty list and another to implement nonempty lists.

In this case, the type at the top of the hierarchy is defined by an abstract class. This class is illustrated in Figure 7.12. It has no instance variables, and there is no constructor since there is no rep. toString and equals are implemented using the elements iterator. Two definitions are given for equals

Figure 7.11   Specification of IntList

```
public abstract class IntList {
    // OVERVIEW: IntLists are immutable lists of Objects. A typical
    //    IntList is a sequence [x1, ..., xn].

    // methods
    public abstract Object first ( ) throws EmptyException;
        // EFFECTS: If this is empty throws EmptyException else
        //    returns first element of this.

    public abstract IntList rest ( ) throws EmptyException;
        // EFFECTS: If this is empty throws EmptyException else returns the
        //    list containing all but the first element of this, in the original order.

    public abstract Iterator elements ( );
        // EFFECTS: Returns a generator that will produce the elements of this,
        //    each exactly once, in their order in this.

    public abstract IntList addEl (Object x);
        // EFFECTS: Adds x to the beginning of this.

    public abstract int size ( );
        // EFFECTS: Returns a count of the number of elements of this.

    public abstract boolean repOk ( );
    public String toString ( )
    public boolean equals (IntList o)
}
```

Figure 7.12   Implementation of `IntList`

```
public abstract class IntList {
   // Overview: IntLists are immutable lists of Objects. A typical
   //   IntList is a sequence [x1, ..., xn].

   // abstract methods
   public abstract Object first ( ) throws EmptyException;
   public abstract IntList rest ( ) throws EmptyException;
   public abstract Iterator elements ( );
   public abstract IntList addEl (Object x);
   public abstract int size ( );
   public abstract boolean repOk ( );

   // methods
   public String toString ( ) { ... }
   public boolean equals (Object o) {
      try { return equals ((IntList) o); }
      catch (ClassCastException e) { return false; }
   }
   public boolean equals (IntList o) {
      // compare elements using elements iterator
   }
}
```

(i.e., `equals` is overloaded) to improve performance in the common case where the calling code is checking the equality of two `IntList` objects. This is similar to the overloading of the subset method for `IntSet`.

Figure 7.13 shows parts of the implementation of the empty list and the nonempty list. In the implementation of the empty list, there is no need for any instance variables, so we save space here. Also, the implementations of the methods are more efficient than would be possible without multiple implementations, since tests are avoided; for example, `first` always throws an exception in `EmptyIntList` and never throws an exception in `FullIntList`.

These implementations illustrate an important point about using hierarchy to obtain multiple implementations: the subclasses in the hierarchy may not be independent of one another. Thus, `EmptyIntList` uses the `FullIntList` constructor (in `addEl`), and `FullIntList` uses the `EmptyIntList` constructor in its constructor. This is different from hierarchies that provide extended

169

Figure 7.13   Partial implementations of full and empty lists

```
public class EmptyIntList extends IntList {

   public EmptyIntList ( ) { };

   public Object first ( ) throws EmptyException {
      throw new EmptyException("EmptyIntList.first"); }
   public IntList addEl (Object x) { return new FullIntList(x); }
   public boolean repOk ( ) { return true; }
   public String toString ( ) { return "IntList: [ ]"; }
   public boolean equals (Object x) { return (x instanceof EmptyIntList); }
   // implementations of rest and size go here
   public Iterator elements ( ) { return new EmptyGen( ); }

   static private class EmptyGen implements Iterator {
      EmptyGen ( ) { }
      public boolean hasNext ( ) { return false; }
      public Object next ( ) throws NoSuchElementException {
         throw new NoSuchElementException("IntList.elements"); }
   } // end EmptyGen
}

public class FullIntList extends IntList {
   private int sz;
   private Object val;
   private IntList next;

   public FullIntList (Object x) {
      sz = 1; val = x; next = new EmptyIntList( ); }

   public Object first ( ) { return val; }
   public Object rest ( ) { return next; }
   public IntList addEl (Object x) {
      FullIntList n = new FullIntList(x);
      n.next = this;
      n.sz = this.sz + 1;
      return n; }
   // implementations of elements, size, repOk go here
}
```

behavior; in that case, subclasses can be implemented independently of one another.

Another point is that it isn't useful for these subtypes to provide an overloaded definition of `equals`; that is, there is no point for `EmptyIntList` to provide:

```
public boolean equals (EmptyIntList x)
```

The whole point of multiple implementations is that using code is written entirely in terms of the supertype, except for creating objects. Therefore, an overloaded definition of `equals` would never be called.

One problem with the implementations shown in Figure 7.13 is that there will be many empty list objects. This is unnecessary since all empty list objects are exactly the same, and lists are immutable. If we can use just one empty list object, this will improve performance by avoiding the creation and later garbage collection of the extra empty list objects. We will show how to have just one empty list object in Chapter 15, when we talk about the *singleton* pattern.

7.8.2   Polynomials

As a second example, consider the `Poly` type whose specification was given in Figure 5.4, and suppose we want to provide different implementations for sparse and dense polynomials. We will use the abstract class shown in Figure 7.14 to provide a partial implementation of `Poly`. Although most methods are abstract, some are not. We have elected to keep the degree as an instance variable of `Poly`, since this is useful information for all `Poly` subclasses. Furthermore, we have made deg protected, so that subclasses can access it directly, although we have provided a constructor to initialize deg. We provide direct access to deg because `Poly` cannot by itself preserve any interesting rep invariant on it.

The implementation of `DensePoly` is similar to what we saw before (in Figures 5.7 and 5.8), including the use of deg. The main difference is that we don't need to implement the methods provided by the superclass. A portion of the implementation is given in Figure 7.15.

Since the point of the hierarchy in this example is to provide efficient implementations for `Poly` objects, we need to decide within the implementations of various `Poly` methods, such as add, whether the new `Poly` object should

Figure 7.14   Partial implementation of `Poly`

```
public abstract class Poly {
   protected int deg;   // the degree
   // constructor
   protected Poly (int n) { deg = n; }

   // abstract methods coeff, repOk, add, mul, minus, terms

   // methods
   public int degree ( ) { return deg; }
   public boolean equals (Object o) {
      try { return equals((Poly) o); }
      catch (ClassCastException e) { return false; }
   }
   public boolean equals (Poly p) {
      if (p == null || deg != p.deg) return false;
      Iterator tg = terms( );
      Iterator pg = p.terms( );
      while (tg.hasNext( )) {
         int tx = ((Integer) tg.next( )).intValue( );
         int px = ((Integer) pg.next( )).intValue( );
         if (tx != px || coeff(tx) != p.coeff(px)) return false); }
      return true; }
   public sub (Poly p) { return add(p.minus( )); }
   public String toString( ) { ... }
}
```

be dense or sparse. This requirement complicates the implementation. For example, the add method of DensePoly in Figure 7.15 lets SparsePoly handle the case of adding a sparse and a dense Poly; otherwise, the result is a dense Poly. However, this latter decision might be wrong, since the addition might introduce many intermediate zeros. Therefore, at the end of add, we might check for this condition and convert to a SparsePoly object, if necessary. The decision could be based on the number of nonzero coefficients relative to the degree. Similarly, in the sparse implementation, we could convert to the dense representation if the new Poly has lots of nonzero coefficients for terms below the degree.

Figure 7.15   Part of the DensePoly class

```
public class DensePoly extends Poly {
   private int[ ] trms; // coefficients up to degree

   public DensePoly ( ) {
      super(0); trms = new int[1]; }
   public DensePoly (int c, int n) throws NegExpException { ... }
   private DensePoly (int n) { super(n); trms = new int[n+1]; }

   // implementations of coeff, add, mul, minus,
   // terms, and repOk go here

   public Poly add (Poly q) throws NullPointerException {
      if (q instanceof SparsePoly) return q.add(p);
      DensePoly la, sm;
      if (deg > q.deg) {la = this; sm = (DensePoly) q;}
         else {la = (DensePoly) q; sm = this;}
      int newdeg = la.deg; // new degree is the larger degree
      if (sm.deg == la.deg) // unless there are trailing zeros
         for (int k = sm.deg; k > 0; k--)
            if (sm.trms[k] + la.trms[k] != 0) break; else newdeg--;
      DensePoly r = new DensePoly(newdeg); // get a new DensePoly
      int i;
      for (i = 0; i <= sm.deg && i <= newdeg; i++)
         r.trms[i] = sm.trms[i] + la.trms[i];
      for (int j = i; j <= newdeg; j++) r.trms[j] = la.trms[j];
      return r; }
}
```

These conversions mean that DensePoly must have an efficient way of creating a SparsePoly and vice versa. For example, we might provide

```
SparsePoly (int[ ] trms)
   // EFFECTS: Initializes this to be same poly as is represented by trms
   //    in the DensePoly implementation.
```

Obviously, such a constructor cannot be public! Making it protected won't work since DensePoly is not a subclass of SparsePoly. Instead, the constructor is package visible, which means that we must place all the implementations in the same package so that they have special abilities to access one another's implementation. When multiple implementations are written with knowledge of one another, this is a reasonable thing to do.

One final point: It would be nice if users could ignore the distinction between dense and sparse representations altogether. If we do this, however, users will need a generic way to create new monomials. This can be provided by another class containing static methods that can be used to create objects; we will discuss this technique further in Chapter 15 when we discuss the *factory* pattern. For example, we might have

```
public class polyProcs {

    public static Poly makePoly ( )
        // EFFECTS: Returns the zero Poly.

    public static Poly makePoly (int c, int n) throws NegExpException
        // EFFECTS: If n < 0 throws NegExpException else returns
        //    the monomial cx^n.
}
```

The first makePoly method returns a DensePoly; the second chooses between a sparse and dense representation based on the value of n.

7.9   The Meaning of Subtypes

Subtypes must satisfy the *substitution principle* so that users can write and reason about code just using the supertype specification. When the code runs, the objects it uses may belong to subtypes; nevertheless, we want the code to behave just as it would have if it used supertype objects, and we want reasoning based on the supertype specification to still be valid.

Thus, the substitution principle requires that the subtype specification support reasoning based on the supertype specification. Three properties must be supported:

- *Signature Rule.* The subtype objects must have all the methods of the supertype, and the signatures of the subtype methods must be *compatible* with the signatures of the corresponding supertype methods.

- *Methods Rule.* Calls of these subtype methods must "behave like" calls to the corresponding supertype methods.

- *Properties Rule.* The subtype must preserve all properties that can be proved about supertype objects.

All of these rules concern *only* specifications: we are interested in whether the supertype and subtype specifications are sufficiently similar that the substitution principle is satisfied.

The signature rule guarantees that every call that is type correct according to the supertype's definition is also type correct for the subtype. This requirement is enforced by the Java compiler. In Java, the subtype must have all the supertype methods, with identical signatures except that a subtype method can have fewer exceptions than the corresponding supertype method. The rule about exceptions makes sense: code written in terms of the supertype can handle the exceptions listed in the method header in the supertype but will also work in a type-correct manner if those exceptions are not thrown.

Java's notion of compatibility is a little stricter than necessary: Java requires that the return type of the sub- and super-method be identical, when, in fact, there would be no type problems if the subtype method returned a subtype of the supertype method. For example, it would be nice if a type Foo had

```
Foo clone ( )
```

since then the result could be used without casts, for example,

```
Foo x = y.clone( );
```

(assume y is a Foo object). However, Java requires clone to have the signature

```
Object clone ( )
```

which leads to using code having to cast the result returned by clone, for example,

```
Foo x = (Foo) y.clone( );
```

The other two requirements guarantee that subtype objects behave enough like supertype objects that code written in terms of the supertype won't notice the difference. These requirements *cannot* be checked by a compiler since they require reasoning about the meaning of specifications.

7.9.1   The Methods Rule

The methods rule is concerned with calls on methods defined by the supertype. Of course, when the objects concerned belong to subtypes, the calls
actually go to the code provided by the implementation of the subtype. The
rule says that we can still reason about the meanings of these calls using the
supertype specification even though the subtype code is running. Here are
some examples of this kind of reasoning:

- For any `IntSet`, if we call `y.insert(x)`, we know x is in the set when the
  call returns.

- For any `Poly`, if a call `p.coeff(3)` returns 6, we know that the degree of
  p is at least 3.

All the examples given so far have obeyed this requirement. In fact, our
subtype methods have all had exactly the same specification as the corresponding supertype method, with one exception, the `elements` method of
`SortedIntSet`. Whenever a method is respecified, there is a potential for doing things wrong. In the case of `elements`, the new behavior is acceptable
because we have taken advantage of the nondeterminism in the specification
of the `elements` method of `IntSet`: its specification allows various orders for
producing the elements, and one of these orders is the sorted order produced
by `SortedIntSet`'s `elements`. When we give new specifications for supertype
methods in subtypes, we often take advantage of nondeterminism like this.

To understand better how the specification of a subtype method is allowed
to differ from that of the corresponding supertype method, we need to consider the pre- and postconditions. The precondition, which is defined by the
requires clause, is what must be guaranteed to hold by the caller in order
to make the call. The postcondition, which is defined by the effects clause, is
what is guaranteed to hold right after the call (assuming that the precondition
held when the call was made).

A subtype method can *weaken* the precondition and can *strengthen* the
postcondition.

- *Precondition Rule:* $\text{pre}_{super} \Rightarrow \text{pre}_{sub}$
- *Postcondition Rule:* $(\text{pre}_{super}\ \&\&\ \text{post}_{sub}) \Rightarrow \text{post}_{super}$

Both conditions must be satisfied to achieve compatibility between the sub-
and supertype methods.

Weakening the precondition means that the subtype method requires less from its caller than the supertype method does. This rule makes sense because when code is written in terms of the supertype specification, it must satisfy the supertype method's precondition. Since this precondition implies that of the subtype, we can be sure that the call to the subtype method will be legal if the call to the supertype method is legal.

For example, suppose we had defined the following `IntSet` method:

```
public void addZero ( )
    // REQUIRES: this is not empty
    // EFFECTS: Adds 0 to this
```

Then in a subtype of `IntSet`, we could redefine the method to have the following specification:

```
public void addZero ( )
    // EFFECTS: Adds 0 to this
```

The subtype definition satisfies the precondition rule because it has a weaker precondition.

Just satisfying the precondition rule is not sufficient for the specification of the subtype method to be correct, since we also need to take the effect of the call into account. This is captured in the postcondition rule. This rule says that the subtype method provides more than the supertype method: when it returns everything that the supertype method would provide is assured, and maybe some additional effects as well. This rule makes sense because the calling code depends on the postcondition of the supertype method, but this follows from the postcondition of the subtype method. However, the calling code depends on the method's postcondition only if the call satisfies the precondition (since otherwise the method can do anything); this is why the rule is stated as it is.

For example, the subtype definition for `addZero` given before satisfies the postcondition rule since its postcondition is identical to that of the supertype method. However, the following definition of `addZero` would also be legal:

```
public void addZero ( )
    // EFFECTS: If this is not empty, adds 0 to this else
    //     adds 1 to this.
```

If the call satisfies the supertype method's precondition, the effect of the subtype method is as expected; if the call doesn't satisfy the precondition, then anything could happen. In the subtype, we have simply decided on a particular thing.

The definition of the elements iterator in SortedIntSet strengthens the postcondition. Here both methods have the same precondition, namely true, meaning that all calls are legal. The postcondition in the subtype promised sorted order; and from this we can deduce the arbitrary order indicated in the specification of the supertype method.

Another example is the following. Suppose we define a subtype of IntSet that, in addition to tracking the current members of the set, also keeps a log of all elements that were ever in the set. The overview section might say

// OVERVIEW: *A* LogIntSet *is an* IntSet *plus a log. The log is also a set;*
//   *it contains all the integers that have ever been members of the set.*

Here is the specification of insert for LogIntSet:

```
public void insert (int x)
    // MODIFIES: this
    // EFFECTS: Adds x to the set and also to the log.
```

This method is legal because its postcondition implies that of the supertype insert method: it does add x to the set, but it does something else as well.

However, suppose that we defined a subtype of IntSet in which we redefined insert:

```
public void insert (int x)
    // MODIFIES: this
    // EFFECTS: If x is odd adds it to this else does nothing.
```

In this case, we have violated the requirement; clearly this postcondition does not imply that of IntSet's insert method. Furthermore, a program written in terms of the IntSet specification would clearly expect even numbers to be added to the set as well as odd ones!

Another example of an illegal subtype method is the following. Ordered-IntList (see Figure 6.10) has an addEl method:

```
public void addEl (int x) throws DuplicateException
    // MODIFIES: this
    // EFFECTS: If x is in this throws DuplicateException else
    //    adds x to this.
```

Suppose we defined a subtype of OrderedIntList in which the addEl method does not throw the exception:

```
public void addEl (int x)
    // MODIFIES: this
    // EFFECTS: If x is not in this adds it to this.
```

This method satisfies the signature rule because it is allowable for the subtype method to throw fewer exceptions than the supertype specification. However, it fails the methods rule because the postcondition rule is not satisfied: the two methods have different behavior in the case where x is already in the list.

An example of a case where not throwing the exception is acceptable is the allPrimes generator. The next method of Iterator throws NoSuch-ElementException if there are no more elements. However, the next method for the allPrimes generator does not throw the exception; this is allowed because there is always a larger prime to be produced.

As a final example, consider int versus long. The ints are 32 bits, while the longs are 64 bits. Furthermore, the two types have different behaviors in certain cases. For example, if adding two ints results in an overflow, the overflow will not happen if the same two values are longs. Therefore int is not a subtype of long, and neither is long a subtype of int.

7.9.2   The Properties Rule

In addition to reasoning about the effects of individual calls, we also reason about properties of objects. Some properties are invariants: they are always true for objects of the type. For example, the size of an IntSet is always greater than or equal to zero. Others are *evolution properties*; they involve reasoning about how objects evolve over time. For example, if we know a polynomial has degree 6, we know it will always have this degree (since polynomials are immutable).

To show that a subtype satisfies the properties rule, we must prove that it preserves each property of the supertype. In the case of an invariant property, we do the normal sort of proof using datatype induction: creators and producers of the subtype must establish the invariant, and all methods of the subtype must preserve the invariant. Note that now we are concerned with the "extra" methods as well as the inherited methods: *all* methods must preserve the invariant. Also, we must consider the subtype constructors and ensure that they establish the invariant.

In the case of an evolution property, we must show that every method preserves it. For example, suppose we want to show that the degree of a `Poly` doesn't change. Before we considered subtypes, the way we would show this is to assume that the degree of some `Poly` object p is a certain value x, and then argue that each `Poly` method does not change this value. With subtypes, we need to make the same argument for all the subtype methods—for example, for all `DensePoly` methods and all `SparsePoly` methods.

The properties of interest must be defined in the overview section of the supertype specification. The invariant properties come from the abstract model. For example, because `IntSet`s are modeled as mathematical sets, they must have a size greater than or equal to zero, and they also must not contain duplicate elements. Also, because `OrderedIntList`s are modeled as sequences that are sorted in ascending order, we know their elements appear in sorted order.

As another example of an invariant property, consider a `FatSet` type whose objects are never empty. This fact would need to be captured in the overview section:

> // OVERVIEW: *A* `FatSet` *is a mutable set of integers whose size*
> //   *is always at least 1.*

Assume that `FatSet` does not have a `remove` method but instead has a `removeNonEmpty` method:

```
public void removeNonEmpty (int x)
    // MODIFIES: this
    // EFFECTS: If x is in this and this contains other elements
    //     removes x from this.
```

and, furthermore, that every `FatSet` constructor creates a set containing at least one element. Therefore, we can indeed prove that `FatSet` objects have size greater than zero.

Now consider `ThinSet`, which has all the `FatSet` methods with identical specifications, plus

```
public void remove (int x)
    // MODIFIES: this
    // EFFECTS: Removes x from this.
```

ThinSet is not a legal subtype of FatSet because its extra method can cause its object to become empty; therefore, it does not preserve the supertype's invariant.

The only evolution property we have seen so far (and the most common one) is immutability. Here is a different example. Consider a type SimpleSet that has only insert and isIn methods so that SimpleSet objects only grow. This fact must be indicated in the overview:

> // OVERVIEW: *A* SimpleSet *is a mutable set of integers.*
> //   SimpleSet *objects can grow over time but not shrink.*

IntSet cannot be a subtype of SimpleSet because its remove method causes sets to shrink.

An immutable type usually will have only immutable subtypes, but this is not a requirement. Saying that a type is immutable means that mutations cannot be observed using supertype methods. For example, suppose a type Point2 represents points in the plane, and the overview section states that Point2 objects are immutable. Point2 could have a subtype whose objects are lines in the plane, consisting of a point in the plane and an angle. This would be a legitimate subtype even if it provided a method that allowed the angle to change, since that change would not be visible using calls on supertype methods.

Sidebar 7.6 summarizes the reasoning about the substitution principle.

Sidebar 7.6   Reasoning about the Substitution Principle

- The *signature rule* ensures that if a program is type-correct based on the supertype specification, it is also type-correct with respect to the subtype specification.

- The *methods rule* ensures that reasoning about calls of supertype methods is valid even though the calls actually go to code that implements a subtype.

- The *properties rule* ensures that reasoning about properties of objects based on the supertype specification is still valid when objects belong to a subtype. The properties must be stated in the overview section of the supertype specification.

7.9.3   Equality

In Chapter 5, we discussed the meaning of the equals method: if two objects are equals, it will never be possible to distinguish them in the future using methods of their type. As discussed previously, this means that for mutable types, objects are equals only if they are the very same object, while for immutable types, they are equals if they have the same state.

When there are subtypes of immutable types, the subtype objects might have more state, or they might even be mutable. Therefore, subtype objects might be distinguishable, even though code that uses them via the supertype interface cannot distinguish them.

For example, consider a type, Point2, which represents points in two-space; its equals method returns true if the x and y coordinates are equal. Now suppose type Point3, which represents points in three-space, is defined to be a subtype of Point2; Point3's equals will return true only if all three coordinates are equal. To implement this behavior properly, Point3 must provide its own extra equals method, and it must also override equals for Point2 and Object, as shown in Figure 7.16. Overriding these methods ensures that equals works properly on Point3 objects regardless of their apparent type.

Figure 7.16   Partial implementation of Point3

```java
public class Point3 extends Point2 {
    private int z; // the z coordinate

    public boolean equals (Object p) { // overriding definition
        if (p instanceof Point3) return equals((Point3) p);
        return super.equals(p); }

    public boolean equals (Point2 p) { // overriding definition
        if (p instanceof Point3) return equals((Point3) p);
        return super.equals(p); }

    public boolean equals (Point3 p) { // extra definition
        if (p == null || z != p.z) return false;
        return super.equals(p); }
}
```

7.10   Discussion of Type Hierarchy

There are three different kinds of supertypes (see Sidebar 7.7). Some are *incomplete*: they serve just to establish constraints on the behavior of subtypes, but their specifications are so loose that using code is unlikely to be written in terms of the supertype specification.

For example, suppose we wanted to define a number of collection types so that similar methods would have similar names. Some collection subtypes might be mutable while others are not. The supertype would define both observers and mutators but, of course, the mutators would not do anything for the immutable subtypes. For example, we might have

```
public void put (Object x) throws NotSupportedException
    // MODIFIES: this
    // EFFECTS: If this is mutable adds x to this
    //    else throws NotSupportedException.
```

Such a supertype is useless as far as using code is concerned, or at least for code that uses the mutators. However, the supertype does serve to standardize the method names so that all the collection subtypes that are mutable will have a method named put that adds its argument to the collection. The collection types in java.util are defined like this.

Sidebar 7.7   Kinds of Supertypes

- *Incomplete supertypes* establish naming conventions for subtype methods but do not provide useful specifications for those methods. Therefore, using code is typically not written in terms of them.

- *Complete supertypes* provide entire data abstractions, with useful specifications for all the methods.

- *Snippets* provide just a few methods, not enough to qualify as an entire data abstraction. However, those methods are specified in a way that allows using code to be written in terms of the supertype.

Other supertypes allow using code to be written in terms of the supertype specification, although that code may actually use subtype objects. Some of these supertypes are *complete*: they define data abstractions with a full complement of methods. For example, `Reader` is like this. Other supertypes define *snippets*: they define one or a few methods but not a complete data abstraction. For example, `Cloneable` is a snippet: it indicates only that subtypes have a `clone` method. Snippets are always defined by interfaces. We will see other examples of snippets in Chapter 8.

Regardless of the kind of supertype, however, subtypes must satisfy the substitution principle. When supertypes aren't complete, this can be easy. For example, supertypes that define snippets typically have only one or two methods and no properties that subtypes must preserve. Also, incomplete supertypes typically have no properties because the whole point is to leave the details up to the subtypes.

The substitution principle precludes the use of inheritance as a simple code-sharing mechanism because it requires that the subtype be similar to the supertype. It is important to keep this in mind because many programming languages (not Java) encourage misuse of inheritance, for example, by allowing objects of the subclass to not provide some methods of the superclass.

7.11   Summary

This chapter has discussed inheritance and how it can be used to define type families and multiple implementations.

The use of type families in program design allows a new kind of abstraction: the designer abstracts from properties of a related group of types to identify what all of those types have in common. When used appropriately, this kind of abstraction can improve the structure of programs in several ways:

- By grouping the related types into a family, the designer makes the relationship among them clear, thus making the program as a whole easier to understand. For example, a program that treats different kinds of windows as a family is easier to understand than one that just has a bunch of different window types because the similarities among the set of types have been carefully delineated.

- Hierarchy allows the definition of abstractions that work over the entire family. For example, a procedure that works on windows will be able to do its job no matter what kind of specialized window is passed it as an argument.

- Hierarchy provides a kind of *extensibility*. New kinds of subtypes can be added later, if necessary, to provide extended behavior. Yet all code defined to work using objects of the existing types in the family will continue to work when actually using objects belonging to subtypes, even subtypes that did not exist at the time the using code was written. This kind of extensibility is similar to that provided by other abstraction mechanisms. For example, it's like the ability to replace the implementation of a data abstraction without affecting the correctness of using code; but it allows the invention of new abstractions, rather than just new implementations.

Sidebar 7.8 summarizes the benefits of hierarchy.

Type families are a valuable tool in designing and structuring programs. However they must be used properly. This requires understanding when to use hierarchy and what it means for one type to be a subtype of another. Such understanding allows type families to be used both correctly and appropriately.

Sidebar 7.8   Benefits of Hierarchy

- Hierarchy can be used to define the relationship among a group of types, making it easier to understand the group as a whole.

- Hierarchy allows code to be written in terms of a supertype, yet work for many types—all the subtypes of that supertype.

- Hierarchy provides extensibility: code can be written in terms of a supertype, yet continue to work when subtypes are defined later.

- All of these benefits can be obtained *only* if subtypes obey the substitution principle.

Exercises

7.1 Define and implement a subtype of `IntList` (see Figures 7.11 and 7.12) that provides methods to return the smallest and largest elements of the list. Be sure to define the rep invariant and abstraction function, and to implement `repOk`.

7.2 Define and implement a type `MaxMinSet`. This type is a subtype of `MaxIntSet` (see Figures 7.4 and 7.5); it provides one extra method

```
public int min ( ) throws EmptyException
   // EFFECTS: If this is empty throws EmptyException else
   //    returns the smallest elements of this.
```

Be sure to define the rep invariant and abstraction function and to implement `repOk`.

7.3 Define and implement a type `ExtendedOrderedIntList`, which is a subtype of `OrderedIntList` (see Figure 6.10). `ExtendedOrderedIntList` provides a big-ToSmall iterator that returns the elements of the list from largest to smallest. Be sure to define the rep invariant and abstraction function and to implement `repOk`.

7.4 Define and implement a type `ExtendedSortedIntSet`, which is a subtype of `SortedIntSet` (see Figures 7.7 and 7.9). `ExtendedSortedIntSet` provides a `reverseElements` iterator that returns the elements of the set in reverse order, from largest to smallest. Be sure to define the rep invariant and abstraction function and to implement `repOk`. Hint: You will probably need to reimplement `SortedIntSet`, and `ExtendedOrderedIntList` may be useful in the implementation.

7.5 Give the rep invariants and abstraction functions for `EmptyIntList` and `FullIntList` (see Figure 7.13).

7.6 Complete the implementation of `DensePoly` and provide the implementation of `SparsePoly`. Decide how to choose the representation for the new objects returned by add and mul and justify your decision.

7.7 Provide multiple implementations for `IntSet`, including at least one that is good for small sets (e.g., it might store the elements in a vector) and one that is good for large sets (e.g., it might store the elements in a `hash table`). (Hash tables are provided in java.util.)

7.8 Consider a type Counter with the following operations:

```
public Counter ( )  // EFFECTS: Makes this contain 0.
public int get ( )  // EFFECTS: Returns the value of this.
public void incr ( )
    // MODIFIES: this
    // EFFECTS: Increments the value of this.
```

Complete the specification of Counter by providing the overview section. Be sure to identify all properties of Counter objects.

7.9 Now consider a potential subtype of Counter, Counter2, with the following extra operations:

```
public Counter2 ( )  // EFFECTS: Makes this contain 0.
public void incr ( )
    // MODIFIES: this
    // EFFECTS: Makes this contain twice its current value.
```

Is Counter2 a legitimate subtype of Counter? Explain by arguing that either the substitution principle is violated (for a non-subtype) or that it holds (for a subtype). Discuss how each operation of Counter2 either upholds or violates the substitution principle.

7.10 Now consider another potential subtype of Counter, Counter3, with the following extra operations:

```
public Counter3 (int n)  // EFFECTS: makes this contain n
public void incr (int n)
    // MODIFIES: this
    // EFFECTS: If n > 0 adds n to this.
```

Is Counter3 a legitimate subtype of Counter? Explain by arguing that either the substitution principle is violated (for a non-subtype) or that it holds (for a subtype). Discuss how each operation of Counter3 either upholds or violates the substitution principle.

7.11 Consider a type IntBag, with operations to insert and remove elements, as well as all the observers of IntSet. Bags are like sets except that elements can occur multiple times in a bag. Is IntBag a legitimate subtype of IntSet? Explain by arguing that either the substitution principle is violated (for a non-subtype) or that it holds (for a subtype).

Polymorphic Abstractions

8

In the preceding chapters, we have defined a number of collection types in which all elements of the collection are ints. Such collections are rather limiting. For example, suppose we wanted a set that contained Strings. We would not be able to use our implementation of IntSet for this purpose. Instead, we would need to provide a separate implementation for a StringSet. And if we later discovered the need for a set of characters, we would need yet another new implementation.

Having to define a new version of a collection abstraction each time we need to store a different type of element is not very satisfactory. Instead, it would be better to define the collection type just once yet have it work for all types of elements.

This goal can be accomplished by defining *polymorphic abstractions*. These abstractions are called *polymorphic* because they work for many types. (See Sidebar 8.1.) A data abstraction might be polymorphic with respect to the type of elements its objects contain—for example, the Vector abstraction is polymorphic with respect to its element type. Or a procedure or iterator might be polymorphic with respect to the types of one or more of its arguments. For example, we could define a routine to remove an element of an arbitrary type from a vector.

Sidebar 8.1 Polymorphism

- Polymorphism generalizes abstractions so that they work for many types. It allows us to avoid having to redefine abstractions when we want to use them for more types; instead, a single abstraction becomes much more widely useful.

- A procedure or iterator can be polymorphic with respect to the types of one or more arguments. A data abstraction can be polymorphic with respect to the types of elements its objects contain.

In Java, polymorphism is expressed through hierarchy. Certain arguments are declared to belong to some supertype, and then the actual arguments can be objects belonging to subtypes of that type. That supertype is often Object. In this case, the polymorphic abstraction is limited to using Object methods such as equals on its parameters. Sometimes the polymorphic abstraction needs to use additional methods, however, and in that case the supertype is chosen to provide those methods.

8.1   Polymorphic Data Abstractions

Figure 8.1 provides a specification of a Set abstraction. Set objects contain heterogeneous collections of elements (similar to Vector). The specification of Set is similar to that of IntSet except that its methods (such as insert and isIn) take Objects as arguments or return them as results. Because objects can be compared in various ways (using either == or equals), the overview states what equality test is being used.

Because the Set stores Objects, the question of whether null can be a legal element comes up. This question is explicitly answered (in the negative) in the overview section of the specification; the restriction is enforced by insert, as indicated in its specification.

A partial implementation of Set is shown in Figure 8.2. This implementation differs little from the one given for IntSet in Figure 5.6, and its rep invariant and abstraction function are similar to those of IntSet:

Figure 8.1   Partial specification of Set

```
public class Set {
    // OVERVIEW: Sets are unbounded, mutable sets of objects.
    //    null is never an element of a Set. The methods use equals
    //    to determine equality of elements.

    // constructors
    public Set ( )
        // EFFECTS: Initializes this to be empty.

    // methods
        public void insert (Object x) throws NullPointerException
        // MODIFIES: this
        // EFFECTS: If x is null throws NullPointerException else
        //    adds x to the elements of this.

    public void remove (Object x)
        // MODIFIES: this
        // EFFECTS: If x is in this, removes x from this, else does nothing.

    public boolean isIn (Object x)
        // EFFECTS: Returns true if x is in this else returns false.

    public boolean subset (Set s)
        // EFFECTS: If all elements of this are elements of s returns true
        //    else returns false specifications of size and elements.

    // Specifications of size and elements
}
```

```
// the abstraction function is:
//    AF(c) = c.els[i] | 0 <= i < c.sz
// the rep invariant I(c) is:
//    c.els != null && for all 0 <= i < c.size ( c.els[i] != null ) &&
//    for all 0 <= i < j < c.els.size ( !c.els[i].equals(c.els[j] )
```

This abstraction function produces the objects in c.els rather than the ints contained within those objects. The rep invariant includes the condition that

Figure 8.2   Partial implementation of Set

```
public class Set {

    private Vector els;

    public Set ( ) { els = new Vector( ); }
    private Set (Vector x) { els = x; }

    public void insert (Object x) throws NullPointerException {
        if (getIndex(x) < 0) els.add(x); }

    private int getIndex (Object x) {
        for (int i = 0; i < els.size( ); i++)
            if (x.equals(els.get(i)) return i;
        return -1; }

    public boolean subset (Set s) {
        if (s == null) return false;
        for (int i = 0; i < els.size( ); i++)
            if (!s.isIn(els.get(i))) return false;
        return true; }

    public Object clone ( ) { return new Set((Vector) els.clone( )); }
}
```

the set not contain null; it depends on the equals method to determine equality of elements.

Note that insert stores its argument object in the set rather than a clone of the object. This behavior is indicated in its specification, which says it adds x to the set, meaning that very object, and not a clone of it; if a clone had been required, the specification would have said so explicitly. Note also that the clone method does *not* clone the set elements but only clones the els vector. Therefore, the cloned set shares its elements with the set being cloned. Neither of these implementations exposes the rep because the state of a set, or, indeed, of almost any polymorphic collection, consists only of the identities of its elements and not their states.

8.2   Using Polymorphic Data Abstractions

Polymorphic data abstractions are used similarly to their nonpolymorphic counterparts, with two main differences. First, only objects can be stored in the collection, and therefore, primitive values like ints must be wrapped in their corresponding object type. Second, observers that return elements of the collection will return `Object`, and therefore the using code will need to cast to the expected type and, in the case of a primitive value, unwrap.

For example, here is code that uses `Set` to store a collection of ints:

```
Set s = new Set( );
s.insert(new Integer(3));
...
Iterator g = s.elements( );
while (g.hasNext( )) {
    int i = ((Integer) g.next( )).intValue( );
    ... }
```

There is one important difference between this code and code using an `IntSet`. An `IntSet` stores only ints, and that guarantee is provided by the compiler: it isn't possible to call `insert` on an `IntSet` object passing something other than an `int` as an argument. No such guarantee is provided for `Set`s. Even though a typical use is to have a homogeneous `Set` in which all elements are of the same type, the compiler will not enforce the constraint. This means that a class of errors is possible when using polymorphic collections that cannot happen when using a specific collection like `IntSet`.

8.3   Equality Revisited

A collection like `Set` determines whether an element is a member of the collection by using the `equals` method. Therefore, the contents of an object of the collection type depends on how `equals` is implemented for the elements.

For example, `equals` for `Vector` actually returns true if the two vectors have the same state; other collection types in `java.util` define `equals` similarly. This means that you have to be careful when you store vectors in a `Set`.

If you are using the set to keep track of distinct vector objects, the implementation in Figure 8.2 won't do what you want. For example, consider the following code:

```
Set s = new Set( );
Vector x = new Vector( );
Vector y = new Vector( );
s.insert(x);
s.insert(y); // y is not added to s since it appears to be in it already
x.add(new Integer(3));
if (s.isIn(y)) // won't get here
```

Since y has the same state as x when it is inserted in s, it appears to already be in s, and therefore it is not added again. However, once the state of x changes, y is no longer equals to x; and therefore the call to isIn returns false.

It may seem that the way to avoid this problem is to use == instead of equals to compare the elements, but this approach won't work properly for immutable types. For example, you probably don't want the set to contain two copies of the string "abc"!

One way to solve the problem is to wrap the vectors in container objects when you intend to distinguish distinct vector objects. Figure 8.3 gives the specification and implementation of such a type. A container is immutable, and two containers are equals if they contain the very same object. Note that Container is itself polymorphic.

Now we can insert both x and y in the set, even when they have the same state:

```
Set s = new Set( );
Vector x = new Vector( );
Vector y = new Vector( );
s.insert(new Container(x));
s.insert(new Container(y));
x.add(new Integer(3));
if (s.isIn(new Container(y))) // will get here
```

This code causes s to contain two elements, one for vector x and the other for vector y. Therefore, even though x is modified, we still find y in the set. Note that now we must pass containers as arguments to Set methods.

Figure 8.3   The Container type and its implementation

```
public class Container {
    // OVERVIEW: A Container contains a single object. Two Containers are
    // equals if they contain the very same object. Containers are immutable.

    private Object el;

    // constructor
    public Container (Object x) {
        // EFFECTS: Makes this contain x.
        el = x; }

    // methods
    public Object get ( ) {
        // EFFECTS: Returns the object in the container.
        return el; }

    public boolean equals (Object x) {
        if (! x instanceOf Container) return false;
        return (el == ((Container) x.el)); }
}
```

8.4   Additional Methods

The Set type, and many other polymorphic data abstractions, use only Object methods on their parameters, but some abstractions need additional methods.

For example, suppose we want to define an OrderedList type, a polymorphic version of OrderedIntList (see Figure 6.10). To define such a type, we need a way to order the elements. Object does not provide a way to do this.

The required ability can be achieved by defining a supertype, all of whose subtypes have a comparison method. Such a type, called Comparable, is defined in java.util; its specification is given in Figure 8.4.

One point to note here is that various objects might not be comparable. compareTo might be called with null or with an argument belonging to a type that is not a subtype of Comparable. But even if the argument belongs to a subtype of Comparable, there can still be a problem. For example, both

Figure 8.4 The Comparable interface

```
public interface Comparable {
    // OVERVIEW: Subtypes of Comparable provide a method to determine
    //    the ordering of their objects. This ordering must be a total order
    //    over their objects, and it should be both transitive and symmetric.
    //    Furthermore x.compareTo(y) == 0 implies x.equals(y).

    public int compareTo (Object x) throws ClassCastException,
        NullPointerException;
        // EFFECTS: If x is null, throws NullPointerException; if
        //    this and x aren't comparable, throws ClassCastException.
        //    Otherwise, if this is less than x returns -1; if this equals
        //    x returns 0; and if this is greater than x, returns 1.
}
```

Integer and String are subtypes of Comparable, yet x.compareTo(s), where x is an Integer and s is a String, does not make sense. Attempts to do comparisons like this will cause compareTo to throw ClassCastException.

Given the Comparable interface, we can define OrderedList. Figure 8.5 provides a partial specification and implementation. As was the case with Set, the specification and implementation are similar to those of the related type, OrderedIntList; its implementation can be found in Figures 6.11 and 6.12. The main differences are: arguments and results are now Comparables, where before they were ints, and the comparison is done using compareTo, as indicated in the overview.

OrderedList actually ensures that the elements of the list are homogeneous. This happens because compareTo throws an exception if the objects aren't comparable—that is, if they don't belong to related types for which a comparison makes sense. The type of element in the list is determined when the first element is added; if the list becomes empty, this type can switch to something different when the next element is added. Note that addEl makes sure the first element is comparable, by rejecting an attempt to add null to the list.

To enable elements of a type to be stored in an OrderedList, the type must be a subtype of Comparable. Every type for which this makes sense should be defined in this way.

Figure 8.5   Partial specification and implementation of ordered lists

```
public class OrderedList {
    // OVERVIEW: An ordered list is a mutable ordered list of Comparable objects.
    //    A typical list is a sequence [x1, ..., xn] where xi < xj if i < j.
    //    The ordering of the elements is done using their compareTo method.

    private boolean empty;
    private OrderedList left, right;
    private Comparable val;

    // constructors
    public OrderedList ( ) {
        // EFFECTS: Initializes this to be an empty ordered list.
        empty = true; }

    // methods
    public void addEl (Comparable el) throws NullPointerException,
            DuplicateException, ClassCastException {
        // MODIFIES: this
        // EFFECTS: If el is in this, throws DuplicateException; if el is null
        //    throws NullPointerException; if el cannot be compared to other elements
        //    of this throws ClassCastException; otherwise, adds el to this.
        if (val == null) throw new NullPointerException("OrderedList.addEl");
        if (empty) {
            left = new OrderedList( ); right = new OrderedList( );
            val = el; empty = false; return; }
        int n = el.compareTo(val);
        if (n == 0) throw new DuplicateException("OrderedList.addEl");
        if (n < 0) left.addEl(el); else right.addEl(el); }

    public void remEl (Comparable el) throws NotFoundException
        // MODIFIES: this
        // EFFECTS: If el is not in this, throws NotFoundException;
        //    otherwise, removes el from this.

    public boolean isIn (Comparable el)
        // EFFECTS: If el is in this returns true else returns false.
}
```

8.5   More Flexibility

Using a supertype like `Comparable` to capture the requirements of a polymorphic abstraction with respect to the methods it uses on its parameters requires preplanning. The supertype must be defined first, before any types that ought to be its subtypes are defined; then those types can be defined to "implement" the supertype.

Such preplanning is not always possible. Sometimes a collection type is defined *after* some of the desired element types. In this case, we need another way to access the methods used in the collection.

This can be accomplished by defining an interface whose objects have the required methods, but now the element types are not subtypes of that interface. Instead, for each type that will be used for elements in the collection, a special subtype of the interface type must be defined.

For example, suppose we wanted a set that maintained a running sum of its elements. Each time an element is inserted, the sum is incremented; when an element is removed, the sum is decremented. To maintain the sum, however, the collection needs to use methods of its element type—one to add, and one to subtract. We can capture this requirement in the `Adder` interface defined in Figure 8.6. In addition to the add and sub methods, note that we also require a way of obtaining the zero object for the element type.

The `Adder` interface is *not* intended to be a supertype of the types whose elements can be added. Instead, it provides objects whose methods can be used to add or subtract elements of some related type. For each related type, a subtype of `Adder` must be defined. Figure 8.7 shows the class defining the subtype of `Adder` that adds `Poly`s. It isn't necessary to provide a specification for this type since it is just an implementation of `Adder`. Here we have chosen to store the zero polynomial in the rep; alternatively, we could create the zero polynomial each time zero is called.

One point to note here is that the `Adder` methods are not identical to methods of the related type. In this case, `Poly` has methods named add and sub, but they have different signatures than the related `Adder` methods; also, `Poly` does not have a zero method. As another example, we could define an `IntegerAdder` class that would add `Integer`s, even though `Integer`s don't have any arithmetic methods.

Figure 8.6   The Adder interface

```
public interface Adder {
    // OVERVIEW: All subtypes of Adder provide a means to add and
    //    subtract the elements of some related object type.

    public Object add (Object x, Object y) throws NullPointerException,
            ClassCastException;
      // EFFECTS: If x or y is null, throws NullPointerException; if x and y are
      //    not addable, throws ClassCastException; else returns the sum of x and y.

    public Object sub (Object x, Object y) throws NullPointerException,
            ClassCastException;
      // EFFECTS: If x or y is null, throws NullPointerException; if x and y
      //    are not addable, throws ClassCastException;
      //    else returns the difference of x and y.

    public Object zero ( )
      // EFFECTS: Returns the object that represents zero for the related type.
}
```

SumSet is defined in terms of the Adder interface; Figure 8.8 provides a partial specification and implementation. SumSet objects are actually homogeneous (like OrderedList), but in this case, the element type is determined when the set is created, by means of the Adder object that is an argument of the constructor.

Here is an example of using this type:

```
Adder a = new PolyAdder( );
SumSet s = new Sumset(a);
s.insert(new Poly(3, 7));
s.insert(new Poly(4, 8));
Poly p = (Poly) s.sum( );
```

SumSet object s will only be able to store Poly objects.

A type like SumSet is somewhat inconvenient to use because of the need to define a related subtype of Adder for each element type. For this reason,

Figure 8.7   The `PolyAdder` class

```
public class PolyAdder implements Adder {

    private Poly z;   // the zero Poly

    public PolyAdder ( ) { z = new Poly( ); }

    public Object add (Object x, Object y) throws NullPointerException,
        ClassCastException {
      if (x == null || y == null)
         throw new NullPointerException("PolyAdder.add");
      return ((Poly) x).add((Poly) y); }

    public Object sub (Object x, Object y) throws NullPointerException,
        ClassCastException {
      if (x == null || y == null)
         throw new NullPointerException("PolyAdder.sub");
      return ((Poly) x).sub((Poly) y); }

    public Object zero ( ) { return z; }
}
```

it can be useful to combine the use of the `Adder` with the use of a type like `Comparable`. For example, we could define a type `Addable`, with the following methods:

```
public Object add (Object x) throws NullPointerException,
    ClassCastException
public Object sub (Object x) throws NullPointerException,
    ClassCastException
public Object zero ( )
```

Then element types defined later can be defined as subtypes of `Addable`. For example, if `Poly` were defined after `Addable` had been defined, we could have it implement `Addable`, although it would need to have additional methods to match the `Addable` interface.

Figure 8.8   Partial specification and implementation of SumSet

```
public class SumSet {
    // OVERVIEW: SumSets are mutable sets of objects plus a sum
    //    of the current objects in the set. The sum is computed using
    //    an Adder object. All elements of the set are addable using the Adder.

    private Vector els;   // the elements
    private Object s;   // the sum of the elements
    private Adder a;  // the object used to do adding and subtracting

    // constructor
    public SumSet (Adder p) throws NullPointerException {
        // EFFECTS: Makes this be the empty set whose elements can be
        //    added using p, with initial sum p.zero.
        els = new Vector( ); a = p; s = p.zero( ); }

    public void insert (Object x) throws NullPointerException,
            ClassCastException {
        // MODIFIES: this
        // EFFECTS: If x is null throws NullPointerException; if x cannot be
        //    added to the other elements of this throws ClassCastException;
        //    else adds x to the set and adjusts the sum.
        Object z = a.add(s, x);
        int i = getIndex(x);
        if (i < 0) { els.add(x); s = z; }
    }

    public Object sum ( ) {
        // EFFECTS: Returns the sum of the elements of this.
            return s; }
```

With this approach, SumSet would have two constructors:

```
public SumSet (Adder p) throws NullPointerException
public SumSet ( )
```

The second constructor would be used for types that are subtypes of Addable.

Some of the collection types in java.util are defined like this. They make use of Comparable and also of a type Comparator:

```
public interface Comparator {
    public int compare (Object x, Object y)
         throws NullPointerException, ClassCastException;
    // EFFECTS: If x or y is null throws NullPointerException;
    //     if x and y aren't comparable throws ClassCastException.
    //     Otherwise, if x is less than y, returns -1;
    //     if x equals y, returns 0; and if x is greater than y, returns 1.
}
```

Comparator is defined in java.util.

8.6   Polymorphic Procedures

All of the examples so far have involved data abstractions, but the same techniques can be used for procedures. Figure 8.9 gives the specifications of some polymorphic procedures. Here there are two definitions of sort. The first works if the elements of v belong to subtypes of Comparable. The second takes a Comparator as an argument.

8.7   Summary

Polymorphic abstractions are desirable because they provide a way to abstract from the types of parameters. In this way, we can achieve a more powerful abstraction, one that works for many types rather than just a single type. Procedures, iterators, and data abstractions can all benefit from this technique.

A polymorphic abstraction usually requires access to certain methods of its parameters. Sometimes the methods that all objects have, the ones that are defined by Object, are sufficient. However, sometimes more methods are needed. In this case, the polymorphic abstraction makes use of an interface to define the needed methods.

There are two different ways of defining this interface. The first uses an interface that is intended to be a supertype of the element types. Comparable is an example of such an interface. We will call this the *element subtype* approach

Figure 8.9   Some polymorphic procedures

```
class Vectors {
    // OVERVIEW: Provides useful procedures for manipulating vectors.

    public static int search (Vector v, Object o)
            throws NotFoundException, NullPointerException
        // EFFECTS: If v is null throws NullPointerException else if o is in v
        //    returns an index where o is stored else throws NotFoundException.
        //    Uses equals to compare o with the elements of v.

    public static sort (Vector v) throws ClassCastException
        // MODIFIES: v
        // EFFECTS: If v is not null, sorts it into ascending order using
        //    the compareTo method of Comparable; if some element of v are
        //    null or aren't comparable throws ClassCastException.

    public static sort (Vector v, Comparator c)
            throws ClassCastException
        // MODIFIES: v
        // EFFECTS: If v is not null, sorts it into ascending order using the
        //    compare method of c; if some elements of v are null or aren't
        //    comparable using c throws ClassCastException.
}
```

since each potential type of element must be defined as a subtype of the interface.

The problem with this approach is that it requires preplanning. If the polymorphic abstraction is invented after some desirable element types have already been defined, it is too late to make those types subtypes of the interface. In this case, another approach is used: the interface is a supertype of types that are related to the element types. Objects belonging to a subtype of the interface have methods that provide the needed functionality for objects of the related element type. Adder is an example of such an interface. We will call this the *related subtype* approach since for each element type a related type that is a subtype of the interface must be defined.

The related subtype approach is less convenient than the element subtype approach because of the need to define the extra subtypes. Furthermore, when element types are defined after the polymorphic abstraction, the element

---

Sidebar 8.2   Requirements of Polymorphic Abstractions

- Almost all polymorphic abstractions need to use methods on their parameters, but sometimes only methods of Object are required.

- Polymorphic abstractions that need more than Object methods make use of an associated interface to define their requirements.

- In the *element subtype* approach, all potential element types must be subtypes of the associated interface.

- In the *related subtype* approach, a subtype of the interface must be defined for each potential element type.

- Some polymorphic abstractions combine the approaches, allowing the user to select the one that works best for the parameter type of interest.

---

subtype approach will work. Therefore, sometimes polymorphic abstractions allow both approaches; the using code selects the approach when it constructs the polymorphic collection or calls the polymorphic procedure. Sidebar 8.2 summarizes this discussion.

Exercises

8.1   Complete the implementation of OrderedList (see Figure 8.5). Be sure to define the abstraction function and rep invariant and to implement toString and repOk.

8.2   Implement IntegerAdder, which is a subtype of the Adder interface (see Figure 8.6).

8.3   Complete the implementation of SumSet (see Figure 8.8). Be sure to define the rep invariant and abstraction function and to implement toString and repOk.

8.4   Specify and implement a version of SumSet that allows users to supply the required methods using either Adder or Addable. Be sure to define the rep invariant and abstraction function and to implement toString and repOk.

8.5   Extend the specification and implementation of Poly (see Figures 5.4, 5.7, and 5.8) to make it a subtype of Addable.

8.6 Specify and implement a polymorphic list; this type is like IntList (see Figure 7.11) except that it stores arbitrary objects rather than ints. Be sure to define the rep invariant and abstraction function and to implement toString and repOk.

8.7 Specify and implement a Bag type that can hold elements of arbitrary types. Bags are like sets except that they can contain multiple copies of an element. Your bags should have insert, remove, elements, and size methods, plus a method

```
public int card (Object x)
    // EFFECTS: Returns a count of the number of occurrences of x in this.
```

Be sure to define the rep invariant and abstraction function and to implement toString and repOk.

8.8 Suppose we want to define a procedure to search an arbitrary collection for a match with an element:

```
public static int search (Object c, Object x) throws
        NullPointerException, NotFoundException,
        ClassCastException
    // EFFECTS: If c is null throws NullPointerException, else if
    //    c is not searchable, throws ClassCastException, else
    //    if x is in c returns an index where x can be found,
    //    else throws NotFoundException.
```

Here we require a notion of *searchable*: search requires a way to find elements of c by their index and to determine the size of c. Define a *related subtype* interface Indexer that provides the needed methods and then implement search using that interface.

8.9 Define and implement VectorIndexer, which is a subtype of Indexer, as defined in the preceding exercise. VectorIndexer allows a vector to be searched.

Specifications

Throughout this book, we emphasize the importance of specifications in all stages of program development. Our main premise is that the proper use of abstraction is the key to good programming. Without specifications, abstractions are too intangible to be helpful. In this chapter, we discuss the meaning of specifications and some criteria to consider when writing them. We also discuss two primary uses of specifications.

9.1 Specifications and Specificand Sets

The purpose of a specification is to define the behavior of an abstraction. Users will rely on this behavior, while implementors must provide it. An implementation that provides the described behavior is said to *satisfy* the specification.

We define the meaning of a specification to be the set of all program modules that satisfy it. We call this the *specificand set* of the specification. As an example, consider the specification

```
static int p (int y)
    // REQUIRES: y > 0
    // EFFECTS: Returns x such that x > y.
```

Sidebar 9.1 Specifications

- A specification describes the behavior of some abstraction.
- An implementation *satisfies* a specification if it provides the described behavior.
- The meaning of a specification is the set of all programs that satisfy it. This set is called the *specificand set*.

This specification is satisfied by any procedure named p that, when called with an argument greater than zero, returns a value greater than its argument. Members of the specificand set include

```
static int p (int y) { return y+1; }
static int p (int y) { return y*2; }
static int p (int y) { return y*3; }
```

Like every specification, this one is satisfied by an infinite number of programs. Sidebar 9.1 summarizes these definitions.

It is important to remember that a specification, its specificand set, and a particular member of the specificand set are very different kinds of things, as different as a program, the set of all possible executions of that program, and an execution of that program on a single set of data.

9.2   Some Criteria for Specifications

Good specifications take many forms, but all of them have certain attributes in common. Three important attributes—restrictiveness, generality, and clarity—are discussed in this section. They are summarized in Sidebar 9.2.

9.2.1   Restrictiveness

There is a vast difference between knowing that some members of a specification's specificand set are appropriate and knowing that all members are appropriate. This is similar to the difference between knowing that a program works on some inputs and knowing that it works on all inputs, a difference we

Sidebar 9.2   Attributes of Good Specifications

- A specification is *sufficiently restrictive* if it rules out all implementations that are unacceptable to an abstraction's users.
- A specification is *sufficiently general* if it does not preclude acceptable implementations.
- A specification should be *clear* so that it is easy for users to understand.

will emphasize in Chapter 10 when we discuss testing. A good specification should be restrictive enough to rule out any implementation that is unacceptable to its abstraction's users. This requirement is the basis of almost all uses of specifications.

In general, discussing whether or not a specification is sufficiently restrictive involves discussing the uses to which members of the specificand set might be put. Certain common mistakes, however, almost always lead to inadequately restrictive specifications. One such mistake is failing to state needed requirements in the requires clause. For example, Figure 9.1 gives three specifications for an `elems` iterator for a bag of integers. (An `IntBag` is like an `IntSet` except that elements can occur in it more than once. For example, a bag could contain 3 twice. Bags are sometimes called *multisets*.) The first specification fails to address the question of what happens if the bag is changed while the generator returned by `elems` is in use. It therefore allows implementations exhibiting radically different behavior. For example, does changing the bag affect the values returned by the generator?

One way to deal with this particular problem is to require that the bag not be changed while the generator is in use, as is done in the second specification. This specification may or may not be sufficiently restrictive since it does not constrain the order in which the elements are returned. It would be better if it either defined an order or included the phrase "in arbitrary order." In addition, the specification fails to make clear what is done when an element is contained in a bag more than once. For that matter, it does not even say explicitly that the generator returns only elements that are in the bag. The third specification corrects these deficiencies.

Other mistakes are failing to identify when exceptions should be signaled and failing to specify behavior at boundary cases. For example, consider a

Figure 9.1   Three specifications of elems

```
public Iterator elems ( )
```
   // EFFECTS: *Returns a generator that produces every element of* this
   //   *(as* Integers*).*

```
public Iterator elems ( )
```
   // EFFECTS: *Returns a generator that produces every element of* this
   //   *(as* Integers*).*
   // REQUIRES: this *not be modified while the generator is in use.*

```
public Iterator elems ( )
```
   // EFFECTS: *Returns a generator that produces every element of* this
   //   *(as* Integers*), in arbitrary order. Each element is*
   //   *produced exactly the number of times it occurs in* this.
   // REQUIRES: this *not be modified while the generator is in use.*

Figure 9.2   Specification of indexString procedure

```
public static int indexString(String s1, String s2)
      throws NullPointerException, EmptyException
```
   // EFFECTS: *If* s1 *or* s2 *is* null, *throws* NullPointerException; *else*
   //   *if* s1 *is the empty string, throws* EmptyException; *else*
   //   *if* s1 *occurs as a substring in* s2, *returns the least index at which*
   //   s1 *occurs; else returns* -1. *E.g.,*
   //   indexString("bc", "abcbc") = 1
   //   indexString("b", "a") = -1

---

procedure indexString that takes strings s1 and s2 and, if s1 is a substring of s2, returns the index at which s1's first character occurs in s2; for example, indexString("ab", "babc") returns 1. A specification that contained only this information would not be restrictive enough because it does not explain what would happen if s1 were not a substring of s2, or if it occurred multiple times in s2, or if s1 or s2 were empty. The specification in Figure 9.2 is restrictive enough.

The moral is that it takes considerable care to write sufficiently restrictive specifications.

9.2.2   Generality

A good specification should be general enough to ensure that few, if any, acceptable programs are precluded. The importance of the generality criterion may be less obvious than that of restrictiveness. It is not essential to ensure that no acceptable implementation is precluded, but the more desirable (that is, efficient or elegant) implementations should not be ruled out. For example, the specification

```
public static float sqrt (float sq, float e)
    // REQUIRES: sq >= 0 && e > .001
    // EFFECTS: Returns rt such that 0 <= (rt*rt - sq) <= e.
```

constrains the implementor to algorithms that find approximations that are greater than or equal to the actual square root. The constraint may well result in a needless loss of efficiency.

It is our desire to make specifications as general as possible that has led us to the *definitional* style of specification used in this book. A definitional specification explicitly lists properties that the members of the specificand set are to exhibit. The alternative to a definitional specification is an *operational* one. An operational specification, instead of describing the properties of the specificands, gives a recipe for constructing them. For example,

```
public static int search (int[ ] a, int x)
            throws NotFoundException, NullPointerException
    // EFFECTS: If a is null throws NullPointerException else examines
    //    a[0], a[1], ..., in turn and returns the index of the first one
    //    that is equal to x. Signals NotFoundException if none equals x.
```

is an operational specification of search, while

```
public static int search (int[ ] a, int x)
            throws NotFoundException, NullPointerException
    // EFFECTS: If a is null throws NullPointerException else returns
    //    i such that a[i] = x; signals NotFoundException if there is no such i.
```

is definitional. The first specification explains how to implement search, while the second merely describes a property that its inputs and outputs must satisfy. Not only is the definitional specification shorter, but it also allows greater freedom to the implementor, who may choose to examine the array elements in some order other than first to last.

Operational specifications have some advantages. Most significantly, they seem to be relatively easily constructed by trained programmers—chiefly because their construction so closely resembles programming. They are generally longer than definitional specifications, however, and they often lead to over-specification. The operational specification of search, for example, specifies which index is to be returned if x occurs more than once in a; this may be more restrictive than is desired. As another example, consider trying to write an operational specification for a square root procedure.

A good check for generality is to examine every property required by a specification, in both the requires and effects clauses, and ask whether it is really needed. If it is not, then it should be eliminated or weakened. Also, any portion of a specification that is operational rather than definitional should be viewed with suspicion.

9.2.3   Clarity

When we talk about what makes a program "good," we consider not only the computations it describes but also properties of the program text itself—for example, whether it is well modularized and nicely commented. Similarly, when we evaluate a specification, we must consider not only properties of the specificand set but also properties of the specification itself—for example, whether it is easy to read.

A good specification should facilitate communication among people. A specification may be sufficiently restrictive and sufficiently general—that is, it may have exactly the right meaning—but this is not enough. If this meaning is hard for readers to discover, the specification's utility is severely limited.

People may fail to understand a specification in two distinct ways. They may study it and come away knowing that they do not understand it. For example, a reader of the second specification of elems in Figure 9.1 may be confused about what to do if an element occurs in the bag more than once. This is troublesome but not as dangerous as when people come away thinking that they understand a specification when, in fact, they do not. In such a case, the user and the implementor of an abstraction may each interpret its specification differently, leading to modules that cannot work together. For example, the implementor of elems may decide to produce each element the number of times it occurs in the bag, while the user expects each element to be produced only once.

Clarity is an important but amorphous criterion. It is easy enough to say that a good specification should be easy to understand but much harder to say how to achieve this. Many factors, of which conciseness, redundancy, and structure are perhaps the most important, contribute to clarity.

The most concise presentation may not always be the best specification, but it is frequently the best starting point. There are valid reasons to increase the size of a specification by adding redundant information or levels of structure, as we shall discuss, but it is important to avoid pointless verbosity. As a specification grows longer, it is more likely to contain errors, less likely to be completely and carefully read, and more likely to be misunderstood.

It is important not to confuse length with completeness. A stream-of-consciousness technique will easily lead to specifications that are both long and incomplete. Like programs, specifications that grow by accretion are often longer than they need to be. Instead of just adding to a specification, it is important to step back from that local change and see whether there is a way to consolidate the information. It takes more time to write a complete short description than to write a complete long one, but the author of a specification owes it to the readers to make this investment.

Any specification containing redundant text is less concise than it could be. Redundancy should not be introduced without a good reason, but it can be justified in two ways: to reduce the likelihood that a specification will be misunderstood by its readers and to catch errors.

In many respects, the role of a specification is like that of a textbook. It should be designed not merely to contain information but to communicate that information effectively. Redundancy can be used to reduce the likelihood that an important point will be missed. The old dictum "Tell 'em what you're gonna tell 'em, tell 'em, then tell 'em what you told 'em" has some pedagogical validity. The key is to present the same information in more than one way, to be redundant without being repetitious. Consider, for example,

```
static boolean subset (IntSet s1, IntSet s2)
        throws NullPointerException
    // EFFECTS: If s1 or s2 is null throws NullPointerException else
    //    returns true if s1 is a subset of s2 else returns false.
```

```
static boolean subset (IntSet s1, IntSet s2)
        throws NullPointerException
    // EFFECTS: If s1 or s2 is null throws NullPointerException else
    //    returns true if every element of s1 is an element of s2 else returns false.
```

```
static boolean subset (IntSet s1, IntSet s2)
        throws NullPointerException
```
// EFFECTS: *If* s1 *or* s2 *is* null *throws* NullPointerException *else*
//   *returns true if* s1 *is a subset of* s2 *else returns false, i.e.,*
//   *returns true if every element of* s1 *is an element of* s2 *else returns false.*

The first specification is concise and, for most readers, quite clear. However, some readers might be left with a nagging doubt: Was the word "subset" carefully chosen, or might the author have meant *proper* subset? The second specification, while a bit harder to read than the first, leaves no doubt on this point. The question it raises is why, if the specifier intended that p be a subset test, was this not stated explicitly? The third specification, of course, answers both of these questions.

By stating the same thing in more than one way, a specification provides readers with a benchmark against which they can check their understanding. This helps to prevent misunderstandings and thus allows readers to spend less time studying a specification. A particularly useful kind of redundancy in this regard is one or more well-chosen examples, such as those given in the specification of indexString in Figure 9.2.

A specification that states the same thing in more than one way also allows for the fact that different readers will find different presentations of the same information easier to understand. Frequently, some critical part of a specification is a concept with a name that will be meaningful to some readers but not to others. For example, consider

```
static float pv (float inc, float r, int n)
```
// REQUIRES: inc > 0 && r > 0 && n > 0
// EFFECTS: *Returns the present value of an annual income of* inc *for*
//   n *years at a risk-free interest rate of* r.
//   *I.e.,* pv(inc,r,n) = inc + (inc/(1+r)) + ... + (inc/(1+r)$^{n-1}$).
//   *E.g.,* pv(100, .10, 3) = 100 + 100/1.1 + 100/1.21

For readers well versed in financial matters, a specification that did not use the phrase "present value" would not be as easy to understand as one that did. For readers lacking that background, the part of the specification following "I.e." is invaluable. The part following "E.g." can be used by either group of readers to confirm their understanding.

If readers are to benefit from redundancy, it is critical that all redundant information be clearly marked as such. Otherwise, a reader can waste a lot of time trying to understand what new information is being presented when, in fact, none is. A good way to indicate that information is redundant is to preface it with "i.e." or "e.g.".

Redundancy does not reduce the number of mistakes in a specification. Instead, it makes them more evident and provides the reader with the opportunity to notice them. For example, consider

```
static boolean tooCold (int temp)
    // EFFECTS: Returns true if temp is <= 0 degrees
    //    Fahrenheit; otherwise returns false.
```

```
static boolean tooCold (int temp)
    // EFFECTS: Returns true if temp is <= 0 degrees
    //    Fahrenheit; otherwise returns false. I.e., returns true
    //    exactly when temp is not greater than the freezing point of
    //    water at standard temperature and pressure.
```

The first specification offers a reader no reason for suspicion, but the second should ring a useful warning bell for most readers. This warning should eventually lead to a revised specification.

One of the primary problems with informal specifications is that each reader brings a somewhat different knowledge and perspective to the task of reading a specification. Introducing redundancy can go a long way toward coping with this problem. For example, consider

```
static int billion ( )
    // EFFECTS: Returns the integer one billion.
```

```
static int billion ( )
    // EFFECTS: Returns the integer one billion, i.e., 10^9.
```

Both American and British readers are likely to find the first specification perfectly unambiguous. Unfortunately, they are also likely to interpret it in completely different ways, for in the United States, a billion is 10^9, whereas in Britain it is 10^{12}. The insertion of what an American author might consider redundant information in the second specification precludes any confusion.

9.3   Why Specifications?

Specifications are essential for achieving program modularity. Abstraction is used to decompose a program into modules. An abstraction is intangible, though. Without some description, we have no way to know what it is or how to distinguish it from one of its implementations. The specification provides this description.

A specification describes an agreement between providers and users of a service. The provider agrees to write a module that belongs to the specificand set. The user agrees not to rely on knowing which member of this set is provided—that is, not to assume anything except what is stated by the specification. This agreement makes it possible to separate consideration of the implementation from the use of a program unit. Specifications provide the logical firewalls that permit divide-and-conquer to succeed.

Specifications are obviously useful for program documentation. The very act of writing a specification is also beneficial because it sheds light on the abstraction being specified. Our experience is that we often profit as much from this activity as from our use of the result. Writing a specification almost always teaches us something important about the specificand set being described. It does this by encouraging prompt attention to inconsistencies, incompleteness, and ambiguities. In some cases, such improved understanding is the most important result of a specification effort.

The goal is to write specifications that are both restrictive enough and general enough. Thus, we pay special attention to requirements, exceptions, and boundary conditions. Doing this involves posing questions about the behavior of the abstractions, questions like those posed about `indexString`—for example, what to do if either string is empty. The point is that posing and answering such questions forces us to think carefully about an abstraction and its intended use.

The construction of a specification focuses attention on what is required of a program. It serves as a mechanism for generating questions that should be answered in consultation with users of a program or a module, rather than by implementors. By encouraging the asking of these questions in the early stages of system development, specification helps us debug our understanding of a system's requirements and design before we start implementation.

As we shall discuss in later chapters, specifications should be written as soon as the decisions they record have been made. Since specifications become irrelevant only when their abstraction is obsolete, they should continue to evolve as long as the program evolves. It is a serious mistake to treat the process of writing specifications as a separate phase of a software project.

Once written, specifications can serve many different purposes. They are helpful to designers, implementors, and maintainers alike. During the implementation phase of the software life cycle, the presence of a good specification helps both those implementing the specified module and those implementing modules that use it. As discussed previously, a good specification strikes a careful balance between restrictiveness and generality. It tells the implementor what service to provide but does not place any unnecessary constraints on how that service is provided. In this way, it allows the implementor as much flexibility as is consistent with the needs of users. Of course, specifications are crucial for users, who otherwise would have no way to know what they can rely on in implementing their modules. Without specifications, all that exists is the code, and it is unclear how much of that code will remain unchanged over time. During testing, specifications provide information that can be used in generating test data and in building stubs that simulate the specified module. (We will discuss this use in Chapter 10.) During the system-integration phase, the existence of good specifications can reduce the number and severity of interfacing problems by reducing the number of implicit assumptions about module interfaces. When an error does appear, specifications can be used to pinpoint where the fault lies. Moreover, they define the constraints that must be observed in correcting the error, which helps us avoid introducing new errors while correcting old ones.

Finally, a specification can be a helpful maintenance tool. The existence of clear and accurate documentation is a prerequisite for efficient and effective maintenance. We need to know what each module does and, if it is at all complex, how it does it. All too often, these two aspects of documentation are intimately intertwined. The use of specifications as documentation helps to keep them separate and makes it easier to see the ramifications of proposed modifications. For example, a proposed modification that requires us only to reimplement a single abstraction without changing its specification has a much smaller impact than one that changes the specification as well.

Sidebar 9.3 summarizes the value of specifications.

9.4   Summary

This chapter has discussed specifications and offered criteria to follow in writing them. We defined the meaning of a specification to be the set of all program modules that satisfy it. This definition captures the intuitive purpose of a specification—namely, to state what all legal implementations

Sidebar 9.3   Benefits of Specifications

- An abstraction is intangible; without a description, it has no meaning. The specification provides this description.

- Writing a specification sheds light on the abstraction being defined, encouraging prompt attention to inconsistencies, incompleteness, and ambiguities. It forces us to pay careful attention to the abstraction and its intended use.

- A specification defines a contract between users and implementors: implementors agree to provide an implementation that satisfies the specification, and users agree to rely on not knowing which member of the specificand set is provided.

of an abstraction have in common. Such a specification tells users what they can rely on and tells implementors what they must provide.

Good specifications should be restrictive, general, and clear. Restrictiveness and generality involve the set of modules that satisfy the specification: no implementations that would be unacceptable to users of an abstraction should be permitted, and desirable implementations (ones that are efficient or elegant, for example) should not be ruled out. Generality is made easier when specifications are written using a definitional approach, which just states properties of the specificand set. An operational approach, which explains a way to implement the abstraction, tends to yield specifications that are too restrictive.

Clarity refers to the ease with which users understand the specification. The main way to enhance clarity is to start with a concise statement and then add some redundancy, often in the form of an example. Redundancy allows readers to check their understanding of the specification. It also makes errors more evident, since these often show up as inconsistencies in the redundant descriptions. To make the reader's job as simple as possible, all redundant information should be clearly marked as such.

Specifications have two main uses. First, the act of writing a specification sheds light on the abstraction being specified by focusing attention on the properties of that abstraction. This use can be enhanced by careful attention to properties that might be overlooked, including what should be stated in the requires clause, exactly when exceptions should be signaled, and the treatment of boundary cases. This use is sometimes the main benefit of a specification because it points out a problem with the abstraction that requires further study.

The second use is as documentation. Specifications are valuable during every phase of software development, from design to maintenance. Of course, they are not the only program documentation required. A specification describes what a module does, but any module whose implementation is clever should also have documentation that explains how it works. Program modification and maintenance are eased if these two forms of documentation are clearly distinguished.

A specification is the only tangible record of an abstraction. Specifications are a crucial part of our methodology, since without them abstractions would be too imprecise to be useful. We shall continue to emphasize them in the chapters that follow.

Exercises

9.1 Provide a concise but readable specification of an IntBag abstraction, with operations to create an empty bag, insert and remove an element, test an element for membership, give the size of the bag, give the number of times an element occurs in a bag, and produce the elements of the bag.

9.2 Take a specification you have given for a problem in an earlier chapter and discuss its restrictiveness, generality, and clarity.

9.3 Is it meaningful to ask whether a specification is correct? Explain.

9.4 Discuss how specifications can be used during system integration.

9.5 Discuss the relationship between an abstraction, its specification, and its implementation.

Testing and Debugging

10

So far we have talked a bit about program design and quite a lot about program specification and implementation. We now turn to the related issues of ascertaining whether or not a program works as we hope it will and discovering why not when it does not.

We use the word *validation* to refer to a process designed to increase our confidence that a program will function as we intend it to. We do validation most commonly through a combination of testing and some form of reasoning about why we believe the program to be correct. We shall use the term *debugging* to refer to the process of ascertaining why a program is not functioning properly and *defensive programming* to refer to the practice of writing programs in a way designed specifically to ease the process of validation and debugging.

Before we can say much about how to validate a program, we need to discuss what we hope to accomplish by that process. The most desirable outcome would be an ironclad guarantee that all users of the program will be happy at all times with all aspects of its behavior. This is not an attainable goal. Such a guarantee presumes an ability to know exactly what it would mean to make all users happy. The best result we can hope for is a guarantee that a program satisfies its specification. Experience indicates that even this modest goal can be difficult to attain. Most of the time, we settle for doing things to increase our confidence that a program meets its specification.

Sidebar 10.1   Validation

- *Validation* is a process designed to increase our confidence that a program works as intended. It can be done through verification or testing.

- *Verification* is a formal or informal argument that a program works on all possible inputs.

- *Testing* is the process of running a program on a set of test cases and comparing the actual results with expected results.

There are two ways to go about validation. We can argue that the program will work on all possible inputs. This activity must involve careful reasoning about the text of the program and is generally referred to as *verification*. Formal program verification is generally too tedious to do successfully without machine aids, and only relatively primitive aids exist today. Therefore, most program verification is still rather informal. Even informal verification, however, can be a difficult process.

The alternative to verification is testing. We can easily be convinced that a program works on some set of inputs merely by running it on each member of the set and checking the results. If the set of possible inputs is small, exhaustive testing (checking every input) is possible. For most programs, however, the set of possible inputs is so large (indeed, it is often infinite) that exhaustive testing is impossible. Nevertheless, a carefully chosen set of test cases can greatly increase our confidence that the program works as specified. If well done, testing can detect most of the errors in programs.

In this chapter, we focus on testing as a method of validating programs. We discuss how to select test cases and how to organize the testing process. We also discuss debugging and defensive programming. Sidebar 10.1 summarizes the remarks on validation.

10.1   Testing

Testing is the process of executing a program on a set of test cases and comparing the actual results with the expected results. Its purpose is to reveal the existence of errors. Testing does not pinpoint the location of errors, however; this is done through debugging. When we test a program, we examine the relationship between its inputs and outputs. When we debug a program, we worry about this relationship but also pay close attention to the intermediate states of the computation.

The key to successful testing is choosing the proper test data. As mentioned earlier, exhaustive testing is impossible for almost all programs. For example, if a program has three integer inputs, each of which ranges over the values 1 to 1,000, exhaustive testing would require running the program one billion times. If each run took one second, this would take slightly more than 31 years.

Faced with the impossibility of exhausting the input space, what do we do? Our goal must be to find a reasonably small set of tests that will allow us to approximate the information we would have obtained through exhaustive testing. For example, suppose a program accepts a single integer as its argument and happens to work in one way on all odd integers and in a second way on all even ones; in this case, testing it on any even integer, any odd integer, and zero is a pretty good approximation to exhaustive testing.

10.1.1   Black-Box Testing

Test cases are generated by considering both the specification and the implementation. In black-box testing, we generate test data from the specification alone, without regard for the internal structure of the module being tested. This approach, which is common across many engineering disciplines, has several significant advantages. The most important advantage is that the testing procedure is not adversely influenced by the component being tested. For example, suppose the author of a program made the implicit invalid assumption that the program would never be called with a certain class of inputs. Acting upon this assumption, the author might fail to include any code dealing with that class. If test data were generated by examining the program, one might easily be misled into generating data based upon the invalid assumption. A second advantage of black-box testing is that it is robust with respect to changes in the implementation. Black-box test data need not be changed even when major changes are made to the program being tested. A final advantage is that the results of a test can be interpreted by people unfamiliar with the internals of the program being tested.

Testing Paths through the Specification

A good way to generate black-box test data is to explore alternate paths through the specification. These paths can be through both the requires and effects clauses. As an example of a path through the requires clause, consider the specification

```
static float sqrt (float x, float epsilon)
    // REQUIRES: x >= 0 && .00001 < epsilon < .001
    // EFFECTS: Returns sq such that x - epsilon <= sq*sq <= x + epsilon.
```

The requires clause of this specification is the conjunction of two terms:

1. $x \geq 0$

2. $.00001 < \texttt{epsilon} < .001$

To explore the distinct ways in which the requires clause might be satisfied, we must explore the pairwise combinations of the ways each conjunct might be satisfied. Since the first conjunct is a disjunct of two primitive terms ($x \geq 0$ is just a shorthand for $x = 0 \mid x > 0$), it can be satisfied in one of two ways. This leaves us with two interesting ways to satisfy the requires clause:

1. $x = 0$ and $.00001 < \texttt{epsilon} < .001$

2. $x > 0$ and $.00001 < \texttt{epsilon} < .001$

Any set of test data for sqrt should certainly test each of these cases.

It can be difficult to formulate test data that explore many different paths through the effects clause of the specification. It may be difficult even to know which paths can be explored. For example, given the preceding specification of sqrt, we might expect the program sometimes to return an exact result, sometimes a result a little less than the square root, and sometimes a result a little greater. However, a program that always returned a result greater than or equal to the actual square root would be a perfectly acceptable implementation. We would not be able to find test data that forced this program to return a result less than the square root, but we could not know this without examining the code. In fact, without examining the code, we would have no idea which classes of inputs would lead to results in the three categories.

Nevertheless, we should always examine the effects clause carefully and try to find test data that exercise different ways to satisfy it. For example, consider the following procedure

```
static boolean isPrime (int x)
    // EFFECTS: If x is a prime returns true else returns false.
```

The effects clause of this specification is a disjunction: either x is in a prime, or it is not. Both conjuncts should be tested by the test cases.

Often paths through the effects clause pertain to error handling. Failing to signal an exception when called with exceptional input is just as serious as failing to do the proper thing with normal input. Therefore, the test data should cause every possible signal to be raised. For example, consider the specification

```
static int search (int[ ] a, int x)
        throws NotFoundException, NullPointerException
    // EFFECTS: If a is null throws NullPointerException else if x is in a,
    //    returns i such that a[i] = x, else throws NotFoundException.
```

Here we must include tests for both the case in which x is in a and the case in which it is not, as well as for the case when a is null. Similarly, if sqrt signaled exceptions rather than having a requires clause, we would want to include test data that should cause the exceptions.

Testing Boundary Conditions

A program should always be tested on "typical" input values—for example, an array or a set containing several elements, or an integer between the smallest and largest values expected by a program. It is also important to test atypical inputs, though; these tend to show up as boundary conditions.

Considering all paths through the requires clause tests certain kinds of boundary conditions—for example, the case in which sqrt is asked to find the square root of zero. A lot of boundary conditions, however, do not emerge from such analysis. It is important to check as many boundary conditions as possible. Such checks catch two common kind of errors:

1. Logical errors, in which a path to handle a special case presented by a boundary condition is omitted

2. Failure to check for conditions that may cause the underlying language or hardware system to raise an exception (for example, arithmetic overflow)

To generate tests designed to detect the latter kind of error, it is a good idea to use test data that cover all combinations of the largest and smallest allowable values for all bounded numerical arguments. For example, tests for sqrt should include cases for epsilon very close to .001 and .00001. For strings, tests should include the empty string and a one-character string; for arrays, we should test the empty array and a one-element array.

Aliasing Errors

Another kind of boundary condition occurs when two different formals both refer to the same mutable object. For example, suppose procedure

```
static void appendVector (Vector v1, Vector v2)
        throws NullPointerException
 // MODIFIES: v1 and v2
 // EFFECTS: If v1 or v2 is null throws NullPointerException else
 //    removes all elements of v2 and appends them in reverse order
 //    to the end of v1.
```

were implemented by

```
static void appendVector (Vector v1, Vector v2) {
   if (v1 == null) throws new NullPointerException
      ("Vectors.appendVector");
   while (v2.size( ) > 0) {
      v1.addElement(v2.lastElement( ));
      v2.removeElementAt(v2.size( ) - 1); }
}
```

Any test data that did not include an input in which v1 and v2 refer to the same nonempty array would fail to turn up a very serious error in appendVector.

Sidebar 10.2 summarizes black-box testing.

Sidebar 10.2   Black-Box Testing

- Black-box tests are based on a program's specification, not its implementation. Therefore, they continue to be useful even if the program is reimplemented.

- Black-box tests should test all paths through the specification, if possible. In addition, they should test boundary conditions and check for aliasing errors.

10.1.2   Glass-Box Testing

While black-box testing is generally the best place to start when attempting to test a program thoroughly, it is rarely sufficient. Without looking at the internal structure of a program, it is impossible to know which test cases are likely to give new information. It is therefore impossible to tell how much coverage we get from a set of black-box test data. For example, suppose a program relies on table lookup for some inputs and computation for others. If the black-box test data happened to include only those values for which table lookup is used, the tests would give no information about the part of the program that computed values.

Therefore, it is necessary to also do glass-box testing in which the code of the program being tested is taken into account. The glass-box test should supplement black-box testing with inputs that exercise the different paths through the program. The goal here is to have a test set such that each path is exercised by at least one member of the set. We say that such a test set is *path-complete*.

Consider the program

```
static int maxOfThree (int x, int y, int z) {
    if (x > y)
        if (x > z) return x; else return z;
    if (y > z) return y; else return z; }
```

Despite the fact that there are n^3 inputs, where n is the range of integers allowed by the programming language, there are only four paths through the program. Therefore the path-complete property leads us to partition the test data into four classes. In one class, x is greater than y and z. In another, x is greater than y but smaller than z, and so forth. Representatives of the four classes are

```
3, 2, 1    3, 2, 4    1, 2, 1    1, 2, 3
```

It is easy to show that path-completeness is not sufficient to catch all errors. Consider the program

```
static int maxOfThree (int x, int y, int z) {
    return x; }
```

The test set containing just the input

```
2, 1, 1
```

Figure 10.1   A program with many paths

```
j = k;
for (int i = 1; i <= 100; i++)
    if (Tests.pred(i*j)) j++;
```

is path-complete for this program. Using this test might mislead us into believing that our program was correct, since the test would certainly fail to uncover any error.

The problem is that a testing strategy based on exercising all paths through a program is not likely to reveal the existence of missing paths, and omitting a path is a fairly common programming error. This problem is a specific instance of the general fact mentioned earlier: no set of test data based solely upon analysis of the program text is going to be sufficient. One must always take the specification into account.

Another potential problem with a testing strategy based upon selecting path-complete test data is that there are often too many different paths through a program to make that practical. Consider the program fragment in Figure 10.1. There are 2^{100} different paths through this program, as can be seen from the following analysis. The if statement causes either the true or the false branch to be taken, and both of these paths go on to the next iteration of the loop. Thus, for each path entering the ith iteration, there are two paths entering the $(i + 1)$st iteration. Since there is one path entering the first iteration, the number of paths leaving the ith iteration is 2^i. Therefore there are 2^{100} paths leaving the 100th iteration.

Testing each of 2^{100} paths is not likely to be practical. In such cases, we generally settle for an approximation to path-complete test data. The most common approximation is based upon considering two or more iterations through a loop as equivalent and two or more recursive calls to a procedure as equivalent. To derive a set of test data for the program in Figure 10.1, for example, we find a path-complete set of test data for the program

```
    j = k;
    for (int i = 1; i <= 2; i++)
        if (Tests.pred(i*j)) j++;
```

There are only four paths through this program. A path-complete set of test data would have representatives in the following categories:

1. pred(k) and pred(2k+2)

2. pred(k) and ¬pred(2k+2)

3. ¬pred(k) and pred(2k)

4. ¬pred(k) and ¬pred(2k)

To sum up, we always include test cases for each branch of a conditional. However, we approximate path-complete testing for loops and recursion as follows:

- For loops with a fixed amount of iteration, as in the example just shown, we use two iterations. We choose to go through the loop twice rather than once because failing to reinitialize after the first time through a loop is a common programming error. We also make certain to include among our tests all possible ways to terminate the loop.

- For loops with a variable amount of iteration, we include zero, one, and two iterations, and in addition, we include test cases for all possible ways to terminate the loop. For example, consider

```
while (x > 0) {
    // do something
    }
```

With a loop like this, it is possible that no iterations will be performed. This situation should always be handled by the test cases because not executing the loop is another situation that is likely to be a source of program error.

- For recursive procedures, we include test cases that cause the procedure to return without any recursive calls and test cases that cause exactly one recursive call.

This approximation to path-complete testing is, of course, far from fail-safe. Like engineers' induction "One, two, three—that's good enough for me," it frequently uncovers errors but offers no guarantees.

Path-complete tests also need to take exceptions into account: for each statement where an exception *could* be raised, there must be a test for that case. For example, consider the statement:

```
int x = a[0];
```

where a is an array of ints. If this statement occurs in a scope where a might be empty, there should be a test to cover this case.

Sidebar 10.3   Glass-Box Testing

- Glass-box tests take the program text into account.

- Glass-box tests should supplement the black-box tests so that the tests are *path-complete*: every path in the code is exercised by at least one test.

- For loops with a fixed amount of iteration, the tests should include one and two iterations of the loop. For loops with a variable amount of iteration, the tests should include zero, one, and two iterations of the loop.

- For recursion, the tests should include no recursion and one recursive call.

Sidebar 10.3 summarizes glass-box testing.

10.2   Testing Procedures

To illustrate the testing of procedures, we consider a simple procedure for determining whether a string is a palindrome. A palindrome is a string that reads the same backward and forward (an example is ''deed''). Figure 10.2 gives a specification and implementation of this procedure. By looking at the specification, we can see that we need a test for the null argument, plus tests that cause both true and false to be returned. In addition, we must include the empty string and the one-character string as boundary conditions. This might lead to the strings " ", "d", "deed", and "ceed". Examination of the code indicates that we should test the following cases:

1. NullPointerException raised by call on length

2. Not executing the loop

3. Returning false in the first iteration

4. Returning true after the first iteration

5. Returning false in the second iteration

6. Returning true after the second iteration.

Cases 1, 2, 3, 4, and 6 are covered already. For case 5, we might add "aaba". At this point, we should ask ourselves whether we have missed any case, and we might notice that the only test string with an odd number of

Figure 10.2   The palindrome procedure

```
static boolean palindrome (String s) throws NullPointerException {
    // EFFECTS: If s is null throws NullPointerException, else returns
    //    true if s reads the same forward and backward; else returns false.
    //       E.g., "deed" and " " are both palindromes.
    int low = 0;
    int high = s.length( ) -1;
    while (high > low) {
        if (s.charAt(low) != s.charAt(high)) return false;
        low ++;
        high --; }
    return true; }
```

characters has just one character. Therefore, we should add a number of odd-length test strings. Finally, we should arrange the test cases in a sensible order, with the shortest first. Such an arrangement helps in finding errors (see Section 10.9).

10.3   Testing Iterators

Generating test cases for iterators is similar to generating them for procedures. The only point of interest is that iterators have paths in their specifications that are similar to those for loops. In other words, we must be sure to include cases in which the generator returned by the iterator produces exactly one result and produces two results; and if it is possible for the generator to not produce any results, we should include a case for that. For example, consider the following iterator:

```
Iterator getPrimes (int n)
    // EFFECTS: Returns a generator that produces all primes less than
    //    or equal to n (as Integers); if there are no such primes (i.e., n < 2)
    //    the generator produces nothing.
```

Test cases here could include calls with n equal to 1, 2, and 3. Whether more tests are needed can be determined by looking at the iterator's implementation. Here we need to consider all paths through the iterator itself, and also through the generator's constructor and its two methods.

10.4   Testing Data Abstractions

In testing data types, we generate test cases as usual by considering the specifications and implementations of each of the operations. We must now test the operations as a group rather than individually, however, because some operations (the constructors and mutators) produce the objects that are used in testing others. In the `IntSet` operations, for example, the constructor and the `insert` and `remove` methods must be used to generate the arguments for the other operations and for each other. (Part of the specification for `IntSet` is repeated in Figure 10.3.) In addition, the observers are used to test the constructors and mutators; for example, `isIn` and `size` are used to examine the sets produced by `insert` and `remove`.

`RepOk` has a special role in this testing: we should call it after each call of an operation of the data type (both methods and constructors). Of course, it must return true (or we have found a bug): it isn't possible to develop tests that will cause it to return false if the implementation is correct.

We begin by looking at paths in specifications. The specifications of `isIn` and `elements` have obvious paths to explore. For `isIn`, we must generate cases that produce both true and false as results. Because `elements` is an iterator, we must look at least at paths of lengths zero, one, and two. Therefore, we will need `IntSet`s containing zero, one, and two elements. The empty `IntSet` and the one-element `IntSet` also test boundary conditions. Thus, to test the observers, we might start with the following `IntSet`s:

- The empty `IntSet` produced by calling the `IntSet` constructor

- The one-element `IntSet` produced by inserting 3 into the empty set

- The two-element `IntSet` produced by inserting 3 and 4 into the empty set

For each, we would do calls on `isIn`, `size`, and `elements` and check the results. In the case of `isIn`, we would do calls in which the element is in the set and others in which it is not.

We obviously do not yet have enough cases. For example, `remove` is not tested at all, and paths in other specifications also have not yet been discussed. These paths are somewhat hidden in our specifications. For example, the size of an `IntSet` remains the same when we insert an element that is already in the set, and we must therefore look at a case in which we insert the same element twice. Similarly, the size decreases when we remove an element only if it is in

Figure 10.3 Partial specification of the IntSet data abstraction

```
public class IntSet {
    // OVERVIEW: IntSets are mutable, unbounded sets of integers.
    //    A typical IntSet is {x₁, . . . , xₙ}.

    // constructors
    public IntSet ( )
        // EFFECTS: Initializes this to be empty.

    // methods
    public void insert (int x)
        // MODIFIES: this
        // EFFECTS: Adds x to the elements of this, i.e., this_post = this + { x }.

    public void remove (int x)
        // MODIFIES: this
        // EFFECTS: Removes x from this, i.e., this_post = this – x .

    public boolean isIn (int x)
        // EFFECTS: If x is in this returns true else returns false.

    public int size ( )
        // EFFECTS: Returns the cardinality of this.

    public Iterator elements ( )
        // EFFECTS: Returns a generator that produces all the elements of
        //    this (as Integers), each exactly once, in arbitrary order.
        // REQUIRES: this must not be modified while the generator is in use.
}
```

the set, so that we must look at one case in which we remove an element after inserting it and another in which we remove an element that is not in the set. We might use these additional IntSets:

- The set obtained by inserting 3 twice into the empty set

- The set obtained by inserting and then removing 3

- The set obtained by inserting 3 and removing 4

To find these hidden paths, we must look explicitly for paths in the mutators. Thus, insert must work properly whether or not the element being inserted is already in the set, and similarly for remove. This simple approach will produce the three cases just given.

In addition, of course, we must look for paths in the implementations of the operations. The cases identified so far provide quite good coverage for the implementation using the vector with no duplicates (see Figure 10.4). One possible problem is in isIn, which contains a loop (implicitly via its call to getIndex). To cover all paths in this loop, we must test the case of a two-

Figure 10.4   Partial implementation of IntSet

```
public class IntSet {
   private Vector els;  // the rep

   public IntSet ( ) { els = new Vector( ); }

   public void insert (int x) {
      Integer y = new Integer(x);
      if (getIndex(y) < 0) els.add(y); }

   public void remove (int x) {
      int i = getIndex(new Integer(x));
      if (i < 0) return;
      els.set(i, els.lastElement( ));
      els.remove(els.size( ) -1); }

   public boolean isIn (int x) {
      return getIndex(new Integer(x)) >= 0; }

   private int getIndex (Integer x) {
      // EFFECTS: If x is in this returns index where x appears else returns -1.
      for (int i = 0; i < els.size( ); i++)
         if (x.equals(els.get(i))) return i;
      return -1; }

   public int size ( ) { return els.size( ); }
}
```

element vector with either no match or a match with the first or the second element. (It is not possible to find such tests cases by considering only the specification. At the level of the specification, we are concerned only with whether or not the element is in the set; its position in the vector is not of interest.) Similarly, in remove, we must be sure to delete both the first and second elements of the vector.

10.5 Testing Polymorphic Abstractions

Testing polymorphic abstractions is similar to testing their nongeneric counterparts. The only new issue is how many different types of parameters need to be included in the test. Just one type per parameter is sufficient because the polymorphic abstraction is independent of the particular parameter type in use.

When the parameterized abstraction uses an interface to express its requirements about methods of parameters, extra black-box tests will be required to handle incompatible objects. For example, tests of OrderedList (see Figure 8.5) would include the case of adding an element of some type, say String, and then later adding an element of some incomparable type, say Integer.

When the parameterized abstraction uses the related subtype approach, it is sufficient to test with one subtype of the interface that expresses the requirements, together with the related element type. Thus for SumSet (see Figure 8.8), we could test with PolyAdder (see Figure 8.7) and Poly. In addition, we must test calls whose arguments are not objects of the related type; for example, the case of attempting to insert a String in a SumSet that uses a PolyAdder.

10.6 Testing a Type Hierarchy

When there is a type hierarchy, the black-box tests for a subtype must include those for the supertype. The general approach is to test the subtype using the following:

- Black-box tests of its supertype augmented by calls to subtype constructors

- Additional black-box tests for the subtype
- Glass-box tests for the subtype

The black-box supertype tests must be based on calls to subtype constructors so that the tests run for subtype objects. In fact, some supertypes (those defined by interfaces and abstract classes) have no constructors, and their tests are simply templates, where the calls to constructors must be filled in.

For example, there would be three tests for Iterator: for the cases where hasNext returns false immediately, or returns false after the first iteration, or returns false after the second iteration. Each test would check that hasNext returns the expected result, and that next behaves consistently with hasNext. To test a particular subtype, we would create a subtype object as the first part of each test case. Thus, to test a specific iterator, there would be a call that creates an empty generator for the first case, a call that returns a generator that produces just one item for the second case, and a call that returns a generator that produces two items for the third case. Of course, it may not be possible to run all tests for some subtypes. For example, for allPrimes it isn't possible to get hasNext to return false! Therefore, the supertype tests may need to be pruned to remove cases that cannot occur.

In addition, there will be extra black-box tests for the subtype. These will, of course, be based on all the subtype constructors.

There are two sources for these tests. First, there must be tests for any inherited methods whose specifications have changed. If the subtype method has a weaker precondition, its black-box tests will include the cases that are allowed by its precondition but not by the supertype's method's precondition. Similarly, if the subtype method has a stronger postcondition, its tests will need to check the extra cases. For example, the tests for the elements iterator for SortedIntSet (see Figures 7.7 and 7.9) must check that the elements are produced in sorted order. Or, for the generator returned by allPrimes, we would want to check that it really produces primes and does not skip any primes.

Second, there must be tests for the extra methods. Here we are interested in two things: how the extra methods interact with the supertype methods, and the effect of the extra methods. For example, for MaxIntSet (see Figures 7.4 and 7.5) there would be tests to ensure that max does not modify the set and also to check that max returns the proper result.

The subtype will also have its own glass-box tests. But note that it is not necessary to test a subtype using the glass-box tests for its superclass.

When the supertype is defined by a concrete class, it will be tested in the normal way, and when it is defined by an interface, it won't be tested at all (since it has no code). A supertype defined by an abstract class has some code, and therefore it has glass-box tests. We would like to test the abstract class so that we can ignore its glass-box tests later when we test its subclasses. However, the test can only be done by providing a concrete subclass! This subclass might be one that you actually intend to implement, or it might be a "stub"—that is, a very simple implementation of a subclass. The implementation must be complete enough that all tests of the superclass, both black-box and glass-box, can run. For example, to test the abstract `IntSet` class (see Figure 7.8), we need to store the elements. Therefore, it may be best to use a real subclass to drive the testing of the superclass.

Extra checking may be needed when hierarchy is used to provide multiple implementations of a type. If the subtypes are independent of one another, testing is particularly simple since there are no extra methods and the behavior of the inherited methods does not change. But when the subtypes are not independent, we need to either test them jointly or simulate one while testing the other. For example, consider the dense and sparse implementations of `Poly` (see Figures 7.14 and 7.15), and suppose we want to test `DensePoly`. The problem is that various `DensePoly` methods make calls on `SparsePoly` methods. We need to handle those calls somehow. Furthermore, extra black-box tests come up, concerning whether the right choice of representation (sparse or dense) is occurring each time a new `Poly` is created (e.g., in the add method). These are black-box rather than glass-box tests because the criteria for the choice is part of the specification of the subtypes.

Sidebar 10.4 summarizes testing for a type hierarchy.

10.7 Unit and Integration Testing

Testing typically occurs in two phases. During *unit testing*, we attempt to convince ourselves that each individual module functions properly in isolation. During *integration testing*, we attempt to convince ourselves that when all the modules are put together, the entire program functions properly.

Integration testing is generally more difficult than unit testing. First, the intended behavior of an entire program is often much harder to characterize than the intended behavior of its parts. Second, problems of scale tend to arise

Sidebar 10.4   Testing a Hierarchy

- Subtypes must be tested using both the black-box tests of their supertypes and their own black-box tests. Their supertype tests must make use of subtype constructors.

- The additional subtype black-box tests cover the extra methods and any changed behavior for the inherited methods.

- Glass-box tests for superclasses need not be used when testing subclasses.

- Testing an abstract class requires a concrete subclass. The pair is tested using black-box tests for both sub- and supertype, and also glass-box tests for both sub- and superclass.

- Testing a hierarchy that provides multiple implementations for a supertype may require testing the subtypes jointly and adding black-box tests to establish that the proper subtype is chosen for various objects.

in integration testing that do not arise in unit testing; for example, it may take much longer to run a test. Finally, specifications play rather different roles in the two kinds of validation.

The acceptance of the specification as a given is a key factor that distinguishes unit testing from integration testing. During unit testing, when a module fails to meet its specification, we generally conclude that it is incorrect. When validating a whole program, we must accept the fact that the most serious errors are often errors of specification. In these cases, each unit does what it is supposed to, but the program as a whole does not. A prime cause of this kind of problem is ambiguous specifications. When this occurs, a module may perform as expected by those doing its unit testing while failing to meet the expectations of those writing some of the modules that call it. This makes errors detected during integration testing particularly difficult to isolate.

Consider a program implemented by module P, which calls module Q. During unit testing, P and Q are tested individually. (To test either individually, it is necessary to simulate the behavior of the other, as will be discussed in Section 10.8.) When each of them has run correctly on its own test cases, we test them together to see whether they jointly conform to P's specification. In doing this joint test, we use P's test cases. Now suppose that an error is discovered. The following are the possibilities:

- Q is being tested on an input that was not covered in its test cases.

- Q does not behave as was assumed in testing P.

It is tempting when dealing with multiple modules like P and Q to test them jointly rather than to do unit tests for each first. Such joint tests are sometimes a reasonable approach, but unit testing is usually better. For example, to test the program shown in Figure 10.1, we care only that each of the four paths be covered; the various ways in which pred produces its results are not of concern. However, testing pred thoroughly probably involves many test cases. Combining all these test cases has many disadvantages: more tests must be run, tests may take longer to run, and if either of these modules is reimplemented, we shall have to rethink the whole set of test cases. Testing each module individually is more efficient.

10.8   Tools for Testing

It is useful to automate as much of the testing process as possible. We usually cannot automate the generation of test data; generating appropriate inputs for testing a program is a nonalgorithmic process requiring serious thought. Furthermore, to automate the process of deciding what outputs are appropriate for any set of inputs is often as difficult and error prone as writing the program being tested.

What we can automate are the processes of invoking a program with a predefined sequence of inputs and checking the results with a predefined sequence of tests for the acceptability of outputs. A mechanism that does this is called a test *driver*. A driver should call the unit being tested and keep track of how it performs. More specifically, it should

1. Set up the environment needed to call the unit being tested. In some languages, this may involve creating and initializing certain global variables. In most languages, it may involve setting up and perhaps opening some files.

2. Make a series of calls. The arguments for these calls could be read from a file or embedded in the code of the driver. If arguments are read from a file, they should be checked for appropriateness, if possible.

3. Save the results and check their appropriateness.

Figure 10.5   Driver for sqrt

```
// accept as inputs the files:
//   file_of_tests, bad_tests, correct_results, and incorrect_results

for { // each test in file_of_tests
    if (test.square < 0 || test.epsilon < .00001 || test.epsilon > .001) {
        // add test to bad_tests
    }
    else {
        result = Num.sqrt(test.square, test.epsilon);
        if (Num.fabsf(square - result*result) <= epsilon ) {
            // add <test, result> to correct_results
        }
        else {
            // add <test, result> to incorrect_results
        }
    }
}
```

The most common way to check the appropriateness of results is to compare them to a sequence of expected results that has been stored in a file. Sometimes, however, it is better to write a program that compares the results directly to the input. For example, if a program is supposed to find the roots of a polynomial, it is easy enough to write a driver that checks whether or not the values returned are indeed roots. Similarly, it is easy to check the results of sqrt by a computation. A driver for testing an implementation of the sqrt specification given previously is shown in Figure 10.5.

In addition to drivers, testing often involves the use of *stubs*. A driver simulates the parts of the program that call the unit being tested. Stubs simulate the parts of the program called by the unit being tested. A stub must

1. Check the reasonableness of the environment provided by the caller.

2. Check the reasonableness of the arguments passed by the caller.

3. Modify arguments and the environment and return values in such a way that the caller can proceed. It is best if these effects match the specification of the unit the stub is simulating. Unfortunately, this is not always possible.

Sometimes the "right" value can be found only by writing the program the stub is supposed to replace. In such cases we must settle for a "reasonable" value.

(If all communication is only via arguments and results, then it is not necessary to check or modify the environment.)

Drivers are clearly necessary when testing modules before the modules that invoke them have been written. Stubs are necessary when testing modules before the modules that they invoke have been written. Both are needed for unit testing, in which we want to isolate the unit being tested as much as possible from the other parts of the program.

In practice, it is common to implement drivers and stubs that rely on interaction with a person. A very simple implementation of a stub might merely print out the arguments it was called with and ask the person doing the testing to supply the values that should be returned. Similarly, a simple driver might rely on the person doing the testing to verify the correctness of the results returned by the unit being tested. Although drivers and stubs of this nature are easy to implement, they should be avoided whenever possible. They are far more prone to error than automated drivers and stubs, and they make it hard to build up a good database of test data and to reproduce tests.

The reproducibility of tests is particularly important. The following testing scenario is all too typical:

1. The program is tested on inputs 1 through n without uncovering an error.

2. Testing the program on input n + 1 reveals the existence of an error.

3. Debugging leads to a fix that makes the program work on input n + 1.

4. Testing continues at input n + 2.

This is an unwise practice, for there is a non-negligible probability that the change that made the program work on input n + 1 will cause it to fail on some input between 1 and n. Whenever any change is made, no matter how small, it is important to make sure that the program still passes all the tests it used to pass. This is called *regression testing*. Regression testing is practical only when tools are available that make it relatively easy to rerun old tests.

It is important to implement drivers and stubs with care. When an error is detected, we want it to be in the code being tested. If drivers and stubs are implemented carelessly, however, they are at least as likely to contain errors

> **Sidebar 10.5   Unit, Integration, and Regression Testing**
>
> - *Unit testing* tests a single module in isolation of the others. It requires:
>   - A driver that automatically tests the module.
>   - Stubs that simulate the behavior of any modules used by the module.
> - *Integration testing* tests a group of modules together.
> - *Regression testing* is the rerunning of all tests after each error is corrected.

as the program being tested. In this case, the programmer wastes lots of time testing and debugging the testing environment.

Sidebar 10.5 summarizes the different kinds of tests.

10.9   Debugging

Testing tells us that something is wrong with a program, but knowing the symptom is a far cry from knowing its cause. Once we know that a problem exists, the tactics to be used in locating and fixing the problem—in debugging—are extremely important. The variance in the efficiency with which people debug is quite high, and we can offer no magic nostrums to make debugging easy. Most of what we have to say on the subject is simple common sense.

Debugging is the process of understanding and correcting errors. When debugging, we try to narrow the scope of the problem by looking for simple test cases that manifest the bug and by looking at intermediate values to locate the responsible region in the code. As we collect evidence about the bug, we formulate hypotheses and attempt to refute them by running further tests. When we think we understand the cause of the bug, we study the appropriate region of code to find and correct the error.

The word *bug* is in many ways misleading. Bugs do not crawl unbidden into programs. We put them there. *Do not think of your program as "having bugs"; think of yourself as having made a mistake.* Bugs do not breed in programs. If a program contains many bugs, it is because the programmer has made many mistakes.

Always keep in mind that debugging consumes more time than programming. It is worth trying very hard to get your program right the first time. Read your code very carefully and *understand exactly why you expect it to work* before you begin to test it. No matter how hard you try and no matter how clever you are, though, the odds against your program working properly the first time are very long. Consequently, you should *design, write, and document your programs in ways that will make them easier to test and debug.* The key is making sure that you have relatively small modules that can be tested independently of the rest of your program. To a large extent, this can be achieved by following the design paradigms outlined earlier in this book. Introduce data abstractions and associate with each the most restrictive possible rep invariant. Write careful specifications for each procedure, so that when it comes time to test it, you know both what input values it should be prepared to deal with and what it should do in response to each of the possible inputs.

Just as you need an overall testing strategy, you also need a careful plan for every debugging session. *Before beginning, decide exactly what you want to accomplish and how you plan to accomplish it.* Know what input you are going to give your program, and exactly what you expect it to do with that input. If you have not thought carefully about your inputs, you will probably waste a lot of time doing things that are not likely to help isolate the problem.

The so-called scientific method provides a good paradigm for systematic debugging. The following is the crux of the scientific method:

1. Begin by studying already available data.

2. Form a hypothesis that is consistent with those data.

3. Design and run a repeatable experiment that has the potential to refute the hypothesis.

Consider a program that accepts a positive integer as input and is supposed to return true if the number is prime and false otherwise. As our first test case, we try 2; and our program returns the correct answer, true. We next try 3, and the program returns the incorrect result, false. We now have two pieces of data on which to form a hypothesis. One plausible hypothesis is that somehow we have failed to reinitialize something after the first input and that the program will always work on the first input and fail on the second. To check this hypothesis, we can test the program on the same two arguments but reverse the order of the tests; that is, we can try 3 and then 2.

Before running the tests, we decide which results would support our hypothesis and which would refute it:

- Results supporting hypothesis: (true, false)
- Results refuting hypothesis: (false, true), (false, false), (true, true)

When we try the experiment, the program returns false and then true. We immediately reject our first hypothesis and look for another—for example, that the program will fail on all odd primes.

When debugging, a good starting goal is to *find a simple input that causes the problem to occur.* This input may not be the test data that first revealed the existence of the bug. It is often possible to find simpler input that is sufficient to provoke a manifestation of the bug. Thus, a good way to start is to pare down the test data and then run the program on variants of that subset.

For example, suppose we are testing the `palindrome` procedure of Figure 10.2; and when we run it on the famous (allegedly Napoleonic) palindrome "able was I ere I saw elba", it returns false. This is a rather long palindrome, so we should try to find a shorter one on which the program fails. We might begin by taking the middle character of this palindrome and seeing whether the program succeeds in recognizing that the single character "r" is itself a palindrome. If it fails on that, we might hypothesize that the program does not work on palindromes containing an odd number of characters, and we should examine our other tests to see whether they support this hypothesis. If it succeeds in recognizing that "r" is a palindrome, we might try "ere" on the hypothesis that it will fail on odd palindromes containing more than one character. If "ere" fails to provoke the error, we should probably try "I ere I". Suppose the program fails on this input. Two hypotheses come to mind: perhaps the blanks are the root problem, or perhaps it is the uppercase letters. We should now test our program on the shortest inputs that might confirm or refute each hypothesis, for example, " " and "I".

Once we have found a small input that causes the error to occur, we use this information to locate where in the program the bug is likely to be. Finding the kind of input necessary to provoke a symptom is often tantamount to locating a bug. If not, however, the next step is to narrow the scope of the problem by examining intermediate results.

The goal is to rule out parts of the program that cannot be causing the problem and then look in more detail at what is left. We do this by *tracing* the program—that is, running it and looking at the values of variables at specific points in its control flow. If the program consists of several modules, our first goal is to discover which module is the source of the bug. We do this by tracing all calls and returns of procedures. For each call, we ask whether the arguments are what they should be; the arguments should satisfy the requires clause of the called procedure and should also follow from what we have learned in the trace so far. If the arguments are not right, then the error is in the calling module. Otherwise, we ask whether the results of the call follow from the arguments. If not, the error is in the called procedure.

Localizing the problem to a single procedure is often enough, since we can then discover the error by examining the code of the faulty module. Sometimes, however, it is useful to narrow the bug to a subpart of the faulty module. To do this, we continue the trace and examine the values of local variables of the module. The goal is to detect the first manifestation of incorrect behavior. It is particularly important to *check the appropriateness of intermediate results* against values computed prior to beginning the trace. If you wait until you see the intermediate results before thinking about what they should be, you run the risk of being unduly influenced by your (erroneous) program.

Consider the following incorrect implementation of palindrome:

```
static boolean palindrome (String s) throws NullPointerException {
    int low = 0;
    int high = s.length( ) -1;
    while (high > low) {
        if (s.charAt(low) != s.charAt(high)) return false;
        low ++;
        if (high $>$ low + 1) high --; }
    return true; }
```

This implementation does not work properly on odd-length palindromes that have more than one character. Therefore, we might trace it on the string "ere". Suppose we expect that low and high equal the low and high bounds of the string at the end of initialization and that low increases and high decreases in each iteration. At the end of initialization, low $= 0$ and high $= 2$, as expected. However, at the end of the first iteration, we notice that low $= 1$ and high $= 2$, which is not expected. We should be able recognize the error at this point.

If you have access to an excellent debugger, it may be possible to examine intermediate results relatively conveniently—for example, merely by telling the debugger which variables you wish to trace. If you don't have access to a debugger, it is worth your while to *write a considerable amount of code whose only purpose is to help you examine intermediate results.* One piece of code that should be written in either case for each type is a method that displays the objects in abstract form. In other words, having a toString method is always desirable. When debugging polynomials, for example, it is much easier to understand what is happening if a Poly is displayed as the string

```
"3 + x**5"
```

instead of the array

```
[3, 0, 0, 0, 0, 1]
```

Such a method can be called either by a user of an interactive debugger or by a print statement. Also, it is sometimes useful to have the reverse routine that accepts a string corresponding to an abstract form for an object and produces an appropriate object of the type.

In planning debugging sessions, keep in mind that *the bug is probably not where you think it is.* If it were, you would have found it by now. It is all too easy to develop and cling to a fixed idea about the location of a bug. The first obvious manifestation of a bug can occur far from the code where the error lies. If you think that you know which procedure contains the error, and you have spent a significant amount of time examining that procedure, you are probably wrong. Keep an open mind. Examine the reasoning that led you to that procedure, and ask yourself whether there is any possibility that it is flawed.

One way to get a slightly different perspective on the problem is to *ask yourself where the bug is not.* It can be much easier to understand where a bug could not possibly be than where it is. Trying to demonstrate that a bug could not possibly be in a particular place will often lead to the discovery that that is exactly where it is. In any event, the systematic elimination of possibilities is frequently the best way to hone in on a bug.

While trying to eliminate possible locations for a bug, *take a careful look at your input* as well as at your code. Every programmer has spent time hunting for a bug in a program when in fact the problem is in the input. As mentioned, you should write your drivers and stubs carefully so as to avoid as many such errors as possible.

Looking carefully at the input is a good example of the more general principle: *Try the simple things first.* Most errors are not particularly subtle. Simple errors that occur frequently include the following:

- Reversing the order of input arguments

- Looping through an array, `String`, or `Vector` one index too far

- Failing to reinitialize a variable the second time through a program segment

- Copying only the top level of a data structure when you intended to copy all levels

- Failing to parenthesize an expression correctly

Remember that in designing your program you went through a reasoning process not unlike that involved in debugging it. The existence of a bug is evidence that your initial reasoning was flawed. It is easy to convince yourself that a procedure does not contain a bug by using the same reasoning that led you to introduce the bug in the first place. It can therefore be invaluable to *get somebody else to help you*. Asking for help is not an admission of failure; it is merely good practice. Try to explain your problem to somebody else. The mere attempt to articulate your reasoning will often lead you to discover the source of the problem. Failing that, a fresh viewpoint is almost certain to prevent you from getting stuck in too deep a rut. In fact, explaining why your program works is such a good way to eliminate errors that it is often worthwhile to do this *before* you run any tests at all!

One of the hardest problems in debugging is *deciding what to take for granted*. The naive thing to say is that one should take nothing for granted, but this is generally counterproductive. When a test yields a faulty result, the problem might lie in one of the modules the program calls, the compiler used to compile the program, the operating system, the hardware, the electrical system of the building housing the hardware, and so on. The most likely location, however, is your program. Begin by taking everything else for granted and looking for a bug in the program. If after a reasonable amount of effort you fail to find any problem with your program, start worrying about the modules your program calls. If after a reasonable amount of effort you can find no problem there, find out whether or not the compiler or operating system has been changed recently. If not, you should be very reluctant to attribute your problems to either of them.

When you encounter a bug that you just cannot track down, *make sure that you have the right source code*. In putting together large systems, you will almost always have to rely on separate compilation facilities. This can easily lead to a situation in which the object code exhibiting the bug does not match the source in which you are trying to find the bug. A particularly vexing variant of this problem can occur when either the compiler or the operating system is changed. When your program's behavior has changed and you are absolutely sure that you have not changed anything, make sure that you are not using code that has been compiled to run on a different version of the operating system.

When you have tried everything you can think of and still have not found the bug, *go away*. The goal of any programming project is to complete the program (including its documentation and testing) expeditiously. The goal is not to find a particular bug as soon as possible. The obsessive pursuit of a particular bug is almost always counterproductive. If you spend too long looking for the same bug, there is a high probability that you will become stuck in a rut. If you try to debug when you are overly tired, you will, at best, work inefficiently. At worst, you will make mistakes, such as making ill-considered changes to the program or accidentally deleting a crucial file.

When you do find a bug, *try to understand why you put it there*. Was it a clerical error, does it reflect a lack of understanding of the programming language, or is it indicative of some logical problem? Knowing why you inserted a bug may help you understand how to fix your program. It may also help you to discover other bugs and even to avoid bugs in the future.

Finally, when you think that you have found a bug and that you know how it got there, *do not be in too much of a rush to fix "the bug."* Make sure that the bug you found could indeed have caused the symptoms that you observed. If you have already spent a lot of time observing the behavior of your program, it may be counterproductive to change that behavior before you have completed your detective work. Not only is it often easier to repair many bugs at once than to repair many bugs one at a time, but it almost always leads to a cleaner and more efficient program.

When you do decide to make a change, *think through all of its ramifications*. Convince yourself that the change really will both cure the problem and not introduce new problems. The hardest bugs to find are often those we insert while fixing other bugs. This is because we are often not as systematic in designing these "patches" as in our original designs. We try to make local changes, when a more global approach might well be called for. It is often more efficient to reimplement a small procedure than to patch an old one.

10.10   Defensive Programming

In preparing to cope with mistakes, it pays to program defensively. In every good programmer is a streak of suspicion. Assume that your program will be called with incorrect inputs, that files that are supposed to be open may be closed, that files that are supposed to be closed may be open, and so forth. Write your program in a way designed to call these mistakes to your attention as soon as possible. Java provides help here via its compile-time type checking and other compiler warnings, by the bounds checking provided for arrays and strings, and by its exception mechanism.

Two standard defensive programming methods not built into any programming language are checking requirements and rep invariants, and exhaustive testing of all conditionals. The violation of a rep invariant or a procedure's requirements is often the first manifestation of a bug. If code to check these explicitly is not included, the first observable symptom of the bug may occur quite far from the place where the mistake actually occurred.

We make it easy to check the rep invariant by including the repOk method in every type. This method can be used to test the rep invariant at the beginning of each operation and before returning if this is new or has been modified. The checks can be put in your test driver or in the type's operations. The latter is particularly robust, but you may need to disable the checks when in production to improve performance. If you do disable the checks, don't remove them from your code; instead, leave them in (e.g., as a comment) so that you can easily reactivate them later if necessary.

As an example of requirements violation, consider a procedure with the specification

```
static boolean inRange (int[ ] a, int x, int y, int e)
        throws NullPointerException
// REQUIRES: x <= y
// EFFECTS: If a is null throws NullPointerException else
//     returns true if e is an element of a[x],...,a[y].
```

Suppose that a caller of this procedure reverses the order of the second and third arguments. inRange will probably return false whether or not e is in a. The first observable symptom of this incorrect call might appear arbitrarily far from the call. In the worst case, the error would never be detected, and the program in which inRange occurs would simply return an incorrect answer. However, if inRange checks the requirement and signals an exception (in particular, FailureException) if it isn't satisfied, the error can usually be found immediately.

Failure to perform exhaustive testing in conditionals can have a similar effect. For example, suppose the receive procedure delivers a string that has been sent over a communications network in a message and that, for this particular call, only the values "deliver" and "examine" are meaningful. The implementation

```
s = Comm.receive( );
if (s.equals("deliver")) { // carry out the deliver request }
    else if (s.equals("examine")) { // carry out the examine request }
    else { // handle error case }
```

is far superior to the marginally more efficient implementation

```
s = Comm.receive( );
if (s.equals("deliver")) { // carry out the deliver request }
    else { // carry out the examine request }
```

Defensive programming generally involves a certain amount of extra overhead—both for the programmer and at runtime. Most of the time, the programming overhead is not an issue, since defensive programming almost always reduces the total amount of programmer time over the course of a programming project. The runtime overhead cannot be dismissed so easily. For programs in which performance is an issue, some defensive programming methods can be prohibitively expensive. If, for example, the hardware does not detect arithmetic overflow, detecting it in software can more than double the cost of doing arithmetic. On a more abstract level, a binary search procedure can hardly afford to check that every array given to it is indeed sorted.

When it seems that defensive programming will be prohibitively expensive in a production version of a program, we should still give serious thought to putting the checks in while the program is under development. Disabling error detection code just before a program is put into production use is much easier than inserting it during debugging. Disabling a program's defenses, however, should not be done as a matter of course. If at all possible, these defenses should be left in the production version. It is almost certain that when the program first goes into production use, it will still contain some bugs and that other bugs will be introduced as it is modified. It is important that these bugs be detected and repaired as expeditiously as possible. The actual economic cost of an undiscovered error in a program may exceed the cost of keeping the checks in during production runs. It is usually worthwhile to retain at least the inexpensive checks.

10.11   Summary

This chapter has discussed the related issues of testing and debugging. Testing is a method of validating a program's correctness. We have described a way to develop test cases methodically by examining both a module's specification and its implementation. The test cases should then be run by a driver that checks the results of each case; the driver either produces the inputs or reads them from a file, and either checks the results by computations or compares them to outputs in a file. If the test being run is a unit test, then lower-level modules are replaced by stubs that simulate their effects. Later, during integration testing, the stubs are replaced by the implementation.

Testing can exhibit the presence of a bug. Debugging is the process of understanding and correcting the cause of the bug. In debugging, we try to narrow the scope of the problem by searching for simple test cases that manifest the bug and by looking at intermediate values to locate the responsible region in the code. As we collect evidence about the bug, we formulate hypotheses and attempt to refute them by running further tests. When we think we understand the cause of the bug, we study the responsible region of code to find and correct the error.

Debugging can be made easier if we practice defensive programming, which consists of inserting checks in the program to detect errors that are likely to occur. In particular, we should check that the requires clause is satisfied. It is also a good idea to check the rep invariant. These checks should be retained in the production code if possible.

The outcome of being methodical about testing, debugging, and defensive programming is a reduction of programmer effort. This work pays off not only when the program is written, but also later when it is modified.

Sidebar 10.6 summarizes the preceding discussion about testing and debugging.

> ## Sidebar 10.6   Testing, Debugging, and Defensive Programming
>
> - *Testing* is a way of validating a program's correctness.
>
> - *Debugging* is the process of finding and removing bugs.
>
> - *Defensive programming* consists of inserting checks to detect errors within the program. It makes debugging much easier.

Exercises

10.1   Develop a set of test cases for partition using the specification and implementation given in Figure 3.6. Do the same thing for quickSort and sort. Write a driver for partition. Run the tests.

10.2   Develop a set of test cases and write a driver for permutations (see Exercise 7 in Chapter 6).

10.3   Implement an iterator that yields all Fibonacci numbers. (A Fibonacci number is the sum of the preceding two Fibonacci numbers, and the first Fibonacci number is 0. For example, the first seven Fibonacci numbers are 0, 1, 1, 2, 3, 5, and 8.) Define test cases in advance of debugging. Then debug your program and report on how successful your tests were.

10.4   Develop a set of test cases for Poly (see Figures 5.4 and 5.7). Write a driver for Poly and run the tests.

10.5   Develop a set of test cases for OrderedIntList (see Figures 6.10, 6.11, and 6.12). Write a driver and run the tests.

10.6   Suppose IntSets were implemented using OrderedIntLists (see Figures 6.10, 6.11, and 6.12). Discuss what kind of stub you would use for ordered lists in testing your implementation of IntSet.

10.7   Develop the test cases needed for MaxIntSet (see Figures 7.4 and 7.5), starting with the test cases for IntSet (see Section 10.4). Write the driver and run the tests.

10.8   Consider the abstract IntList class shown in Figures 7.11 and 7.12. Develop the black-box and glass-box tests for this class. Then develop a testing strategy including selection of the subclass (or subclasses) that will be used in the tests. Develop a driver for the pair of classes and run the tests.

10.9 Consider the abstract `Poly` class shown in Figure 7.14. Develop a strategy for testing this class including selection of the subclass that will be used in the tests. Write a driver for `Poly` and this subclass and run the tests.

10.10 Develop test cases for `Adder` (see Figure 8.6). Then develop test cases for `PolyAdder` (see Figure 8.7). Write a driver for `PolyAdder` and run the tests.

10.11 Develop test cases for `SumSet` (see Figure 8.8). Note that this includes deciding what parameter types to use in the test. Write the driver for `SumSet` and run the tests.

10.12 Develop an error profile for yourself. Keep a log in which you record errors in your programs. For each error, record the reason for it and look for patterns.

Requirements Analysis

11

So far we have concentrated on the specification, implementation, and validation of program modules. These individual modules form the components of programs, the building blocks out of which programs are constructed. The remainder of the book deals with issues related to programs as a whole and with the process of program development.

This chapter begins by describing the software life cycle: the activities that occur during the lifetime of a software project. Then it discusses the requirements phase in which a description of the product being produced is developed. It gives an overview of the issues that must be addressed during this phase and illustrates the ideas by means of a short example. The topics covered are complicated. Our discussion of them is abbreviated, oversimplified, and intended to serve only as an introduction.

11.1 The Software Life Cycle

Program development is usually broken up into a number of phases: requirements analysis, design, implementation and testing, acceptance testing, production, and modification and maintenance. The process typically begins with someone we shall call the *customer* who wants a program to provide a particular service. Sometimes the service is well understood and described a priori in a complete and precise manner, but this is quite rare. More often customers do not fully understand what they want the program to do. Even if the desired service is well understood, it is probably not described precisely enough to serve as a basis for constructing a program. The purpose of the requirements analysis phase is to analyze the needs of the customer and produce a document describing a program that will meet those needs. This process will require communication with the customer to make sure the needs are understood.

The document that results from requirements analysis is the input to the design phase. In this phase, a modular decomposition of a program satisfying the specification is developed. In the next phase, the individual modules are implemented and then tested to ensure that they perform as intended. As discussed in Chapter 10, we use two kinds of tests: unit tests, in which individual modules are tested in isolation, and integration tests, in which modules are tested in combination.

At best, integration testing shows that the modules together satisfy the implementor's interpretation of the specification. The implementor may have misinterpreted the specification or neglected to test some portion of the program's behavior, though, and the customer therefore needs some other basis for deciding whether or not the program does what it is supposed to do. This typically takes the form of *acceptance tests*. Acceptance tests provide an evaluation of the program behavior that is independent of the design, and they are generally performed by an organization other than the one that worked on the design and implementation. They should include both trial runs under conditions approximating those the customer will actually encounter and tests derived directly from the requirements specification.

When the program has passed the acceptance tests, it enters the production phase and becomes a product that the customer can use. The useful life of the program occurs during this phase, but the program is unlikely to remain unchanged even here. First, it almost certainly harbors undetected errors that must be corrected during production. Correcting such errors is called *program maintenance*. Second, the customer's requirements are likely to change. Responding to such changes requires *program modification*.

Figure 11.1a illustrates the *waterfall model*, an idealized form of the software development process previously described, in which each phase is completed before work starts on the next phase. The waterfall model is neither realistic nor practical: the software development process is unlikely to proceed sequentially through the phases. There are two reasons for this. First, some work can be done in parallel. For example, even before requirements analysis

Figure 11.1 Life cycle models

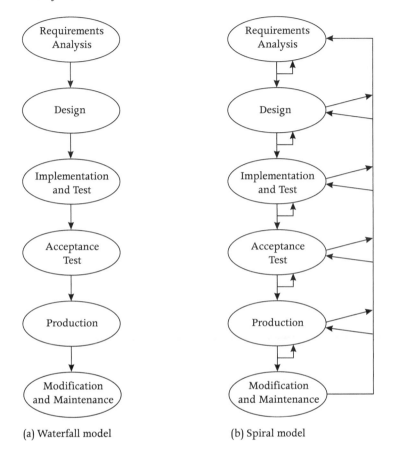

(a) Waterfall model   (b) Spiral model

is complete, certain features of the product may be well enough understood that it makes sense to begin the design for that part. A similar situation occurs during design: a portion of the design may be complete enough that implementation work can begin for that part, even though the entire design is not yet finished. However, it is important to work on the phases roughly in order. For example, it isn't a good idea to expend lots of effort implementing modules before the design is firm enough to ensure those modules are needed.

The second reason that development isn't entirely sequential is errors, which may make it necessary to go back to an earlier stage of the process. During design, we often uncover problems with the requirements specification. When this happens, it is necessary to redo part of the requirements analysis. Similarly, if a problem with the design is found during implementation, the relevant parts of the system must be redesigned. Therefore, iteration through these phases is inevitable. Figure 11.1b illustrates the more realistic *spiral model*. In this model, phases can start before their predecessor phase is complete, and the process includes many feedback loops.

Errors are a problem throughout the entire development process. The earlier the phase in which an error occurs, the more wasted effort results, unless the error is caught quickly. For example, an error made in the requirements analysis can lead to a totally useless program, since it is not the program the customer wants. If this is not discovered until the acceptance tests, an enormous amount of design and implementation may have to be redone. An error made during design can result in the implementation of unusable modules and failure to create needed modules. By contrast, an error made in implementing a single module affects only that module and can be corrected simply by reimplementing it.

The earlier an error is detected, the less serious its consequences. If an error in the requirements analysis is caught during that phase, it may be necessary to rethink parts of the requirements specification but not to discard design work. Similarly, if an error in design is caught before implementation begins, it may be necessary to rethink a number of design decisions but not to discard work done in implementing and testing unneeded modules.

Clearly, it is important to make use of error-detection methods and techniques during requirements analysis and design, and not just during implementation. But how can this be done? Program verification can ensure that a program meets its specification, but it is not generally practical today, and even if it were, it would still find errors much too late in the program development process. As was just noted, the errors made in the early phases matter most, and it is important to find these errors quickly to minimize wasted effort.

One way to uncover errors in requirements is to build a prototype of the system. The customer can use the prototype and then provide feedback on its suitability and acceptability, so that when the product is delivered, it is more likely to be what the customer wants. For this approach to be practical, however, the prototype needs to be built quickly. Fast prototyping can work well for simple systems, since the prototype can be produced without much effort. But for more complex systems, building a prototype is difficult, and in the end, its implementation can be too valuable to throw away. This can be unfortunate since the prototype may be a poor basis for the real implementation, and reusing prototype code in the implementation can lead to a system that isn't very robust. One technique that can sometimes work is to produce a very simple prototype that contains only a small subset of the desired features. Throwing away a small prototype might be acceptable, and if the subset is well chosen, the prototype can provide substantial insight into the real product requirements.

Another way to catch errors in early phases is to document all decisions explicitly and then carefully review the decisions; we will discuss such an approach in Chapter 14. While better than nothing, however, these methods are far from adequate. Identification and invention of better methods is an important area for research in programming methodology.

11.2 Requirements Analysis Overview

Recall that a program is developed to satisfy the needs of a customer. The customer might be someone outside of the organization that will develop the program, or it might be someone on the inside. Products are frequently developed in expectation of customers before any actual customer exists. In this case, some group in the development organization needs to act as a kind of "model" of the customer, whose needs are identified through market analysis.

The original product description produced by a customer is unlikely to be either complete or precise. The purpose of requirements analysis is to analyze the customer's needs so that we can identify and carefully describe the customer's requirements. This analysis must involve consultation, since the customer is the ultimate judge of what is wanted.

A good way to get started on requirements analysis is to examine how the customer does things at present. Almost always a product is intended to replace an existing system, possibly noncomputerized, or consisting of some combination of programs and external processes, or even a program in which the performance was not satisfactory. The current system will contain methods for normal processing and for coping with errors and a variety of contingencies. It can be a source of ideas not only about how to do things, but about what needs to be done. Additionally, the product must be compatible with other systems already in use. Studying the environment in which the new product will be used can help ensure that it will fit in smoothly. For example, studying the customer's organization will help insure that the program will fit well into that organization and will be compatible with current practices.

Requirements analysis must consider both normal situations and errors. Studying normal case behavior means defining the effect of all nonerroneous user interactions with a program under the assumption that the program is in a normal state. Normal case behavior is often the easiest part of the problem, so that focusing on it is a good way to get started.

Cases with no errors represent only a small part of program behavior, however, and it is essential to consider and describe how a program behaves in the presence of errors. This part of the analysis should never be neglected or underemphasized. The analyst must try to uncover all possible errors that might occur and develop the appropriate responses for each case. Errors come from two sources: users interacting with the program, and hardware and software malfunctions.

A good approach to studying both normal case behavior and behavior in the presence of user errors is to work out *scenarios* (see Sidebar 11.1). A scenario is step-by-step walk-through of an interaction with the system, consisting of use/response pairs: the user or environment requests some action, leading to a particular response by the system. We shall give an example of the use of scenarios in Section 11.3.

You can begin with scenarios that capture typical interactions with the system in the absence of errors: both the user and the system are functioning correctly. Next you can use scenarios to study user errors; scenarios are useful here since they can pinpoint the ways in which these errors might be made. Proper interface design can sometimes prevent user errors—for example, by presenting an interactive user with a menu containing only legal commands. Another possibility is for the system to recognize erroneous input and reject it. Of course, it is not possible to avoid all errors. For example, if a bank clerk

Sidebar 11.1   Scenarios

- A scenario is a step-by-step walk-through of an interaction with the system, assuming the system itself is functioning properly.

- A good place to start is to focus on what the user does during a session, assuming the user does not make errors.

- Then, you can consider additional scenarios that cover user errors.

makes an error entering an account holder's deposit, it might not be noticed until the account holder examines a monthly statement. The analyst must identify all such situations and decide what should be done to handle them. Often these decisions require consultation with the customer since business policy is involved, and the solution may require actions outside the program (for example, consider the question of how to compensate an account holder whose check has bounced because of a bank error).

The use of scenarios focuses attention on how the system responds to the user when the system itself is working properly. But the system may not be working properly, and the requirements analysis needs to examine the possibilities here as well. In this situation, scenarios are no longer so useful; instead, you need to enumerate possibilities.

As far as software errors are concerned, the analyst must decide how much effort should be expended to detect and cope with such errors. For example, if it is important to limit the scope of software errors, the output of critical modules can be checked for reasonableness, and the system shut down if the checks fail; the shutdown might simply terminate processing until the problem is fixed, or it might be followed by a restart in a clean state, which is often sufficient for continued service. If this approach is taken, it is important to log information about failures so that information about the errors that led to them is not lost.

The analyst must also decide what to do about hardware failures. It may be important for a system to be *highly available*; that is, it should be highly likely that the system is up and running all the time (or at certain times). Satisfying such a requirement may involve the use of redundant hardware and software. A related requirement is that the system be *highly reliable*. Here we are concerned with avoiding loss of information because of failures. Determining how ambitious the system must be in trying to recover from hardware and software malfunctions is an important aspect of requirements analysis.

In addition to functional requirements, a program must satisfy performance requirements. These requirements should be considered as the functional requirements are developed, and also on their own, just to double-check that nothing has been forgotten. Time and space efficiency should be considered together since it is often necessary to trade one off against the other. The first thing to do is to find out whether or not there is a hard limit in either dimension. For example, the program might have to run on a micro-computer with limited memory. Alternatively, it might have to satisfy some real-time constraint (for example, computing the current altitude of a plane every tenth of a second). In considering time efficiency, it is important to distinguish between *throughput* and *response time*. Throughput refers to the amount of data processed by a system over an interval of time. Response time refers to the amount of time between interactions with the system. Optimizing one of these characteristics often has a deleterious effect on the other. A communications network, for example, might maximize throughput at the cost of response time by batching messages.

The customer's space and time requirements must be checked for compatibility with the functional requirements, the hardware the customer intends to use, and the price the customer is willing to pay for the system. For example, the customer may want some activity to satisfy performance requirements that are either not possible given the hardware or can be satisfied only with very sophisticated software. If an incompatibility is discovered, negotiations may be necessary to produce new requirements.

These issues affect the content of the requirements specification directly. A number of other issues should be considered during requirements analysis, not because they affect the specification, but because they provide useful input for the designers. Two such issues are *modifiability* and *reusability*. There will usually be areas with fixed requirements, and others in which changes are likely. Information about likely changes is useful because a design can be shaped in such a way as to make certain changes easy. This information can sometimes be obtained by careful study of earlier systems designed to do a similar job. Changes are likely in places where those systems differ from the current one. The specified system might also be intended to be the first of many systems that will be similar but will differ in details. Or the specified system might contain only a subset of features that are intended to be provided in later systems. The job of building the additional systems can be simplified if all or part of the software produced for the first system is designed to be reusable. If the designers know what the similarities are, they can shape the design to accommodate them. An outstanding example of this is the isolation of target-machine dependencies in a compiler, which allows the compiler to be mostly independent of the machine for which it is producing code, so that it can be retargeted to another machine with minimal effort.

Pinning down constraints on the delivery schedule is another important part of requirements analysis. Knowing that the customer is in a hurry, for example, may encourage the designer of the software to trade noncritical features for simplicity. Knowing that a program providing a proper subset of the functionality of the entire system should be available early would have an impact on the implementation schedule as well as on the design.

Sidebar 11.2 summarizes the issues that must be considered during requirements analysis.

The result of the requirements phase is a requirements document (see Sidebar 11.3). This document contains the requirements specification, which describes the program behavior, including its behavior in the presence of errors. In addition, the document should explain the performance requirements, the decisions made during analysis, and if it can be done with a reasonable amount of effort, the alternatives that were rejected (and why they were rejected). The latter information is useful when requirements must be rethought because of errors or changing customer needs.

The requirements document can be the input to two activities in addition to the design. It can be used to produce acceptance tests and as a basis for a system user's manual. The user's manual is something that must be produced anyway, but its production can provide an independent check on the suitability of the specification. If the system is hard to use, this may be evident when the manual is written. Also, by reading the manual, the customer may notice deficiencies in the specification that were overlooked earlier.

Sidebar 11.2   Goals of Requirements Analysis

- Identify the *functional requirements*:
  - How a correctly functioning program responds to both correct and incorrect user interactions
  - How the program responds to both hardware and software errors
- Identify the *performance requirements*: how fast certain actions must be, and any constraints on the amount of primary and secondary storage that can be used.
- Identify potential modifications: changes or extensions to the product that are likely in the future.
- Pin down the delivery schedule.

Sidebar 11.3   The Requirements Document

The requirements document contains:

- The requirements specification, which describes the functional requirements

- A description of the performance requirements, potential modifications, and scheduling constraints

- A discussion of alternatives that were considered and a rationale for decisions

---

11.3   The Stock Tracker

To illustrate this discussion, we now investigate an example, a program called StockTracker that keeps track of a user's investments. The program is required to store information about all stocks owned by a user, including the amount owned and other information that the user may want to record, such as the date and price when purchased. In addition, the program needs to be able to find out the current price of any stock in the portfolio and to compute the current value of the user's investments. To simplify the example, we will assume that only stocks are tracked but not, for example, mutual funds.

To gain an understanding of what this program should do, we begin by considering the normal case behavior. A good way to do so is to sketch a sample session; this session will be one of our scenarios. Trying to sketch the scenario points out the first major decision: what style of interaction will the program provide? In general, there are two ways of interacting with a program: the user either waits for the program to demand information or offers it spontaneously—for example, as arguments when the program is called. Deciding between the two choices is something that must be done in consultation with the customer. Let's assume the customer decides that the program will request responses from the user. In other words, it is an interactive program that allows the user to examine information about many stocks in a single session.

Now we can develop the scenario. Clearly, the user must start by invoking the program. How this is done depends upon the computing environment in which the stock tracker is to run. The details of the syntax to be used are not of concern at this point. What does matter, however, is whether the user must supply any arguments. In particular, the stock tracker needs access to information about stocks that has already been created on the user's behalf in earlier sessions; how does it find this information? It might receive it as an argument (e.g., names of one or more files); it might ask the user for the information via the user interface; or it might "know where to look." Any of these choices is a viable option. The third choice seems best, however, since it avoids errors due to the user mistyping a filename. Therefore, we make the third choice (after consulting the customer).

Once the program has obtained the information from the previous session, it is ready to accept user commands. There are two basic kinds of commands: ones used to examine the stored information, and ones used to add new information.

Presumably, when a user wishes to examine stored information, he or she is interested in looking at a single investment or perhaps a group of related investments. In the latter case, how would a user indicate that a group of investments is related? It seems unlikely that any decision the system might make here will match the needs of an arbitrary user and, therefore, a way for users to group investments should be provided. Grouping could be done by allowing users to define separate *portfolios*, each containing a group of investments that are related as far as the user is concerned. An alternative might be for users to associate keywords with investments, which would allow the user to examine all investments marked with a particular keyword. Either of these choices is plausible, but providing separate portfolios is simpler (it effectively provides one keyword per investment) and easier for users to manage, and it seems adequate for this application. Therefore, let's choose the separate portfolio approach. A portfolio contains *positions*, each of which provides information about a particular stock.

At this point, it is helpful to list the commands and consider them one-by-one. Here are some of them:

- Identify a particular portfolio for further examination.
- Browse the information in the identified portfolio.
- Create a portfolio or delete one.
- Add or remove a position from the open portfolio.

The first command requires a way to name portfolios. These names can be alphanumeric strings, since such strings are easy for users to enter (or to show to users in a menu). The user can use a name to identify a portfolio of interest; we will refer to this portfolio as the *open* portfolio.

To carry out the second command requires deciding how information about a portfolio's contents is presented to the user. One possibility is to present all of it; a second is to highlight the contents by indicating what stocks are in the portfolio, and then allow the user to indicate where more information is desired. The latter approach seems better since it allows the user to get a general sense of what is in the portfolio. Let's assume that the customer chooses this approach, which implies that we need a way to identify the stocks. An obvious way to identify them is to use the name of the stock: we can use its "ticker" name, the name used by the stock market. However, this approach is possible only if a portfolio can contain at most one entry for a specific stock; let's assume this is true. Thus, the program informs the user of the stocks in the open portfolio, and the user can indicate a stock of interest. Let's refer to this stock as the *current* position.

We also need to decide what other information (besides the name of its stock) is maintained in each position. We need to know the number of shares being held for that stock. In addition, the user might want to store notes about the stock (e.g., the date and price when the stock was purchased), but let's assume that at present the customer does not want to store such notes.

The customer does want the system to provide stock price information, however. This requirement brings up the question of how price information is obtained and how often it is refreshed. One possibility is to have the user enter the information, but this is error prone and inconvenient. Instead, it would be better to obtain price information automatically. Suppose that in investigating this requirement, we discover that such quotes can be obtained by getting in touch with a particular Web server. Therefore, we decide to obtain the information by communicating with this server; each communication will give us the price of a single stock.

However, remote communication has a cost, and it seems reasonable to retain price information that isn't too old. Therefore, we will allow the user to indicate when he or she wants information to be refreshed. This can be done for a single stock (the "current" stock in the current portfolio) or for all stocks in the current portfolio. An implication of this approach is that price information is not necessarily very current; to convey this information to the user, it seems appropriate to associate price information with the time at which that information was obtained.

Now let's consider the remaining commands. We need to be able to record the buying or selling of some stock within a portfolio. This could cause an entry to be added to the portfolio or removed from the portfolio. Or it could simply change the number of shares for some stock in the portfolio; this kind of change probably should be limited to affect just the current position. We also need to create and delete portfolios. Creating a portfolio could make the new portfolio be the open one; this seems reasonable since the user most likely will immediately want to put some stocks into the new portfolio. Similarly, deleting the open portfolio makes sense since the user probably has been working on that portfolio (e.g., moving its positions to other portfolios).

Finally, let's consider what happens when the user terminates the current session. At that point, we must store the portfolios back into the file if they contain any modified information that has not already been written to disk.

Now that we have finished looking at how the program behaves in the normal case in which the user makes nonerroneous requests and the program is behaving properly, the next step is to consider user errors. To do so, we simply continue with our scenario, but now we include user commands that are wrong for some reason. The user might make a number of errors. For example, the user might type the wrong ticker name when inserting or deleting a stock or might enter the wrong number of shares. As another example, the user might ask to delete a portfolio that contains investments.

The system can reduce the potential for errors in several ways. First, it can check whether the arguments are correct. For example, when the user adds a new stock to a portfolio, the program could determine whether a ticker name is legitimate, consulting with the Web server if the name is one that it doesn't already know. However, not all incorrect arguments can be recognized; for example, as long as the number of shares being bought is plausible (e.g., positive), the program can't recognize whether the number is correct. Second, the system can refuse to carry out potentially erroneous requests (such as deleting a nonempty portfolio). Third, it can double-check with the user before carrying out a request. Fourth, it might allow changes to be undone after the fact.

To decide how to respond to user errors, we must prepare a list of options and consult with the customer. For this version of the program, let's assume the customer has decided that the program should check for obvious errors (such as a nonexistent ticker name) and should disallow deletion of nonempty portfolios. To help in emptying a portfolio, the user needs a way to move a position from one portfolio to another.

We also need to consider problems due to system malfunctions. It would be unfortunate if the modifications in today's session were lost in a computer crash. This loss can be avoided if each modification is recorded on disk immediately (assuming that disk crashes are rare and that a computer crash doesn't cause a disk crash). Or the loss can be limited if the user has the ability to cause writing to disk while the session is active. Either of these options is plausible, but writing immediately (after the user has approved the change) is safer; and in an interactive system, the cost of writing to disk at this point is not an issue. We might want to be even more fault-tolerant—for example, writing the information to a second disk just in case there is a media failure. Here is another question to ask the customer. Let's assume that writing to one disk right after each change is what is wanted.

One point to note about the preceding analysis is that we have been considering performance as we go along. For example, we explicitly decided that logging information to disk immediately is acceptable. And we decided that since communication with the Web server is costly, we would do so on user request only.

To finish the requirements analysis, we need to think about ways in which the requirements are likely to change in the future. Viable alternatives that were rejected are potential changes, but we need to look for other changes as well. Here are some potential changes:

- Providing an undo facility. For example, we could maintain a log of user updates and provide a way to display the log and to undo the change recorded in a particular log entry.

- Allowing the use of additional Web servers to look up prices. The difficulty here is that different Web servers may expect different communication formats. The advantage, of course, is that if one server is down (or ceases service) another can be used.

- Allowing users to indicate buy and sell levels for various stocks; the system would alert the user if the current price exceeded the level indicated.

- Extending the system to allow handling of mutual funds.

- Allowing the user to specialize the system in various ways (e.g., to indicate a preferred Web server).

- Extending the system so that users can actually purchase and sell stock through it.

11.4   Summary

We began this chapter with a description of the software life cycle. While conceding that it is indeed a cycle, and that it is desirable to start later phases before earlier ones are complete, we emphasized the importance of doing a careful requirements analysis of some part of the program before starting design for that part and a careful design of some portion of the implementation before starting that implementation work.

The bulk of the chapter was devoted to a discussion of requirements analysis. We usually start requirements analysis with an incomplete understanding of what the customer really wants. The goal of analysis is to deepen our understanding so that we end up with a product that matches the customer's needs. Customers should be consulted during analysis because they are the ultimate judges of what is required.

A number of issues must be considered during requirements analysis:

- The program's behavior must be defined for both correct and incorrect inputs.

- Issues related to hardware and software errors, such as availability and reliability constraints, must be explored.

- Constraints on time and space efficiency must be pinned down. Performance is not an add-on feature. It must be designed in from the start.

- Scheduling constraints must be addressed. The customer's desired delivery schedule for the software or part of the software may well have an impact on the design and implementation.

- It is useful to try to identify those parts of the requirements that are most likely to change.

- It is useful to know whether the system being specified is the first of a number of similar systems, so that it can be designed in a way that will allow components to be reused.

We suggested the use of sample sessions or scenarios to drive the analysis. Scenarios are useful because they provide a way to methodically walk through how the system behaves, considering first the case of no errors and then the case of user errors. Finally, we considered system errors; here we don't use scenarios, but rather make up a list of possibilities. We illustrated our approach by a simple example, the stock tracker. In addition to determining system behavior, we also considered its performance and identified potential modifications.

The requirements analysis process is a difficult one. Our discussion was far from thorough. Involving customers in a productive way is perhaps the most difficult and critical aspect of requirements analysis. It involves many issues that are beyond the scope of this book.

The outcome of requirements analysis is a description of the product to be built. However, the description we ended up with in this chapter was very vague, much too vague to be confident that designers could understand what to do. What we need now is a more precise description. The next chapter describes how to provide requirements specifications.

Exercises

11.1 Program xref produces an index for a document: For each word containing more than one letter, it lists the word followed by the lines in which it appeared, for example,

```
compiler 3, 17, 25, ...
```

Carry out a requirements analysis for this program and describe the result.

11.2 Consider a spelling checker that will compare the words in a document with a dictionary to identify spelling errors. Carry out a requirements analysis for this program and describe the result.

11.3 Consider a path finder program that gives directions on the best way to get from point A to point B. The program has access to a database that identifies points of interest, how to get from one adjacent location to another, and the distance involved. Carry out a requirements analysis for this program and describe the result.

Requirements
Specifications

12

In the preceding chapter, we discussed how to do requirements analysis. This activity involved interacting with a customer to discover what the product being developed is supposed to do. The result of the analysis is a requirements document that captures this understanding. The most important part of the requirements document is a *requirements specification*. This chapter describes how to write a requirements specification.

As we shall see, a program is a data object, and its specification will be similar to those we have already seen for abstract types. Specifications for abstract types rely on the overview section to define a model for the states of their objects. In those specifications, we were able to make use of simple models that were based on a small set of mathematical concepts. For requirements specifications, however, such simple models aren't sufficient. Now we need to model the state of an entire program. This state often has a complex structure, even when we limit our concerns to just that part of the structure that is visible to users of the program. For example, users of a file system need to understand about files and directories and how they are connected to one another.

Thus, we need a way to describe the program state. This could be done informally, in English, but such a definition is likely to be both imprecise and verbose. Therefore, we make use of a different technique: we define the program state by means of a *data model*. The model is then used in the requirements specification.

The result is a reasonably precise definition of what is required. Such a specification is a good basis for program design, since now the designer is likely to understand what to build. Furthermore, the exercise of defining the model and then using it to write the specification is a valuable part of the requirements analysis process since it brings problems to the attention of the analyst. This leads to a specification that reflects more careful thinking about the issues and is more likely to meet the customer's needs as a result.

12.1   Data Models

A data model consists of a graph and a textual description (see Sidebar 12.1). The graph defines the kinds of data being manipulated and how they are related to one another. The graph and textual description together define constraints on what the program does. Defining these constraints forces us to pay attention to details that might otherwise be overlooked during requirements analysis.[1]

The graph contains nodes and edges. The nodes represent the kinds of data being manipulated by a program. Each node is a named set of items. For example, a data model for a file system would contain a `File` node, representing files, and a `Dir` node, representing directories. Each set contains all items that exist at a particular moment (e.g., all files in existence at this time).

The items in the sets are structureless; no detail is given for them, except by means of relationships to other sets. The edges represent these relationships. The purpose of the graph is to provide a convenient pictorial mechanism for showing the relationships. The notation also allows the relationships to be constrained in ways that will be explained later. Thus, a graph expresses certain kinds of invariants.

The model describes the state of the system. This state may change over time (e.g., as a result of the program responding to a user request). The model expresses this mutability in two ways. First, the sets themselves can change:

---

1. The data model we are using is based on Alloy, a modeling technique defined in more detail in Jackson, Daniel, *Alloy: A Lightweight Object Modeling Language*, MIT Laboratory for Computer Science Technical Report 797, Cambridge, Mass., Feb. 2000.

Sidebar 12.1 Components of a Data Model

A data model contains:

- Definitions of domains, subsets, and relations
- A graph that shows how sets and relations interrelate and defines constraints on them
- Definitions of derived relations and additional constraints

---

as the program state changes, items may be added to or removed from sets. Second, the relationships between the sets can change.

12.1.1   Subsets

Some sets represented by nodes in the graph are subsets of other sets. We will call sets that have no supersets *domains*. Each domain is disjoint from all other domains.

Subset edges are used to indicate that one set is a subset of another. We represent this information with an arrow with a closed head. The arrow goes from the subset to the superset. The arrowhead indicates whether the subset contains all elements of its superset (a filled arrowhead) or just some elements of the superset (an unfilled arrowhead).

Subsets can share an arrow; in this case, they are mutually disjoint, and the arrowhead indicates whether or not their union exhausts the superset. Subsets that don't share an arrow are not necessarily disjoint.

Three constraints are useful to define for subsets. First, subsets can sometimes be *fixed*. This means that the subset's membership is fixed for all time; the subset never gains or loses elements. A fixed subset is indicated by double lines on both sides of its node.

Second, a subset can be *static*. This means its membership is determined statically: an element never switches between belonging to the subset and not belonging to the subset. We will indicate a static subset by double lines on the left side of its node. Note that a subset that is fixed is also static.

Third, it is sometimes useful to state explicitly how many elements a subset contains. This can be done by writing the size of the subset within the box for its node; for example, a "1" means that the subset contains exactly

Figure 12.1 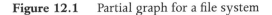 Partial graph for a file system

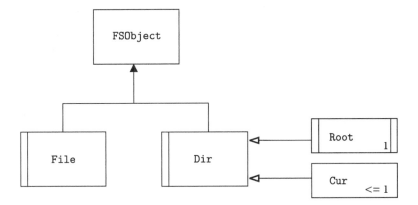

one element, while "<=1" means the subset is either empty or contains one element.

Figure 12.1 shows some of the subset relations and constraints for a file system. An FSObject (file system object) can be either a file or a directory. These two subsets are disjoint and exhaust their superset. Furthermore, they are both static: a file system object cannot switch from being a directory to being a file or vice versa.

In addition, there are two interesting subsets of Dir. Root represents the root directory; this directory is fixed for all time (and thus its node is marked as fixed), and there is exactly one root directory. Cur represents the current directory. There is at most one current directory, and different directories can be chosen as current while the file system is in use. Note that since Root and Cur do not share an arrow, they need not be disjoint; and therefore the root directory could be the current directory.

12.1.2   Relations

Relations are used to indicate how items of a set are related to items in other sets. They are represented by arrows with open heads. Each relation arrow is labeled with a name. Each relation has a *source* (the node it comes from) and a *target* (the node it points at). For example, there might be a contents arrow from the node DirEntry (representing entries in directories) to the node FSObject, indicating that a directory entry names a file system object. Here DirEntry is the source, and FSObject is the target.

Relation names needs not be unique within a diagram, except that if two relations have the same source, they should have distinct names.

Sometimes it is useful to define the *inverse* of a relation. For example, we might have a `parent` relation that maps a directory to its parent directory (each directory except for the root directory has a parent directory). But it is also useful to define a `children` relation that is the inverse of `parent`: if directory d1 is the parent of d2, then d2 is a child of d1. A single arrow can represent both a relation and its inverse. The label on the arrow names the *primary* relation and the inverse relation. We use the notation `r1(~r2)` to mean that `r1` is the primary relation and `r2` is its inverse. Thus, for a file system, we would have `parent(~children)`.

The graph also defines the multiplicity and mutability of the relations. *Multiplicity* defines the number of items a relation maps to or from. A relation actually maps to a set: it maps an item in the source to a set of items in the target. The relation's multiplicity defines how many items are in the set. For example, the `parent` relation maps to at most one directory (since root has no parent, and all other directories have a single parent). Multiplicity is indicated by annotating the relation arrow with one of the following symbols:

`!`:	*means exactly one*
`?`:	*means zero or one*
`*`:	*means zero or more*
`+`:	*means one or more*

Multiplicity annotations must appear on both ends of the arrow. An annotation on the target end explains how many target items are in the set a particular source item maps to. An annotation on the source end explains how many source items are in the set mapped to a particular target item.

To decide what symbols to use, we consider the ends separately. First, we consider the symbol at the target end of the arrow and determine the size of the set that a single source item maps to. For example, each directory entry object is mapped by `contents` to a single file system object, and therefore the target end of the `contents` arrow will be labeled with `!`. Then we consider the source end of the arrow. We simply invert the relation, considering it a map from the target node to the source node, and we ask the question: how many source items are in the set mapped to a single target item? For example, a file system object might be referred to by several directory entries, but the root directory is not referred to by any directory entry; therefore, we would mark the source end of the `contents` arrow with a `*`.

Relations can be mutable or immutable. A relation is mutable if the mapping can change—for example, if a source item can be associated with a different target at some point in the future. Mutability is also applied at both ends of the arrow: if the target associated with a source item can change, the target end is mutable, while if the source item associated with a particular target can change, the source end is mutable.

Here are some examples to illustrate these constraints, using a textual representation that indicates both multiplicity and mutability:

```
location: Airport?  ⇒ | Location!
socialSecurityNumber: Person! | ⇒ SSN*
parent(~children): Dir*  ⇒ Dir?
```

These relations can be explained as follows. Each airport is located at a distinct location, but many locations aren't associated with any airport; also an airport won't move, but a new airport could be built at some location at some future point. Each person can have many social security numbers and can add some later, but any particular number is associated with a single person and that association can't change. Finally a directory has at most one parent but can be the parent of many directories; furthermore, both of these associations can change. Note that in the case of an inverse, we give the constraints for the primary relation, but this immediately defines them for the inverse as well.

Figure 12.2 gives a simple data model for a file system. In addition to the sets already discussed (FSObject, File, Dir, Root, and Cur), we have DirEntry, which models entries in directories; Name, which models the names used within directories to name files or directories; and PathName, which models pathnames for files and directories.

There are also a number of relations in the model in addition to the parent relation and its inverse children, which were discussed earlier. entries maps a directory to its entries. An entry is an association between a name and a file system object; name maps an entry to the name it contains, while contents maps the entry to the file system object it refers to. Furthermore, first selects the first name in a pathname, and rest produces the rest of the pathname after the first name has been removed.

The diagram also shows the decisions we made about constraints on the relations. For example, a directory contains zero or more entries, and entries cannot be shared among directories. Each entry contains exactly one name and one file system object, but the same name or file system object can appear in many entries. Furthermore, an entry is immutable: its mappings to Name

Figure 12.2   Graph for the file system

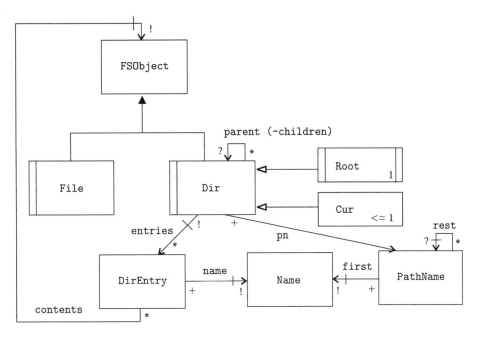

and FSObject cannot be changed. This last point reflects a decision: users can't change the binding of a name within a directory entry. However, they can replace an entry with a new one that contains a different binding (since entries is mutable).

Annotating the relations forces us to think about issues that might otherwise be overlooked, but that are important for the requirements. For example, in deciding what the associated symbols are for the parent relation, we needed to decide whether the parent of a directory can change. We have decided that it can change (since we did not mark the relation as immutable).

Relations map source elements to target elements without any additional arguments. When arguments are needed, there are two ways to handle them. First, we can introduce an extra node that effectively associates the argument with the result. This is what we did when we introduced DirEntry; we are using it to model a map from a name in a particular directory to a file system object. The other approach is to use recursion. For example, we might like to think of a pathname as a sequence of names, but modeling this would require a relation that takes an integer as an argument. In this case, we instead use recursion, effectively treating the pathname as a linked list rather than a sequence.

Expressing constraints as part of defining the diagram is particularly useful because the process is so methodical: we simply consider every subset node and every relation. For each relation, we decide for each end what its multiplicity is and whether it is mutable. Similarly for each subset, we decide about its mutability (whether it is fixed, static, or unconstrained) and its size. However, the graph does not usually capture all constraints that a model must satisfy. These extra constraints will be defined textually, as explained in the next section.

12.1.3   Textual Information

The textual information consists of two parts. The first part simply explains in English the intended meaning of each set and relation. Figure 12.3 shows this

Figure 12.3   Descriptions of sets and relations for the file system

Domains
FSObject: *all the files and directories in a file system*
File: *all files in a file system*
Dir: *all directories in a file system*
Root: *the root directory*
Cur: *the current directory*
DirEntry: *entries in directories*
Name: *string names within directory entries*
PathName: *pathnames for directories and files*

Relations
parent(~children): *gives the parent directory of a directory*
entries: *gives the entries (name/file system object pairs) of a directory*
name: *gives the name of a directory or file within a directory entry*
contents: *gives the file system object associated with a name in a* directory
first: *gives the name at the start of a pathname*
rest: *gives the rest of the pathname (all but the first name)*
pn: *gives the pathnames for all paths starting from a directory*

information for the file system. Note that the explanations omit information in the graph, such as the subset relationships among the sets.

The second part defines additional constraints. There are two forms of constraints. First, some relations are *derived*. A derived relation is one that can be defined in terms of other relations. It's important to identify derived relations because this reduces the size of the model, making it easier for people to understand. Also, identifying derived relations reduces the number of additional constraints. Derived relations will automatically be constrained by constraints on the relations that define them and vice versa.

The way to recognize derived relations is to consider each relation in turn and ask whether it can be defined in terms of the other relations. For the file system model, such an analysis leads to identifying two derived relations. The first is parent(~children): a directory's parent is the directory that contains an entry for it:

> *A directory's parent is the directory that contains an entry for it*
> *for all* d: Dir [d.parent = { d2 | d2 *in* Dir &&
>   *there exists* e: DirEntry (e *in* d2.entries &&
>   d = e.contents) }]

This definition makes use of a notational shorthand: when a set has just one member, we use the set name to also name that member. Thus, e.contents is used to stand for the directory that is the single element of that set.

Note that d.parent is defined to be a set; this, of course, is necessary since every relation maps to a set. Furthermore, this set must have at most one element, since the graph constrains the parent relation to map to a set containing at most one element. Once we have defined how parent is derived from the other relations, this constraint applies to them as well, so that now we know that a directory can be contained in at most one other directory.

The second derived relation is pn:

> d.pn *contains all pathnames that name a path from directory* d
> *for all* d: Dir [d.pn = { p | p *in* PathName &&
>   *there exists* e: DirEntry (e *in* d.entries &&
>   p.first = e.name &&
>   (p.rest = { } || (e.contents *in* Dir &&
>   p.rest *in* e.contents.pn))) }]

Now we are ready to define the constraints. Let's begin by constraining the structure of the directory hierarchy. We want to express the fact that the root directory is an ancestor of every directory (except itself), and there are no cycles in an ancestor chain. To capture this constraint precisely, it is useful to define a helping function:

A directory's ancestors are its parent and its parent's ancestors
    `ancestors(d) =` *if* `d = Root` *then* `{ }`
                  else `d.parent + ancestors(d.parent)`

(Recall that "+" denotes set union.) Here again we use the notational shorthand: `Root` is used to denote its single element, the root directory.

Given this definition, we can state the following:

A directory is not its own ancestor and every directory but
the root has the root as an ancestor
    for all `d: Dir [ !(d` *in* `ancestors(d)) &&`
        `( d = Root ||  Root` *in* `ancestors(d) ) ]`

This constraint is interesting because it tells us that the file system contains only the root directory and other directories accessible from the root. A similar constraint limits the files contained by the system:

Every file has an entry in some directory
    for all `f: File [` *there exists* `d: Dir, e: DirEntry`
        `( e` *in* `d.entries && f = e.contents ) ]`

Together these constraints say that the only file system objects that exist are those accessible by a path from the root directory. For a user, this means that files and directories that become unreachable from the root cannot be used; for an implementor, this means that it is not necessary to provide storage for unreachable objects.

We also want to constrain the contents of directories.

A directory contains at most one entry with a given name
    for all `d: Dir, e1,e2: DirEntry [`
        `e1, e2` *in* `d.entries && e1.name = e2.name => e1 = e2 ]`

A directory can contain at most one entry for a subdirectory
    for all `d: Dir, e1,e2: DirEntry [ e1, e2` *in* `d.entries &&`
        `e1.contents` *in* `Dir && e1.contents = e2.contents`
            `=> e1 = e2 ]`

Note that we have written the constraints both informally, in English, and by using mathematical notation. As was the case with rep invariants, it is

Figure 12.4   Constraints for the file system

Derived relations and helping functions
A directory's parent is the directory that contains an entry for it
 for all d: Dir [d.parent = { d2 | d2 *in* Dir &&
  there exists e: DirEntry (e *in* d2.entries && d = e.contents) }]
d.pn *contains all pathnames that name a path from directory* d
 for all d: Dir [d.pn = { p | p *in* PathName &&
  there exists e: DirEntry (e *in* d.entries && p.first = e.name &&
   (p.rest = { } || (e.contents *in* Dir && p.rest *in* e.contents.pn))) }]
A directory's ancestors are its parent and its parent's ancestors
 ancestors(d) = *if* d *in* Root *then* { } *else* d.parent + ancestors(d.parent)

Constraints
A directory is not its own ancestor and every directory but
the root has the root as an ancestor
 for all d: Dir [!(d *in* ancestors(d)) && (d = Root || Root *in* ancestors(d))]
Every file has an entry in some directory
 for all f: File [*there exists* d: Dir, e: DirEntry
  (e *in* d.entries && f = e.contents)]
A directory contains at most one entry with a given name
 for all d: Dir, e1,e2: DirEntry [e1, e2 *in* d.entries && e1.name = e2.name
  => e1 = e2]
A directory can contain at most one entry for a subdirectory
 for all d: Dir, e1,e2: DirEntry [e1, e2 *in* d.entries && e1.contents *in* Dir &&
  e1.contents = e2.contents => e1 = e2]

---

acceptable to give only the informal definition, providing your definitions are precise and understandable.

Figure 12.4 gives the constraints for the file system. The constraints do not include everything that is true about the file system. For example, it is true that the root directory does not have a parent, and that every other directory has exactly one parent. However, this fact can be proved from the constraints already stated, namely, the constraint on ancestors and the multiplicity constraint on parents.

It's easier to forget about a textual constraint than those expressed directly in the graph because there is no way to be as methodical about them. Instead, you need to think about all groups of relations and whether any other constraints are needed for them.

12.2   Requirements Specifications

A requirements specification is concerned with describing how the program interacts with its state to carry out *operations*, where each operation corresponds to a user request. For example, a specification of a file system must explain what happens to files and directories as users read and write files, and access and modify directories. Sidebar 12.2 summarizes the contents of a requirements specification.

There are two kinds of operations. *Static operations* start "from scratch"— that is, when the application is not already running. *Dynamic operations* are used only after the application is already running. The former correspond roughly to static methods and constructors, while the latter correspond roughly to instance methods. For example, in a file system there will be static operations to create a new file system, or to recover a file system after a system failure, and there will be dynamic operations to interact with the file system once it is running—for example, to create or remove a directory or to make a directory the current directory.

Thus, an application corresponds to a data abstraction, although in addition there might be some static operations that do not correspond to constructors, and sometimes all operations will correspond to static methods (and in this case, there might be just one method). In any case, the data model is used to explain the behavior of the operations.

Before we can write the specification, we need to consider two issues. The first concerns how the application is intended to be used. If the operations are intended to be called by programs, each operation will be defined as a static

---

Sidebar 12.2   Contents of a Requirements Specification

- A requirements specification contains specifications for *static* and *dynamic* operations.

- If the specification is for an interactive program, the operations are limited to string arguments and no results, and their specifications can include a *checks* clause to identify conditions that must hold for the operation to run.

- The operation specifications are based on the data model, and they must satisfy its constraints.

method, constructor, or instance method. In this case, the specification will be like what we have seen before, except that it will refer to the model, since this defines the state of the abstraction's objects.

However, if the program is only intended to be used interactively, we do not specify it in the usual way. In this case, the operations are limited. They are allowed to have string arguments, but they have no other types of arguments and no results; instead, their result is made visible to the user by some change in the user interface. Furthermore, the specifications do not give details about how the operations are used via the user interface; we avoid giving these details because they are likely to change (e.g., if the application is provided for more than one platform).

A program is sometimes intended to be used interactively and also to be called by programs. In this case, we must provide specifications of both the interactive operations and the normal methods.

The second issue concerns the selection of external data formats for use in communicating with users; all such formats are constraints on strings. For example, we want formats for names and pathnames in a file system. For some applications, the choice of format might be left up to the provider of the user interface, but generally it is a good idea to define the formats in the requirements specification to provide uniformity from one user interface to another.

Figure 12.5 defines some simple formats for a file system and then presents specifications of a few simplified file system operations that are intended to be used from the user interface. We use different notation and conventions in these specifications because these operations are somewhat different from normal methods. First, operations almost always modify the state, and therefore we omit the modifies clause since it conveys little information. Second, operations must be total; if a problem exists, they must find out about it and notify the user. Since operations are total, their specifications will not include requires clauses. However, they make use of a new kind of clause, a *checks* clause. This clause identifies the conditions that the operation must check for; if the conditions do not hold, the operation must bring the problem to the attention of the user via the user interface. We do not specify the form of the interaction with the user since this will differ with the form of the user interface.

In the specifications, the operations are divided into the two categories of static and dynamic operations. Their specifications refer to the model (e.g., the specification of makeDirInCur refers to Cur) and make use of the

Figure 12.5   Specifications of some file system operations

// Format restrictions:
// NAME: *A nonempty string of printable characters not containing the character* /
// PATHNAME: *A nonempty sequence of* NAMEs *separated by* / *and beginning*
//   either with / *(meaning the name starts from the root) or with*
//   a NAME, *meaning the pathname starts from the current directory.*

// Static Operations
start( )
    // EFFECTS: *Creates a new file system consisting of just the root*
    //   directory, and this directory is empty.

// Dynamic Operation
makeDirInCur(String n)
    // CHECKS: NAME(n) *and there is a directory* c *in* Cur *and* n *is not defined in* c
    // EFFECTS: *Creates a new directory and enters it with name* n *in* c.

makeCurFromRoot(String p)
    // CHECKS: p *is a pathname leading from the root to a directory* d
    // EFFECTS: *makes* d *be the current directory.*

deleteDir( )
    // CHECKS: *There is a directory* c *in* Cur *and* c *is empty and is not the root*
    // EFFECTS: *Removes entry for* c *from its parent and sets* Cur = { }.

---

format constraints for Name and PathName, using the notation NAME(n) or
PATHNAME(p); these predicates return true if their argument has the proper
format.

All operations must preserve the constraints of the data model, including
both constraints defined in the graph and ones defined textually. Each operation definition should be examined and its impact on the state validated
against the constraints to ensure that all of them are preserved; as usual in
doing such an analysis, the constraints can be assumed to hold on the state
when the operation starts running. In doing the analysis, start with the checks
clause; it must contain enough checks to rule out conditions that if not checked
would cause the operation to violate some constraint or otherwise not make
sense. Then consider whether the modifications described in the effects clause
will lead to a state that satisfies the constraints. The effects clause must de-

scribe all modifications made by the operation except for modifications to derived relations; modifications to derived relations follow from modifications to relations they depend on.

For example, makeDirInCur enters the new directory under name n in the current directory. Its checks clause rules out erroneous situations, such as no current directory or name already in use; the operation will check for these conditions and notify the user if they occur. Since the effects clause does not state that Cur changes, we can assume that it stays the same (i.e., the same directory c that was the current directory before the operation ran is still the current directory when it finishes). However, we also know that c.pn changes and that c is the parent of the new directory, since these relations are derived from relations that do change. As another example, consider the deleteDir operation, and note how it explicitly answers the question of what happens to Cur.

If an operation does not preserve a constraint or does not explain the effect on the state completely, its specification needs to change, or perhaps some constraints in the model need to be redefined. In either case, interaction with the customer may be required to figure out what to do. The result will be a specification that is more likely to describe what the customer wants.

The specification in Figure 12.5 is incomplete; many other operations are needed; and in addition, since a file system is also used from programs, there must be specifications of the methods used by programs. These methods will have specifications that follow our normal conventions: they must have a modifies clause if they modify anything, and they do not have a checks clause. However, their specifications are similar to those of their counterparts that are used from a user interface, with changes to reflect obvious differences (e.g., they may take different types of arguments, and they may return results or throw exceptions).

In addition to the specification of the data abstraction that corresponds to the application as a whole, we must give specifications of any new object types that are externally visible in the sense that their objects will be used by other programs. For example, the requirements specification for a file system would define file and directory types, with a full set of methods that allow them to be used conveniently. These types will correspond to certain sets in the model, and the model can be used as a guide to defining methods. But one needs to go beyond the model since it is necessary to think about user needs in interacting with the type being defined, just as was discussed earlier in the book. The specifications for these types will be like specifications of normal abstract types except that they can be written in terms of the data model. For example, the specification of the method that creates a subdirectory of directory d might state that d is the parent of the new directory.

12.3   Requirements Specification for Stock Tracker

This section gives the data model and requirements specification for the stock tracker.

12.3.1   The Data Model

The requirements analysis for the stock tracker (see Section 11.3) determined that there could be many portfolios, each with a distinct name. One of the portfolios could be *open*. The user could inspect or modify the open portfolio, make a position in the open portfolio be the *current* one, and could then inspect or modify the current position. The user could also create or delete a portfolio.

Figure 12.6 explains the domains and relations for the stock tracker, and Figure 12.7 gives its graph. The graph indicates that there is at most one open portfolio and at most one current position. The multiplicity constraints are mostly obvious and uninteresting, but some reflect decisions that weren't discussed previously but that must be made during requirements analysis; defining the model brings these decisions to the attention of the analyst. For example, should we allow more than one name for a portfolio? The graph indicates that this is not allowed and also that the name of a portfolio cannot change. Another decision reflected in the graph is that every position has an associated quote; this constraint is interesting because it implies that when a position is added to a portfolio, the system will need to obtain a quote for it.

The constraints for the stock tracker are given in Figure 12.8. The figure indicates that value and folioValue are derived (the notation fToD denotes a function that converts the price given as a fraction into a decimal dollar amount). As was the case in the graph, some of the textual constraints reflect previously made decisions, while others require the analyst to make additional decisions. For example, we had already decided that a portfolio contains at most one position for a given ticker name and that the open portfolio must belong to the current position. The other constraints represent new decisions. They indicate that different positions for the same stock have the same price

Figure 12.6   Domains and relations for the stock tracker

Domains
Folios: *the set of named portfolios*
Name: *names of portfolios*
Folio: *a portfolio*
Open: *the open portfolio*
Position: *a position within a portfolio*
Cur: *the current position within a portfolio*
Ticker: *stock ticker names*
Quote: *a price for a stock at a particular time*
DateTime: *a date and time*
Price: *prices of stocks*
Num: *numbers of shares*
Dollar: *dollar values*

Relations
name: *the name of a portfolio*
folio: *the portfolio associated with a name in Folios*
contents: *the positions in a portfolio*
ticker: *the ticker name of a position*
quote: *the quote for a position*
price: *the price of a position*
time: *the date and time of a quote for a position*
amount: *the number of shares of a position*
value: *the dollar value of a position*
folioValue: *the dollar value of a portfolio*

---

and that all positions have non-negative amounts of stock and non-negative price. Both of these constraints are interesting. The first one implies that when the tracker obtains a price for a stock, this information must be reflected in positions in other portfolios that are for the same stock. The second constraint allows a position that contains zero shares; this makes it possible for a user to track the quote for a stock without owning any of that stock. The second constraint also implies that the tracker must cope somehow with a negative price (should it ever receive one from the Web server); it could either set the price to zero or leave the old price in place. Let's assume the former since it will work even for a newly purchased stock.

Figure 12.7   Graph for the stock tracker

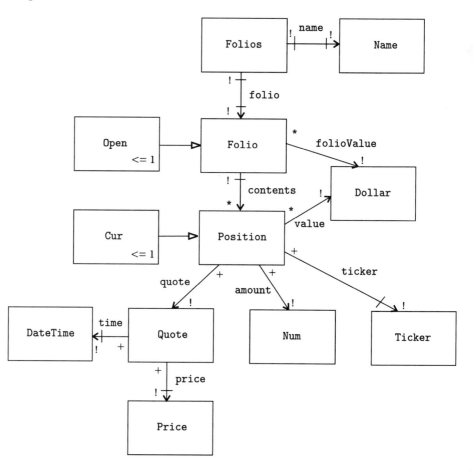

The constraints record decisions that must be made as part of requirements analysis. For example, we might have decided that different portfolios could not contain positions for the same stock, or alternatively that the same portfolio could contain more than one position for the same stock. The constraints document the decisions that were actually made, and the need to consider constraints helps the analyst to focus on issues that must be resolved during the requirements phase.

Figure 12.8   Constraints for the stock tracker

Derived Relations
The value of a position reflects its amount and price
   for all p: Position [p.value = p.amount * fToD(p.quote.price)]
The value of a portfolio reflects the values of its positions
   for all f: Folio [f.folioValue = sum(p.value for all p in f.contents)]

Constraints
A portfolio contains at most one position for a particular stock
   for all f: Folio, p1,p2: Position [p1, p2 in f && p1.ticker = p2.ticker
      => p1 = p2]
The current position must belong to the open portfolio
   Cur != { } => (Open != { } && Cur in Open.contents)
All positions for the same stock have the same quote
   for all p1,p2: Position [p1.ticker = p2.ticker => p1.quote = p2.quote]
All positions have a non-negative amount and a non-negative price
   for all p: Position [p.amount >= 0 && p.quote.price >= 0]

12.3.2   Stock Tracker Specification

Since the stock tracker is a purely interactive program, there is no need to define any types for things like portfolios and positions, since they will not be used by other programs. We do need to define the formats for data items that users must enter. There are only three such formats. NUM must be a non-negative integer, and NAME must be an alphanumeric string. We don't need to define a format for TICKER since that is defined elsewhere (by the stock market). Note that no format is provided for the file that stores the state of the stock tracker when it isn't running, since no program except the stock tracker ever needs to examine that file.

The requirements specification for the stock tracker is shown in Figures 12.9 and 12.10. Note how the specification ensures that the operations satisfy the constraints. For example, the specification of addStock preserves the constraint that there is at most one entry in a portfolio for a particular stock. Also, the specifications for getPrice and getPrices ensure that all positions for a particular stock have the same quote.

Figure 12.9   First part of specification of tracker operations

// *Modifications are written to disk as they occur. When the stock tracker*
// *runs, it starts in the end state from the last time it ran.*

// *Static Operations*
startTracker( )
    // EFFECTS: *Starts the tracker running with the end state from its last run.*

// *Dynamic Operations*
createFolio(String f)
    // CHECKS: NAME(f) *and* f *not in use in* Folios
    // EFFECTS: *Creates an empty portfolio named* f *and makes it be the*
    //   *open portfolio.*

deleteFolio
    // CHECKS: *There exists a portfolio* f *in* Open *and* f *is empty*
    // EFFECTS: *Deletes* f, *removes its entry from* Folios, *and sets* Open = { }.

openFolio(String f)
    // CHECKS: f *names a portfolio*
    // EFFECTS: *Makes* f *be the open portfolio and sets* Cur = { }.

selectStock(String t)
    // CHECKS: *There exists a portfolio* f *in* Open *and* t *names a stock in* f
    // EFFECTS: *Makes* t's *position in* f *be the current position.*

buyStock(String n)
    // CHECKS: NUM(n) *and there exists a position* p *in* Cur
    // EFFECTS: *Increases shares for* p *by* n.

sellStock(String n)
    // CHECKS: NUM(n) *and there exists position* p *in* Cur *and* n <= p.amount
    // EFFECTS: *Decreases shares of* p *by* n.

addStock(String t, String n)
    // CHECKS: NUM(n) *and there exits a portfolio* f *in* Open *and* t *names*
    //   *a stock that is not in* f
    // EFFECTS: *Adds a position for* t *with* n *shares to* f *and gets a quote for*
    //   t *from the web server if no quote for that stock is currently known.*

deleteStock
    // CHECKS: *There exists position* p *in* Cur
    // EFFECTS: *Removes* p *from* Open *and sets* Cur = { }.

Figure 12.10 Rest of specification of tracker operations

```
moveStock(String f, String t)
```
   // CHECKS: f *names a portfolio and there exists portfolio* f1 *in* Open *and* f != f1
   //   *and* t *names a position in* f
   // EFFECTS: *Removes* t'*s position from* f. *If* t *has a position in* f1, *adds*
   //   n *shares to that position, where* n *is the number of shares in the*
   //   *deleted position, else adds a position for* t *to* f1 *with* n *shares.*

```
getPrice
```
   // CHECKS: *There exists a position* p *in* Cur
   // EFFECTS: *Uses the Web server to update the price of* p *and*
   //   *all other positions for that stock.*

```
getPrices
```
   // CHECKS: *There exists portfolio* f *in* Open
   // EFFECTS: *Uses the Web server to update the prices of all positions in* f.
   //   *Also updates prices of all other positions for those stocks.*

12.4 Requirements Specification for a Search Engine

This section explores a second example, a search engine that allows the user to run queries against a collection of documents. It describes both an abbreviated requirements analysis and the resulting requirements specification.

As usual, we begin our analysis by a scenario representing normal case behavior. Suppose the user starts a session with the search engine. The first question that comes up concerns whether the engine already has a collection of documents that it remembers from the last time it ran. Let's assume that the customer is interested only in new searches. Therefore, the first thing the user must do is identify some documents of interest. Let's assume that this is done by presenting a URL of a site containing documents; the engine will run searches against all of those documents. Furthermore, the customer is interested in multisite searches; therefore, the user can present additional URLs of document-containing sites, and the engine will increase its collection as a result. The customer indicates that the collection can be enlarged at any time, not just at the start of a session, and that there is no interest in removing documents from the collection.

The customer indicates that a user should be able to search the collection for a document with a particular title. However, the main purpose of the engine is to run queries against the collection, which means we have to decide what a query is. In consultation with the customer, we determine that a query begins by the user presenting a single word, which we will refer to as a *keyword*. The customer indicates that many words are uninteresting (e.g., "and" and "the") and will not be used as keywords. The customer expects the search engine to know what the uninteresting words are without any user intervention; thus, it must have access to some storage, such as a file, that lists the uninteresting words.

The system responds to a query by presenting information about what documents contain the keyword. This information is ordered by how many times the keyword occurs in the documents. The system does not present the actual documents, but rather provides information so that the user can examine the matching documents further if desired.

However, the ability to query using a single keyword is quite limited, and the customer also requests the ability to "refine" a query by providing another keyword; the matching documents must contain all the keywords. The customer rules out more sophisticated queries, such as queries that match documents containing any one of their keywords or queries that require the keywords to be adjacent in the document in order for there to be a match. However, such queries are likely in a later release of the product.

Now we need to consider user and system errors, and also performance. The main performance issue is how to carry out the queries; the customer wants it to be done expeditiously. This requirement has two implications. First, the program must contain data structures that speed up the process of running a query. Second (and more important) is the question of whether querying requires visiting the Web sites containing the documents. The customer indicates that this should not happen; instead, the query should be based on information already known to the search engine. One implication of this decision is that the collection might not be up to date. A site might have been modified since the search engine was told about it, and queries will not reflect the modifications: they will miss newly added documents or find documents that no longer exist. The customer indicates that this is acceptable but that tracking modifications might be desired in a future release. The customer also indicates that all information about documents should be stored at the search engine, so that if a query matches a document, the user will be able to view the document even if it no longer exists at the site from which it was fetched. One point to note about these decisions is that a trade-off is being made between speed of processing queries versus the space taken for storing documents at the search engine.

Now let's consider errors. There aren't any interesting system errors: the system has some persistent storage containing information about uninteresting words, but this storage is not modified and the customer is not concerned about media failures. Furthermore, the customer indicates that it is acceptable for the search engine to simply fail if something goes wrong.

There are interesting user errors, however. The user could enter an uninteresting word as a keyword or could enter a word not in any document; the customer indicates that the user should be told about the error in the first case, but that in the second case, the response will simply be an empty set of matches. The user might also present a URL for a site that doesn't exist, that doesn't contain documents, or that has already been added to the collection; all of these actions should result in the user being notified of the error. The customer indicates that it is acceptable if a document is found at multiple sites and that, in this case, the document will end up in the collection just once. Two documents are considered to be the same if they have the same title; again, a later release might handle things differently.

Now that we have a rough idea of what the search engine is supposed to do, we are ready to write the requirements specification. As we do so, we will uncover a number of issues that were overlooked in the analysis but must be resolved to arrive at a precise specification. Thus, the process of writing the requirements specification, including the definition of the data model, is an intrinsic and important part of the requirements analysis process.

The sets and relations for the search engine are defined in Figure 12.11 and the graph is given in Figure 12.12. A document has a title, some URLs (of the sites from which it was obtained), and a body; a body is a sequence of words. The NK node represents the uninteresting words; this set is fixed (its membership never changes). Match represents the set of documents that match the current query; Key is the set of keywords used in this query. Key and NK are disjoint (a keyword is never an uninteresting word), but they do not exhaust Word (since at any moment, many words in documents are neither keywords nor uninteresting words). Cur is a document that was identified by title as being of current interest; CurMatch is a Match that is currently being examined.

The constraints for the search engine are given in Figure 12.13. We can see that sum is a derived relation: it is the sum of the number of occurrences

Figure 12.11 Sets and relations for the search engine

Domains
Doc: *the set of documents*
URL: *the URLs of sites where documents were found*
Title: *the title of a document*
Entry: *the entries (word/index pairs) in a document*
Num: *positive integers*
Word: *words in documents*
NK: *uninteresting words*
Key: *keywords used in current query*
Match: *documents matching keywords of current query*
Cur: *document currently being examined*
CurMatch: *match currently being examined*

Relations
site: *the URLs of sites containing a document*
title: *the title of a document*
body: *the entries that make up the contents of a document*
index: *the index of an entry in Entry*
wd: *the word of an entry in Entry*
doc: *the document of an entry in Match*
ind: *the index of an entry in Match*
sum: *the count of the occurrences of keywords in a match.*

of each keyword in the document. The constraints indicate that the indexes in Match and Entry are unique, that documents are in Match only if a query is occurring, that the documents in Match are exactly those that contain all the words in Key, and that the ordering of documents in Match reflects the number of occurrences of keywords in the documents.

The requirements specification for the search engine is given in Figure 12.14. The specification does not give information about formats; we are assuming a standard format for URLs and a simple format for documents. For example, words in documents are whatever appears between white space or HTML control characters, and the sections of a document (title, authors, body) are separated in a simple way. The specification indicates that the search engine knows about uninteresting words via some private file and that it has no other persistent state.

Figure 12.12 Graph for the search engine

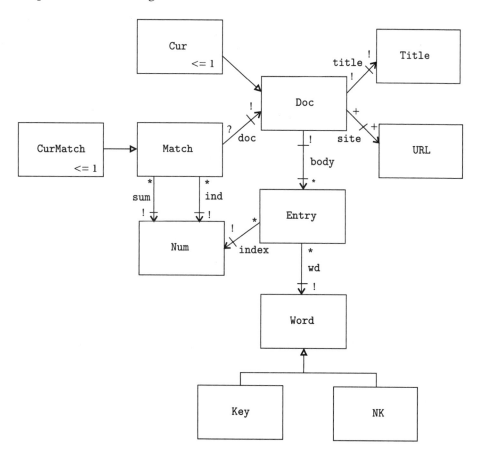

There are a number of potential extensions to the search engine. We list some of them here:

- We might want to support a more sophisticated notion of words and documents.

- We might allow several distinct documents to have the same title.

- We could support more sophisticated queries—for example, disjunctions that match all documents containing one of several words.

- We could provide more information about specific documents such as a count for various words. Or we might show all the places where a particular word occurs in a document.

Figure 12.13   Derived relations and constraints for the search engine

Derived relations and helping functions
The sum for a match is the total count of occurrences of all
keywords in that document
> *for all* m: Match [m.sum = $\sum_{k \in Key}$ sumKey(m.doc, k)]

sumKey *is the count of occurrences of* k *in* d
> sumKey(d, k) = | {e: Entry | e *in* d.body && e.wd = k } |

Document d *matches if it contains all keywords in* Key
> matches(d) = Key != { } && (*for all* k: Key (sumKey(d, k) > 0))

Constraints
Every entry in a document has a distinct index
> *for all* d: Doc, e1,e2: Entry [e1, e2 *in* d.body &&
> e1.index = e2.index ⇒ e1 = e2]

Every match has a distinct index
> *for all* m1, m2: Match [m1.ind = m2.ind => m1 = m2]

If there are no keywords, there are no entries in Match
> Key = { } => Match = { }

Match *contains exactly the documents that match*
> *for all* m: Match [matches(m.doc)] &&
> *for all* d: Doc [matches(d) => *there exists* m: Match (d = m.doc)]

Match *is ordered by keyword count*
> *for all* m1, m2: Match [m1.ind < m2.ind => m1.sum $\geq$ m2.sum]

- We might provide a way for users to see a list of all the interesting words occurring in documents in the collection.

- We might allow the set of uninteresting words to be changed.

- We might have the engine periodically revisit the sites where its documents came from to obtain any new documents that have been added to the sites.

- We might want to have the engine record the URLs of sites persistently so that it can refetch the documents when it starts up or even store the documents persistently as well.

- We might want to have the engine not store the documents but rather simply record information about them and then refetch ones that the user wants to examine.

Figure 12.14   Requirements specification for the search engine

> *// The engine has a private file that contains the list of uninteresting*
> *// words.*
>
> *// Static Operations*
> `startEngine( )`
>> *// EFFECTS: Starts the engine running with* NK *containing the words*
>> *//   in the private file. All other sets are empty.*
>
> *// Dynamic Operations*
> `query(String w)`
>> *// CHECKS: w not in* NK
>> *// EFFECTS: Sets* Key = { w } *and makes* Match *contain the documents*
>> *//   that match w, ordered as required. Clears* CurMatch.
>
> `queryMore(String w)`
>> *// CHECKS:* Key != { } *and w not in* NK *and w not in* Key
>> *// EFFECTS: Adds w to* Key *and makes* Match *be the documents already*
>> *//   in* Match *that additionally match w. Orders* Match *properly.*
>> *//   Clears* CurMatch.
>
> `makeCurrent(String t)`
>> *// CHECKS: t in* Title
>> *// EFFECTS: Makes* Cur *contain the document with title t.*
>
> `makeCurMatch(String i)`
>> *// CHECKS:* NUM(i) *and i is an index in* Match
>> *// EFFECTS: Makes* CurMatch *contain the ith entry in* Match.
>
> `addDocuments(String u)`
>> *// CHECKS: u does not name a site in* URL *and u names a site that*
>> *//   provides documents*
>> *// EFFECTS: Adds u to* URL *and the documents at site u with new*
>> *//   titles to* Doc. *If* Key *is non-empty adds any documents*
>> *//   that match the keywords to* Match *and clears* CurMatch.

12.5   Summary

The main result of requirements analysis is a requirements specification. This specification needs to be complete and precise: complete so that it captures all decisions about the requirements, and precise so that the designers can understand what product to build. This chapter has discussed a way to write requirements specifications that makes it more likely that we will meet these goals.

The approach is to base the specification on a data model. The model defines the program state and how it changes over time. It does so using a notation that allows constraints to be specified. Constraints are defined at several points: when defining the graph, when defining the textual constraints, and when specifying the operations. Defining constraints is useful both during analysis, where they help the analyst to think of details that might otherwise be overlooked, and in writing the requirements specification, where they provide a double-check on whether the operations are specified correctly.

The need to define constraints often points out a place where the requirements need more thought. This can lead the analyst to further dialog with the customer to work out the details. Thus, the need to define constraints leads directly to a more complete specification. The constraints can also lead to improved understanding on the part of designers because the use of the data model allows a more precise specification than would otherwise be possible. As a result, we can move into the design phase with more confidence that the product we will construct is the one the customer wants.

Exercises

12.1   Define more operations for the file system. In particular, add operations to add and remove entries from directories and to read and write files.

12.2   Extend the data model for the file system to take account of soft links. These are pathnames that are stored in files; they can be used to access file system objects but do not guarantee that the objects exist.

12.3   Look at the operations provided by a file system you are familiar with and compare them to definitions developed in the preceding two exercises. Then modify the data model to match your system and define some of its operations in terms of the new model.

12.4 Extend the stock tracker so that it provides a log of user updates and the ability to make use of information in the log to undo changes. Modify the data model and requirements specification to support this upgrade.

12.5 Extend the stock tracker so that it provides "alerts": warnings when a stock price exceeds a stated upper bound or falls below a stated lower bound. Modify the data model and the requirements specification to support this change.

12.6 Extend the stock tracker so that it keeps its information about stock prices reasonably up to date (e.g., its quotes are all obtained within the last hour). Modify the data model and the requirements specification to support this change.

12.7 Extend the search engine so that it allows distinct documents to have the same title and so that it revisits document sites periodically to obtain recent information. Modify the data model and requirements specification to support these changes.

12.8 Produce a data model and requirements specification for the xref program discussed in the exercises in Chapter 11.

12.9 Produce a data model and requirements specification for the spelling checker discussed in the exercises in Chapter 11.

12.10 Produce a data model and requirements specification for the path finder program discussed in the exercises in Chapter 11.

Design

13

In preceding chapters, we have discussed the specification and implementation of individual abstractions. We have emphasized abstractions because they are the building blocks out of which programs are constructed. We now discuss how to invent abstractions and how to put them together to build good programs. Our approach will rely heavily on material presented earlier, especially our discussions of good abstractions and good specifications (for example, see Chapter 9).

13.1 An Overview of the Design Process

The purpose of design is to define a program structure consisting of a number of modules that can be implemented independently and that, when implemented, will together satisfy the requirements specification. This structure must provide the required behavior and also meet the performance constraints. Furthermore, the structure should be a good one: it should be reasonably simple and avoid duplication of effort (for example, it should not contain two modules that do almost the same thing). Finally, the structure should support both initial program development and maintenance and modification. The ease of modification will depend on the sort of change desired. A particular decomposition cannot accommodate all changes with equal ease. This is why likely

---

Sidebar 13.1 Design Goals

- Meet functional and performance requirements
- Define a modular structure such that
  - The components are all good abstractions
  - The structure is reasonably simple and relatively easy to implement and modify
  - The structure makes it relatively easy to incorporate the modifications identified by the requirements analysis

---

modifications should be identified prior to design—so that a decomposition can be developed that facilitates them. Sidebar 13.1 summarizes these design goals.

We start a design with the requirements specification. Sometimes it describes a single abstraction, sometimes several that together make up the system (e.g., the file system abstraction plus the file and directory abstractions). We pick one of these abstractions to start work on. It becomes the initial *target abstraction*.

In designing a program, we carry out three steps for each target:

1. Identify *helping abstractions*, or *helpers* for short, that will be useful in implementing the target and that facilitate decomposition of the problem.

2. Specify the behavior of each helper.

3. Sketch an implementation of the target.

The first step consists of inventing a number of helping abstractions that are useful in the problem domain of the target. The helpers can be thought of as constituting an abstract machine that provides objects and operations tailored to implementing the target. The idea is that if the machine were available, implementing the target to run on it would be straightforward.

Next, we define the helpers precisely by providing a specification for each one. When an abstraction is first identified, its meaning is usually a bit hazy. The second step involves pinning down the details and then documenting the decisions in a specification that is as complete and unambiguous as is feasible.

Once the behavior of each helper is defined precisely, we can use them to write programs. In principle, the target can now be implemented, but we

Sidebar 13.2   The Design Process

1. Select a *target* abstraction whose implementation has not yet been studied.
2. Identify *helper* abstractions that would be useful in implementing the target and that facilitate decomposition of the problem.
3. Sketch how the helpers will be used in implementing the target.
4. Iterate until the implementations of all abstractions have been studied.

generally do not do it at design time. Instead, we merely sketch enough of an implementation to convince ourselves that an acceptably efficient and modular implementation can be constructed. For example, for a data abstraction, we might list some items that need to be in the rep.

If the abstract machine existed, we would now be finished; but in reality, the helpers need to be considered in more detail. The next step is to select one helper and design its implementation. This process continues until all the helpers have been studied. (See Sidebar 13.2 for a summary of the design process.)

The design process is concerned with efficiency of two sorts. First is finding an economical design: one that is not overly complex and that will be relatively easy to implement and to modify. Equally important, however, is finding a design that will lead to a program that performs well. A concern for performance permeates the process: at each stage we want to implement the target efficiently. This will lead us to select certain helpers and not others; specifically, we want to select helpers that will do the work required by the target in a cost-effective way.

For large programs, we usually do not know in advance what the structure of the program ought to be. Instead, the discovery of this structure is a major goal of the design. As the design progresses, sometimes a choice must be made between a number of structures, none of which is well understood. Later, the decision may be found to be wrong. This is especially likely for choices made early in design, when the structure of the program is least understood and least constrained by other decisions, and when the effect of an error on the global structure is most significant.

When errors are discovered, we must correct them by changing the design. We often must discard all later work that depends on the error. That is why we are reluctant to start implementation until after we have a complete design, or at least a complete design of the part of the program being implemented. Of course, no matter how careful we are about our design, we are likely to uncover problems with it during implementation. When this happens, we must rethink the part of the design related to the problem.

Our discussion so far has outlined how design occurs but has neglected a number of questions, such as:

- How is decomposition accomplished? That is, how do we identify subsidiary abstractions that will help to decompose the problem?

- How do we select the next target?

- How do we know whether we are making progress? For example, are the helpers easier to implement than the target that caused them to be introduced?

- How are performance and modification requirements factored into a design?

- How much decomposition should be done?

These and other, similar questions will be addressed as we carry out an example. First, however, we discuss how to document a design.

13.2   The Design Notebook

The decisions made during design must be recorded. This documentation should be done in a systematic manner and kept in a *design notebook* (see Sidebar 13.3). The notebook contains an introductory section describing the overall design of the program and a section for each abstraction.

13.2.1   The Introductory Section

The introductory section lists all the abstractions identified so far. It also indicates which helpers are to be used in the implementations of which targets. This documentation takes the form of a *module dependency diagram*, which identifies all the abstractions encountered during design (those present when

Sidebar 13.3   The Design Notebook

The design notebook contains:

- The module dependency diagram
- A section for each abstraction containing:
  - Its specification
  - Its performance requirements
  - A sketch of its implementation
  - Other information including justification of design decisions and discussion of alternatives, potential extensions or other modifications, and information about expected context of use

the design starts or introduced as helpers) and shows their relationships. The module dependency diagram shows the code modules (e.g., the classes and interfaces) that will exist in the program when it is implemented. It also shows their dependencies, where module *M1 depends on module M2 if a change to M2's specification might cause a change in M1*. The module dependency diagram will be especially useful for tracking the impact of a change in a specification, since it will allow us to identify all modules that must be reconsidered because of the change.

A module dependency diagram consists of nodes, which represent abstractions, and arcs (see Sidebar 13.4). There are three kinds of nodes, one for each of the three kinds of abstractions we use. Each node names its abstraction. Nodes like the one labeled C1.P in Figure 13.1 represent procedures, ones like C2.I represent iterators, and the remainder represent data abstractions. A data abstraction will be implemented by either a class or interface. Procedures and iterators will be implemented by static methods in some class; the node name will indicate the class as well as the method name (e.g., C.P indicates that procedure P will be implemented in class C).

There are two kinds of arcs. The first kind, an arc with an open head, is a *using arc*; it shows which modules are to be used in implementing which other modules. The arc goes from a *source abstraction* to a *helper abstraction*; it means that the implementation of the source abstraction will use the helper. We say that the source abstraction *uses* or *depends on* the helpers. In the case

---

Sidebar 13.4   Components of a Module Dependency Diagram

- The nodes of the diagram represent abstractions; each node names its abstraction, and this name identifies a program entity that will implement the abstraction.

- The arcs represent dependency, where abstraction A depends on abstraction B if a change to B's specification means that A's implementation or specification must be reconsidered. aboveskip=17pt

  - An arc with an open head indicates that abstraction A's implementation *uses* or *weakly uses* B.
  - The arcs with closed heads indicate *extensions*: a subtype extends its supertype.

---

of an arc to a data abstraction, we do not indicate what methods will be used because typically the source abstraction will use many of the helper's methods. Recording more detailed information would result in an overly cluttered diagram that would be hard to read.

Sometimes, an abstraction uses objects of a data abstraction without calling any of their methods. In such a case, we say the source abstraction *weakly uses* the helper. A special dashed arc is used to indicate this kind of dependency.

A module dependency diagram is a directed graph. It is not a tree, since one abstraction can be used in implementing several others. The graph may contain cycles, which occur when there is recursion. We indicate only mutual recursion; if an individual abstraction is recursive, the recursion does not show up in the diagram. In general, it is acceptable for a program to include recursion if the problem being solved has a naturally recursive structure. However, if the cycles get very long and involve many arcs, it is wise to be suspicious of the program structure.

In Figure 13.1, data abstraction D is to be implemented by three helpers, procedure P, and data abstractions E and G. Furthermore, E uses G and iterator I. Also E and I are mutually recursive.

The second type of arc, an *extension arc*, indicates a subtype relationship; this arc has a closed head. Extension arcs occur only between data abstraction nodes. They lead from the subtype to the supertype and indicate that the subtype extends the behavior of the supertype, as discussed in Chapter 7. For

Figure 13.1   A module dependency diagram.

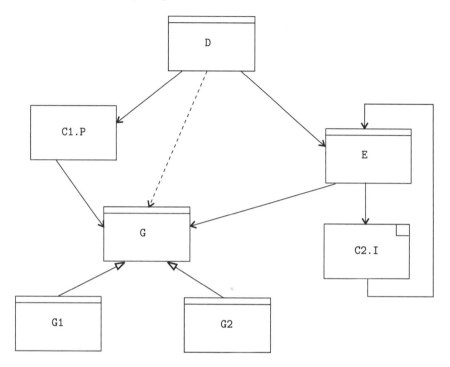

example, Figure 13.1 indicates that data abstraction G has two subtypes, G1 and G2. There cannot be any cycles involving just extension arcs.

The module dependency diagram is useful when errors are detected. A design error shows up as a flaw in an abstraction—for example, an efficient implementation becomes impossible or needed arguments are missing. The result is that the abstraction's interface, and therefore, its specification, must change. The potential impact of the change can be determined from the diagram. All abstractions that use the erroneous one must be reconsidered in light of the new interface and its specification. (That reconsideration may find some of those abstractions erroneous, and so on.) An abstraction that weakly uses an erroneous data abstraction is affected if the abstraction disappears entirely but not if its specification changes or it is replaced by another type. For example, if we found a problem with G in Figure 13.1, we would have to rethink the implementations of E and P, but D would not be affected. Of course, if rethinking E prompted us to change its specification, we would be forced to reexamine the implementation of D.

The extension arrows are used in a similar way. If the specification of a data abstraction with subtypes changes, all its subtypes must be examined; either their specifications will also change, or they can no longer be its subtypes. Thus, a change to the specification of G means that we must examine G1 and G2. Also, if a data abstraction with supertypes changes, we must examine the supertypes. It is possible that the change will have no impact on a supertype; this would happen if the change affects only the subtype's new methods, and the subtype still satisfies the substitution principle (as defined in Chapter 7). If, however, the substitution principle is no longer satisfied, the supertype must be redefined, or the changed abstraction can no longer be its subtype, and the diagram must be changed to reflect this. Thus, if the specification of G1 changes, we must examine G; either the substitution principle still holds, or we must redefine G, or G1 can no longer be a subtype of G.

Although a module dependency diagram looks a bit like a data model graph, the two are very different. A module dependency diagram describes the structure of a program; its nodes are program modules, and its arcs define relationships among these modules. A data model, on the other hand, is abstract; its nodes define sets and do not correspond to program modules. We will discuss this issue further in Section 13.11.

13.2.2   The Abstraction Sections

We partition the notebook entry for an individual abstraction into four parts:

1. A specification of its functional behavior

2. A description of performance constraints it must observe

3. Information about how it is to be implemented

4. Miscellaneous information that does not fit into any of the previous four categories

The specification is, of course, the most important item in this list. However, we have already said a great deal about specifications and will say no more about them here.

Performance constraints are generally propagated top-down through a program. The requirements specification may constrain the time the program can take to perform certain tasks, the amount of primary and secondary memory it can use, and its use of other resources such as the network. To convince ourselves that the implementation of a target abstraction will meet its performance constraints, we have to make assumptions about the efficiency of its helpers. These assumptions show up as performance constraints in the parts of the design notebook detailing each helper.

Performance constraints can be expressed in a variety of ways. We frequently express them as functions of the size of the input. We might, for example, require that a set abstraction use memory that is linear in the size of the set (Order(n), where n is the number of elements in the set); this means that the amount of space occupied by a set object should never exceed some constant times the size of the set. Furthermore, we might constrain the time to perform various methods on the set, such as lookup and insert, to be constant (Order(1)). Such constraints would be imposed so that an abstraction that uses the set can meet its own performance constraints. The constraints in turn affect the way the set is implemented; in particular, we need to use a hash table to meet the constraints just given.

For many applications, it suffices to supply relative performance constraints such as those just given. Sometimes, however, it is useful to bound the multiplicative constants or even to impose an absolute bound. An absolute upper bound on time is needed in real-time applications. Analogously, we put absolute bounds on the space used in programs that are to be run on small machines or machines that do not support virtual memory.

The section of the notebook entry containing information about how the abstraction is to be implemented should include a list of its helpers. It might also include a description of how the implementation works. This description can be omitted if the implementation is straightforward, but it is necessary if the implementation is clever. For example, for the set abstraction discussed previously, the implementation section might indicate that a hash table should be used.

As its name implies, the section of the abstraction entry labeled "miscellaneous" might contain almost anything. Typical items are

- A justification for the decisions documented elsewhere in the entry

- A discussion of alternatives that were considered and rejected

- Potential extensions or other modifications of the abstraction

- Information about the context in which the designers expect the abstraction to be used

In closing this section, we should note that if the design is very large, it may be useful to structure the notebook by introducing subsidiary notebooks. In a module dependency diagram, any subgraph can be viewed as an independent subsystem. However, the most convenient choice is a subgraph in which only one node is used from outside. In this case, the entire substructure simply corresponds to a single abstraction as far as the rest of the program is concerned.

13.3   The Structure of Interactive Programs

In the next several sections, we illustrate the design process by developing a Java program to implement the simple search engine described in Section 12.4. Our presentation idealizes the design process; for example, very few design errors are made. We discuss this point further in Section 13.12.

The requirements specification for an interactive application like the search engine describes operations that are intended to be used through a user interface. Thus, an implementation of such a specification will include both code to implement the user interface and code to carry out the work of the application. Although it is possible to build a monolithic structure in which the two parts are not separated, we will instead make a clean separation between them. Thus, our designs will always have two parts: a *functional part* (the FP) and a *user interface* part (the UI). The UI will take care of interacting with the user; it will display information to the user (e.g., the current list of keywords) and accept user input (e.g., an additional keyword for a search). The FP will carry out the user commands when informed of a user input and will notify the UI of the results.

There are several important reasons for separating a program into a UI and an FP (see Sidebar 13.5). The first is that this structure allows us to keep the FP free of all UI details and the UI free of FP details. This means we can change the FP implementation (e.g., to speed it up) without having to change the UI. Also, we can change the UI (e.g., to make use of a different library to interact with the display and keyboard) without affecting the FP. Therefore, if the library changes (e.g., is replaced with a different library with more advanced features), the application can be modified to make use of the new library by changing only the UI code.

Sidebar 13.5 Benefits of Separating the UI and FP

Separating the UI and FP is beneficial because:

- We can change the FP (e.g., to correct an error or improve performance) without having to change the UI.

- We can change the UI (e.g., to provide a different look and feel) without having to change the FP.

- We can have several different UIs for the same FP, including a UI that acts as a driver for the FP. This allows thorough regression testing of the FP.

The second reason for having the separation is that it allows us to change the way the user interface appears to the user (the "look and feel") without changing the functional part. For example, this makes it relatively easy to replace a simple UI with a more sophisticated one. In fact, we can have several different UIs; all of them can make use of the same FP.

The third reason for the separation is that it allows us to develop thorough regression tests (see Chapter 10) for the functional part. The regression test code will be programmed to interact with the FP just like a UI does, but rather than interacting with a user, it will act as a driver of the FP.

There are two ways to connect the UI and FP, as illustrated by the module dependency diagrams in Figure 13.2. In the first structure, the FP provides methods that the UI calls when user inputs happen; the FP methods carry out the user request and return some information to the UI that informs it of the result. The second structure extends the first: the UI still calls the FP to inform it of user inputs, but the FP can either return a result or call a UI method, whichever is more convenient. In doing a design, we always start with the first structure, since it will be adequate for many applications. We will switch to the second structure if we discover the need for it as the design progresses.

We begin our design by considering the UI since it drives the application by interacting with the user. We do not concern ourselves with the form of the user interaction, and in fact UI design is beyond the scope of the text. Our concern instead is to come up with a design of the FP that is independent of

Figure 13.2   Two structures

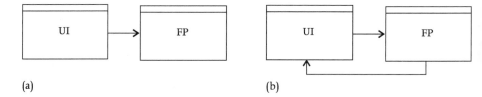

(a)   (b)

any particular UI. We focus on specifying the FP methods that are used by a UI to carry out user requests. These methods will be independent of the particular UI, so that we can change the UI as desired.

To determine the FP interface, we consider each operation in the requirements specification. In most cases, we will invent an FP method that will be called by a UI to perform the operation. The FP will do all the actual work of the application; the UI is responsible only for the interaction between the user and the FP.

Figure 13.3 gives a specification for our FP, Engine. This specification is derived from the requirements specification for the search engine shown in Figure 12.14. A first point to note is that the methods are similar to the associated operations but with two differences. First, they do not have checks clauses (nor requires clauses); instead, they throw NotPossibleException when a check would be violated. The value of this exception will be a string explaining the problem; the idea is that the UI will simply present the string to the user to explain what the problem is. The second difference from the operations is that methods return results that can be used by the UI to display information to the user.

A second point is that the specification of Engine makes use of the data model. We will continue to use the data model as we develop the design.

A third point is that the methods return objects of two data abstractions, Doc and Query, and we need to define these data types. Doc is the way the UI gets hold of a document; to display a document, it needs access to its title and text. Query is the way the UI gets hold of a query result; here it needs access to the keywords of the query and the documents that match the query, but it does not need to know the sum for each match since this information is not displayed to users. Figure 13.4 gives specifications for these two types. The specifications are preliminary: they are missing constructors

Figure 13.3   Specification of Engine

```
class Engine {
```
// OVERVIEW: *An engine has a state as described in the search engine*
//   *data model. The methods throw the* NotPossibleException
//   *when there is a problem; the exception contains a string explaining*
//   *the problem. All instance methods modify the state of* this.

// *constructors*
```
Engine( ) throws NotPossibleException
```
// EFFECTS: *If the uninteresting words cannot be retrieved from the*
//   *persistent state throws* NotPossibleException *else creates* NK *and*
//   *initializes the application state appropriately.*

// *methods*
```
Query queryFirst (String w) throws NotPossibleException
```
// EFFECTS: *If* ¬WORD(w) *or* w *in* NK *throws* NotPossibleException *else*
//   *sets* Key = { w }, *performs the new query, and returns the result.*

```
Query queryMore (String w) throws NotPossibleException
```
// EFFECTS: *If* ¬WORD(w) *or* w *in* NK *or* Key = { } *or* w *in* Key *throws*
//   NotPossibleException *else adds* w *to* Key *and returns the query result.*

```
Doc findDoc (String t) throws NotPossibleException
```
// EFFECTS: *If* t *not in* Title *throws* NotPossibleException
//   *else returns the document with title* t.

```
Query addDocs (String u) throws NotPossibleException
```
// EFFECTS: *If* u *is not a URL for a site containing documents or* u *in* URL
//   *throws* NotPossibleException *else adds the new documents to* Doc.
//   *If no query was in progress returns the empty query result else*
//   *returns the query result that includes any matching new documents.*
```
}
```

---

and methods that will be invented when we consider the implementation of
Engine.

A fourth point is that some operations do not have associated Engine
methods. This occurs when the UI can easily do the work by itself or by calling
methods of subsidiary types. In the search engine, for example, the FP does
not need to have a method for the makeCurMatch operation because the UI can

Figure 13.4   Preliminary specifications of Doc and Query

```
class Doc {
    // OVERVIEW: A document contains a title and a text body.

    // methods
    String title ( )
        // EFFECTS: Returns the title of this.

    String body ( )
        // EFFECTS: Returns the body of this.
}

class Query {
    // OVERVIEW: Provides information about the keywords of a query and
    //    the documents that match those keywords. size returns the number
    //    of matches. Documents can be accessed using indexes between 0 and
    //    size. Documents are ordered by the number of matches they
    //    contain, with document 0 containing the most matches.

    // methods
    String[ ] keys ( )
        // EFFECTS: Returns the keywords of this.

    int size ( )
        // EFFECTS: Returns a count of the documents that match the query.

    Doc fetch (int i) throws IndexOutOfBoundsException
        // EFFECTS: If 0 <= i < size returns the ith matching document else
        //    throws IndexOutOfBoundsException.
}
```

implement this operation by using methods of Query and Doc. However, as stated previously, all the application work is done by the FP. For example, the UI for the search engine obtains a keyword from the user, but it calls an FP method to compute the query result.

A final point is that we do not include toString and repOk in the specifications. However, all the abstractions will have these methods.

13.4   Starting the Design

The first step is to construct an initial module dependency diagram and enter it, and the specifications of the FP and other abstractions, in the design notebook. The initial module dependency diagram for the search engine is shown in Figure 13.5.

The diagram is laid out so that if one abstraction uses another, the used abstraction is positioned lower in the diagram than the using abstraction. We deduce the uses relations for the helpers from their specifications, in particular from the headers of standalone procedures and iterators or, in the case of data abstractions, from the headers of their methods and constructors. If a header for an abstraction indicates that an object of some type is passed in as an argument or returned as a result, the abstraction uses that type. Thus, Engine uses both Query and Doc, and Query uses Doc. We assume strong dependencies among helpers (i.e., that abstractions will call methods of types they use). When we study the implementation of an abstraction, we may discover that the dependency is weak rather than strong.

Then we choose our first target, the FP for the application. The first step is to invent helpers. There is one main heuristic to guide us in this process: *Let the problem structure determine the program structure*. This means that we should concentrate on understanding the problem being solved (namely, how to implement the target) and use the insights we gain into the problem to help us develop the structure of the program.

Figure 13.5   First module dependency diagram

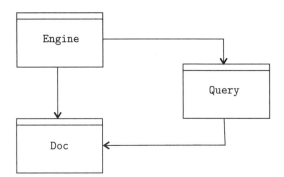

315

A good way to study the problem structure is to make a list of the tasks that must be accomplished. In the case of a data abstraction like Engine, each method is a task, so we begin by considering each of them in turn. We can choose to consider them in any order, but some of them are more interesting than others. For example, considering queryFirst will force us to think about how we do query processing, and considering findDoc will force us to think about how we find a document given its title.

When a method has lots of work to do, we list the tasks it must accomplish. Here is a list for queryFirst:

1. Check the input string w to be sure it's a word.

2. Make sure it's an interesting word.

3. Start a new query with w as the only keyword.

4. For each document, determine whether it is a match (contains w).

5. For each match, determine the number of occurrences of w.

6. Sort the matches by number of occurrences of w.

7. Return the information about the matches and query.

We do *not* assume that the final program will have subparts that correspond to the listed tasks. Listing the tasks is just a first step toward a design. Also, although we have listed the tasks in approximately the order in which they might be carried out, we do not assume that this order will exist in the final program. As we continue the design, we might reorganize the way the tasks are carried out.

Instead, the next step is to use the list as a guide in inventing the abstractions that will determine the program structure. In looking for abstractions, we seek to hide details of processing that are not of interest at the current level of the design. Although we can use procedures and iterators to hide details, data types (and sometimes families of types) are most useful for this.

Let's start by considering task 4 since it is critical to the performance of the queryFirst method. One way to proceed is to examine all the words of all the documents, or at least all the words of a single document, until we find a match. However, this is going to be very time consuming if the collection is large. Furthermore, as we look at a document, we will look at many words that are not the current keyword but that might be keywords in later queries. If we can record the information we learn about them, we can avoid work in future queries. To record the information, we need a data abstraction, ITable, that keeps track of what interesting words are in documents. Information can be added to `ITable` either when documents are fetched (by `addDoc`) or when a query is run after documents have been fetched; the former decision is better because it avoids a test in `queryFirst`. This decision means that `queryFirst` doesn't need to iterate through the documents at all! It just uses the prestored information by calling a `lookup` method of `ITable`.

Now consider task 5. Although there are presumably many fewer documents that match a query than there are documents in the collection, processing the matching documents to count occurrences of the keyword is still lots of work. Furthermore, it is redundant work: when information about a document was added to the `ITable`, we had to look at every word of every document, so we might as well count occurrences at the same time and store this information in the `ITable` too. The `lookup` method can then return information about counts as well as matches.

Next let's consider task 6. We need to sort the matches by count, but this can be accomplished in many ways. Rather than deciding how to do this now, let's instead introduce a data abstraction, `MatchSet`, to take care of the details. In fact, it is probably a good idea for `MatchSet` to perform the query: this provides flexibility for its implementation (e.g., the chance to sort as documents are added to the set), and it allows us to defer deciding about the kind of information the `ITable` `lookup` method returns until we consider what form will be most useful for implementing `MatchSet`. Having `MatchSet` perform the query means that all of tasks 3–6 will be handled by a `MatchSet` method; this method can return the `Query` object that contains the result for the query.

Finally, let's consider the first two tasks. For the second task, we need to preprocess the information about uninteresting words when the program starts up so that we can quickly look up whether a proposed word is uninteresting. This information could be stored in a separate data abstraction, or we might merge the information with that about interesting words. The latter choice gives us a table that keeps track of all words, both interesting and uninteresting; its lookup method can return all this information. An advantage of this choice is that it allows each word in a new document to be added to the table with just one call, rather than having to check first in another table to see whether the word is uninteresting. Therefore, let's make this choice and rename `ITable` to be `WordTable` to better match its function. Another point is that `WordTable` methods can also detect nonwords; a nonword is just a special kind of uninteresting word.

Thus, just by considering the queryFirst method, we have introduced a number of subsidiary abstractions. These abstractions allow the method to be implemented very simply, by calling a method of WordTable and then a method of MatchSet. Yet the implementation can also be efficient, assuming WordTable and MatchSet are implemented efficiently.

To continue the design, we need to consider the other methods. queryMore is similar to queryFirst; the only difference is that we are now interested in documents that have already matched (and therefore are in MatchSet). However, there are two ways to handle the new keyword. We could build another MatchSet matching the new keyword and then merge the two sets to obtain the matches in common. Or we could have another MatchSet method that adds the new keyword to the existing query. The latter choice seems better because, again, it provides flexibility for the MatchSet implementation that might lead to better performance.

Next let's consider the findDoc method. This method cannot be implemented by using the WordTable to look up each word in the title because that could produce many matches, not just the document of interest. Therefore, we need another way to find a document given its title. Since it would be inefficient to look at all documents when findDoc is called, we want to preprocess documents as they are added to the collection. Let's call the data abstraction that stores the information about titles the TitleTable.

Finally, let's consider the addDocs method. This method needs to obtain the new documents by getting in touch with the site named by the URL. The interaction with the site can be handled by an iterator, getDocs, that provides the documents (as text) one after another. addDocs creates the new document and adds it to TitleTable and WordTable; the document itself will simply exist in heap and be accessible from both tables. Then addDocs must add the document to the query if one is in progress; this should be done by calling a method of MatchSet. Finally, addDocs must return the new query result, or the empty query if no query was in progress; this implies that we need an empty Query object.

Now that we have looked at all the methods, we are ready for the second step of the design, namely, firming up and documenting these abstractions. In the process of producing the documentation, we often uncover loose ends. Some are simply details that need to be worked out, but some might be design errors that require modifications. That is to say, a lot of design work is done during this step; this process is similar to what hap-

Figure 13.6   Specification of getDocs iterator

```
class Comm {
    static Iterator getDocs (String u) throws NotPossibleException
        // EFFECTS: If u isn't a legitimate URL or the site it names does not
        //     respond as expected throws NotPossibleException else returns a
        //     generator that will produce the documents from site u (as strings).
}
```

pened during requirements analysis when we defined the requirements specification.

Figure 13.6 gives the specification of getDocs. Note that this procedure doesn't know anything about URLs of sites that have provided documents earlier; therefore, addDocs must check the provided URL against a list of URLs it maintains.

Figure 13.7 gives specifications for WordTable, and TitleTable. For WordTable, we could either process the file of uninteresting words in Engine and add the words to the table one at a time, or we could have the WordTable constructor handle this processing. Having the WordTable constructor do the processing limits knowledge of the filename and format to WordTable so that we can change them easily. Another point about WordTable is that its addDoc method requires that its argument not be null; this is reasonable since the method is called by the search engine only after it creates the document. A similar requirement exists for the addDoc method of TitleTable (and in many of the specifications given later in this chapter). Note also that the TitleTable addDoc method checks whether the document is a duplicate.

The specification for WordTable is incomplete. When inventing data abstractions, we define only the operations used by the implementations studied so far. Additional operations will be defined when we study other implementations that use the type; this is what happened for Query as a result of studying the implementation of Engine.

Now let's consider the specification for MatchSet. One question that arises here is how MatchSet relates to Query. There does not seem to be any good reason to have two separate abstractions here. Instead, the MatchSet methods we identified in the design of Engine are simply ways of constructing queries, while the methods we mentioned earlier are the ways of accessing information about queries once they have been constructed. Therefore, we should merge

Figure 13.7   Specifications of WordTable and TitleTable

```
class WordTable {
```
    // OVERVIEW: *Keeps track of both interesting and uninteresting words.*
    //   *The uninteresting words are obtained from a private file. Records*
    //   *the number of times each interesting word occurs in each document.*

    // *constructors*
```
    WordTable ( ) throws NotPossibleException
```
        // EFFECTS: *If the file cannot be read throws* NotPossibleException
        //   *else initializes the table to contain all the words in the file*
        //   *as uninteresting words.*

    // *methods*
```
    boolean isInteresting (String w)
```
        // EFFECTS: *If* w *is* null *or a nonword or an uninteresting word*
        //   *returns false else returns true.*

```
    void addDoc (Doc d)
```
        // REQUIRES: d *is not* null
        // MODIFIES: this
        // EFFECTS: *Adds all interesting words of* d *to* this *with a count*
        //   *of their number of occurrences.*
```
}
```

```
    class TitleTable {
```
    // OVERVIEW: *Keeps track of documents with their titles.*

    // *constructors*
```
    TitleTable ( )
```
        // EFFECTS: *Initializes* this *to be an empty table.*

    // *methods*
```
    void addDoc (Doc d) throws DuplicateException
```
        // REQUIRES: d *is not* null
        // MODIFIES: this
        // EFFECTS: *If a document with* d's *title is already in* this *throws*
        //   DuplicateException *else adds* d *with its title to* this.

```
    Doc lookup (String t) throws NotPossibleException
```
        // EFFECTS: *If* t *is* null *or there is no document with title* t *in* this
        //   *throws* NotPossibleException *else returns the document with title* t.
```
}
```

these abstractions into a single abstraction that we will call Query to be consistent with the specification of Engine.

Finally, we must consider the specification for Doc. All we have identified is the need for a constructor, which takes the document as a string and returns a Doc provided the string can be interpreted as a document. Our processing requirements here are very slight: the constructor must determine that the document has a title and a body, but it need not actually scan the body. This is important; we would not want the constructor to process the entire document, since we will have to do this work when we find the document's keywords.

Figure 13.8 shows the specifications for Query and Doc. Note that a query based on a new keyword is actually computed using a constructor, not a method, and that there is a second constructor to make the empty query (which is needed by the addDocs method of Engine). Note also that Query operations do not require an interesting keyword; if the keyword is uninteresting, the resulting query will not have any matches.

The specifications in the figures do not give any performance constraints. However, for Engine to perform well, it is important for all the tables to provide efficient ways of looking up information. In fact, they should all provide constant time lookups (and therefore we can expect heavy use of hash tables as we proceed with the design).

The extended module dependency diagram is shown in Figure 13.9. Note that we do not show Engine having a dependency on Iterator although it uses a generator; this dependency is omitted because we consider iterators to be part of the base language. Exception types are also treated this way, and so are most abstractions defined in standard libraries, such as java.util; for example, we take Vector for granted.

As before, we determine levels in the diagram based on dependencies. Also, we assume strong dependencies; as we continue the design, we might discover that some of these dependencies are weak.

Just to firm up the design of Engine, here is a sketch of its rep:

```
WordTable wt;
TitleTable t;
Query q;
String[ ] urls;
```

Thus, its rep just stores the state of the engine and the tables that will be used to process future user requests. The actual rep may be different from what is shown here but will contain the information shown in the sketch.

Figure 13.8 Specifications of Query and Doc

```
class Query {
```
   // OVERVIEW: *as before plus*

   // *constructors*
```
   Query ( )
```
      // EFFECTS: *Returns the empty query.*

```
   Query (WordTable wt, String w)
```
      // REQUIRES: wt *and* w *are not* null
      // EFFECTS: *Makes a query for the single keyword* w.

   // *methods*
```
   void addKey (String w) throws NotPossibleException
```
      // REQUIRES: w *is not* null
      // MODIFIES: this
      // EFFECTS: *If* this *is empty or* w *is already a keyword in the query*
      //   *throws* NotPossibleException *else modifies* this *to contain the*
      //   *query for* w *and all keywords already in* this.

```
   void addDoc (Doc d)
```
      // REQUIRES: d *is not* null
      // MODIFIES: this
      // EFFECTS: *If* this *is not empty and* d *contains all the keywords of*
      //   this *adds it to* this *as a query result else does nothing.*
```
}
```

```
class Doc {
```
   // OVERVIEW: *As before plus*

   // *constructors*
```
   Doc (String d) throws NotPossibleException
```
      // EFFECTS: *If* d *cannot be processed as a document throws*
      //   NotPossibleException *else makes* this *be the* Doc
      //   *Corresponding to* d.
```
}
```

Figure 13.9 Extended module dependency diagram for Engine

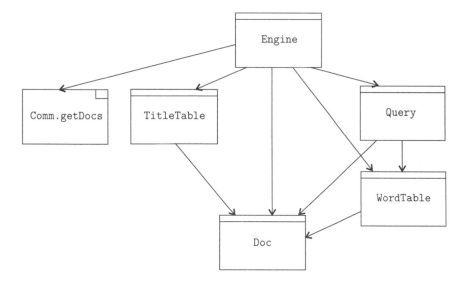

13.5   Discussion of the Method

In constructing our design, we have used a single method for focusing our attention on what needed to be done—we broke the work into subtasks and then investigated how we might accomplish the subtasks. We did not simply introduce a procedure for each subtask, however. Instead, we looked for abstractions, especially data types, to take care of the details of the tasks. This results in a better design, by making it easier to hide details until later stages of the design and to see and exploit connections among different tasks.

We introduced abstractions to hide details that we deemed inappropriate at the current level. This raises the question of how to decide what is appropriate at a given level. Such a decision is largely a matter of judgment, but there are some guidelines. An implementation should accomplish something, but it should not do too much. Our goal is to end up with small modules; implementations of data abstractions should be no more than a few pages, and method implementations should usually be shorter than a page. For example, if Engine had taken care of all details of carrying out user requests, it would have been much too big. In addition, the different parts of the implementation

323

of a module should be at roughly the same level of detail. Finally, each abstraction should be focused on a single purpose; we discuss this issue further in Chapter 14. See Sidebar 13.6 for a summary of our design method.

The design of Engine is typical of the design of a top-level abstraction in a system. The implementations of such abstractions are concerned primarily with organizing the computation, while the details of carrying out the steps are handled by helpers. Introducing partially specified data types like Doc and Query is also typical. In the early stages of design, we frequently know that two modules must communicate with each other, but we do not know exactly how this communication is to take place. In particular, we know that modules are to communicate through objects of some type, but we do not know what methods on those objects will be useful. Therefore, the specification of the shared type is necessarily incomplete. It will be completed as we continue with the design.

13.6   Continuing the Design

We now have a module dependency diagram containing several abstractions. How do we select the next target? (See Sidebar 13.7.) The first thing to notice is that not all abstractions are suitable as the next target; those that are suitable we shall call the *candidates*. Clearly, Engine itself is not a candidate since we have already designed its implementation. In addition, Doc and WordTable

Sidebar 13.7 Selecting the Next Target

- Identify all *candidates*; these are abstractions whose implementation has not yet been studied but whose specification is complete.
- Choose the target T from among the candidates. Reasons for choosing a particular target include exploring an uncertainty, increasing insight into the program structure, or finishing up a part of the design.

are not candidates since we have not yet studied how to implement modules that use them; and therefore we cannot be certain that their specifications are complete. (Actually, we shall occasionally select an incomplete abstraction as a candidate, as discussed a bit later in this section.)

Therefore, we have three candidates: getDocs, TitleTable, and Query. How do we choose between them? There are no hard and fast rules here; either candidate could be studied. However, there are several reasons why we might prefer one of several candidates:

1. We are uncertain about how to implement the abstraction. For example, we might need to implement an abstraction very efficiently, and we are not sure how to achieve this efficiency or even whether it can be achieved.

2. We are uncertain about its appropriateness.

3. One candidate may be more central to the design than another, so that studying its implementation will provide more insight into the design.

4. We may have been working on some area of the design and would like to finish that area.

The first two rules concern the investigation of areas considered to be questionable; choosing an abstraction for one of these two reasons is likely to expose design errors quickly. If such an uncertainty exists, it is almost always best to investigate it immediately. In fact, we might even investigate a data abstraction that is not yet a candidate, if we felt sufficiently uncertain about it. The other two rules are really opposites: finishing up an area is unlikely to lead to further insights, but it may nevertheless be useful (not to mention psychologically comforting) to get part of the design fully out of the way.

Furthermore, doing this might allow us to start implementing that part of the program.

In our example, all candidates are central to the design, although getDocs raises issues about how to communicate with other sites, whereas the other two candidates will expose details about data structures. To shorten the presentation, we will not go into the design of getDocs; instead, we will assume that it is provided by some library (e.g., a class Comm). Therefore, we need to choose between TitleTable and Query. Both will provide insight; we will start with TitleTable since it seems a bit simpler, and also it will shed some light on Doc.

There are two main issues in TitleTable: how to get a title from a document (in the addDoc method), and how to organize the table so that lookup will be fast. The title can be obtained by calling the title method of Doc. A fast lookup can be achieved by using a hash table, either one we implement directly within TitleTable or the one provided by java.util. However, we need to decide what types to use for the keys and values. In this case, the values are Docs. Either we can use a string for the key or we can introduce a Title data abstraction. The former decision seems acceptable, assuming that titles are random enough that the hash method for strings will produce sufficiently random results; we will make this assumption since it seems to be reasonable.

We do not need to extend the module dependency diagram at this point because we have not introduced any new abstractions. Even if we had decided to use the hash table in java.util, it isn't necessary to add it to the diagram since it is in a standard library. However, we do need to explain in the documentation about the implementation of TitleTable that we intend to use a hash table mapping from strings to Docs. And if we decided to use the hash table in java.util, we should also state this. In this case, using the hash table in java.util should be adequate.

13.7 The Query Abstraction

Now we have only one abstraction, Query, to consider, since there are no other candidates. Query has four interesting tasks to accomplish:

1. Compute a new query given a keyword.

2. Extend a query with a new keyword (the addKey method).

3. Extend a query with a new document (the addDoc method).

4. Provide access to the information about the query (in the observers). Of particular interest is providing access to the documents sorted by number of occurrences of the keywords.

In addition, Query must create an empty query, but that task is trivial.

Probably a good place to start is by considering how to make a query given a keyword. To do so, Query must

1. Find all the documents that contain the keyword with its count.

2. Keep track of the keyword.

3. Sort the documents based on number of occurrences of keywords.

The first task can be accomplished by calling a lookup method of WordTable. If lookup returned the matching documents sorted by a count of matches, the third task would be trivial. However, having this work done in WordTable is not a good idea for two reasons. First, many words will never be used as keywords yet sorting would have to happen for them anyway. Second, sorting is not useful for extended queries since there we care about the sum of the counts for all the keywords. Therefore, lookup will return the documents unsorted, and Query must take care of the sorting.

If we could assume that the number of matching documents is small, the technique used to do sorting is not important. However, this assumption is unlikely to be true, and therefore we need to be careful. A possible way to do the sorting is to use a sorted tree like the one discussed in Chapter 6. That technique will work efficiently provided the ordering of the documents in the list returned by WordTable is random in the number of matches: this assumption does seem reasonable. Therefore, using a sorted tree is a reasonable choice.

Now let's consider the addKey method. Here the tasks are

1. Check whether the new key is already in use.

2. Find the documents that contain the new key.

3. Find the documents matching the new key that are already in the query.

4. Sort the remaining documents by the sums of the matches.

Task 2 can be done using the WordTable lookup method. To do a good job of task 3, we need a quick way to check whether a document that matches the new key is already in the query. This cannot be done efficiently using the sorted tree, since that is sorted on number of matches with the previously known keywords, not on something that identifies the document. Instead, we need to store the previous matches (or the new matches) in a hash table so that we can look them up efficiently. Using a hash table will give us a constant rather than a linear lookup.

Next let's consider the addDoc method. This method must check whether each of its keywords is in the new document; if they are, it must add the document to the matches in the proper sorted order (i.e., it just adds the document with its sum to the sorted tree). However, there is a problem with this scheme: how does addDoc find out whether the keywords are in the new document? We could look up each keyword, and then determine whether the new document is in the list; but since these lists can be long, the test will be expensive. As an alternative, we could provide another WordTable method to look up a document and return its interesting words, but either that method requires a more complex implementation for WordTable, or it will be time consuming. Also, we don't really need this method; the only time we are interested in looking up the words of a document is when it is first added to the database. Therefore, instead let's have the addDoc method of WordTable return a hash table that tracks the keywords of the new document. This table can be constructed in time linear in the document size, and testing whether the document matches the query will be linear in the number of keywords. The table can actually map each word in the document to its number of occurrences so that in case the document matches the query, the sum of matches can be computed easily. The table will need to be an argument to the addDoc method of Query.

Thus, we have identified a need to change the specification of Query and also of WordTable, which means we need to re-examine Engine to determine the impact of these changes. But there is no problem: Engine simply passes the table returned by the call of the addDoc method of WordTable to the addDoc method of Query.

Finally, let's consider the observers. Keeping the documents in a sorted tree or a hash table will not allow an efficient implementation for fetch. Although we could imagine replacing the fetch method with an elements iterator (over the sorted tree), fetch is really what is needed for the UI. Therefore, after we sort, we should move the documents into an array so that fetch can be implemented efficiently.

However, if we are going to move the documents into an array, it doesn't make sense to use the sorted tree to sort them! Instead. we should store them in an array and sort them in place, using a good sorting algorithm such as quickSort. Actually, we'll use a vector so that in the addDoc method, we can simply insert the new document into the proper location in the vector (using the Vector method insertElementAt). The implementation of the addKey method will move the documents into a hash table, store the documents containing all keys in a vector, and then, as in the constructor, sort the vector.

Thus, we end up with approximately the following rep for a nonempty query:

```
WordTable k;
Vector matches; // elements are DocCnt objects
String[ ] keys;
```

DocCnt is a record-like type with two fields, the document and the count of the occurrences of keywords in the document. The rep invariant will state that matches is sorted by count, that the sums are correct, and that the matches contain all the keywords—in other words, it will state some of the constraints from the data model!

Since the implementation of Query is not obvious, it's useful to document our decisions by making sketches of some of the methods. Figure 13.10 shows these sketches. They can be used to help in developing the specifications for

Figure 13.10   Sketches of some Query methods

for the constructor (of a non-empty query):
    look up the key in the WordTable
    sort the matches using quickSort

for the addKey method
    look up the new key in the WordTable
    store the information about matches in a hash table
    for each current match, look up the document in the hash
       table and if it is there, store it in a vector
    sort the vector using quickSort

for the addDoc method
    use the argument table to get the number of occurrences
       of each current key
    if the document has all the keywords, compute the sum
       and insert the <doc, sum> pair in the vector of matches

Figure 13.11 Extended specifications for `Query` and `WordTable`

```
class Query {
    // As before except the addDoc method specification has changed.

    void addDoc (Doc d, Hashtable h)
        // REQUIRES: d is not null and h maps strings (the interesting words
        //    in d) to integers (the count of occurrences of the word in d).
        // MODIFIES: this
        // EFFECTS: If each keyword of this is in h, adds d to matches of this.
}

class WordTable {
    // As before plus

    Vector lookup (String k)
        // REQUIRES: k is not null.
        // EFFECTS: Returns a vector of DocCnts where the Doc contains k cnt times.

    Hashtable addDoc (Doc d)
        // REQUIRES: d is not null
        // MODIFIES: this
        // EFFECTS: Adds information about d's interesting words and their
        //    number of occurrences to this; also returns a table mapping each
        //    interesting word in d to its number of occurrences.
}
```

newly identified methods and abstractions, and they can also be entered in the design notebook (in the section for the Query abstraction).

The extended specifications for Query and WordTable are given in Figure 13.11. Figure 13.12 gives the specification for quickSort and related abstractions. quickSort is a generic abstraction that requires that elements of the vector belong to a type that extends the Comparable interface (this interface was defined in Figure 8.4). Since the actual vector being used in Query contains DocCnt objects, this means DocCnt must extend this interface. Note that the specification of DocCnt does not contain details about the methods for accessing the components since these are standard for record-like types, as explained in Chapter 5.

The extended module dependency diagram is shown in Figure 13.13. The most interesting point here is the use of hierarchy to explain how DocCnt

Figure 13.12   Specifications of quickSort and DocCnt

```
class Sorting {
    // OVERVIEW: Provides a number of procedures for sorting vectors.

    static void quickSort (Vector v) throws ClassCastException, NullPointerException
        // MODIFIES: v
        // EFFECTS: If some member of v is null throws NullPointerException; if
        //     elements of v aren't comparable, throws ClassCastException; else
        //     uses the quick sort algorithm to sort the elements of v so that
        //     elements with larger indexes are less than those at smaller indexes.
}
```

```
class DocCnt implements Comparable {
    // OVERVIEW: DocCnt is a record like type with two fields, a Doc
    //     and an integer.

    // methods
        int compareTo (Object x) throws ClassCastException, NullPointerException
        // EFFECTS: If x is null throws NullPointerException; if x isn't a DocCnt
        //     object, throws ClassCastException. Otherwise, if this.cnt < x.cnt
        //     returns -1; if this.cnt = x.cnt returns 0; else returns 1.
}
```

Figure 13.13   Extended module dependency diagram

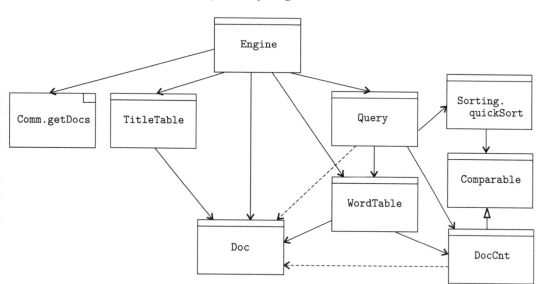

satisfies the dependence of quickSort on Comparable. Note that quickSort does *not* depend on DocCnt since it is generic; it depends only on Comparable. Another point is that we now know that Query has only a weak dependency on Doc (since it doesn't call any Doc methods), whereas in Figure 13.9, we assumed a strong dependency. DocCnt also has a weak dependency on Doc.

13.8   The WordTable Abstraction

At this point, we have only one candidate, WordTable, under the reasonable assumption that quickSort is provided in a library. The implementation of WordTable is fairly clear. It will use a hash table that maps strings that represent uninteresting words to null and strings that are interesting words to vectors, where each element of the vector is a DocCnt.

The addDoc method will get each word from Doc and use the hash table to determine whether the word is interesting. It will store interesting words both in the hash table, H, it is returning and in the hash table that records the state of the WordTable. Probably the best approach is for addDoc to store information in H as it processes the document, and then add the information to its rep at the end.

Implementing WordTable does require a way of iterating over the words in the documents. Thus, Doc needs to provide an iterator that can be used for this purpose (or size and fetch methods).

We have not yet considered one additional issue for WordTable: it concerns canonical forms for words. For example, we would not want to have entries for both "hash" and "Hash" in the WordTable. One possibility is to have an extended equality test that would recognize, for example, that "hash" and "Hash" are the same word, but that sounds expensive. A better solution is to have a canonical form for each word—for example, all lowercase. Another point is that canonicalization is needed in other places—for example, in the queryFirst and queryMore methods of Engine and also in the addDocs method of TitleTable. This suggests that a good approach is to have a canon procedure that produces a canonical form. This procedure can be called by Engine methods so that a word entered by a user can be converted to canonical form just once, and by WordTable when it enters words in the table, including in its constructor, since it needs to keep the uninteresting words in canonical form as well. Having a single procedure that is used everywhere for canonicalization allows us to localize knowledge of what the canonical form is so that

Figure 13.14 Specifications of Doc and canon

```
class Doc {
    // As before plus we now know that Doc is immutable and that
    // it provides an iterator.

    Iterator words ( )
        // EFFECTS: Returns a generator that will yield all the words in the
        //     document as strings in the order they appear in the text.
}

class Helpers {
    // Provides various helping procedures; at present only canon is defined.

    String canon (String s) throws NotPossibleException
        // EFFECTS: If s is null throws NotPossibleException else
        //     returns a string that is the canonical form of s.
}
```

we can change it easily if necessary. Thus, this design is better than one in which, for example, both Engine and WordTable needed to produce canonical forms.

Another point is that the words iterator of Doc simply returns words. It does not determine whether those words are keywords. This design is more desirable than one in which Doc knows about keywords since it represents a clean separation of concerns.

The specification of canon and the extended specifications for Doc are given in Figure 13.14. Figure 13.15 shows the extended module dependency diagram.

13.9 Finishing Up

Now we have only the canon and Doc abstractions left. canon is trivial to implement, and we need not consider it further. Doc parses its input string as needed. When a Doc is constructed, the constructor finds the title by parsing the first part of the string; if it can't find a title, it throws the NotPossible-Exception. The rest of the parsing is done by the words iterator; at each

Figure 13.15 Extended module dependency diagram.

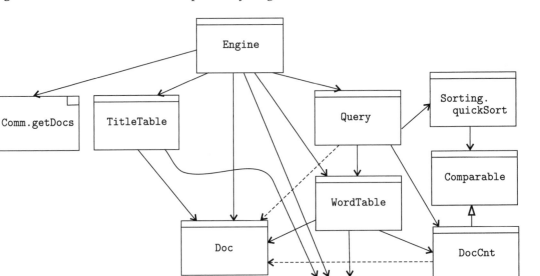

iteration it finds the next word and returns it. It terminates when it reaches the end of the document.

13.10   Interaction between FP and UI

Our design for the search engine used only the simple form of interaction between the FP and UI: the UI calls FP methods (or methods of some of the auxiliary types). Now we consider a more complicated interaction.

The addDocs operation may take a long time to complete since it involves interaction with a remote site; and, in addition, there may be lots of documents to retrieve. When an operation takes a long time, users generally like to be reassured that the program is making progress. This reassurance might take the form of telling the user periodically what is going on—for example, how many documents have been retrieved.

Suppose we decide to add this to our design. A simple way to do it is to have the FP call the UI with progress reports. For example, each time the addDocs

Figure 13.16 UI Hierarchy

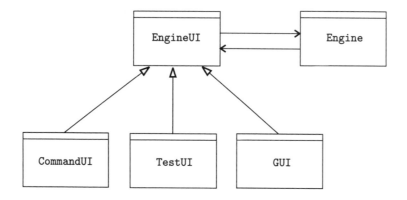

method of Engine gets another document from getDocs, it could call a UI method to report the current count; the UI can then display this information to the user. The UI method might be

```
void docProgress (int n)
    // REQUIRES: An addDocs operation is in progress
    // EFFECTS: Informs the user that n documents have been retrieved.
```

Now we have the structure (b) in Figure 13.2.

When we have structure (b), the FP will need to have access to the UI object to call its methods. This can be accomplished by passing the UI object as an argument to the FP's constructor.

When the UI and FP interact as in structure (a) in Figure 13.2, the FP is not dependent on the UI. With structure (b) the FP is dependent on the UI. Since our goal is to have many UIs, we need a way to relate them so that the FP will work with any of them. This is easily accomplished using hierarchy: the FP depends on an abstract UI, and real UIs are subtypes of that UI. A module dependency diagram illustrating this situation for the search engine is shown in Figure 13.16 where we see that there are three actual UIs: one that does regression testing of the FP, one providing a command-line interface, and one providing a GUI interface. In the diagram, we have omitted the structure of the Engine; one way to think about this is that in this diagram, the node labeled Engine stands for the entire module dependency diagram shown in Figure 13.15.

Actually, we might also want to have a hierarchy for the FP, so that the UI can be used with variants of the FP. We will discuss this issue further in Chapter 15.

The extension of the search engine to inform the user about progress in fetching documents does not address another user need: when an operation takes a long time to carry out, the user may want to terminate it. When this happens, the user generally requires a speedy response to the termination command. Our current design allows the termination to happen each time the engine calls the docProgress method, but this may not be fast enough, for example, if communication is very slow or the site containing the documents is not responding well.

To provide faster response, however, requires the use of concurrency. An FP method that runs for a long time would fork a thread to do the lengthy work and then return to the UI. The UI can then call some other FP method if the user indicates that it is time to abandon that work. For example, in the search engine, the body of the addDocs method would fork a thread; the thread would carry out the fetching and processing of documents, while the addDocs method would return immediately. Engine would need to provide another method that the UI can call to terminate fetching of documents:

```
void stopFetch ( )
    // EFFECTS: Terminates the current fetching of documents.
```

This structure allows the search engine to go on to the next user command immediately, even though document fetching is in progress. (To find out how to use threads in Java, consult a Java text.)

13.11 Module Dependency Diagrams versus Data Models

A data model defines the abstract state of a program at the level of the requirements specification. It does not say anything about the modular structure of the program. The sets in the model are *not* types. We do not produce a program design by introducing a data abstraction for each set. Instead, we consider what the program needs to do and introduce abstractions that allow it to be accomplished in an economical way. Furthermore, in our design process, we did not pay much attention to the model except indirectly: the model helps keep the design focused on what is wanted because it plays an important role in clarifying the requirements specification. The end result of the design is a structure that is quite different from the model. This can be seen for the search engine by comparing Figures 12.12 and 13.15.

However, the data model can be used to check on the correctness of the design. First, every set in a data model must show up somewhere in the program, or the design cannot be correct. For example, here is an explanation of what happened to the sets for the search engine:

`Cur`, `Curmatch`: *these are in the UI*
`Doc`: *there is no set of all documents, but all documents are*
    accessible from `WordTable` *and* `TitleTable`
`Title`: `TitleTable`
`Entry`: *handled within the* `Doc` *abstraction*
`Word`: *part of* `WordTable`
`NK`: *part of* `WordTable`
`Key`: *handled by* `Query`
`Match`: *handled by* `Query`
`URL`: *just part of the rep of* `Engine`
`Num`: `int`

In addition, we need to explain what happened to the relations and the constraints. Some relations will disappear; for example, this is what happens to the `index` relation (since Doc provides an iterator rather than access by index) and the `site` relation (since there is no need to determine the site that provided a document). The constraints on relations that remain must be enforced. For example, the `Query` abstraction is responsible for ensuring that there are no matches when Key is empty. It's ideal when a constraint ends up being enforced within a single abstraction, but that is usually not the case. For example, the `TitleTable` contains an entry for each document only if Engine enters each document in the table and the table stores every document that is entered. Thus, it is useful to determine which modules must work together to enforce each constraint. Here is some of this information for the search engine:

Every document has a title: enforced by `Engine` *and* `TitleTable`
Every word in each document is in `Word`: *enforced by* `Doc`,
    `WordTable`, *and* `Engine`
`NK` *is a subset of* `Word`: *enforced by* `WordTable`
`Key` *is a subset of* `Word` − `NK`: *enforced by* `Engine`, `Query`,
    and `WordTable`

> ### Sidebar 13.8 Data Models and Design
>
> - A module dependency diagram identifies program modules that will be used in the implementation. A data model defines sets that do not correspond to program modules.
>
> - Every set in a data model must show up somewhere in the design. One check on the completeness of the design is to explain how it handles each set.
>
> - Furthermore, the design must enforce all the constraints of the model. A good check on the correctness of the design is to explain how this is accomplished.

Exactly the matching documents are in `Match`: *enforced by* `Query`, `WordTable`, `Doc`, *and* `Engine`

`Key = { } ` $\Rightarrow$ `Match = { }`: *enforced by* `Query`

    matches are sorted properly: enforced by `Query`, `WordTable`, `Doc`, *and* `Engine`

Note that several modules are usually involved in enforcing a constraint and, furthermore, that `Engine` is often involved. For example, `Engine` is involved in keeping `Key` disjoint from `NK` because it tests whether a word is interesting and forms a query with it only if it is; `WordTable` is also involved since it must provide the correct answer when the `isInteresting` method is called; and `Query` is involved since it must produce the answer for the word given to it as an argument and not for some other word. The reason `Engine` is involved so often is that it orchestrates the running of the entire program; this is typical of a top-level module, and as a result, such modules will play a role in enforcing many of the constraints.

Sidebar 13.8 summarizes this discussion.

13.12 Review and Discussion

The design of `Engine` was accomplished in stages. We selected a new target at each stage and investigated its implementation by carrying out two main activities. First, we invented some helping abstractions that were useful in the problem domain of the target. Then we defined the properties of the helpers precisely and described those properties in specifications.

13.12.1   Inventing Helpers

The hardest part of program design, and the place where the greatest creativity is required, is in the invention of the helpers. The primary method used here is to study the problem structure and derive from it a structure for the program. Our study of the problem structure takes the form of a list of tasks to be accomplished. However, we do not simply invent a program structure that carries out those tasks one after another. Instead, we use the list as a way of focusing attention on what needs to be done and then invent abstractions to accomplish the needed work.

Abstractions are introduced in each case to hide detail. For example, Query hides the details of how a query is processed, while Doc hides the details of how a document is interpreted. It is desirable to hide detail for two reasons: control of complexity and modifiability. We control complexity by delaying decisions and thus limit the number of concerns that must be dealt with at any particular level of the design. We support modifiability because the hidden details can be changed later without affecting other abstractions.

In developing the design, we are guided by several factors:

- Knowledge of what abstractions are already available. This includes abstractions present in the programming language and in any available library of programs, as well as those already identified during this design. For example, we knew that java.util provided hash tables and that quickSort was also available in a library.

- Knowledge of preexisting algorithms and data structures. It is necessary to know about the methods that have already been developed. For example, the designer should be familiar with existing sorting and searching techniques and not have to reinvent them.

- Knowledge about related programs and their structure. As we get deeper into the design, this knowledge is likely to become more and more useful, since even radically different applications are likely to have some similar subtasks.

For example, our decision to process the words in a document as we added them to the WordTable was based on our knowledge that one-pass algorithms are usually better in both space and time than two-pass algorithms. Also, we relied on the existence of Java types, including those in packages such as java.io, and made explicit choices between them and data abstractions; for example, we might have defined an abstraction for the title of a document, but it seemed sufficient to use a string in this case.

Role of Data Types

Types usually have the most impact on the shape of the design, with procedures and iterators as methods, but independent procedures and iterators are also important. We look for types in four areas: input, output, internal data structures, and individual data items. Most of our data abstractions in Engine hide details of internal data structures. (The design of Engine is somewhat unusual in its repeated use of the same data structure—a hash table; more typically, a program will make use of several different data structures.) However, Doc is an abstraction of a data item, and WordTable abstracts from details of input (the structure of the file defining the uninteresting words). We might have had an abstraction of output if there were a way for a user to request the search engine to write information about matching documents to a file; in this case, an InfoStream, where information about an entire document is added at once, might have been useful.

Encapsulating input and output permits us to consume input or produce output in terms of abstract quantities. Input and output are often handled with procedures or iterators, since we typically just read or write the next item. The getDocs iterator is an example. It could be doing fancy buffering— for example, fetching documents in batches or fetching the next document while we are processing the current one. Since it is an abstraction, these details are hidden from us, and we need not be concerned with them.

13.12.2   Specifying Helpers

In inventing helpers, we are concerned only with concepts; the details of those concepts are usually left ill defined. In the second step of design, we firm up those details and document them by means of specifications. During this activity, we commonly uncover cases that have been overlooked, especially error cases and end cases (for example, the empty input). We may discover missing arguments or results, or find that arguments or results are of the wrong type. In the case of data types, we may discover missing operations. Moreover, if an abstraction has become overly complex, this may be evident when we try to write the specification. A complicated specification leads naturally to the question of how things can be simplified. A better, simpler abstraction is often the result.

We can use sketches of the implementation as an aid to identifying and specifying the helper abstractions and to document our implementation decisions. These sketches are written in English and contain descriptions of subtasks to be accomplished. We can then identify for each subtask what standalone procedure or iterator, or operation of a type, is to be used and what its arguments are. Unlike the list of tasks used to start the design, the order in which subtasks are carried out in the sketch is significant. These sketches are worth doing only when something complicated is going on; we used them only for the Query abstraction.

After we have specified all the helpers precisely, we document our design decisions in the notebook by extending the module dependency diagram, and by adding or extending definitions of the helpers. Although we have shown only the new parts of specifications in the figures in this chapter, the entire specification will appear as a unit in the notebook. We will also include a sketch of the implementation of the target if one was made; as mentioned, this is done only if the implementation is clever. Also, for data abstractions, we will record decisions made about what data structures to use in the rep, and we may provide a sketch of the rep (what it will contain).

One issue we have not yet discussed is how thorough the design of an abstraction implementation must be. At each stage, the investigation must be thorough enough that all helpers are identified and specified precisely. It is not necessary to go further than this. For example, we did not look closely at the implementation of WordTable since it was clear what to do. By contrast, the design of Query was carried out in detail since we needed to understand what it did and how the helpers should be defined. However, in general, we expect more design (but of a localized nature) to be needed during implementation, including possibly the recognition of the need for private methods within data abstractions.

13.12.3   Continuing the Design

As soon as one target has been studied, the next step is to select a new target. First, the candidates are identified; these candidates are abstractions whose implementations have not yet been studied but whose using abstractions have all been analyzed. One candidate is then chosen as the next target. While there are guidelines for making this choice, there are no rules. For example, there is no requirement that all abstractions at one level in the design must be studied before those at lower levels. Instead, common sense should be used, with the goal of finishing the entire design as quickly as possible. This is why we look at questionable abstractions as soon as possible and even study them before they are complete.

If, while studying the implementation of some target, we discover an error in the abstraction itself (i.e., a change in its specification), we must correct the error before proceeding further with the current target. We use the arcs in the module dependency diagram to discover all implementations affected by the error. Then we correct the design for those implementations. In the process, we may discover more errors that must also be corrected. We saw several examples of such errors in our design, but all of them were easy to handle. In a real design, we are likely to find more significant problems that may lead us to back up through several abstractions before the problem can be fixed. In fact, some design errors may not be found until the implementation is underway. The data model can be used to check for design errors as discussed in Section 13.11; other techniques for finding errors early will be discussed in Chapter 14.

When there are no more candidates, then ordinarily the design is finished. There is one special case, however. When two or more abstractions are mutually recursive, then none can be a candidate, since each is used by another abstraction that has not yet been studied. When dealing with mutually recursive abstractions, we must proceed with caution. One must be selected as a candidate and studied first. Since this candidate is used by another abstraction that has not been studied, we may discover later that its behavior is not what is needed. This problem is another indication of why mutual recursion must be viewed with suspicion.

13.12.4   The Design Notebook

The result of a finished design is a design notebook containing the completed module dependency diagram and sections for each abstraction. It is important that this notebook contain not only the decisions that were made, but also the reasons for them. Ideally, this part of the documentation will explain both what problems are being solved by a particular structure and what problems are being avoided that would have been introduced by other structures studied during the design.

Because such documentation is difficult and time consuming to produce, it is often neglected. It is important in the later stages of program development, however, whenever a situation arises in which a design decision must be reconsidered or changed. The new decision can best be made by someone who fully understands the design. The documentation makes the needed information available, both to people other than the original designers and even to the original designers, who will forget it as time goes by.

13.13 Top-Down Design

Our design process is a top-down; that is, we always reason from what is wanted to how to achieve it. In this way, we keep our goal (the required program) firmly in view and are free to use our intuition about programs to guide us to a solution. Through experience in writing programs, programmers develop intuition about what is implementable with what efficiency. They also come to know what program structures are appropriate to various problems. This knowledge can be used to good effect in top-down design.

An alternative to top-down design is bottom-up design, which starts with what is known to be implementable and somehow proceeds from there to achieve what is wanted. Bottom-up design is not really a tenable process for any but the smallest programs. For large programs, the gap between what is available and what is wanted is large and must be bridged by the introduction of many abstractions. This gap is easier to bridge top-down because we can concentrate on the thing that is least understood (the program that is wanted) and use what we know to help us. With top-down design, our intuition about what is implementable tells us whether we are making progress: the helpers should be easier to implement than the target. With bottom-up design, it is much harder to measure progress since it is hard to evaluate how close we are to what is wanted.

In reality, we tend to go back and forth between top-down and bottom-up design. For example, we may investigate the implementation of key abstractions or questionable abstractions even when all uses are not yet understood. However, it is important that the design be driven from the top and that we avoid actually implementing any abstractions until their design and that of their helpers is complete; doing implementation before then is truly a waste of effort, since the chances of all the details being right are small.

13.14   Summary

This chapter has discussed program design. Design progresses by modular decomposition based on the recognition of useful abstractions. We discussed how this decomposition happens and illustrated the design process with an example. We also discussed a method of documenting a design in a notebook.

The example used was a simple search engine, and the resulting program was small. In addition, the presentation of the design process was unrealistic: we made very few errors as we went along, and these errors had little impact on the overall design. In the real world, any design, even of a simple program, requires a great deal of iteration, and many errors will be introduced and corrected as it progresses. Nevertheless, the basic methods we presented still apply, even to much larger programs. We have used them in such programs ourselves.

We do not claim that the search engine design is the best possible. In fact, the goal of the design process is never a "best" design. Instead, it is an "adequate" design, one that satisfies the requirements and design goals and has a reasonably good structure. We discuss this issue in the next chapter.

This chapter carried out the design in its entirety, without any implementation occurring until the design was finished. It is often desirable to start the implementation earlier. If some portion of the design is complete, those modules can be implemented while the remainder of the design is carried out. For example, we might have implemented the `TitleTable` while we were working on the design of query processing. Starting the implementation early is desirable because it can lead to earlier completion of the program or to the early release of a product that provides some features. However, before doing any implementation, it is important to evaluate the design to determine whether it is "correct"—that is, will lead to a program that meets the requirements. Techniques for determining this are discussed in the next chapter.

Exercises

13.1 In many places in the design of Engine, we chose to require that arguments were not null rather than having the called method throw an exception if the argument was null. What do you think of this approach versus having the called methods throw exceptions?

13.2 In the design of Query, sorting matches using a sorted tree was rejected in favor of sorting a vector. Compare the performance differences between these two alternatives.

13.3 Suppose we change the design so that the addDoc method of WordTable is passed an extra argument, an Iterator that it uses to get the words of the document:

```
Hashtable addDoc (Iterator e, Doc d)
```

Provide a specification for this method. Also discuss its ramifications on the design and how it affects the module dependency diagram. Discuss whether this change is an improvement over the design presented in the chapter.

13.4 Suppose the search engine is no longer going to store documents once they have been entered in the word and title table; instead, if a user wants to view a document (selected through a match on a title or a query), the engine will refetch the document. Modify the requirements specification and the design to accommodate this change.

13.5 Modify the search engine to support disjunctive queries—that is, queries that match all documents that contain at least one keyword in a list of keywords. First, change the requirements specification, including changes to the data model if any are needed. Then change the design.

13.6 Modify the search engine requirement specification and design to allow more than one document to have the same title.

13.7 Design and implement the stock tracker program specified in Chapter 12.

13.8 Design and implement the xref program specified in the exercises of Chapter 12.

13.9 Design and implement the spelling checker specified in the exercises of Chapter 12.

13.10   Design and implement the path finder program specified in the exercises of Chapter 12.

13.11   Form a team of three or four people and design and implement a moderately large program.

Between Design and Implementation

14

In this chapter, we discuss briefly the two considerations that arise between the completion of a design and the start of implementation—namely, evaluation of the design and choice of a program development strategy.

14.1   Evaluating a Design

During the design of a large program, it is worthwhile to step back periodically and attempt a comprehensive evaluation of the design so far. This process is called *design review* (see Sidebar 14.1). Design reviews should always be conducted by a team composed of some people involved in the design and others who are not. Those not involved in the design should be familiar with both the program requirements and the technology that will be used in implementing the design. They should also be familiar with the design itself.

It is important that both the designers and the outside reviewers understand that the point of a design review is not to discover the perfect design, but rather to discover whether the existing design is adequate—will do the job with acceptable performance and cost. While the designers will inevitably find themselves attempting to justify their design decisions to the outside reviewers, they should not view this as their primary goal. In addition, both the reviewers and the designers must keep in mind that the purpose of

---

Sidebar 14.1   Goals of a Design Review

A design review evaluates the correctness, performance, and quality of a design:

- The design must enable an implementation that satisfies the requirements both functionally and with respect to performance.

- The design structure must be relatively easy to implement, and it must accommodate potential modifications relatively easily.

---

the review is only to find errors, not to correct them. Errors should be recorded in an error log, and then the review should continue (unless so many errors have been found that continuing is no longer productive).

It is useful for the designers to present not only the design but also the alternatives that were considered and rejected. This will give the outside reviewers a context for evaluating the chosen design. It may also help the reviewers to find flaws in the design. A common problem is failure to apply design criteria uniformly. Explaining that an alternative was rejected because it failed to meet some criterion may well prompt the reviewers to notice that some other part of the design fails to meet that same criterion.

There are three critical issues to address in evaluating a design:

1. Will all implementations of the design exhibit the desired functionality? That is, will the program be "correct"?

2. Are there implementations of the design that will be acceptably efficient?

3. Does the design describe a program structure that will make implementations reasonably easy to build, test, and maintain? Also, how difficult will it be to enhance the design to accommodate future modifications, especially those identified during the requirements phase?

14.1.1   Correctness and Performance

Earlier in this book, we discussed two approaches, testing and informal verification, to increasing our confidence that a program will behave as desired. Unfortunately, neither of these approaches can be applied to designs. Since designs cannot be run, testing is out of the question. If designs were presented completely in a formal language, some verification might be possible. However, formal specification of designs of large programs is beyond the current state of the art.

While there are no completely rigorous techniques for reviewing a design, it is important that design reviews be systematic. They should examine both local and global properties of the design. Local properties can be examined by studying the specifications of individual modules, global properties, by studying how the modules fit together.

Two important local properties are consistency and completeness, which were discussed in Chapter 9. Another important local property is performance. The first step in estimating the overall performance of a system is to construct for each abstraction an expression relating its running time and storage consumption to its arguments. How accurately this can be done depends upon the completeness of the design. Consider the sort procedure:

```
void sort (Vector v) throws ClassCastException
    // MODIFIES: v
    // EFFECTS: If v is not null, sorts it into ascending order using
    //     the compareTo method; if some elements of v
    //     are null or aren't comparable throws ClassCastException.
```

If the design does not specify any performance constraints for sort, relatively little can be said about the performance of its implementations or about the performance of abstractions to be implemented using sort. The problem is that implementations of sort span a wide range with respect to performance. Considerably more can be said about the performance of implementations if the design includes the following criterion:

```
// worst case time = n*log(n) comparisons, where n is the size of a
```

and more yet if the design states

```
// worst case time = n*log(n) comparisons, where n is the size of a.
// Maximum temporary main memory allocated is a small constant.
```

An important function of a design review is to discover places where the design needs to be more specific about what is required of implementations.

After each module has been evaluated in isolation, we examine the design as a whole. A good way to begin is by discussing the relationship of the module dependency diagram to the data model. As discussed in Chapter 13, it must be possible to explain how the implementation handles every set and preserves each constraint.

The next step is to trace paths through the design that correspond to the various operations. We select some test data and then trace how both control and data would flow through an implementation based on the design. This tracing process is sometimes called a *walk-through*. The test data are chosen in much the same way as described in Chapter 10. However, since "testing" a design is labor intensive, we must be very selective in choosing our test data.

Since the point of tracing the design is to convince ourselves that all implementations of the design will have the desired functionality, the success of this method is related to the completeness of the test cases. We are using the test cases to carry out an informal verification process. During the design review, it is also important to discuss the completeness of the process—that is, to argue that all cases have been considered. Both normal and exceptional cases should be considered.

Picking test cases for a design review is simplified by the fact that the data can be symbolic. We need only identify properties that the test data should have; we do not need to invent data with those properties.

As an example, consider the search engine program designed in Chapter 13. We start with the call of the constructor of Engine. If an error occurs in creating the "WordTable" (because the file of uninteresting words is ill formed), the program will terminate. Otherwise, the table will be initialized, and we can proceed with user commands. At this point, no documents are in the collection; and therefore an attempt to look up a document using its title will fail, and queries will either fail (if the input is uninteresting or not a word) or give no matches.

Now suppose the user requests the fetching of some documents. Here we can define some symbolic data: the fetch produces three documents:

- d1 contains w1 6 times and w2 12 times and has title t1

- d2 contains w1 10 times and has title t2

- d3 contains w2 4 times and has title t3

All of these words are interesting words; in addition, the documents contain some uninteresting words.

We use these data to walk through the design of Engine. The walk-through is, in effect, a hand simulation of the design. The main thing we want to examine is the flow of information through the program. Here is how we might start a walk-through based upon the previous data:

1. Processing the fetch causes three Docs to be created. The Docs are then added to the title and word tables. When the Doc is passed to the WordTable addDoc method, its words are added to the table if they are interesting. This work is done efficiently since the title table and the word table are hash tables, and the documents are processed incrementally.

2. Suppose the user performs a query for w1. This word will be canonicalized, found to be interesting, and passed to Query. Query looks up the word in the WordTable and finds that it is contained in d1 and d2. It will sort in the order d2, d1. Now the user can examine the documents via the UI. The lookups in the word table are fast since it is a hash table, and the sort is also efficient.

3. Next the user adds w2 to the query. This is canonicalized, found to be interesting, and passed to the addKey method of query. The method looks up the word in the WordTable and finds that it matches d1 and d3. It combines this information with its previous query results to determine that only d1 has both words.

4. Next the user looks up a title t. This is looked up in the title table, which returns the appropriate match or throws an exception if t is not a title of an existing document.

The walk-through continues in this fashion until the behavior of the entire program has been explored. In the process, we estimate the performance of each module, so that we can construct estimates of worst-case and average efficiencies for the whole program.

Walk-throughs are a laborious and imprecise process. Experience indicates that designers are seldom able to examine their own designs adequately. The process works best when it is performed by a team of people including, but not dominated by, the designers.

Tracing through the entire design with a small set of inputs helps us to uncover gross errors in the way the abstractions that make up the design fit together. A good next step is to work bottom-up through the module dependency diagram, isolating subsystems that can be meaningfully evaluated independently of the context in which they will be used. Since these subsystems are likely to be considerably smaller than the system as a whole, we can trace more sets of test data through them. For example, if canonicalization had been left out of the design, the error might be noticed during a review of the WordTable because, at that point, we could look in more detail at the words in documents.

The modifiability of the design should be addressed explicitly during the review. A discussion of how the design must be changed to accommodate each expected modification should take place. A plausible measure of how well the design accommodates modifications is how many abstractions must be reimplemented or respecified in each case. The best situation is one in which only a single abstraction needs to be reimplemented.

For example, suppose the search engine were modified to not store the text of documents; instead, when a user wanted to examine a document, the document would need to be refetched from its site. This requires our design to be changed in a number of ways. First, we would probably like to refetch the document using its URL, but this means that we need to obtain that URL and to relate it to its document (e.g., by storing it in the Doc). One way to do so is to replace the getDocs iterator with an iterator that produces the URLs of the documents and then use a procedure to fetch a document given its URL; this procedure can also be used to refetch documents. We also need to decouple the production of words in the body of the document from the objects stored in the title and word tables so that the storage for the body can be deleted once the document's words have been added to the word table. One way to handle this change is to introduce a FullDoc abstraction, with a words iterator, and also a method that will return a Doc. The Engine creates a FullDoc and passes it to the addDoc method of the title and word tables, but both tables map to Docs and not to FullDocs. Therefore, the FullDoc can be garbage collected once information about it has been added to the two tables. The Doc stores only the URL of the document and perhaps other identifying information (e.g., the title), but not the full contents. Thus, this modification requires quite a few changes, but they are reasonably straightforward.

A walk-through forces us to look at the design from a different perspective than the one that characterized the design process. During design, we focused on identifying abstractions and specifying their interfaces. These abstractions arose from considering what steps were to be carried out, but our attention was focused on parts of the program separately. Now we go back over the steps carried out by the whole program as it uses the abstractions, and this exercise forces us to address the question of whether the abstractions can be composed to solve the original problem.

Sidebar 14.2 summarizes this part of the design review.

Sidebar 14.2   A Design Review: Evaluating Functionality

- Explain how the design captures the sets and constraints of the data model.
- Do a walk-through of the program on symbolic test data to show that the design will be able to perform correctly and with the required performance.
- Do the same process on individual modules or groups of related modules, to show that their arguments are sufficient and that their performance can be adequate.
- Discuss how the design will accommodate potential modifications.

14.1.2   Structure

The most important structural issue to address in evaluating a design is the appropriateness of the module boundaries. There are two key questions to ask:

1. Have we failed to identify an abstraction that would lead to a better modularization?

2. Have we grouped together things that really do not belong in the same module?

We can provide no formula for answering these questions. What we can provide is a list of symptoms that occur when a program has been badly modularized. We shall concentrate on local symptoms—that is, problems that can be detected by looking at a single module or at the interface between two modules.

Coherence of Procedures

Each procedure in a design should represent a single coherent abstraction. The coherence of an abstraction can be examined by looking at its specification. A procedure should perform a single abstract operation on its arguments. (Our discussion applies to iterators too. An iterator maps its inputs to a sequence of items; this mapping should be a single abstract operation.)

Some procedures have no apparent coherence. They are held together by nothing more than some arbitrarily placed bracketing mechanism. In the early days of "structured programming," many people failed to understand that good program structure is basically a semantic notion. They looked for simple syntactic definitions of "well-structured." Many of these simplistic definitions included an arbitrary upper bound, such as one page, on the size of procedures. Another example of an arbitrary size restriction occurs in programs that must manage their own memory and are divided into modules to facilitate overlays. Such arbitrary restrictions frequently led to procedures totally lacking in coherence.

A second cause of lack of coherence is hand optimization of programs. An eagle-eyed programmer may notice that some arbitrary group of statements appears several times. In an attempt to save space, the programmer may bundle these statements into a procedure. In the long run, however, such optimizations are generally counterproductive because they make the program harder to modify.

There are two reliable indicators of a total lack of coherence. If it seems that the best way to specify a procedure involves describing its internal structure (that is, how it works), the procedure is probably incoherent. The second good tip-off is difficulty in finding a suitable name for a procedure. If the best name we can come up with is "procedure1," there is probably something wrong with our design. If there is no apparent coherence to a procedural abstraction, we should rethink the design with the goal of eliminating that procedure.

Conjunctive coherence is a step up from no coherence at all. It is indicated by a specification of the form:

```
A && B && C && ...
```

Conjunctive coherence usually occurs when a sequence of temporally contiguous actions is combined into a single procedure. A typical example is an abstraction whose job is to initialize all data structures. The specification of such an abstraction is likely to be a conjunction:

```
initialize A && initialize B && ...
```

Note that such a structure can make it more difficult to identify data abstractions since part of the job of each type is taken over by the procedure.

The isInteresting method of WordTable could be viewed as exhibiting conjunctive coherence because it checks for both nonwords and uninteresting words. However, it seems reasonable to view a nonword as uninteresting, and therefore combining these checks within a single method seems acceptable. However, we might have gone further and had isInteresting canonicalize its input and return the canonical form if the word is interesting. Making this change means that the query and queryMore methods of Engine need to make just one call where now they make two calls (first to canon and then to isInteresting). Nevertheless, this grouping seems undesirable because canonicalizing a word and checking whether a word is interesting do not seem closely related.

In an environment in which procedure calls are unduly expensive, conjunctive coherence may be useful since it can eliminate some calls. However, unless the actions have a strong logical connection, it is generally better not to combine procedures. The more we put into a procedure, the harder it will be to debug and maintain it. Furthermore, as we maintain a program, we are likely to discover occasions when it would be useful to perform some subset of the conjuncts. If this happens, the appropriate thing to do is probably to break up the original procedure. What people often do instead, however, is to add another procedural abstraction. This leads to more code to debug and maintain, and to a program that occupies more space at runtime. Alternatively, the programmer might modify the original abstraction to take a flag that controls what subset of the work is to be performed. This is also a bad idea since it leads to disjunctive coherence, which is discussed next.

Disjunctive coherence is indicated by a specification with an effects clause of the form:

```
A || B || ...
```

often in the guise of an if-then-else or a conjunction of implications. A robust procedure is likely to involve some disjunctive coherence to separate the normal return from exceptions. However, if the specification of what happens when the procedure returns normally involves disjunction, one should be concerned. Consider the specification in Figure 14.1. If getEnd returns normally, it can do one of two different things. Each of these two would have been a perfectly reasonable abstraction in its own right; that is to say, we could have had the two abstractions of Figure 14.2.

Combining these two procedures into one has no advantage and several disadvantages. First, a call of the form getEnd(a, 1) is likely to be harder for a reader to understand than a call of the form getFirst(a). Second, a new class of errors is possible—for example, a call of the form getEnd(a, 3). Third, a program using getEnd is less efficient than one using the two abstractions of Figure 14.2. Whenever a call to getEnd is made, the caller knows which of the procedures is wanted. However, this information must

Figure 14.1   An example of disjunctive coherence

```
public static int getEnd (List a, int j)
        throws EmptyException, NullPointerException
    // REQUIRES: 0 < j < 3 and all elements of a are Integers
    // EFFECTS: If a is null throws NullPointerException
    //    else if a is empty throws EmptyException
    //    else if j = 1 returns the first element of a
    //    else if j = 2 returns the last element of a.
```

Figure 14.2   Two coherent procedures

```
public static int getFirst(List a)
        throws EmptyException, NullPointerException
    // REQUIRES: All elements of a are Integers.
    // EFFECTS: If a is null throws NullPointerException
    //    else if a is empty throws EmptyException
    //    else returns the first element of a.

public static int getLast(List a)
        throws EmptyException, NullPointerException
    // REQUIRES: All elements of a are Integers.
    // EFFECTS: If a is null throws NullPointerException
    //    else if a is empty throws EmptyException
    //    else returns the last element of a.
```

be encoded into the second argument of the call, and getEnd must test this argument to figure out what to do. This extra work requires both time and space. Also, we may implement getEnd using subsidiary abstractions such as getFirst and getLast, thus increasing the number of procedure calls that get executed.

Disjunctive coherence often arises from a misguided attempt to generalize abstractions. When a program design contains two or more similar abstractions, it is always worthwhile to consider whether a single more general abstraction might replace all or some of the similar ones. If successful, generalization saves space and programmer effort with little cost in execution speed or complexity in the implementation of the generalized abstraction. However, if the result is an abstraction with disjunctive coherence, then it is usually better not to do the replacement.

Occasionally, the appearance of excessive disjunctive coherence indicates failure to introduce appropriate data abstractions into the design. In such cases, combining several distinct functions into one procedure may be an attempt to encapsulate representation information that should have been encapsulated in a missing type. In effect, the type is implemented by a single procedure, and extra arguments are used to identify the operation being called.

Disjunctive coherence isn't always bad (and neither is conjunctive coherence). For example, a compiler might take an environment object as an argument and produce somewhat different outputs depending on the environment. This represents a kind of disjunctive coherence. However, it also represents a generalization of the compiler (to handle several kinds of environments); here the benefits outweigh the disadvantages. In general, conjunctive or disjunctive coherence is permissible in a design but only if there is a good explanation of why it is worthwhile.

Coherence of Types

Each method of a type should be a coherent procedure or iterator. In addition, a type should provide an abstraction that its users can conveniently think of as a set of values and a set of methods intimately associated with those values. One way of judging the coherence of a type is to examine each method to see whether it really belongs in the type. As discussed in Chapter 5, a type should be *adequate*—that is, should provide enough methods so that common uses are efficient. In badly designed types, one frequently finds additional methods that do not seem particularly relevant to the abstraction and whose implementation can take little or no advantage of direct access to the representation. It is generally better to move such methods out of the type. If fewer operations have access to the representation, it is easier to modify the representation if it becomes desirable to do so.

Consider, for example, a stack type containing sqrtTop method:

```
float sqrtTop ( ) throws EmptyException
    // EFFECTS: If this.size = 0 throws EmptyException else returns the
    //    square root of this.top.
```

sqrtTop has little to do with stacks, and its implementation can run just fine without access to a stack's representation. Therefore, this method should be moved out of the stack abstraction.

Communication between Modules

A careful examination of how much and what kind of information is exchanged between modules can uncover important flaws in a design. Throughout this book, we have stressed the importance of narrow interfaces: a module should have access to only as much information as it needs to do its job. Our methodology is designed to encourage narrow interfaces—for example, by not allowing procedures to refer to global variables—but it is still possible to pass too much information to a module.

A module may be passed too much information because a type has not been identified. In the absence of a type, all modules that would have communicated in terms of the abstract objects instead communicate in terms of the representation. The result is modules that have much wider interfaces than necessary; instead of being related only through the type, they share knowledge of how that type is implemented. This includes the abstraction function and representation invariant in addition to the representation itself. Note that all using modules must be considered in reasoning that the implementation of the (missing) type is correct. Furthermore, if the implementation of the type changes, every using module must also change.

Even if all needed types have been identified and are implemented by their own classes, some interfaces may still be wider than necessary. Well-designed programs frequently have types that include a great deal of information. Some modules may not need to access all of this information. Yet many designs call for passing the entire abstract object when a small piece of it would be sufficient. For example, we might have a type StudentRecord that includes, among other things, a student's name, social security number, residence, and transcript. A procedure, printAddress, that prints an address label might need only a student's name and residence. Such a procedure should not be passed the whole student record; instead, the information it needs should be extracted from the student record by its caller and passed to it explicitly. There are several good reasons for this:

- If printAddress is passed an object of type StudentRecord, its implementor will have to know how to extract the needed information—that is, what methods to call. If the specification of StudentRecord changes, the implementation of printAddress may have to change. None of this would be necessary if the needed information were passed explicitly.

- The implementation of printAddress may have a bug that causes it to mutate the StudentRecord. Such bugs can be very hard to find.

Reducing Dependencies

A design with fewer dependencies is generally better than one with more. Having fewer dependencies can result from narrower interfaces; for example, passing an element instead of a set can mean that the called abstraction no longer depends on Set. It can also result from changing strong dependencies into weak ones. Such a change can be an improvement because the module with the dependency is not affected by changes to the specification of the data abstraction it depends on.

For example, in the design of Engine, the WordTable depends on Doc because its addDoc method calls the Doc words method; a similar situation exists for TitleTable. We can reduce these dependencies to weak dependencies by changing the design slightly. First, rather than having the addDoc method of WordTable call the words iterator, we could instead pass it the generator returned by the words iterator:

```
Hash table addDoc (Iterator e, Doc d)
    // REQUIRES: e produces strings
    // MODIFIES: this
    // EFFECTS: Adds each interesting word w produced by e
    //    to this, mapped to d and the number of occurrences of w in e;
    //    also returns a table mapping each interesting word produced by e
    //    to a count of its occurrences in e.
```

Second, we can change the specification for the addDoc method of TitleTable to:

```
void addDoc (String t, Doc d) throws DuplicateException
    // REQUIRES: d and t are not null
    // MODIFIES: this
    // EFFECTS: If a document with title t is already in this throws
    //    DuplicateException else adds d to this with title t.
```

The module dependency diagram that results from these changes is shown in Figure 14.3. One advantage of this structure over the one shown in Figure 13.15 is that TitleTable no longer needs to canonicalize the title since

Figure 14.3   Module dependency diagram for modified design

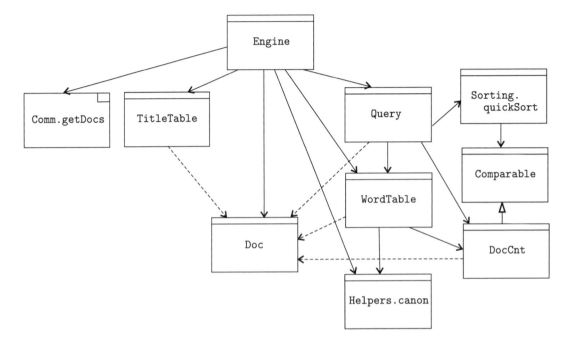

this can be done in Engine, and therefore there are fewer dependencies in the design. Another advantage is that the structure more easily accommodates the modification discussed in Section 14.1.1 in which document bodies are discarded and refetched when needed. With the revised structure, changes to the title and word tables are not needed to accommodate the modification.

Sidebar 14.3 summarizes the desiderata for program structure.

14.2   Ordering the Program Development Process

Throughout this book, we have stressed a program development strategy that is basically top-down. While we recognize that program development is an iterative process, we have argued that in each iteration, specification and design should precede implementation, at least for the part of the implementation that is underway. We have not yet discussed how to order the process of going from a design to an implementation. The basic choice is between a top-down strategy and a bottom-up strategy (see Sidebar 14.4).

Sidebar 14.3   A Design Review: Evaluating Program Structure

- Each abstraction should be coherent: it should have a well-defined purpose, and if its specification exhibits conjunctive or disjunctive coherence, there should be a plausible explanation. Furthermore, data types should not contain methods that are irrelevant to their purpose.

- The interfaces of abstractions should be no wider than necessary.

- A design with fewer dependencies is usually better than one with more, and weak dependencies are better than strong ones.

Sidebar 14.4   Top-Down and Bottom-Up Development

- In a top-down development, all modules that use module M are implemented and tested before M is implemented.

- In a bottom-up development, all modules used by module M are implemented and tested before M is implemented.

The traditional mode of development is bottom-up. In bottom-up development, we implement and test all modules used by a module M before we implement and test M. Consider, for example, implementing a design with the module dependency diagram shown in Figure 14.4. We might begin by implementing and unit testing D and E. We might then implement and test B and C; here we might use D and E to avoid writing stubs. Finally, we would implement and test A. Note, by the way, that this is not the only possible bottom-up order. We might equally well have used the order D, B, E, C, A.

When we use D and E in testing B and C we are no longer performing unit testing, since we are not testing a single module in isolation. This is both good and bad. It's bad because B and C might depend on implementation details (and errors) in the actual code of D and E. However, it's good because it can be

Figure 14.4   A simple module dependency diagram

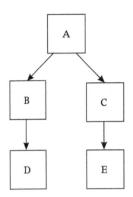

difficult to write stubs for some abstractions, and one advantage of bottom-up implementation is that we can avoid writing stubs.

In top-down development, we implement and test all modules that use a module M before implementing and testing M. Possible top-down orders for the previous example include A, B, C, D, E and A, C, E, B, D. Just as bottom-up development reduces our dependence on stubs, top-down development reduces our dependence on drivers. It is important, however, that top-down development be accompanied by careful unit testing of all modules. If we tested B only as it is used by A, we might see only part of B's specified behavior. Were we to change A later, new bugs might be revealed in B. Therefore, if we choose to use A as a driver for B, we must make sure that A tests B thoroughly. Otherwise, we must use a separate driver to test B.

Neither development strategy strictly dominates the other. Most of the time, it seems best to work top-down. However, there can be compelling reasons to pursue a bottom-up approach. We advocate a mixed strategy in which one works top-down on some parts of the system and bottom-up on others.

Top-down development has the advantage of helping us to catch serious design errors early on. When we test a module, we are testing not only the implementation of that module, but also the specifications of the modules that it uses. If we follow a bottom-up strategy, we might easily spend a great deal of effort implementing and testing modules that are not useful because there is a problem with the design of one of their ancestors in the module dependency diagram. A similar problem can occur in top-down development if we discover that some crucial descendent module is unimplementable or cannot be implemented with acceptable performance. Experience indicates, however, that this problem occurs less often. This may be because lower-level abstractions are often similar to things we have built before, whereas higher-level abstractions tend to be more idiosyncratic.

In top-down development, it is always possible to integrate one module at a time. We merely replace a stub by the module it is intended to simulate. In bottom-up development, on the other hand, we tend to integrate several modules at once; in most cases, a single higher-level module corresponds not to one but to several drivers. For example, when A is integrated into the program of Figure 14.4, it will be replacing drivers for both B and C. Since system integration tends to proceed more smoothly if we can add one interface at a time, top-down development has a significant advantage in this regard. Furthermore, system integration can be the real bottleneck in completing the development: with bottom-up development, a system that is "90 percent implemented" can require much more than 10 percent of the time to complete because what is left is system integration.

When the design contains a type hierarchy, top-down development is required. In this case, we must consider the implementation of supertypes before subtypes, so that we can decide what parts of the implementation of the entire family are handled by the supertype and what must be deferred to the subtypes.

Top-down development increases the likelihood of bringing up useful partial versions of the program being developed. Suppose a program to compute income tax payments has the (partial) module dependency diagram of Figure 14.5. By working top-down, it is possible to bring up many useful partial implementations of this design. A system without the investment and itemized procedures, for example, might be quite useful to some people.

Even if partial versions of the system cannot be used productively by the customer, bringing partial versions up early in the development process may have some important benefits. If implementors are able to demonstrate something early, they can get feedback that may reveal problems with the requirements for the program. Furthermore, on lengthy projects, the ability to produce a series of working partial systems seems to help the morale of both the customer and the developers.

While bottom-up development delays the point at which one has a working partial system, it does lead to the earlier completion of useful subsystems. These subsystems generally have wider applicability than do the partial

Figure 14.5   Module dependency diagram for an income tax program

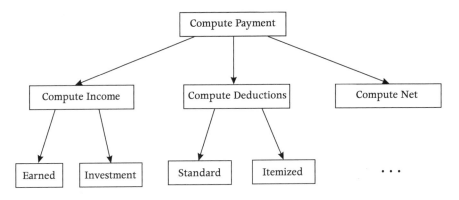

systems we get when working top-down. This is particularly true of low-level subsystems (for example, input/output subsystems). In an environment in which several related systems are being developed simultaneously, it can be helpful to bring up shared subsystems by working bottom-up. Moreover, it is sometimes easier to build a low-level subsystem than to build a stub to simulate it.

Another potential advantage of bottom-up development is that it may place less of a load on machine resources than does top-down development. Top-down development tends to use more machine time because we are running a larger part of the system during many phases of development. Typically, full tests of the system are developed and then run each time a new module is added. Such tests may exercise many other parts of the system besides the module being added, and thus consume much time and space that really is not needed for this step of the integration. On the other hand, such a systematic approach to testing is bound to uncover more errors and be more thorough than a more ad hoc approach.

A related advantage of bottom-up development is that it may allow us to proceed in the absence of some computational resource. Consider building a system that is to run on a machine with a very large amount of memory. If that machine has not yet arrived, but a similar machine with less memory were available, we might be able to do quite a bit of bottom-up development before memory becomes a problem. We might run out of memory sooner working top-down.

Generally, it's best to use a mixed strategy in which top-down development is favored but not followed entirely. In working out this strategy, both technical and nontechnical factors should be taken into account. The most important point is that a development strategy should be defined explicitly before implementation begins.

Sidebar 14.5 summarizes the issues that arise in choosing a development order.

Some insight into implementation and testing order can be gained by considering the search engine:

1. Doc should be implemented and unit tested so that we can deal with real documents throughout the testing process.

2. Now we can implement Engine. It will use Doc and also the real getDocs iterator (since this is provided by a library) but stubs for canon, Query, and the title and word tables. canon just returns its input. The addDoc methods of the two tables will simply record the document in an array. In addition, the isInteresting method of WordTable returns false, and the lookup method of TitleTable throws the exception. Only the empty Query will be implemented since all words are uninteresting. Now we can test a fair amount of the logic of Engine; we will be able to see that the right calls are made on the two tables, and we can also test certain base cases (e.g., bad and uninteresting words in queries, titles that don't match).

Sidebar 14.5 The Development Strategy

- A development strategy should be defined explicitly before implementation begins.

- It should be primarily top-down, with bottom-up used mainly for modules that are easier to implement than to simulate, because the advantages of top-down development outweigh those of bottom-up development:
    - Top-down development greatly simplifies system integration and test.
    - Top-down development makes it possible to produce useful partial versions of the system.
    - Top-down development allows critical high-level design errors to be caught early.

3. Next we implement and unit test the canon procedure. Then we implement TitleTable and unit test it using Doc and canon. This allows us to test searches based on titles.

4. Next we implement and unit test the WordTable using Doc and canon.

5. Next we extend the stub for Query so that size returns 0, and the various mutators record their arguments. This will allow us to complete testing the logic of Engine.

6. Finally we implement DocCnt and Query and unit test them using Doc and WordTable. Then we can run the entire Engine.

This strategy allows us to get an early version of the engine: we can do searches on titles after step 3.

The strategy is typical of testing strategies in that either we implement the entire data abstraction, or we use very simple stubs: some methods record their input, others return canned responses, and still others are not implemented because they are not called at this stage of the development. For example, in step 2, the addDoc method of WordTable records its argument, isInteresting has a canned response, and the lookup method isn't called. Sometimes, however, we implement a data abstraction in stages. For example, we might provide a complete implementation of the empty query (as a subtype of Query) in step 2; nonempty queries are implemented later.

The testing of Engine should be done using the regression test code (i.e., the TestUI of Figure 13.16). In addition, of course, the actual UI must be implemented and run against the Engine, but testing the UI will be simpler if we can separate it from tests that determine that Engine is functionally correct. The UI tests will focus on how the display looks, and whether user inputs lead to the right calls on Engine methods; these tests could even be done with a simple stub for Engine (e.g., using a predefined set of documents).

14.3   Summary

In this chapter, we discussed some things that should be done between the completion of a design and the start of implementation. The key points to take away are the importance of conducting a systematic evaluation of the design and developing a plan specifying the order of implementation and testing of the modules comprising the design.

In a design review, one considers whether or not implementations of the design will exhibit the desired behavior and performance, and whether or not the program structure described by the design will be reasonably easy to build, test, and maintain. We suggested conducting design reviews by tracing the path of symbolic test data through the design. We also suggested several criteria that could be used in evaluating structural issues. All of the criteria were related to the appropriateness of module boundaries.

We did not give fixed rules for picking an order of implementation and testing. We discussed the relative merits of top-down and bottom-up development and testing. Our conclusion was that most of the time, it is best to follow a mixed strategy but with an emphasis on proceeding top-down.

In our discussion of design reviews, we presented an extremely abbreviated review of the search engine designed in Chapter 13. The reader should not infer from this that design reviews should be conducted only after a design is complete. For larger programs, it is imperative that we conduct careful reviews during the design phase. If we want to start the implementation of some subsystem before the design is complete, it should happen only after the design at that point has been carefully reviewed. But even if we are not planning to start implementation early, we need reviews before design is complete since it is critical to catch design errors early.

It is also important to start considering how the implementation effort is to be organized early in the design. A need for early completion of subsystems, for example, can have a significant impact on design decisions and on the order in which abstractions are studied during the design process.

Exercises

14.1 A Map abstraction might provide an insert method to add a string with its associated element to the Map and a change method to change the element associated with the string. Suppose these two operations were replaced by a single method that adds the association if it does not already exist and changes it if it does. Discuss the coherence of this modified abstraction. How does the modified abstraction compare with the original?

14.2 Consider the effect of various potential modifications for the search engine on its design. For example, suppose we want to support more sophisticated queries, or we want to allow several documents to have the same title, or we want the engine to record persistently the sites where documents are located so that they can be refetched the next time it runs.

14.3   One could argue that having a single word table that keeps track of both interesting and uninteresting words is less coherent than a design with two separate tables. Discuss this point and compare the two alternatives.

14.4   Consider an alternative design for Query in which a query object is initially empty and keywords are added to it. Discuss the advantages and disadvantages of this design relative to the one that was presented in Chapter 13.

14.5   Perform a design review for some program that you have designed. Be sure to include a discussion of the structure and modifiability of the program as well as a discussion of its correctness.

14.6   Define an implementation strategy for a program that you have designed.

Design Patterns

15

When designing a program, it is useful to understand the ways that people have organized programs in the past, since these approaches might speed up the design process or lead to a better program in the end. This chapter discusses a number of such *design patterns*.[1] Each pattern provides a benefit: some patterns improve performance, while others make it easier to change the program in certain ways.

In this book we have already used several design patterns. One is the *iterator pattern*. As explained in Chapter 6, we use iterators as a basic part of our methodology since it allows us to provide efficient access to elements of collection objects without either violating encapsulation or complicating the abstraction. Another is the *template pattern*. This pattern captures the idea of implementing concrete methods in a superclass in terms of abstract methods that will be implemented in subclasses; the concrete method defines a template for how execution proceeds, but the details are filled in later, when the subclasses are implemented. Examples of the use of this pattern can be found in the implementations of IntSet (see Figure 7.8) and Poly (see Figure 7.14).

---

1. More information about design patterns can be found in Gamma, Erich, Richard Helm, Ralph Johnson, and John Vlissides, *Design Patterns*, Addison-Wesley, Reading, Mass., 1995.

Design patterns often take advantage of type hierarchy to accomplish their goals. They abstract from detail to certain commonalities, which are captured in a supertype. Using code is written based on the supertype specification and is intended to work correctly regardless of which subtype is actually in use. Therefore, it is critical that the subtypes obey the substitution principle: a subtype's objects must behave like those of the supertype as far as using code can tell by calling supertype methods.

The downside of patterns is that some of them can increase program complexity. The most common mistake made by novice programmers is over-design: the program is more complicated than is necessary to accomplish its job. Therefore, your motto should be "When in doubt, leave it out." In other words, you should use a pattern only when its benefits outweigh any additional complexity it introduces.

Design patterns are like a bag of tricks that every competent programmer should understand. This doesn't mean that you use them indiscriminately; rather it means that you can recognize situations where they might apply and then decide whether their use is merited in that particular case. An additional point is that patterns can help you understand other people's programs more easily, and you can also use them to explain both your own and other people's programs. They provide a vocabulary that can make it easier to both develop and describe designs. Sidebar 15.1 summarizes this discussion.

Sidebar 15.1   Design Patterns

- Design patterns provide a vocabulary for understanding and discussing designs.
- Design patterns can improve the performance or flexibility of code. They can increase complexity, however, and should be used only when analysis indicates the benefits outweigh the disadvantages.
- Patterns should always be used in a way that observes the substitution principle.

15.1   Hiding Object Creation

Much of the code in an object-oriented program does not depend directly on the particular class that implements an object it uses. Instead, it depends only on the object's behavior—that is, the object's methods with their associated behavior as defined in the specification of the object's type. However, not all code has such a loose connection to the class implementing an object: any code that calls a constructor depends on the class.

Limiting dependencies on classes is desirable for two reasons. First, it makes it easier to replace the class currently implementing an object with another one, since all code that depends only on the object's type and not its class is unaffected by the change. Second, it provides a way to hide details associated with selecting what class to use, in the case where multiple classes implement a type.

For example, we discussed multiple implementations for polynomials in Chapter 7. Two implementations were provided, DensePoly and SparsePoly, and programmers writing code that used polynomials had to decide for each new polynomial whether its representation should be sparse or dense. But why should users need to make this decision? A better approach would be to shield them from this detail by providing some code that they could call to create a polynomial, where the code would decide what to do. In this way, the existence of two implementations for polynomials is completely hidden from using code, which, as a result, becomes less complex. In addition, if we decide to add a third implementation, or to change the parameters that are used to determine which implementation to choose, we can change just the code that actually creates the polynomials; no other code needs to be changed.

Object creation can be hidden by using the *factory pattern*. The name "factory" captures the idea that the factory manufactures the objects. The factory pattern is based on *factory methods*. A factory method creates an object of some class, but it is not a constructor for that class.

We have seen many examples of factory methods already. For example, every iterator is a factory method: it creates a generator object, but it is not a constructor of some subclass of Iterator. The iterator hides the exact type of generator being used, and using code depends only on the Iterator interface. This structure is illustrated in Figure 15.1. The figure shows how a program P that uses the set elements iterator depends only on the Iterator interface

Figure 15.1   Iterators are factory methods

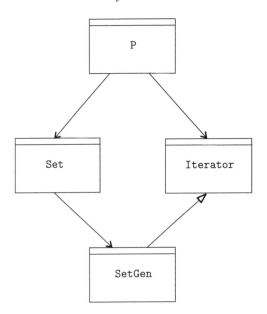

and not on the particular type of generator (SetGen in this case). This structure is flexible because we can change the type of generator by just reimplementing the elements method; the using code does not need to change at all.

Factory methods are sometimes gathered together in their own *factory class*. A factory class might provide static methods, or it might have objects of its own. Such objects are called *factory objects*.

The methods of a factory class might create objects of a single type or of several types. For example, Figure 15.2 shows a factory class containing static factory methods that create polynomials: one method creates the zero polynomial, and the other creates an arbitrary monomial. This class creates objects of only one type (Poly). In a symbolic manipulation program, you might have a factory class with methods to create polynomials, matrices, vectors, and so on. Such a factory has an additional benefit; it provides an easy way to ensure that the objects it creates all work together properly. For example, suppose there are several types whose implementations differ depending on the environment in which the system is supposed to run. The factory can ensure that all these types' objects are created for the same environment. Thus, the use of the factory not only hides complexity so that using code is simpler;

Figure 15.2   A factory class for Poly

```
public class PolyProcs {

    public static Poly makePoly( )
        // EFFECTS: Creates the zero polynomial.

    public static Poly makePoly(int n, int c) throws NegativeExponentException
        // EFFECTS: If n < 0 throws NegativeExponentException else returns
        //    the polynomial cx^n.
}
```

Sidebar 15.2   The Factory Pattern

- A *factory method* creates an object of some class.

- A *factory class* provides a number of factory methods. If the class has objects, they are called *factory objects*.

- Methods of a factory class might create objects of several different types. The factory class can ensure that these objects come from compatible classes (e.g., ones that all work in a particular environment).

it also ensures that certain errors aren't possible since using code cannot create incompatible objects based on different environments.

Sidebar 15.2 summarizes the preceding discussion.

Factory objects are useful when many places in a program need to use the factory methods. In such a case, a single module creates the factory object, which is passed to other modules. The advantage of this structure is that the dependency on the particular implementation choice is limited to that one module. The rest of the code will depend only on the interface of the factory object and not its class!

Figure 15.3 shows the module dependency diagram for a program that uses factory objects. The figure shows a factory interface with two implementations, Factory1 and Factory2. Objects of two types, S and T, are created by the factory; Factory1 creates one "flavor" for these types (S1 and T1),

Figure 15.3   The factory pattern hierarchy

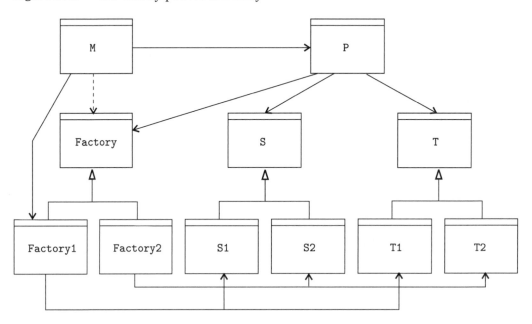

while Factory2 creates another. Module M creates the factory objects by using Factory1 and/or Factory2. It passes a factory object to module P, which stands for the rest of the program; P is shown as a single module but will actually consist of many modules. P then uses the factory object passed to it by M to create S and T objects of the "flavor" selected by M. Note that because there are factory objects, they need to be passed to code in the rest of the program. Thus, this code (e.g., P) takes a factory object as an extra argument.

The figure illustrates the way that factories reduce dependencies. P does not depend on the specific implementation of the factory (i.e., Factory1 and Factory2) since this information is limited to M. M weakly depends on Factory since it uses none of its methods; instead, it only uses constructors of Factory1 and Factory2. Neither M nor P depends on the implementation choices for S and T since that information is limited to the factory implementation. Yet we can be certain that P will use compatible implementations of S and T.

Factories aren't needed when all you want to do is to reimplement some types, replacing old implementations with new ones. In this case, you can just relink your code to use the new classes rather than the old ones. However, fac-

---

Sidebar 15.3 When to Use Factories

- A factory is *not* needed when all you want to do is reimplement some type. In this case, you can just relink your code with the new class.

- A factory is useful when you use multiple implementations of a type within a program.

- A factory is also useful when you want several different versions of a program, each using a different implementation for one or more types.

- Using a factory object can limit dependency on the factory class to a single module.

---

tories are useful when a single problem uses several implementations for a type or when each of several versions of a program uses a different implementation choice for some set of types.

Two other patterns are closely related to factories. A *builder* is a method that not only hides implementation choices for one or more types but also constructs a collection of objects of these types. A *prototype* is an object that can be used to create other objects of its type. The prototype is created by one module; the rest of the code calls a method of the prototype to obtain other objects of the prototype's type. The new objects will be in an initial state, rather than a clone of the prototype (in case the prototype has been modified). Sidebar 15.3 summarizes the uses of factories.

15.2   Neat Hacks

A number of patterns are useful for either speeding up a computation or reducing its storage requirements. Every competent programmer should know about them; they should be part of your bag of tricks, so that you can use them when the right situation arises.

15.2.1   Flyweights

Sometimes you will encounter a situation where you have many instances of identical objects. When this happens you can greatly reduce your storage requirements if you can manage to use just one object per set of identical ones.

Sidebar 15.4   The Flyweight Pattern

- The *flyweight pattern* allows one object to be used to represent many identical instances.

- Flyweights *must* be immutable.

- Flyweights always depend on an associated table, which maps identical instances to the single object that represents all of them. This table can either be hidden within the flyweight class or can be visible to users.

- Flyweights should be used when there is a sufficiently large amount of sharing to justify the extra complexity of maintaining the related table.

The technique for accomplishing this sharing is called the *flyweight patter* the shared objects are called *flyweights* (see Sidebar 15.4). The name com from the fact that the pattern makes even very small objects, such as individu characters, practical. The overhead for such an object is high relative to th information it stores, but the cost is insignificant if there is enough sharin However, the use of the pattern is not restricted to small objects; for exampl it might be used for font objects in a document processing system.

You can take advantage of the savings provided by using flyweights on if the objects are immutable. This is clearly necessary since the objects a going to be shared. If the flyweights were mutable, they could not be share since modifications made because of the needs of one using context would t visible to the others.

For example, flyweights might be useful in the search engine. Each docu ment is potentially very large, yet a document contains many occurrences the same word, and the same word may occur in many different document Rather than storing a document as a (very long) string, or as a collection strings with one string per word, why not have just one object for each uniqu occurrence of a word? Having one object is acceptable since strings are im mutable.

Thus, there would be just one object for the word "the", even though "the occurs many times in the documents. A document might be represented as a array (or vector) of Words; the objects representing the unique words woul be shared both within the array representing a single document and betwee arrays representing different documents.

To use this pattern, there must be a way to avoid creating duplicate objects. This implies that we cannot create the objects using a constructor since a new object is created each time a constructor is called. Therefore, we need another way to create new objects. But we know how to do this—by using a factory method. The factory method needs access to a table that keeps track of already existing objects. When a new object is requested, the method checks whether the desired object already exists in the table; it returns the preexisting object if one exists and otherwise, creates a new object.

There are two structures for providing flyweights. In the first, the table is inaccessible to users. In this case, the flyweight class provides a static factory method that is used to create flyweights, and the table is maintained within the class, in a static variable. Figure 15.4 illustrates this structure. When make-Word encounters a string that is not in the table, it calls the constructor to create a new word, but users can't create words directly since the constructor is private.

The mapWord method shown in the figure provides different results depending on a context. For example, a context might indicate that the resulting

Figure 15.4   Flyweight pattern with a hidden table

```
public class Word {
// OVERVIEW: Words are strings that provide methods to produce them
//    in various forms. words are immutable, and for each unique string
//    there is at most one word.

private static Hashtable t; // maps strings to words

public static makeWord (String s)
    // EFFECTS: Returns the word corresponding to s.

private Word(String s)
    // EFFECTS: Makes this be the word corresponding to s.

public String mapWord(Context c)
    // EFFECTS: Returns the string corresponding to this in
    //    the form suitable for context c.

// other word methods
}
```

string should have all alphabetic characters capitalized. Having the context information be an argument enhances sharing: a word can be shared even in different contexts. Another point is that the context might be mutable—for example, the using code might have a context object that it changes to reflect the current constraints. Obviously, a mutable context could not be part of the flyweight, since flyweights must be immutable. This type of mutable information is referred to as the *extrinsic* state; the idea is that it is related to the flyweight object but not inside it since flyweights cannot contain mutable information. The information inside the flyweight is referred to as its *intrinsic* state.

The second structure for flyweights makes the table accessible to users: there is a table object, and the factory method is a method of this object. This structure is useful when there are other things to do with the table (e.g., iterate over its elements) or if more than one table is needed. This structure is illustrated in Figure 15.5, which shows a type Ident and an associated table type IdentTable. The Ident type might be used in implementing a compiler. An Ident is a string, but there are two kinds of identifiers: reserved words (e.g., "class", "for"), which have a predefined meaning, and all the other words, which are used for naming variables, methods, and so on. The main point to notice is that tables have a number of methods. A second point is that Ident's constructor is package visible, which means it is not accessible to users but is accessible to IdentTable provided they are defined in the same package.

A final point about flyweights is that it may be necessary to remove entries from the associated table when they are no longer in use. For example, if documents were removed from the search engine, some words might no longer appear in any document, in which case we might want to be sure they no longer consumed storage. This can be accomplished in Java by having the table refer to its elements using *weak pointers*; details can be found in a Java text.

15.2.2   Singletons

Sometimes a type needs just a single object (or a few objects). In this case, we may want to ensure that additional objects aren't created. This can be important for performance: for example, if there were more than one IdentTable, we would not be able to guarantee just one object for a unique identifier. The

Figure 15.5 Flyweight pattern with a visible table

```
public class IdentTable {
```
// OVERVIEW: *A* IdentTable *is a mutable collection of* Ident
// *objects; each distinct string has at most one entry in the table.*

// *constructors:*
```
public IdentTable( )
```
   // EFFECTS: *Makes* this *be the empty* IdentTable.

// *methods:*
```
public Ident makeReserved (String s) throws WrongKindException
```
   // MODIFIES: this
   // EFFECTS: *If* s *is already in* this *as a reserved word returns*
   // *the prestored object else if it is in* this *as a nonreserved word*
   // *throws* WrongKindException *else adds* s *to* this *as a reserved word.*

```
public Ident makeNonReserved (String s) throws WrongKindException
```
   // MODIFIES: this
   // EFFECTS: *If* s *is already in* this *as a nonreserved word returns*
   // *the prestored object else if it is in* this *as a reserved word throws*
   // WrongKindException *else adds* s *to* this *as a nonreserved word.*

```
public Iterator idents ( )
```
   // EFFECTS: *Returns a generator that will produce all identifiers in* this,
   // *each exactly once, in arbitrary order.*
   // REQUIRES: this *not be modified when generator is in use.*
```
}
```

```
public class Ident {
```
   // OVERVIEW: *An* Ident *is an identifier that occurs in a program.*
   // Idents *are immutable. They are created by using an* IdentTable.

   ```
   Ident(String s) // package visible
   ```

   // *various methods*
```
}
```

Sidebar 15.5   The Singleton Pattern

- When a type has just one object, that object is called a *singleton*.

- Using a singleton can improve performance or eliminate errors.

- To enforce singleton-ness, the constructor must be made private and access to the object provided through a static method.

- Although the static method makes it possible to access the object without having it be a parameter, this structure is undesirable since it increases dependencies. Making the entire class static is even less desirable.

constraint can also be important for correctness. For example, we might implement equals for Ident by simply checking whether the two objects are the same object:

```
boolean equals (Object x) { return this == x; }
```

(Actually this is the definition of equals provided by Object.) This test is very efficient, but it will work correctly only if both identifier objects come from the same IdentTable. This condition will certainly be true if we can guarantee there is just one IdentTable.

The notion of a type with just one object is captured by the *singleton pattern*, and the single object is called a *singleton* (see Sidebar 15.5).

The way to ensure that there is just one object of a type is to make the constructor unavailable to using code. Instead, using code can access the object by calling a static method of the class that implements the type. This method is a factory method. It will return the single object, creating the object if this is the first time it has been requested. The structure is illustrated in Figure 15.6. The main points to notice are that the implementation maintains a pointer to the object in a static variable and that the constructor is private.

The static method used to access a singleton provides a kind of global variable: the method names the singleton. For example, IdentTable.getTable names the singleton IdentTable object (given the code in Figure 15.6), which means we can avoid passing the singleton as a parameter. However, even if the singleton object is not passed explicitly, any module M that uses it, either directly or indirectly by calls on other modules, still depends on the singleton.

Figure 15.6   The singleton pattern

```
public class IdentTable {
    // OVERVIEW: As before except there is just one IdentTable object, which
    //    can be obtained by calling the getTable procedure.

    private static IdentTable t; // the single table

    public static IdentTable getTable( ) {
        if (t == null) t = new IdentTable( );
        return t; }

    private IdentTable( ) { ... }
    // methods go here
}
```

This means that M's specification must explain its use of the singleton, and the module dependency diagram must show the dependency.

For example, exactly one WordTable and exactly one TitleTable are used in the search engine. We could make these tables singletons and thus eliminate a potential source of errors. However, the search engine will still have the module dependency diagram shown in Figure 13.15 even if the word table object is a singleton and is not passed explicitly to Query. Also, the specification of Query would still need to describe its use of the word table.

Since the dependencies and specifications need to reflect the use of the singleton object, it is better to pass it as an explicit parameter. Not only does this make the code cleaner, but it also provides better modifiability: if we should later change the way to access the singleton, all code that receives it as an argument will be unaffected by the change. This really is just an argument in favor of abstraction by parameterization: code is more general if it uses parameters rather than depending on specific objects.

One final point: it is possible to use a class as the singleton object. In this case, there are only static methods; for example, makeReserved, makeNon-Reserved, and elements would all be static methods of the IdentTable class shown in Figure 15.6. However, doing things this way is less desirable than having an actual object because classes cannot easily be treated as objects in Java.

There is a connection between singletons and flyweights: sometimes a singleton is a special kind of flyweight. For example, since lists are immutable, we can use the flyweight pattern to represent specific lists. This might be worthwhile for the empty list, which is likely to be created and then discarded many times. Since there is just one empty list, we can implement it as a singleton. (It's not clear, however, that use of the pattern is justified here. It saves storage and less garbage needs to be collected, but the program structure is a bit strange: we no longer have a public constructor for creating an empty list but have to use a static [factory] method instead.)

15.2.3   The State Pattern

It is sometimes worthwhile to change how an object is represented dynamically. This might happen because the object changes state from time to time, and in different states, different information needs to be stored. Or it might happen because as the object changes state, its performance can be improved by changing its representation.

For example, we might implement a set by starting with a vector that stores the elements in consecutive locations. However, this representation is suitable only for relatively small sets. Therefore, when the size of the set passes a threshold, we switch the implementation to use a hash table. Later, if the set shrinks, we switch back to the vector; this typically will happen at a smaller threshold than the one that causes the switch in the reverse direction since otherwise, the implementation might be unstable: it would end up switching between the vector and the hash table repeatedly, in the case of a set whose size remains around the threshold.

To support a representation that switches from one form to another, we might simply have the rep contain an Object. For example, the rep of a Set object might contain

```
Object els; // a vector or a hash table
```

The object would be a vector for a small set and a hash table for a large one. However, this approach has the disadvantage that the code of each method needs to determine what the current state is and then cast els to either a vector or a hash table—for example, each method would have roughly the following form:

```
if (els instanceof Vector) {
   Vector v = (Vector) els; } // process the vector
else { Hashtable t = (Hashtable) els; } // process the hash table
```

This is both inconvenient and expensive (since casts are relatively costly).

The *state pattern* provides a better approach. It separates the type being implemented from the type used to implement it. The type being implemented is called the *context*; the type used to implement it is called the *state type*. The structure is illustrated in Figure 15.7, which shows a portion of the set

Figure 15.7   The state pattern

```
public class Set {
   private SetState els;
   private int t1; // the threshold for growing
   private int t2; // the threshold for shrinking

   public Set( ) {els = new SmallSet( );} // set the thresholds
   public boolean empty ( ) { returns (els.size( ) == 0); }

   public void insert (Object x) {
      int sz = els.size( );
      els.insert(x);
      if (sz == t1 && els.size( ) > t1)
         els = new BigSet((Vector) els);
   }

   // other methods go here
}

public interface SetState {
   // OVERVIEW: SetState is used to implement Set; it provides most of the Set
   //     methods. SetState objects are mutable.
}

public class SmallSet implements SetState {
   // implementation similar to that shown in Figure 5.6
}

public class BigSet implements SetState { ... }
```

implementation. The implementation makes use of a `SetState` type; this type has two implementations, `SmallSet`, which uses a vector, and `BigSet`, which uses a hash table.

There are three points to note here. First, the implementation of `Set` does not need to determine the type of its `els` object; instead, its calls on methods of `els` go directly to the code of `els`'s current implementation, which, of course, knows its type. Second, the state type is not in the same hierarchy as the type being implemented and therefore need not have the same methods; instead, we can choose methods as needed for the implementation of the context type.

The third point concerns changing the implementation of an object of the context type from one state to another. Figure 15.7 shows how to do this: the work is done in the context type's implementation. The figure shows how the switch occurs in the `Set insert` method; the implementation of `remove` would be similar, except that it would check for the set becoming smaller than threshold `t2`.

There is another way of causing the state change to happen: the subtypes of the state type could detect the need for change and modify the containing object accordingly. But to do this, the state objects would have to use the context object; and therefore the state type would depend on the context type. The structure shown in Figure 15.7 is better because the dependency is not needed.

Sidebar 15.6 summarizes the discussion about the state pattern.

Sidebar 15.6 The State Pattern

- The *state pattern* allows the representation of an object to change as the object's state changes. It uses a *state type* to implement objects of a *context type*.

- The pattern applies only to mutable types.

- The pattern is worthwhile if there is a significant benefit to using different implementations as state changes (e.g., because different reps are suitable for large and small objects).

- Having the context type's implementation control when objects change their implementation provides better modularity than having this be controlled by subtypes of the state type.

15.3   The Bridge Pattern

We use hierarchy for two different purposes: to extend behavior and to provide multiple implementations. These two uses can interfere.

For example, suppose you want to define ExtendedSet, a subtype of Set with more methods (e.g., union and intersection methods). But suppose, in addition, that you had already defined SmallSet and BigSet to be subtypes of Set. How do these types interact with ExtendedSet? What we would really like is to use them to implement ExtendedSet as well as Set. However, to do so, we would need to move them down in the hierarchy, so that they are subtypes of ExtendedSet. And this really does not capture our intent because there is no reason for SmallSet and BigSet to have the extra methods of ExtendedSet.

We can solve this problem by keeping implementations outside the hierarchy used to define the type family. The resulting structure for this example is shown in Figure 15.8. The implementation hierarchy has been separated from the type family for Set. Set and ExtendedSet objects refer to SetState objects, and their methods will be implemented by using SetState methods. However, as discussed in Section 15.2.3, since SetState is not part of the Set hierarchy, its objects need not provide the same methods as set objects.

The pattern shown in Figure 15.8 is the *bridge pattern* (see Sidebar 15.7). The name implies that a relationship (a "bridge") exists between the two hierarchies but they are not the same hierarchy.

Figure 15.8   Structure of the bridge pattern.

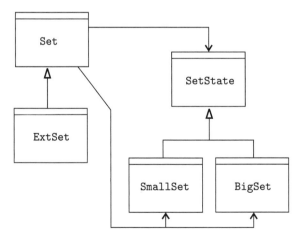

> ## Sidebar 15.7   The Bridge Pattern
>
> - The *bridge pattern* separates the implementation hierarchy from the subtype hierarchy.
> - The pattern occurs naturally when the state pattern is used, but it can be used more generally.
> - The bridge pattern adds complexity, and therefore it should be used only in conjunction with the state pattern, or when there is a need for *both* multiple implementations and subtype hierarchy.

The bridge pattern occurs naturally for mutable types whose objects change their implementation over time, since we needed to introduce this structure for them anyway. The pattern can be used whenever there are multiple implementations; for example, we could use it for Poly. However, the pattern does add complexity: we now have two hierarchies where before we had just one. Therefore, the pattern should be used only when there is a need for the state pattern, or when there is a need for *both* multiple implementations and extension subtypes.

15.4   Procedures Should Be Objects Too

Many object-oriented languages, including Java, do not allow procedures to be used as objects. In particular, there is no easy way to store a procedure in a data structure or to pass it as an argument or result of a call. However, sometimes you need to do these things.

The only practical way to obtain a procedure object in Java is to create an object that has the procedure as its method; that object can then be passed as an argument or result, or stored in a data structure. Of course, many procedures belong to objects already: they are regular methods rather than static methods. If the object's type is a subtype of an interface that describes the needed procedures, no extra mechanism is needed. Comparable (see Figure 8.4) is an example of such an interface; it allows the use of the compareTo method for objects belonging to its subtypes.

When the procedure in question is a static method, however, or when the object does not belong to a subtype of the needed interface, we must fall back on a different approach: we define an interface that describes the needed procedures, and each subtype of that interface implements the procedures. We saw examples of how to do this in Chapter 8. For example, Figure 8.6 defined the Adder interface; objects belonging to subtypes of Adder provide methods to add and subtract their arguments. Similarly, objects belonging to subtypes of the Comparator interface, which is defined in java.util and also in Section 8.5, provide a compare method that defines an ordering on its arguments.

As another example, suppose a collection has a doWork method that performs some operation on those elements of the collection that satisfy a certain check. The idea here is that doWork doesn't define the check; instead, its user does this by passing doWork a procedure argument. Having a procedure argument gives the user the ability to control what doWork does.

Figure 15.9 shows an interface that defines the needed procedure. doWork uses this interface, for example,

```
public void doWork (Filterer f)
    // MODIFIES: this
    // EFFECTS: Changes all elements of this that match filter f.check.
```

(The exact change will depend on what is going on in the collection.)

Figure 15.9 also shows two subtypes of the Filterer interface. Pos-Filterer accepts only positive integers. Here is an example of its use:

```
Filterer f = new PosFilterer( );
c.doWork(f); // call the collection method, using f as the filter
```

The second subtype, LTFilterer, accepts all integers less than a predefined value. The point to notice here is that LTFilterer's check method actually requires a second argument, the integer bound that it is checking against. However, doWork expects a check method that takes just one argument, the object being checked. We resolve this incompatibility by having the bound be part of the rep of the LTFilterer object. An example of a use is:

```
Filterer g = new LTFilterer(100);
c.doWork(g);
```

Here the filter will accepts all elements of c that are less than 100.

Figure 15.9   Defining a filter

```
public interface Filterer {
   public boolean check (Object x) throws ClassCastException
      // EFFECTS: If x cannot be checked throws ClassCastException;
      //    if x passes the check returns true else returns false.
}

public class PosFilterer implements Filterer {
   // OVERVIEW: Accepts all positive integers.
   public PosFilterer ( ) { }
   public boolean check (Object x) throws ClassCastException {
      if (!x instanceof Integer) throw ClassCastException;
      return ((Integer) x).intValue( ) > 0; }
}

public class LTFilterer implements Filterer {
   // OVERVIEW: All Integers less than some bound pass the check;
   //    the bound is an argument to the constructor.
   private int b;
   public LTFilterer (int x) { b = x; }
   public boolean check (Object x) throws ClassCastException {
      if (!x instanceof Integer) throw ClassCastException;
      return ((Integer) x).intValue( ) < b; }
}
```

The class LTFilterer implements a *closure*. A closure is a procedure, some of whose formal arguments are already bound. In this case, the upper bound is the extra argument. The value selected for this extra argument is bound when the LTFilterer object is created, by providing it as an argument to the constructor. The check method of the newly created object then uses this prebound value to do the computation.

There are two design patterns whose purpose is to make up for the lack of procedure objects. The *strategy pattern* is used when the using context has some expectation about what the procedure will do. All the examples discussed so far are examples of strategies; the using code expects to do addition (with the Adder interface), comparisons (with the Comparator interface), or

Figure 15.10 The Runnable interface

```
public interface Runnable {

    public void run ( )
        // MODIFIES: Anything
        // EFFECTS: Anything
}
```

filtering (with the Filterer interface). Note also that in all cases, the calling context expects there to be no side effects (since the specifications of the interfaces indicate modifies nothing).

The *command pattern* is used when there is no expectation about the behavior of the procedure. All the calling context expects is a particular signature; the effects clause does not constrain what the procedure does, and the modifies clause allows arbitrary modifications. Typically, the modifications will be to objects that are accessible from the rep of the command object, and at least some of these objects are likely to have been provided when the command object was created (i.e., the command object is highly likely to be a closure).

An example of such an interface is the Runnable interface shown in Figure 15.10. This interface is used in Java to start up new threads. (See a Java text for information about how to use threads in Java.) When a new thread is created, the creating thread provides a procedure for the new thread to run by supplying a Runnable object. The new thread runs the procedure by calling the run method on this object. The procedure is almost certainly a closure; for example, it may know of certain objects that it uses to communicate with its creating thread.

Both the strategy pattern and the command pattern have the structure shown in Figure 15.11. Here S specifies the interfaces for the needed procedures; its subtypes S1 and S2 implement the procedures. The Creator module creates an object of subtype S1 and passes it to the using module U. Note that U depends only on interface S and not on its subtypes.

Sidebar 15.8 summarizes the discussion about these two patterns.

Figure 15.11   Structure of strategy and command patterns

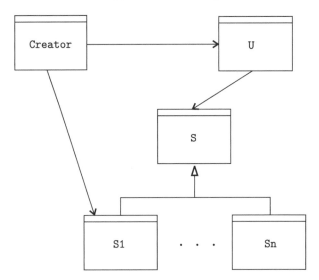

Sidebar 15.8   Strategy and Command Patterns

- The *strategy pattern* and the *command pattern* allow the use of procedures as objects.

- With the strategy pattern, the using context expects a certain behavior from the procedure; with the command pattern, it expects only a certain interface.

- In either pattern, the procedure may be a *closure*. A closure makes use of some prebound arguments, which are provided when the procedure's object is created.

- Both patterns are defined via an interface that specifies the procedures as methods. Subtypes of the interface implement the procedures.

15.5   Composites

Certain applications use a tree of objects to store their information, where all the objects in the tree belong to types in a type hierarchy. The top object in the tree belongs to such a type; it has descendants (its children) that also belong to such types; they in turn have such descendants, and this continues until you reach the leaves of the tree. This sort of structure arises in user interfaces; for example, the entire display is a window, which has other windows as subcomponents, and so on, and all these windows, such as plain windows and bordered windows, belong to the same type family.

Another place where the structure arises is in compilers and interpreters. In these programs, the text to be compiled or interpreted is processed to arrive at a *parse tree*. Then the tree is manipulated in various ways. For example, an interpreter might first walk over the tree to determine whether the program it represents is type correct, and then each time the interpreter is asked to run the program, it walks over the tree to carry out the execution. A compiler would also do a tree walk to carry out type checking, but then it would do another tree walk for each later processing phase. There typically will be many optimization phases in which the compiler gathers information about the program that can be used to produce efficient code in the later, code generation phases.

The nodes of a parse tree are entities that represent portions of the program. For example, in the tree corresponding to a Java program, there would be a node for an if statement, and this node would contain references to its components—namely, a node for the expression being tested, a node for the statement to execute if the test is true, and possibly a node for the statement to execute if the test is false (if the statement has an else part). Similarly, the expression node would point to other nodes for its components, which might be subexpressions, variables, or literals. An example of such a tree is shown in Figure 15.12; it corresponds to the program fragment:

```
if (x > 6) return; else z = x;
```

The figure shows that the node for the if statement has three descendants: the node for the if-expression (x > 6), the node for the then-part (the return statement), and the node for the else-part (the assignment statement). The if-expression is a binary expression consisting of the variable x, the operator >, and the literal 6. The assignment statement consists of the variable being assigned to (z) and the variable being assigned (x).

All the types appearing in a parse tree are similar in the sense that as the compiler or interpreter interacts with them, it does so in similar ways; that is, it calls the same methods. Therefore, all these types are members of a hierarchy. A part of the hierarchy for our fragment of Java is shown in Figure 15.13.

Figure 15.12   A parse tree

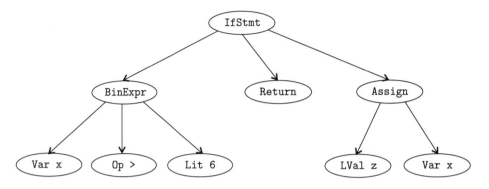

Figure 15.13   Partial hierarchy for Java

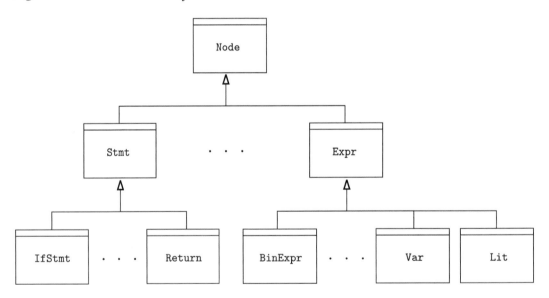

Higher levels in the hierarchy are abstract—that is, the types have no objects. This might be true, for example, for the types Node, Expr, and Stmt.

Such a hierarchy is an example of the *composite pattern* (see Sidebar 15.9). All types in the hierarchy have certain methods. However, the types may also differ; for example, internal nodes, which are called *components*, might have methods to access their descendants, while the *leaf* nodes do not need such methods.

Sidebar 15.9 The Composite Pattern

- The *composite pattern* composes objects in trees containing nodes, all of which belong to the same type family. *Component* nodes have descendants in the tree, while *leaf* nodes have no descendants.

- This pattern occurs naturally in certain applications, ranging from user interfaces to compilers and interpreters.

Sidebar 15.10 Ways of Traversing Composites

There are three ways of traversing the trees that arise when using the composite pattern:

- The *interpreter pattern* uses a method in each node for each phase. With this pattern, it is easy to add a new node type but more difficult to add a new phase.

- The *procedural approach* has a class per phase, with each class containing a static method per node type. This pattern makes it easy to add a new phase but requires lots of casts.

- The *visitor pattern* also has a class per phase, with each class containing a (nonstatic) method for each concrete node type. This pattern makes it easy to add a new phase, and it does not require casts. But it is more complex than the interpreter or procedural approaches.

15.5.1   Traversing the Tree

Gathering all the node types into a common family helps to regularize the processing of the tree. The code that carries out a computation over the tree interacts with each node in a similar way. In general, there will be many types of such computations—for example, one for each phase in a compiler.

There are three different ways to organize how the code of a phase interacts with the nodes (see Sidebar 15.10). The first approach is to have each node type

Figure 15.14   The interpreter pattern

```
public class IfStmt implements Stmt {
    private Expr e;   // the if expression
    private Stmt s1;  // the then statement
    private Stmt s2;  // the else statement

    public boolean typeCheck( ) {
        // EFFECTS: Returns true if this type checks else returns false.
        if (!e.typeCheck( ) || !s1.typeCheck( ) ||
                (s2 != null && !s2.typeCheck( ))) return false;
        return e.type( ).equals("boolean"); }

    public node optX( )
        // EFFECTS: If there is a way of reorganizing this to reflect
        //     this optimization, returns a new node that reflects the
        //     optimization else returns this.

    // methods for other optimizations and for code-generation
}
```

provide a method for each phase. This is called the *interpreter pattern*. This structure is illustrated in Figure 15.14. The figure sketches the implementation of IfStmt, the node type for the if statement. IfStmt provides a method for each phase carried out by the compiler; the implementations of other node types are similar.

The figure shows how methods on node objects are implemented—by calling the corresponding method on the node's descendants. Thus, the code for the typeCheck method of the IfStmt object first checks that each of its child nodes is type correct, and then it checks that the expression returns a boolean result.

The interpreter pattern allows new types of nodes to be defined with only localized effort: just define the class for the new node type. However, it doesn't work so well when a new phase is added to the compiler because, in this case, every class that implements a node type must be modified. And, unfortunately, the latter kind of modification is more likely than the former because compilers are often improved by adding additional phases.

The second way of traversing the tree is to implement a class per phase: a class to do type checking, a class for each optimization phase, and a class for

Figure 15.15 The procedural approach to traversing a composite tree

```
public class TypeCheck {
    // handles the type-checking phase

    public static boolean ifStmt(IfStmt n) {
        if (!TypeCheck.expr(n.expr( )) || !TypeCheck.stmt(n.thenStmt( )) ||
            (n.elseStmt( ) != null && !TypeCheck.stmt(n.elseStmt( )))) return false;
        return n.expr( ).type( ).equals("boolean"); }

    public static boolean stmt(Stmt n) {
        if (n instanceof IfStmt) return TypeCheck.ifStmt((IfStmt) n);
        if (n instanceof Return) return TypeCheck.returnStmt((Return) n);
        if (n instanceof Assign) return TypeCheck.assign((Assign) n);
        if ...
    }

    // methods for other node types go here
}
```

each code generation phase. Each class contains a static method for each node type, and these methods call one another recursively. Figure 15.15 illustrates the structure for the type-checking phase. Each static method is passed a node of the tree as an argument. It uses methods of that node object to obtain the node's descendants; it then passes each descendant as an argument to the static method for the descendant's type. Thus, TypeCheck.ifStmt calls TypeCheck.expr, passing it the node corresponding to the if-expression as an argument.

Using this approach, we have effectively moved the knowledge about how to perform a phase such as type checking out of the nodes and into the class implementing that phase. This means that when we add another phase, we merely need to implement another class; the classes implementing the node types need not change. However, if we add another node type, we need to add procedures to each class, so this kind of change is more difficult than it was with the interpreter pattern.

A problem with the procedural approach is that many methods must do casts, which is both inconvenient and expensive. For example, to type check the statement in the then part, TypeCheck.ifStmt must call TypeCheck.stmt, since it does not know what kind of statement it is dealing with. Type-Check.stmt must then figure this out by using casts, as shown in Figure 15.15. These casts are avoided with the interpreter approach since the call on the s1.typeCheck method shown in Figure 15.14 goes to s1's object, which knows what kind of statement it is. (For example, for the structure in Figure 15.12, it is a return statement.)

The third way of traversing the tree is intermediate between these forms. This technique is called the *visitor pattern*. With this pattern, the knowledge about what the tree structure is like below a node is localized to the node, as in the interpreter pattern, but the knowledge about what phase is being executed is localized in a separate class, as in the procedural approach. The classes that implement the phases are the *visitor classes.*

The visitor pattern is illustrated in Figure 15.16. As in the procedural approach, there is a class for each phase, and within that class is a method for each node type. However, these methods are not static; there is an actual visitor object instead. Furthermore, we need methods only for concrete node types—that is, those that actually have objects. With the procedural approach, methods are needed for some abstract types as well since the code must handle such nodes; for example, Stmt is such a type.

Figure 15.16 also shows part of the IfStmt class. Every node class provides an accept method that takes a visitor object as an argument. This method traverses the tree beneath its node by calling accept methods on its child nodes, each of which will call its own method on the visitor as part of its processing. When all child nodes have been traversed, the parent calls the method associated with its node's type on the visitor. Thus, the IfStmt accept method calls accept on the if-expression node, the then-statement node, and the else-statement node if there is one. Then it calls the ifStmt method on its visitor.

The visitor object keeps track of what has been learned in the processing so far. In the case of type checking, this is information about type correctness up to this point. The information is shown as being kept on a stack within the visitor object. For statements, the only possibilities are "correct", meaning the statement type checked correctly, or "error", meaning it did not type check correctly. For expressions, the information is the actual type of the expression or "error" if there is a mismatch in the types of subexpressions.

The module dependency diagram for the visitor pattern is shown in Figure 15.17 (page 398). The figure shows that in this pattern there is a mutual dependency: the nodes use the visitors, and the visitors use the nodes. Note

Figure 15.16 The visitor pattern

```
public class TypeCheckVisitor implements Visitor {
    // implements the type-checking phase
    // provides a method for each concrete node type
    private StringStack els; // stores the types of expressions as strings

    public void ifStmt (IfStmt n) {
        String s2 = null;
        if (n.hasElse( )) s2 = els.pop( );   // the else stmt
        String s1 = els.pop( ); // the then stmt
        String e = els.pop( ); // the if expression
        if (e.equals("boolean") && s1.equals("correct") &&
            (s2 == null || s2.equals("correct")))
        els.push("correct"); else els.push("error");
    }

    public void var (Var n) { els.push(n.type); }

    // other methods go here
}

public class IfStmt implements Stmt {
    private Expr e; // the if expression
    private Stmt s1; // the then statement
    private Stmt s2; // the else statement

    public void accept (Visitor v) {
        e.accept(v);
        s1.accept(v);
        if (s2 != null) s2.accept(v);
        v.ifStmt(this); }

    // other IfStmt methods
}
```

that the node types depend only on the Visitor interface, but the visitor types depend on various node subtypes: each visitor method depends on the related node type (e.g., the ifStmt visitor method depends on the IfStmt node type). (It's possible to make the visitor types depend only on Node, but

Figure 15.17 Dependencies in the visitor pattern

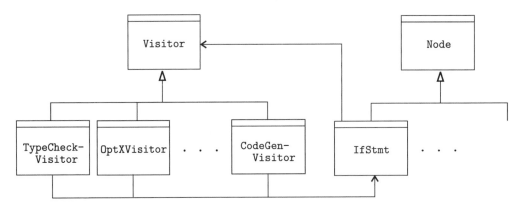

this complicates the code of the visitor methods and makes them more costly since they need to do casts.)

The visitor pattern is similar to the procedural approach in the way it accommodates change: a new phase requires writing a new visitor class, but a new node type requires implementing a new method in every existing visitor class. The pattern avoids the need for the casts used in the procedural approach because a node object calls the visitor method for its type, which it knows. The pattern implements a form of what is called *double dispatch*: it gets to the right code based on *both* the type of the node being traversed and the phase being run.

However, the visitor pattern is more complicated than either the interpreter pattern or the procedural approach, and it has a problem that arises from the fact that all phases do not have identical structure. For example, for type checking, we want to return a boolean; but for optimization, we might modify the parse tree, and for code generation, we might modify the object storing the code being generated. In the interpreter and procedural approaches, these differences showed up as different types of results in different phases. The visitor pattern doesn't allow different kinds of results; instead, information about what has happened so far must be stored within the visitor (e.g., the els stack in Figure 15.16), and the code can be more complex as a result.

An additional problem is that sometimes more interaction is required between a node and the visitor. For example, the node might need to call a visitor method both before it starts calling accept on its child nodes and after. To allow this interaction, we would need to have two visitor methods associated with each node type (the "before" method and the "after" method). Furthermore, we probably would want a different accept method for each way of interacting with a visitor, since if there were just one accept method, it would sometimes make unnecessary calls (e.g., to the "before" method in a phase that doesn't need it).

The visitor classes are more closely coupled to the node classes than was the case in the procedural approach because of the callbacks from the node to the visitor methods. Furthermore, if a new phase is added that needs to have nodes interact with the visitor in a new way, all node types must be modified to accommodate the change. Such changes are not necessary with the procedural approach.

15.6   The Power of Indirection

Suppose you are adding code to a system that is already using objects of some type T and will continue to do so. Your new code will use these preexisting objects but in a different way than they are already being used. This different way might correspond to a different interface, or it might simply be an augmented implementation of some of the methods of the original object.

In such a situation, you can customize the original object to provide the desired behavior by interposing an object between it and the using code. The using code interacts with the interposed object, which does some work itself and forwards most of it to the original object. The structure is illustrated in Figure 15.18: the using code makes use of the interposed object, which in turn makes use of the original object.

Three patterns capture this paradigm (see Sidebar 15.11). The *adaptor pattern* covers the situation where the interface required by the new code does not match that provided by the object; in other words, the interposed object does not belong to the same type family as the original object. In the other two patterns, *proxy* and *decorator*, the interposed object supports the same interface as the original object. In the case of the proxy pattern, the interface is identical to that of the original object; the goal with this pattern is to control access to the object in some way. With the decorator pattern, the behavior is enhanced: the existing methods might do more, and there might

Figure 15.18   Using indirection

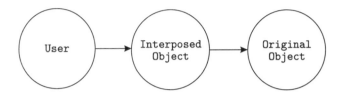

Sidebar 15.11   The Adaptor, Proxy, and Decorator Patterns

The adaptor, proxy, and decorator patterns all interpose an object between using code and the original object.

- In the *adaptor pattern*, the interposed object has different behavior than the original object, and therefore it can be used only by new (or modified) code.

- In the *proxy pattern*, the new object has identical behavior to the original object, while in the *decorator pattern* the new object has extended behavior. In both patterns, the new object can be used by either new or preexisting code.

---

be some extra methods. All these patterns have the object structure shown in Figure 15.18.

To illustrate these patterns, consider a Registry type that provides a mapping from strings to objects and assume at least one registry object is already in use. A registry object has a lookup method:

```
public Vector lookup (String s) throws NotFoundException
    // EFFECTS: If there is a mapping for s in this returns a vector that
    //    contains all the associated objects else throws NotFoundException.
```

If you decide that you need to also do the reverse lookup (from an object to the string that maps to it), you can accomplish it by using a decorator. This decorator has all the registry methods plus the new reverseLookup method; it forwards calls on all the old methods to the original object, and it implements the new method itself, using the original object as needed. (The reverse lookup won't be very efficient, but that may not matter, for example, if the registries are small.)

Alternatively, if you decide that you want the `lookup` method to retrieve only the first matching object, you can use an adaptor. In this case, the specification of the `lookup` method changes to:

```
public Object lookup (String s) throws NotFoundException
   // EFFECTS: If there is a mapping for s in this returns the object
   //    first associated with s else throws NotFoundException.
```

and, therefore, the adaptor type cannot be a subtype of the type of the original object.

Finally, suppose the new code is going to run at a different computer than the rest, yet it needs to access one of the preexisting registries. In this case, you can use a proxy. The proxy resides on the same machine as the new code, which makes calls on it as if it were making calls directly on the real registry object at the other computer. The proxy forms a packet that represents the call and sends it across the network to the registry object using some remote procedure call mechanism. When the reply packet arrives, the proxy extracts the result and returns to the caller.

Since the adaptor changes the observable behavior of the original object, its type is unrelated to that of the original object. The proxy and decorator do not change the observable behavior of the original object, and therefore their types can be subtypes of the type of the original object. This allows them to be used in another situation: where a system is being extended with a new kind of object that needs to fit in with existing code.

For example, adding a new kind of window to a window system can be done with the decorator pattern. Since the new window type (e.g., "bordered window") is a subtype of the some preexisting window type, it can be placed in an existing tree of windows (e.g., a composite structure), and it can be manipulated with the preexisting code that already interacts with existing types of windows.

On the other hand, suppose you need to redistribute objects, so that an object that at present runs at the same machine as the code that uses it is moved to some other machine. In this case, you can use the proxy pattern: a proxy is left behind on the original machine, and it forwards all the calls made by the preexisting code to the machine where the original object now resides.

15.7   Publish/Subscribe

A change in one object is sometimes of interest to a number of other objects. We will refer to the object of interest as the *subject* and to the other objects as *observers*. For example, when a document changes, one observer might print a new copy, while another might send e-mail to an interested user. Or, when e-mail arrives in your mailbox, one observer might add its header to a list, while another might cause your terminal to alert you by making a noise. Another example arises in a distributed file system; when a file is modified, all remote sites that have cached the file need to be notified.

In this kind of situation, it is desirable to decouple the subject from the observers, since it allows the observers to change without having to modify the subject. The number of observers might change over time, and the observers need not all belong to the same type.

The *observer pattern* captures this structure. The subject maintains a list of interested parties; it provides methods that allow observers to add and remove themselves from the list. When the subject's state changes, it notifies every observer in the list by calling its update method.

The structure is illustrated in Figure 15.19 where S is a particular subtype of Subject and O is a subtype of Observer. Some object of type S would act as a subject in a program, and it might be observed by objects of type O (and of other types not shown in the diagram). In addition to the nodes representing the subject and observer types, the figure also shows a User type; an object of this type causes the state of the subject to change.

Note that very loose coupling exists between the subject and its observers: the observer depends on the subject only to support the Subject interface, and the subject depends on the observers only to support the Observer interface. Other details about the actual subject and observer objects—that is, their other methods—are hidden.

Either the update method takes no arguments, in which case the observer must call other methods on the subject to find out about its current state, or the observer can be passed information about the subject's state directly as extra arguments of the update method. The former structure is called a *pull* structure because the observers explicitly ask for the information they need (this asking is the "pull"); the latter structure is called a *push* structure, since information is given to observers directly (it is "pushed" to them). Each form

Figure 15.19 The observer pattern

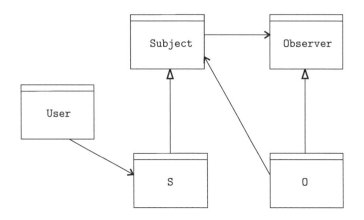

has advantages and disadvantages. The pull approach requires extra calls to methods of the subject, but the push approach might provide more arguments than a particular observer needs. These issues are especially significant if subject and observers are on different machines: the pull method requires extra remote communicate, while the push method can consume bandwidth unnecessarily.

The observer pattern is sometimes referred to as *publish/subscribe* because the subject publishes information to the subscribers (which are the observers).

Sidebar 15.12 summarizes this discussion.

15.7.1   Abstracting Control

In the observer pattern, the subject does not know the types of the observer objects (other than that they are all subtypes of the observer interface), but it does know what objects are observing it. Furthermore, it controls the order in which the observers are notified of a change. The subject and observers can be further decoupled by removing these relationships.

This decoupling can be accomplished by using the *mediator pattern*. In this pattern, the subject and observers communicate via a shared *mediator* object. Each observer registers with the mediator. Then when the subject wants to communicate with the observers, it calls a method of the mediator,

Sidebar 15.12 The Observer Pattern

- The *observer pattern* captures a situation in which changes in the state of some *subject* object are of interest to other *observer* objects. It abstracts from the number of observers and defines a standard way for subjects and observers to interact.

- With the *pull* structure, the observer is notified of a change and then it communicates further with the subject to determine the details of what happened.

- With the *push* structure, all information about the change is sent to the observer as part of the notification.

- The pull structure causes more communication, since the observer must make calls on methods of the subject to find out the details, but the push structure can cause more information to be sent to an observer than it needs.

and the mediator forwards the information to the observers. The structure is illustrated in Figure 15.20.

In this structure, the subject and observers know nothing about one another; they are related only through their use of the mediator. Of course, complete decoupling works only with a push model. If we used the pull approach instead, the observers would depend on a Subject interface that provided the methods used to get the additional information.

Although we have described the mediator pattern as a way for the subject to communicate with the observers, the communication need not be asymmetric. Instead, the mediator can be used by a group of "colleagues"; each communication goes from one of them to all the others.

In addition to decoupling the subject and observers, the mediator pattern also centralizes control over the details of communication. For example, the mediator might prioritize the observers and communicate with them in priority order. Or, it might use a "first acceptor" approach: rather than communicate with all observers, it communicates with them one-by-one and stops as soon as one "accepts" the information. Since the communication details are localized to the mediator, they can be changed just by reimplementing the mediator; the code of subjects and observers that use the mediator need not change.

Figure 15.20 The mediator pattern

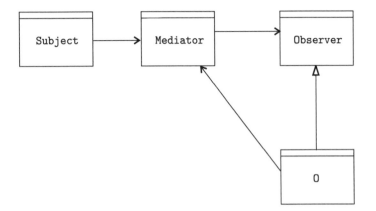

The mediator pattern can be generalized further into a *white board*. A white board is a place where information is posted; it provides a naming mechanism that is used to control interactions. For example, one group of interacting objects might communicate using the names A and B, while another group uses different names. The object wanting to communicate writes information to the white board under some name. Either this information is automatically disseminated to interested parties (the subscribers) or interested parties periodically examine the white board to see what has changed.

Communication through a white board is sometimes proposed as an alternative to direct calls on methods; the caller publishes a request to the white board, and producers of the desired service find out about the request from the white board. One advantage of this structure compared to direct calls is that the publisher need not know who the subscribers are, nor even how many of them there are; in other words, the white board easily generalizes a call into a multicast to a group of service providers. A second advantage is that synchronization is not necessary. The publisher need not wait for some subscriber to handle its request. Instead, it can do something else and check for the result later by looking somewhere else on the white board.

Sidebar 15.13 summarizes this discussion.

Sidebar 15.13   Abstracting Control

- A *mediator* decouples subjects from observers by providing an intermediary that allows them to communicate. It localizes details of how communication takes place and allows these details to be changed without having to change subjects or observers.

- A *white board* provides a place for posting and looking for information. It can be used as an alternative to procedure calls: it allows the caller to be independent of the identities and number of objects that provide the desired service, and it allows asynchronous communication.

15.8   Summary

This chapter has discussed a number of design patterns. Patterns typically impose a level of indirection since it allows something to be changed. For example, a factory object is interposed between the code that uses some types and the code that implements them; the indirection allows us to easily switch to different implementations for the types. Similarly, the state pattern uses a level of indirection between the object being implemented to the one that represents it, so that we can change to a different implementation. And, a mediator is interposed between a subject and its observers so that the subject does not depend on the observers nor on the order in which they receive the information.

Patterns can be used to improve the flexibility or performance of a program. However, they can also make a program more complex and more difficult to understand. For example, the down side of using a mediator is that it is not clear from reading the code of the subject what communication paradigm (e.g., broadcast or first acceptor) is in use. Therefore, it is important to have a sound motivation for using a pattern. In general, a pattern should be introduced into a program only when a substantial benefit can be gained by using it.

Even though restraint is necessary when using patterns, they are a useful design tool. They provide a vocabulary for design. They are useful when you design yourself, since they give you more options; and they are useful for explaining designs and for understanding the designs of others.

Exercises

15.1 Analyze the design of the stock tracker (see Chapter 13) to identify places where patterns might be used and decide whether the use of the pattern is justified in each case.

15.2 Analyze some program you have designed to identify places where patterns would be useful and decide whether the use of the pattern is justified in each case.

Glossary

Abstract class A class that has no objects.

Abstract method A method without an implementation; an abstract method is defined in an interface or abstract class.

Abstraction The process of forgetting information so that things that are different can be treated as if they are the same. Also, the program entity that results from the abstraction process.

Abstraction by parameterization The process of abstracting from the identity of specific data items by replacing them with parameters.

Abstraction by specification The process of abstracting from how a program module is implemented to what the module does.

Abstraction function A mapping from the rep of an object to the abstract state that the rep is intended to represent.

Abstract state The state of an object at the abstract level, as determined by its specification.

Acceptance test phase A phase of the software life cycle in which a program is validated by having it pass the acceptance tests.

Acceptance tests A set of tests used to determine whether a program is acceptable.

Activation record A block of storage containing a procedure's actual parameters; the activation record is pushed on the program stack when the procedure is called and popped when it returns.

Actual parameters The arguments passed to a procedure when it is called.

Actual type The type an object receives when it is created.

Adaptor pattern   A design pattern in which an object is interposed between using code and the original object in order to change the behavior of the original object.

Adequacy   A data type is adequate if it provides enough operations that whatever users need to do with its objects can be done conveniently and with reasonable efficiency.

Aliasing errors   Errors that arise when two different formal parameters refer to the same actual parameter.

Apparent type   The type of an expression that can be deduced by a compiler from information available in declarations.

Assertion   A predicate that applies to the state of a program.

Basis step of data type induction   The step that starts an inductive proof by showing that a predicate holds when each constructor returns.

Behavioral equivalence   Two objects are behaviorally equivalent if it is not possible to distinguish between them using any sequence of calls to the objects' methods.

Benevolent side effect   A change to the rep of an object that does not affect its abstract state. Benevolent side effects are possible only when the abstraction function is many-to-one.

Black box tests   Tests based on a program's specification, not its implementation.

Bottom-up development   A development process in which all modules used by module M are implemented and tested before M is implemented.

Bridge pattern   A design pattern that separates the implementation hierarchy for a type from its subtype hierarchy.

Builder pattern   A design pattern that provides a method called a builder, which is a kind of factory method that constructs a collection of new objects.

Call by value   A mechanism for passing arguments to a procedure in which the result obtained from evaluating an argument expression is assigned to the associated formal parameter.

Candidate   An abstraction whose implementation has not yet been studied during a design, but whose specification is complete.

Casting   The runtime action of changing the type of an object; in Java, casting succeeds only if the actual type of the object is a subtype of the type to which it is being cast.

Checked exception   A category of exception types in Java. Checked exception types are subtypes of `Exception` but not of `RuntimeException`. Java requires that a checked exception must either be handled by the calling procedure or be listed in its header.

Checks clause   Part of the specification of an operation in a requirements specification. The checks clause identifies illegal inputs; the operation is required to check for such an input and provide an appropriate error message if it occurs.

Class   The Java entity used to implement a data type or a group of standalone procedures.

Closure   A procedure with prebound arguments.

Coherence   A property of an abstraction; an abstraction is coherent if its specification indicates that it has a single well-defined purpose.

Command pattern   A design pattern that provides procedure objects, where the using context expects only a certain interface for the procedure. This pattern is related to the strategy pattern.

Compatible signatures   The signature rule of the substitution property requires that signatures of subtype methods be compatible with those of corresponding supertype methods. Java enforces this by requiring identical signatures except that the subtype method can have fewer exceptions than the supertype method.

Complete supertype   A data type with a full complement of methods, each having a sufficiently complete specification so that using code can be written based on the supertype's specification.

Component in the composite pattern   An interior node in a tree formed according to the composite pattern.

Composite pattern   A design pattern that defines a tree of objects, where each object in the tree belongs to the same type family, so that every node of the tree can be treated uniformly.

Composite tree   The tree of objects that results from the composite pattern.

Concrete class   A class that has objects.

Concrete state   The state of an object at the rep level.

Conjunctive coherence   A property of an abstraction; an abstraction exhibits conjunctive coherence if its specification indicates that it does more than one thing.

Constraint in a data model   A predicate that limits some relations in the model.

Constructor   A constructor is a special kind of method that is used to initialize a newly created object.

Constructors part of a specification   The part of a specification of a data abstraction that specifies the behavior of the abstraction's constructors.

Context type   In the state pattern, this is the type whose objects are represented differently when they are in different states.

Creators   Operations of a data abstraction that produce objects "from scratch"; these operations are constructors that do not have arguments belonging to their type.

Dangling reference   A reference to storage that has been deallocated. Dangling references are not possible in a garbage-collected language such as Java.

Data abstraction   An abstraction that hides details about the way data objects are implemented.

Data model   A model describing the state of a program. It consists of sets and relations with associated constraints, expressed both graphically and textually.

Data type induction   A way of proving invariants for data abstractions by using an inductive proof. The basis step shows that the invariant holds for each newly created object. The inductive step shows that the invariant holds after each method call, assuming it holds just before the call.

Debugging   The process of finding and removing errors (bugs) from programs.

Decomposition   A way of dividing a large problem into smaller subproblems. We do decomposition through the recognition of useful abstractions.

Decorator pattern   A design pattern in which an object is interposed between using code and the original object in order to extend the behavior of the original object. The interposed object will belong to a subtype of the type of the original object.

Defensive programming   Writing code to defend against errors.

Definitional style   A way of writing specifications by describing properties that specificands are intended to have. We use this style in this book.

Derived relation   A relation in a data model that is not independent but can be defined in terms of other relations.

Design   The process of deciding a structure for the implementation of a program. We use a design technique based on the recognition of useful abstractions.

Design notebook   A document describing a design; it consists of a module dependency diagram and a section for each abstraction containing its specification, its performance requirements, a sketch of its implementation, and other information including a justification of design decisions.

Design pattern   A way of organizing a program to obtain some benefit such as improved performance or flexibility.

Design phase   The phase of the software life cycle in which a design for a software product is developed.

Design review   A process to evaluate the correctness, performance, and quality of a design.

Deterministic implementation   An implementation of a procedure is deterministic if any two calls with identical inputs produce the same result. Implementations of underdetermined procedures are almost always deterministic.

Disjunctive coherence   A property of an abstraction; an abstraction exhibits disjunctive coherence if its specification indicates that it does one of a number of things.

Dispatching   Causing a method call to go to the code provided by the method's object—that is, the code provided by its class.

Dispatch vector   A way of implementing dispatching by using a vector that points to an object's methods.

Domain in a data model   A set in the model that is not a subset of any other set in the model.

Domain of a procedure   The number and types of a procedure's arguments.

Driver   A test driver; a driver runs a module through a series of tests.

Effects clause   Part of a procedure's specification. It states what the procedure does, assuming its requires clause is satisfied. The effects clause gives the procedure's postcondition.

Element subtype approach to polymorphism   A way of using hierarchy to define polymorphism. The polymorphic abstraction is defined in terms of an interface, and all its elements must belong to subtypes of the type defined by that interface.

Encapsulation   The hiding of implementation details so that they are inaccessible outside of the module providing the implementation.

Evolution property   A property of a data type that holds in future states: if the property is true for an object of the data type at a particular point in a program, then it is true for that object at all future points.

Exceptional termination   Terminating the execution of a procedure by throwing an exception.

Exception mechanism   A mechanism that allows a procedure to terminate either by returning or by throwing exceptions.

Exposing the rep   An implementation exposes the rep if it provides users of its objects with direct access to some mutable component of the rep.

Extensibility   The process of adding code to a system later, thus extending its behavior.

Extension arc in a module dependency diagram   This kind of arc indicates that one module is a subtype of another.

Extension subtypes   Subtypes that extend the behavior of their supertype —for example, by providing extra methods.

Extra method   A method of a subtype that is not also a method of its supertype.

Extrinsic state   State that is retained in the context from which a flyweight is used.

Factory class   A class providing a number of factory methods.

Factory method   A method that returns a newly created object, but the method is not a constructor of that object's class.

Factory object   An object whose methods are factory methods.

Factory pattern   A design pattern that allows object creation to be hidden through the use of factory methods, classes, and objects, thus reducing dependencies on the classes of objects.

Fixed subset A subset in a data model whose membership never changes.

Flyweight An object in the flyweight pattern that represents many identical objects.

Flyweight pattern A design pattern that allows a single object to represent many identical objects.

Formal parameters The declared arguments of a procedure. The declaration for the procedure defines the name and type of each formal parameter.

Formal specification A specification written in a specification language with precise semantics.

Formals Formal parameters.

FP The functional part of a program. Its job is to carry out the tasks of the program as instructed by the UI (user interface) part of the program.

Full encapsulation The implementation of a data abstraction is fully encapsulated if code outside the abstraction's implementation cannot access components of the rep.

Fully populates A class fully populates the type it implements if, for every abstract state of the type, the class has an object containing a corresponding concrete state.

Functional requirements In a requirements specification, a description of how a program behaves both in the presence and absence of errors.

Garbage collection The automatic collection of unused storage in the heap; the collected storage contains objects that are no longer accessible by the program.

Generality A property of a specification: one specification is more general than another if it can handle a larger class of inputs.

Generator A generator is an object that produces a sequence of elements. It is returned by an iterator; its type is a subtype of Iterator.

Glass box tests Tests based on the program text.

Graceful degradation A program degrades gracefully if, in the presence of an error, it provides an approximation to its normal behavior.

Handle an exception Provide code to catch an exception. The code might mask or reflect the exception.

Header The first part of a method declaration, which defines the method name, the types of its arguments and result, and the types of any exceptions it throws. The header defines the method's signature.

Heap The storage area in which objects reside.

Helper abstractions Abstractions invented while investigating the design of a target abstraction; helpers are abstractions that would be useful in implementing the target and that facilitate decomposition of the problem.

High availability A program is highly available if it is very likely to be up and running all the time.

High reliability A program is highly reliable if it is unlikely to lose information even in the presence of hardware failures.

Immutability An object is immutable if its state never changes. A data type is immutable if its objects are immutable.

Implementation and test phase The phase of the software life cycle in which the abstractions identified during design are implemented and tested.

Incomplete supertype A data type whose specification is so weak that using code is highly unlikely to be written in terms of it. Such a supertype is used to establish naming conventions for methods of its subtypes.

Induction step of data type induction The step that shows for each method of the type that a predicate holds when the method returns, assuming the predicate holds when the method is called.

Informal specification A specification written in an informal specification language (e.g., English). The specifications in this book are informal.

Inheritance A way of obtaining code without writing it. In particular, a subclass can inherit the implementations of its superclass's methods.

Instance An object.

Instance method A method belonging to an object.

Instance variable A variable that is part of the rep of an object.

Integration testing Testing a group of modules together.

Interface The interface of an abstraction is what it makes visible to other program modules. Also, in Java, an interface is an entity used to define a data type by declaring its methods.

Interpreter pattern   A design pattern in which a traversal of a composite tree is accomplished by calling a method for that traversal on each node in the tree.

Intrinsic state   The information stored in a flyweight object.

Invariant   A predicate on the program state that is always true, or always true except when the program is running some particular piece of code.

Invariant property   A property that holds for each object of a data type whenever control is not inside one of the object's methods.

Inverse of a relation   The inverse of a relation in a data model is a map that goes in the opposite direction, mapping items in the target set of the relation to the source items that the original relation mapped to that target item.

Iteration abstraction   An abstraction that hides details about how items in a collection are obtained; it allows using code to iterate over the items in the collection in an abstract way.

Iterator   An iterator is a procedure that returns a generator. The generator belongs to a subtype of type Iterator.

Iterator pattern   A design pattern that uses iterators to provide efficient access to elements of collection objects without either violating encapsulation or complicating the abstraction.

Leaf in the composite pattern   A leaf node in a tree formed according to the composite pattern.

Locality   A property of a program module; a module exhibits locality if its code can be read or written without needing to examine the code of any other module. A module exhibits locality only if its rep is not exposed.

Maintenance   Maintaining a program once it is in production by modifying it to correct errors.

Many-to-one map   A function that maps many items to the same result. In particular, an abstraction function is many-to-one if it maps many concrete states to the same abstract state.

Masking an exception   Responding to an exception thrown by a call by handling the exception and resuming normal processing.

Mediator pattern   A design pattern that allows objects to communicate through an intermediary.

Method The entity used in Java to implement a procedure. A method can either belong to an object or be static.

Methods part of a specification The part of a specification of a data abstraction that specifies the behavior of the methods of the abstraction's objects.

Methods rule A part of the definition of the substitution principle, requiring that subtype methods behave like the corresponding supertype methods.

Minimality A property of a specification: one specification is more minimal than another if it contains fewer constraints on allowable behavior.

Modifiability A property of a program module; a module exhibits modifiability if it can be reimplemented without requiring changes to any code that uses it. A module exhibits modifiability only if it is fully encapsulated.

Modification and maintenance phase A phase of the software life cycle that occurs once a program is in production; in the modification and maintenance phase, the code is changed either to correct errors or to satisfy new requirements.

Modifies clause Part of a procedure's specification. It identifies all inputs that might be modified by the procedure.

Modular decomposition A design technique in which a program is subdivided into a number of interacting modules. We use a decomposition technique that is based on the recognition of useful abstraction.

Module A unit of a program. In this book, modules implement abstractions.

Module dependency diagram A graph showing how abstractions in a design are related. The nodes represent program modules, each corresponding to an abstraction.

Multiple implementations Several classes that implement the same type. These classes define subtypes of the type they implement.

Multiplicity of a relation The number of items a relation in a data model maps to or from.

Mutability An object is mutable if its state can change. A data abstraction is mutable if its objects are mutable.

Mutability of a relation A relation in a data model is immutable if the mapping it defines cannot change over time; otherwise, it is mutable.

Mutator   A method of an object that modifies the object's state. An object is mutable if and only if it has some mutator methods.

Normal termination   Terminating the execution of a procedure by returning.

Object   An entity in a program that encapsulates its state and allows access via its methods.

Observer   A method of an object that observes its state—that is, provides information about the object's state.

Observer object in the observer pattern   An object that must be informed when the state of the subject object changes.

Observer pattern   A design pattern that captures a situation in which changes in the state of some subject object are of interest to other observer objects.

Operational style   A way of writing specifications by giving a recipe for constructing specificands.

Overloading   Several method definitions with the same name.

Overriding   A subclass overrides a method of its supertype when it provides its own implementation for that method.

Overview clause   Part of the specification of a data abstraction. It gives a brief description of the data abstraction including a model for its objects in terms of well-understood concepts or in terms of a data model.

Package   The Java mechanism for grouping together a number of classes and interfaces.

Partial procedure   A procedure is partial if there are some inputs for which its behavior is not specified.

Path-complete tests   Tests that exercise every path in the code at least once.

Performance requirements   Requirements on program performance—for example, how fast certain actions must be.

Polymorphic abstraction   An abstraction that works for many types. A procedure or iterator can be polymorphic with respect to the types of one or more arguments. A data abstraction can be polymorphic with respect to the types of elements its objects contain.

Postcondition   An assertion that holds when a procedure returns, assuming that the precondition held when the procedure was called.

Postcondition rule   A part of the methods rule of the substitution principle, requiring that the postcondition of a subtype method not be weaker than the postcondition of the corresponding supertype method.

Precondition   An assertion that must hold when a procedure is called.

Precondition rule   A part of the methods rule of the substitution principle, requiring that the precondition of a subtype method not be stronger than the precondition of the corresponding supertype method.

Preserving the rep invariant   An implementation preserves the rep invariant if it guarantees that the invariant holds for its objects whenever one of their methods is not running.

Priming a generator   Consuming some of the items produced by a generator before looping over the rest of them.

Procedural abstraction   An abstraction that hides details associated with executing an operation or task.

Procedural approach to traversing trees   A way of traversing a composite tree by using a class per traversal. The class contains a static method for each node type, and the traversal is accomplished by calling the static method for its type for each node of the tree.

Procedure   A procedural abstraction.

Producers   Operations of a data abstraction that produce new objects given objects of that type as arguments.

Production phase   The phase of the software life cycle in which the program is used.

Programming in the large   Programming entire systems that are made up of many individual modules.

Programming in the small   Programming individual modules.

Program maintenance   The activity of making changes to a program to correct errors after it has entered the production phase.

Program modification   The activity of making changes to a program after it has entered the production phase. The changes might be to correct errors or to provide additional features.

Properties rule   A part of the definition of the substitution principle, requiring that the specification of the subtype must preserve all properties that can be proved about supertype objects.

Property   A predicate.

Prototype pattern   A design pattern in which an object provides a factory method that produces a new object of its own class; the new object is in an initial state, similar to what would normally be obtained by calling a constructor.

Proxy pattern   A design pattern in which an object is interposed between using code and the original object in order to control access to the original object. The interposed and original objects are both members of the same type.

Publish/subscribe   A way of communicating in which an object publishes information, and other objects (the subscribers) are informed about the new information.

Pull structure in the observer pattern   With this structure, the observer is notified of a change and then communicates further with the subject to determine the details of what happened.

Push structure in the observer pattern   With this structure, the observer is informed about the state of the subject object as part of the notification.

Range of a procedure   The type of a procedure's result.

Record type   A data type consisting of a set of visible fields. Its abstraction function is the trivial map, and its rep invariant is "true".

Reflecting an exception   Responding to an exception thrown by a call by throwing another exception; this typically will be a different exception than the one thrown by the call.

Regression testing   The process of methodically rerunning all tests after each error is corrected.

Related subtype approach to polymorphism   A way of using hierarchy to define polymorphism. The polymorphic abstraction is defined in terms of an interface, and a subtype of this interface must be defined for every element type. The interface is an example of the strategy pattern.

Relation in a data model   A mapping between sets in a data model, indicating how items in one set are related to items in another set.

Rep   The representation of a data abstraction.

Representation invariant A predicate that accepts only legal representations for objects of some class. It defines which representations are legal by mapping each rep to either true (if it is legal) or false (if it is not legal).

Requirements The things that a software product must do in order to satisfy the needs of a customer.

Requirements analysis A process for discovering the requirements for a proposed software product.

Requirements analysis phase The phase of the software life cycle in which the requirements for a software product are defined.

Requirements document A document describing the requirements for a software product, including its behavior under both normal and error conditions, its performance requirements, information about potential modifications, and a schedule for producing the product.

Requirements specification A specification of the behavior of a software product, consisting of specifications of the operations provided by the product.

Requires clause Part of a procedure's specification. It states any preconditions that must hold when the procedure is called. In addition, in an iterator specification, a requires clause can constrain the behavior of using code while the returned generator is in use.

Robust program A program that continues to behave reasonably even in the presence of errors.

Satisfying a specification An implementation satisfies a specification if it provides the described behavior.

Scenario A step-by-step walk through of a user interaction with a software system, assuming the system itself is functioning properly. Scenarios are used during requirements analysis.

Semantics The meaning of an abstraction. The semantics are captured by a specification.

Sharing An object is shared by two variables if it can be accessed through either of them.

Side effect A program has a side effect if it modifies some of its inputs.

Signature A description of the argument types, result type, and exception types of a procedure.

Signature rule A part of the definition of the substitution principle. It requires that subtype objects have all the methods of the supertype, and these methods must have signatures compatible with those of the corresponding supertype methods.

Similarity Two objects are similar if it is not possible to distinguish between them using calls to their observers.

Singleton The single object of its class in the singleton pattern.

Singleton pattern A design pattern that is used to ensure that a class has just one object.

Snippet A snippet is a supertype that has just a few methods, but these methods have sufficiently complete specifications that using code can be written in terms of the supertype.

Software life cycle The set of activities that occurs during the lifetime of a software product.

Source in a data model The source is the set in the model that a relation maps from.

Specificand A program that satisfies a specification.

Specificand set The set of all programs that satisfy the specification.

Specification A description of the intended behavior of an abstraction. A specification can be either formal or informal.

Specification language The language used to write a specification.

Spiral model A software life cycle model in which a development phase can start before its predecessor phase is complete and the process contains many feedback loops.

Stack The storage area in which program variables reside; the storage is managed in a LIFO (last-in, first-out) manner.

Standalone procedure A procedure that is not a method of an object.

State of an object The current value of the object.

State pattern A design pattern that allows the representation of a mutable object to change as the object's state changes.

State type In the state pattern, this type is used to implement the object whose state is changing.

Static inner class A class nested inside another class. We use static inner classes to implement iterators.

Static method A method that belongs to a class rather than to an object.

Static subset A subset in a data model whose potential membership is determined statically.

Strategy pattern A design pattern that allows the use of procedures as objects, where the using context expects a certain behavior from the procedure. This pattern is related to the command pattern.

Stronger predicate Predicate A is stronger than predicate B if we can prove that B holds assuming A holds.

Strong type checking Type checking done at compile time that catches all type errors.

Stub A program that simulates the behavior of some module.

Subclass A class that inherits the rep and methods of its superclass. The subclass implements a subtype of the type implemented by its superclass.

Subject object in the observer pattern The object whose state changes are being observed by other objects.

Substitution principle A principle that governs the behavior of types in a hierarchy. It requires that subtypes behave in accordance with the specification of their supertype.

Subscriber The object that receives published information is the one in the publish/subscribe communication pattern.

Subtype A type that extends another type, which is called its supertype.

Sufficiently general specification A specification is sufficiently general if it does not preclude acceptable implementations.

Sufficiently restrictive specification A specification is sufficiently restrictive if it rules out all implementations that are unacceptable to an abstraction's users.

Superclass A Java class that can have subclasses—that is, classes that can inherit its rep and methods. The superclass implements a supertype of the types implemented by its subclasses.

Supertype A type that has subtypes.

Target abstraction   The abstraction whose implementation is currently being investigated in a design.

Target in a data model   The target is the set in the model that a relation maps to.

Template pattern   A design pattern that captures the idea of implementing methods in a superclass in terms of other methods that will be implemented in subclasses; the method implemented in the superclass defines a template for how execution proceeds, but the details are filled in later, when the subclasses are implemented.

Test driver   A program that runs a module through a series of tests.

Testing   The process of running a program on a set of test cases.

Top-down design   A design process in which the design progresses by considering how to implement abstractions whose specifications are complete.

Top-down development   A development process in which all modules that use module M are implemented and tested before M is implemented.

Total procedure   A procedure is total if its behavior is specified for all inputs that could be given to it at runtime.

Type checking   The process of checking the types of expressions and variables to determine whether a program is type correct.

Type correctness   A program is type correct if it contains no type errors.

Type error   A type error occurs when code accesses an object as if it belongs to a type that it does not belong to.

Type family   A group of related types; together the types form a type hierarchy.

Type hierarchy   A grouping of types into a type family consisting of a supertype and its subtypes; the subtypes may in turn have subtypes.

Type safety   A property of a program or a programming language. A program is type safe if it contains no type errors; a language is type safe if its compiler is able to recognize and reject all programs containing type errors at compile time.

UI   The user interface part of a program. Its job is to interact with the user and make calls on the FP (functional part) to carry out requested tasks.

Unchecked exception   A category of exception types in Java. Unchecked exception types are subtypes of `RuntimeException`. Java allows an unchecked exception to not be handled in the calling code.

Underdetermined behavior   A procedure is underdetermined if, for certain inputs, its specification allows more than one possible result.

Unit testing   Testing a single module in isolation from the others.

Using arc in a module dependency diagram   An arc that maps a module to the modules that will be used in its implementation.

Validation   A process designed to increase confidence that a program works as intended. Validation can be done through verification or testing.

Value   A primitive item of data such as an integer or a character.

Verification   A formal or informal argument that a program works on all possible inputs.

Visibility   The scope in which a variable or method is accessible.

Visitor class   A class defining a particular traversal according to the visitor pattern.

Visitor object   An object belonging to a visitor class.

Visitor pattern   A design pattern in which a traversal of a composite tree is accomplished by passing a visitor object to each node of the tree. In this pattern, there is a visitor class per kind of traversal.

Walk-through   A process for evaluating a design in a design review by walking through how the program performs on a set of test data.

Waterfall model   An unrealistic software life cycle model in which each development phase completes before the next one starts.

Weaker predicate   Predicate A is weaker than predicate B if we can prove that A holds assuming B holds.

Weakly uses   In a module dependency diagram, a module weakly uses another module if it depends on that module's existence but not on its specification.

White board   A way for code to communicate by posting and looking for information in a shared data base.

Wrapper   An object that contains within it another object or value. For example, an object of type `Integer` wraps the contained `int`.

Index

Index

Index

Index

Index

Index

Index